NURSING AND THE INJUSTICES OF THE LAW

To make a deep change in something that, once it exists, apparently has never not existed . . . requires a new way of thinking, not just thinking about new things.

Catharine A. MacKinnon (1987) *Feminism unmodified: discourses on life and law*, Harvard University Press, Cambridge, Mass., p. 9.

NURSING AND THE
INJUSTICES
OF THE LAW

MEGAN-JANE JOHNSTONE

RN, BA (Waikato), PhD (La Trobe),
FRCNA, FCN (NSW)

W. B. Saunders
Baillière Tindall

Harcourt Brace & Company
Sydney   Philadelphia   London   Toronto

To Darren, Annika, Sean and Elaine

W.B. Saunders/Baillière Tindall

An imprint of
Harcourt Brace & Company, Australia
30–52 Smidmore Street, Marrickville, NSW 2204

Harcourt Brace & Company
24–28 Oval Road, London NW1 7DX

Harcourt Brace & Company
Orlando, Florida 32887

National Library of Australia Cataloguing-in-Publication Data

Johnstone, Megan-Jane, date– .
  Nursing and the injustices of the law.

  Bibliography.
  Includes index.
  ISBN 0 7295 1418 8.

  1. Nursing — Law and legislation.   2. Nursing — Law and
  legislation — Australia.   I. Title.

344.0414

Typeset in Times Roman by Harcourt Brace & Company
Printed in Australia by Star Printery

CONTENTS

3 The Nursing Profession's Quest for Legal Status: A Brief Historical Overview

4 The Pyrrhic Victory of State Registration

5   The Medical Construction of Nurse Subordination

6   The Legal Construction and Reinforcement of Nurse Subordination

9 The Legal Invalidation of Professional Nursing Ethics

10 Conclusion: Towards a New Nursing Jurisprudence

FOREWORD

NURSING IS A METAPHOR for subordinated femininity. In patriarchal societies, woman has been constructed as affective and caring in order to provide succour for men in the interludes between war and work. This role has been traditionally performed for love, not money, within the domestic sphere.

Women's affective and caring skills have been regarded as the *natural* corollary of their reproductive role. This socio-biological construction has been a significant factor in the undervaluation of women's work, of which nursing is a preeminent example. It contrasts with the characterisation of medicine as a technology of reason over which men have claimed a monopoly. The arrogation by men of rationality to themselves and non-rationality to women is a central dualism enmeshed within our cultural heritage. If women are less rational than men, they need to be under male control. Hence, the idea of a male head of the household permeates the Western intellectual tradition.

Similarly, when women move from the private sphere into the public sphere, women's non-rationality must be curbed in order to harness their affective and caring skills for the benefit of the common good. Rational man, who is invariably Anglo-Celtic and middle class, must occupy an authoritative position in order to suppress the irrational and the subversive within the rational world of work. Productivity could be threatened by disorder. Accordingly, there have to be limitations on the authority exercised by women in the public sphere.

An understanding of the fictional character of Rational man facilitates an understanding of the gendered relationship between doctors, who are paradigmatically men, and nurses, who are paradigmatically women. It is the voice of rationality, epitomised by the authoritative figure of the doctor, bolstered by a technology increasingly distant from nature, which invariably trumps that of the nurse, with scant regard for what might be deemed to be reasonable nursing practice. The seeds of invidiousness attaching to femaleness have not disintegrated with the advent of equal opportunity laws and occasional changes in the gender of medical and nursing personnel.

Law has been of remarkably little help to date in disrupting the ordering and the gendered assumptions underlying the male/female, mind/body, public/private dualisms. However, it is frequently forgotten in the search for effective mechanisms of change, that law is a master discourse and, hence, a primary means of transmitting dominant social values within the Western intellectual tradition. The idea that law is autonomous and neutral will serve those who are subordinate equally as well as dominant is an enduring social myth. Law's facade of neutrality occludes its ideological role. Thus, when judges pontificate as to the appropriate degree of deference to be exercised by the nurse towards her liege lord, the doctor, law assumes the mystical power of truth.

Through recourse to the insights of feminist jurisprudence, this book demonstrates persuasively that it is naive for nurses to adopt an uncritical approach to law reform. Reforms which purport to improve the position of nurses vis-à-vis doctors may actually redound against nurses. Hegemonic masculinity is inherent within law, no less than within medicine. Minor tinkering, therefore, cannot reverse the presumption of rationality in favour of the doctor.

Despite her clear-eyed critique of the nexus between law and the role of nurse authority, Dr Johnstone does not recommend that law be jettisoned altogether because law reform is an important public site of contest. Nurses should nevertheless be aware of law's sometimes treacherous allure. It is to this task that the author devotes herself.

This is an important book which goes far beyond an instrumental view of law. I have great pleasure in commending it to you.

Margaret Thornton
Professor of Legal Studies
La Trobe University, Melbourne
February 1993

PREFACE

HISTORICALLY, NURSES IN THE common law countries of Australia, England and the United States of America have looked to the law to improve their status and authority as autonomous professionals. This book seeks to examine critically nursing's historical relationship to and experience of the law, and to demonstrate that the law has failed nurses in a number of important ways. In particular, the law has failed to provide nurses with the remedies they have sought in their historical quest for improved legal status, and has played a major role in reinforcing and maintaining nursing's subordinate and subservient position in the health care system. Furthermore, rather than facilitate the professional development of nursing, the law has in fact hindered it — and in a way that has been not only to the detriment of the nursing profession, but also to those requiring and receiving nursing care.

In the chapters to follow, arguments are advanced to support the view that the law's treatment of nurses has been paradigmatic of its treatment of women. The law has tended to regard nurses (over 90 per cent of whom are female, world-wide) as being rationally incompetent, and as being naturally inferior and subordinate to medical men. This is evident in the fact that nurses lack the legal authority necessary to match their responsibilities, are not permitted to exercise independent (medically unauthorised) professional judgment in patient care matters, and are subject to the legitimated control and dominance of doctors — the majority of whom are men.

It is contended that if nurses are to free themselves of the legitimated subordinate and subservient position they are in — and are to gain the legitimated authority they need to practise their profession in a safe, effective and morally responsible manner — they need to develop a new and radically different way of thinking about the law. Specifically, nurses need to examine critically the nature and adequacy of traditionally accepted legal doctrines and concepts, legal rules and principles, legal processes, and the way in which the law operates in the specific field of nursing. Nurses must also examine critically the law's unjust treatment of nurses and nursing practice, and the role the law has historically played not only in obstructing the professional development of nursing but also in supporting and maintaining generally nursing's continued subordination to the (male dominated) medical profession. As well as this, nurses need to engage in legal activism and to fight for law reforms that are more responsive to the lived experiences of nurses, and the realities and complexities of nursing practice.

The issues examined in this book provide a critical basis upon which a better understanding of nursing's relationship to and experience of the law can be gained and developed. It should be noted, however, that the issues examined are by no means exhaustive. There are several other issues relevant to developing a better understanding of nursing's relationship to and experience of the law, which, owing to restrictions of length and time, could not be included. These issues concern industrial law, disciplinary action by statutory authorities, the legal regulation of other fields of nursing and nursing specialties,[1] the patriarchal biases of other Acts and statutes (that is, other than nurse practice/registration Acts) which have a bearing on nursing practice,[2] the general physical and verbal abuse of nurses (for example, by doctors, employers, and patients), private agency nursing, men in nursing, and overseas qualified nurses. Another extremely important topic warranting attention is the whole question of the personal and professional consequences to nurses who have had to face either a disciplinary board or court hearing. It is well known, for example, that the whole process of disciplinary action and/or litigation can be traumatic. Anecdotal evidence has shown that nurses can and do suffer a range of quite severe health problems — including severe reactive depression (also called exogenous depression) — prior to, during, and/or after going through a disciplinary or court hearing. However, there is very little publicly available material on nurses' actual experiences in these types of situations, making it very difficult for the nursing profession to identify problematic areas and to initiate reforms needed to change the status quo. Since this and the other issues given above are important and lengthy issues in their own right, their investigation and consideration must be left for another time.

---

1 For example, psychiatric nursing, midwifery, community nursing, maternal and child health nursing, occupational health nursing, remote area nursing, nurse education and nurse administration. (See also Styles 1989.)

2 For example, Acts pertaining to drugs and poisons, the giving of evidence in criminal and civil court proceedings, human tissue transplantation and anatomy, statutory provisions for consent to treatment, and statutory protection of children at risk.

ACKNOWLEDGMENTS

WHILE UNDERTAKING MY RESEARCH for and preparing this text I have become indebted to several people. Foremost among these people is Professor Margaret Thornton of the Legal Studies Department, La Trobe University, Melbourne, who supervised my original PhD thesis upon which this text is based. Professor Thornton's critical comments and discussion of my research as it progressed contributed enormously to its development. The end result of my thesis and this text are, however, entirely my own, as are any omissions, weaknesses or mistakes.

In researching local and overseas material, I have become indebted to a number of individuals who, in their organisational capacities, were of great assistance: the staff of the interlibrary loan section of the Borchardt Library, La Trobe University; the staff at the Abbotsford Campus Library, La Trobe University; the Australian Nursing Federation (Victorian Branch); the New South Wales Nurses' Association, Sydney; Pam Stamm of the Bundoora Campus Library at Royal Melbourne Institute of Technology; the Victorian Nursing Council; Kevin McMahon, Chief Nursing Officer of the Victorian Nursing Council; the International Council of Nurses, Geneva; the Philippine Nurses' Association; June Cochrane and Pam Ryan (formerly of the Royal College of Nursing, Australia); Professor Margaret Bennett, Dean of the Faculty of Nursing, Royal Melbourne Institute of Technology, Bundoora; Jenny Cramer (formerly of the Council of Remote Area Nurses of Australia); Bart Schultz (retired nurse and historian); Sophia Heathcote; Jean Steel and Jennifer Lang of Shrew Women's Bookshop, Fitzroy, Melbourne; and Bernadette Brennan.

Acknowledgment and thanks is also due to those at Harcourt Brace & Company who have helped enormously in the successful production of this text. Jeremy Fisher (who was once again the epitome of enduring patience), Fiona Sim (for her meticulous editing of the manuscript), Mary Fuller, Pamela Horsnell and Cecily Courtney. Thanks are also due to Jenny Curtis (formerly of Harcourt Brace & Company) for her interest and support of this work.

Finally, these acknowledgments would not be complete without naming friends and colleagues whose unwavering personal and moral support has contributed enormously to facilitating the development of my work and thinking over the years, and, hence, ultimately to the successful completion of this project. Thanks are particularly due to Olga Kanitsaki, Bill McArthur, Maureen Leong, Elaine Henry, Theo Horsley, Esther Whittington.

ABBREVIATIONS

(Journal titles are in italics)

ADON	Assistant Director of Nursing
AORN	*American Operating Room Nurses*
A&E	Accident and Emergency Department
AMA	American Medical Association
AMA	Australian Medical Association
ANA	American Nurses Association
ANF	Australian Nursing Federation (formerly Royal Australian Nursing Federation)
ANJ	*American Nurses Journal*
ANJ	*Austral[as]ian Nurses Journal*
ATNA	Australasian Trained Nurses Association
BMA	British Medical Association
BMJ	*British Medical Journal*
CCU	Coronary Care Unit
CNA	(see RCNA below)
CPR	Cardio-pulmonary resuscitation
COHSE	Confederation of Health Service Employees
CRASS	Contribution Related to Adjustment Salary Scheme
DGM	District General Manager
DHSS	Department of Health and Social Security
DNR	'Do not resuscitate' order (see NFR below)
DON	Director of Nursing
GNC	General Nursing Council
HDV	Health Department Victoria
ICN	International Council of Nurses
ICU	Intensive Care Unit

IV	Intravenous (for example, intravenous therapy)
JAMA	*Journal of the American Medical Association*
NCVQ	National Council for Vocational Qualifications
NFR	'Not for resuscitation' order (see DNR above)
NHS	National Health Service
NICU	Neonatal Intensive Care Unit
NM	*Nursing Mirror*
NP	Nurse Practitioner
NSWNA	New South Wales Nurses' Association
NT	*Nursing Times*
NZNA	New Zealand Nurses' Association
ODA	Operating Department Assistants
OTC	Over the counter (drugs)
RANF	(see ANF above)
RCN	Royal College of Nursing
RCNA	Royal College of Nursing, Australia (formerly College of Nursing, Australia)
RN	Registered Nurse
RVTNA	Royal Victorian Trained Nurses Association (formerly VTNA)
SEN	State Enrolled Nurse
SM	Service Manager
TUC	Trades Union Congress
UKCC	United Kingdom Central Council for Nursing, Midwifery and Health Visiting
UGM	Unit General Manager
VNC	Victorian Nursing Council
VTNA	(see RVTNA above)
WHO	World Health Organisation
YTS	Youth Training Scheme

Introduction

'The nurse question is the woman question'

IN 1887, MRS ETHEL BEDFORD FENWICK, a distinguished English nurse reformer and the 'originator and prime mover' of the International Council of Nurses — currently the oldest international association of professional women in the world[1] — founded the first nurses' organisation in the world, the British Nurses Association (Dock and Stewart 1938, pp. 252–253; Kelly 1985, p. 629). The establishment of this association (which later became the Royal British Nurses Association), and the very idea of professional autonomy for nurses that it represented, was regarded by many outside nursing (for example, the medical establishment and hospital administrators) to be totally objectionable. Mrs Fenwick, an ardent feminist and friend of the suffragist Mrs Pankhurst, was unperturbed by the swell of opposition to nurses obtaining professional autonomy. Determined that 'the emerging nursing profession should be led and organised by nurses' (Bendall and Raybould 1969, p. 2), Mrs Fenwick responded by declaring 'the nurse question is the woman question', and by setting out to fight, single-mindedly, for the nursing cause (Dock and Stewart 1938, p. 254).

Although Mrs Fenwick's views and the opposition to them were expressed over a century ago, they continue to be of relevance today. Despite the professional and educational advancements made over the past 130 years, 'the nurse question' remains very much 'the woman question'. Today, world wide, approximately 90 per cent of nurses are women (Morrow 1986, p. 216). And, as in the past, nursing is still popularly regarded as being quintessentially 'women's work' (*The Lamp* 1976, pp. 15–17; Austin 1977a, 1977b; Dachelet 1978; Thornton 1984; Salvage 1985, p. 4; Gamarnikow 1991, p. 110). Furthermore, rather than being a paradigmatic example of 'female success'

> nursing is the paradigmatic example of a predominantly female occupation which is undervalued vis-à-vis predominantly male occupations which involve a comparable degree of skill, effort and responsibility.
> (Thornton 1984, p. 11)

In the 1990s, political opposition to nurses obtaining legitimated professional autonomy remains just as strong as it was in the early days of the profession, and many (mostly male doctors, hospital administrators, and politicians) continue to resist actively any thought that nurses 'should take their destiny into their own hands' (Salvage 1985, p. 20). Thus, to borrow from Riane Eisler (1987, p. 25) writing on the broader struggle for women's rights:

> Rather than steadily advancing, we are constantly forced to refight the same battles. Instead of becoming firmly rooted, even gains we have already made are chronically in jeopardy.

Explaining nursing's subordinate and oppressed position

Many attempts have been made to try and explain the subordinate and oppressed position in which the nursing profession seems to have found itself (see in particular Ashley 1976a; Melosh 1982; Muff 1982; Salvage 1985; Reverby 1987; Savage 1987; Williams 1989; Achterberg 1990; Holden and Littlewood 1991). Literature on the subject (which is now vast and too numerous to list here) has borrowed heavily from feminist theories and discourse on a wide range of social phenomena, including male dominance, the 'natural disorder' (rational incompetence and inferiority) of women, female oppression, the gender division of labour, the devaluing generally of women's work, the marginalisation, 'manipulated passivity' and 'constructed silence' of women, and so on.[2] While discourse on these and other factors has been enormously helpful in explaining the so-called 'nurse question', it is evident that there is another factor that needs to be considered, namely, *the law*. Indeed, upon a closer examination of the modern history of the nursing profession's quest for legal status and its ongoing struggle for legal recognition as an autonomous health profession, it is evident that many of the nursing profession's problems — including its exploitation by the state, and its failure to obtain legitimated authority as an autonomous profession — have a firm legal basis, something which has not yet been fully appreciated either by nurses or their representative professional organisations.

It is hoped that this text will help to improve nurses' understanding of the (patriarchal) nature of law and the extent to which it has been instrumental in obstructing the development of nursing as a predominantly female profession. It is also hoped that this text will help to show nurses that the law cannot be relied upon as a beneficent agent of positive nursing reform, and further, as Professor Margaret Thornton (1990) argues persuasively in her outstanding book *The liberal promise*, 'blind faith in the law as a beneficent agent of social change is misplaced'.

The question of male nurses and female doctors

It might be objected at this point that the presence of men in nursing, and the presence of women in medicine, stands to weaken substantially the underlying assumptions of and the central arguments being advanced in this book. There are, however, firm grounds for rejecting this objection.

Although it is true there are men in the nursing profession, it should be noted that their relatively low statistical representation (of between only 3.5 and 7.8 per cent) has not been and is not sufficient to alter either the stereotypical view of nursing being a 'women's profession', or indeed, stereotypical views of nursing's 'rightful' (read 'low' and 'poorly valued') social position and status as a predominantly female profession (London 1987; Savage 1987, p. 68; Williams 1989, p. 88; Griffin 1990, p. 9). Instead, the presence of men in nursing (who, interestingly, are statistically over-represented in the top nursing jobs) has tended to reinforce rather than redress stereotypical views about nursing as a predominantly female profession and the apparent 'need' to have men in nursing to help improve its (nursing's) low professional status (Austin 1977a, 1977b; Dachelet 1978, p. 37; Flanagan 1982, p. 171; Levine 1983; Thornton 1984; Kelly 1985, pp. 308, 356; Salvage 1985, pp. 35–36; London 1987; Savage 1987; Delamothe 1988e, p. 346; Williams 1989; Griffin 1990). Furthermore, being 'male' is not sufficient to alter the legitimated position of the nurse as a subordinate and 'servant' of the medical practitioner (female or male). The point being here that, whether male or female, a nurse still lacks legitimated authority as a nurse, and is legally bound to 'obey' the lawful and reasonable orders of his or her superiors — the majority of whom either directly or indirectly are medical practitioners.

In regard to the presence of women in the medical profession (as in the case of women in the legal profession) the presence of women in medicine has not been sufficient to alter the stereotypical view of medicine (like law) being a male dominated profession — or indeed sufficient to change significantly the gender relation between medicine and nursing. There are a number of reasons for this:

1. Although the percentage of women in medical courses has risen dramatically in recent years to between 47 and 50 per cent respectively in Australia, the United Kingdom, and the United States of America, women doctors still have not been fully accepted by, and still do not have parity with, their male medical colleagues (Walsh 1977; Leeson and Gray 1978; Eisner and Wright 1986; Altekruse and McDermott 1988; Kirov 1991). Further to this, it must be remembered that the increased numbers of women entering medicine is a relatively recent

phenomenon, and its impact (if any) on the profession and practice of medicine generally has yet to be fully realised and measured. At present, however, women remain statistically under-represented in the upper echelons of the medical profession, and, as Eisner and Wright (1986, p. 120) point out, the 'lady doctor' is often regarded as a 'second-class citizen' among the male doctors she works with. Eisner and Wright (ibid.) conclude: 'medicine, like other professions, has a place for women — provided the women know their place'.

2. Women entering medicine are very often forced (for reasons of personal and professional survival) to assimilate to the masculinist medical culture into which they have entered, and to adopt the patriarchal, paternalistic and authoritarian values that are commonly associated with and upheld by that culture. Not surprisingly, this has often resulted in woman doctors treating nurses (male and female) in much the same patriarchal and paternalistic way that their male colleagues have historically treated nurses.

3. Even in instances where woman doctors are aware of the traditional patriarchal relationship between nursing and medicine, and desire to change the status quo, the legitimated hierarchical structures of the health care settings in which they practise (not to mention their legitimated power and authority as doctors) make it genuinely difficult for them to develop democratic and 'equal' working relationships with nurses (see, for example, Eisner and Wright 1986, p. 118).

Thus, in the ultimate analysis, it can be seen that even with the 'feminisation' of the medical profession, medicine as a whole (as in the case of law) remains very much a 'man-dominated decision-making system' (Altekruse and McDermott 1988, p. 85).

The problem of the nursing hierarchy

It might also be objected at this point that many of nursing's problems are related to and could be explained by its own hierarchical nature, and may not necessarily be attributable to legitimated patriarchal medical dominance per se. As in the previous case, however, there are firm grounds for rejecting this objection.

While it is certainly true that nursing has a hierarchical structure and that nurses are subject to the directives of nurse superiors, ultimately it is still the doctors who have overriding (legitimated) authority in health care contexts, and it is the medical hierarchy that reigns supreme over the nursing hierarchy. Doctors are generally regarded as having superior knowledge and experience to nurses, and therefore as being in a better position to decide what is the 'right' course of action in clinical, administrative (for example, patient admissions and discharges), ethical, and other matters. Where a doctor's directives are at odds with a nurse's judgment, there is often very little a nurse (whether a superior or a subordinate) can do if the doctor is not responsive to changing his or her directives. This is primarily because 'nurses are employees and must work as directed' (Peterson 1990). Although a nurse may refuse to carry out either a medical or nursing superior's orders, such an act is not without legal risk. In a 1978 Canadian case, for example, nurses argued that they declined to accept a medical directive to admit a patient into an intensive care unit (ICU), fearing it would expose them 'to potential civil liability and professional discipline' because the ICU was grossly understaffed and 'no nurse felt capable of taking responsibility' (*Re Mount Sinai Hospital and Ontario Nurses' Association* (1978); Sklar 1979a, pp. 14–15). The nurses' defence was not accepted, however. Instead, it was characterised as being 'dangerous' because of 'the uncertainty with respect to legal liability' in the case at hand and because the question of 'legal responsibility' was a matter for the court — not the nurses — to decide (*Re Mount Sinai Hospital and Ontario Nurses' Association* (1978)).

In difficult situations, such as where a doctor wishes to admit a patient despite a lack of qualified nursing staff being available to provide nursing care, it is not uncommon for nurses to be instructed by a nursing supervisory authority to 'cope' and to 'do the best that you can', as happened in the above case (Sklar 1979a, pp. 14–15). Thus, although nurse superiors can and do have authority over subordinate nurses, and subordinate nurses are obliged to follow the directives of a nurse superior (unless obviously unlawful or unreasonable), in the final analysis, nurse superiors and nurse subordinates alike share the commonality of legitimated powerlessness: neither has ultimate control in the realm of nursing, and neither has any real influence over the legitimated power and authority of doctors.

While it is true that nurses have experienced certain personal and professional hardships on account of questionable directives being given by nurse superiors (for example, when nurses are directed to 'float', that is, to work in or cover an area for which they are neither educationally prepared nor practically experienced (see the end of the section entitled 'The nurse's lack of sovereignty in her own realm of practice' in chapter 7 of this book), or to work in an area where there is an unsafe nurse–patient ratio (see, for example, Sklar 1979a, 1979b; M.A.B. 1979)), most of the problems experienced by nurses have been, and are, primarily owing to medical dominance in the work place, and the legitimated power that doctors (and more recently non-nurse general managers (see the section entitled 'The Griffiths Report' in chapter 4 of this book)) have as 'masters' and 'superiors' over nurses and over nursing practice. For this reason, attention in the following chapters is mostly given to the nurse–doctor relationship, rather than to the nurse–nurse relationship. Furthermore, as already stated, since the majority of nurses (93–97 per cent) are women, and because many of the problems experienced by nurses can be linked to the fact that nursing is a predominantly female profession and to stereotypical views of nurses as women, this book takes as its primary focus the female nurse. Where relevant, however, examples involving men in nursing are also considered.

Synopsis of chapters

This book is divided into ten chapters. Chapter 1 considers the early modern nursing reforms and why these reforms were, at the time, politically threatening to the profession and practice of orthodox medicine. It is suggested that the spectacular successes of the early modern nursing reforms threatened not only the medical profession's dominance and control in the emerging public health care sector, but the very credibility of medicine as a healing art. It is further suggested that in an attempt to contain the 'nurse threat' and to reassert its dominance and control in the health care arena, the medical establishment actively exploited two key things:

- Gender (and, more particularly, the gender division of labour between medicine and nursing (Gamarnikow 1991)).
- The law (and, more particularly, the law's traditional role in structuring and reinforcing the subordination of women to men).

Chapter 2 focuses on the question of law and on the nursing profession's traditional but questionable reliance on law (its processes, procedures, and discourse) to advance nursing's goals. It is argued that the law (interpreted broadly here as 'a core doctrine, as a system and as an approach to the social world' (Naffine 1990, p. 1), and as 'a dominant discourse' (Eisenstein 1988, pp. 43–47; Fineman 1990, p. xii; Smart 1990)) has not only failed nursing as an instrument of professional and social reform, but has also been an important influence in obstructing the development of nursing as an autonomous profession. Drawing on feminist jurisprudential scholarship (which has, over the past two to three decades, successfully identified and exposed the genderisation of law and its historical failure to be responsive to the needs and lived experiences of women), it is argued that the law's treatment of nurses has, in almost every respect, been paradigmatic of its oppressive and unjust treatment of women generally; and that even in the case of law reforms and court cases which appear to have gone 'for' nurses, have in reality gone against them. The conclusion of this chapter is that nurses' blind faith in the law as a beneficent agent of professional nursing reform is misplaced and that if the status quo is to improve for the nursing profession, nurses will need to adopt a radically different way of thinking about the law to the way they have historically done so. In short, nurses need to re-think the law, and the traditional role it has been given in adjudicating nursing's affairs.

Chapter 3 investigates respectively the Australian, English and American nursing professions' historical quest for legal status through state registration laws. Factors motivating this quest are examined briefly. Examples are given to show how the processes of law-making used during this time effectively prevented nurses achieving the legal remedies they had hoped to achieve.

Chapter 4 examines further the question of state registration. Arguments are advanced to support the view that the state registration that was granted to nurses in the United States of America, England, and Australia respectively was not 'real' and, in the ultimate analysis, has proved to be little more than a Pyrrhic victory for the nursing profession in those countries. It is further contended that rather than challenge the status quo, state registration laws merely reinforced and legitimated it in so far as the public interest was not protected (unqualified people could still 'nurse' for gain), the status of nursing did not improve (nurses were still vulnerable to exploitation and abuse by doctors, hospital administrators and the state), and nursing was not given its independence (state registration laws in fact legitimated medical dominance and control of statutory nursing boards, nurse education and nurse employment). It is concluded that to this day state registration laws have failed both the public and the nursing profession. For instance, the public is still vulnerable to being cared for by unqualified people 'nursing' for gain (there is much to suggest that hospitals may even be reverting to using the exploitative nurse apprenticeship system of 100 years ago), and nursing still has not gained legitimated status as an autonomous profession. Nurses remain subject to abuse and exploitation by the hospital system and by their superiors, and still lack the legitimated authority to match their responsibilities. Even more disturbing, however, is what appears to be the state supported de-professionalisation and devolution of contemporary nursing.

In chapter 5 the debate takes a slightly different direction with attention focusing on the medical establishment's attempt to contain the 'nurse threat' by constructing and reinforcing patriarchal assumptions about the rational incompetency and inferiority of nurses (women), and the need for nurses (women) to be controlled by — and to be loyal and obedient to — medical men. In chapter 6 attention is given to the extent to which patriarchal medical views and assumptions about nurses (women) and nursing practice have been legitimated and reinforced by law. A number of legal cases are examined to show how the law has historically structured and reinforced the principles of nurse legal incompetence (note that the law has tended to regard nurses as 'non-persons'), nurse subordination, and the establishment of medical supervision and guardianship over nurses. Examples are also given to demonstrate that, historically, the law has tended to view (and continues to view) the nurse as a 'servant' who performs only 'routine and ministerial' duties (as opposed to discretionary professional duties) and thus, in the main, must work as directed (by doctors).

Chapter 7 looks at the question of whether, given contemporary trends in nursing law (including increased litigation against nurses, and so-called 'progressive' law reforms favouring the 'expanded' practice of nursing), the legal status of the nurse has improved. A number of legal cases are examined to show that, contrary to popular commentary, the legal status of the nurse as an authoritative and autonomous professional has not significantly improved. It is contended that the rise in litigation against nurses is more a reflection of nurses being given increased responsibility, rather than authority, and a reflection of nurses being used increasingly as 'scapegoats' by more powerful others (for example, doctors, hospitals and the state) whose competing self interests have been at stake. It is argued that nurses still lack sovereignty in their own realm of practice, and still lack the legitimated authority to exercise independent (medically unauthorised) professional judgment in matters of life and death — a position which has often proved to be to the detriment of patient care. Examples are given to show that in many instances law reforms have merely reinforced rather than redressed the gender inequalities between doctors and nurses, and have served to legitimate further the authority of doctors over nurses. This chapter concludes by contending that regardless of legal trends in nursing which appear to indicate that the legal status of the nurse has improved, on a closer analysis of legal cases and law reforms involving nurses, and indeed of the realities of nursing practice generally, it is evident that nurses still have not acquired legitimated status and authority as autonomous professionals.

Still on the theme of the legal status of the nurse, chapter 8 examines the role and dominance of medical men as expert witnesses in professional negligence cases involving nurses. A number of legal cases are examined to demonstrate that the dominance and prominence of male doctors as expert 'nurse' witnesses is not so much a reflection of judicial ignorance about the distinctive nature of nursing practice, but a reflection of a much broader political motive to 'keep nurses (women) in their proper place', to uphold and reinforce the cultural hegemony of medical men, to ensure that nurses (women) do not 'overstep their authority' as (subordinate) health-care providers, and indeed to protect and maintain generally the patriarchal political status quo. The chapter concludes by arguing that an improved legal status of nursing is dependent not just on nurses 're-thinking' the law and its traditional role in adjudicating nursing's affairs, but also on a radical (and revolutionary) reform of the entire legal system itself.

Chapter 9 looks at the nurse–patient relationship, and the law's reluctance to recognise the moral dimensions of that relationship. Examples are given to show that courts have been inclined to disregard and invalidate professional nursing ethics, and in so doing have effectively eliminated a reliable basis (that is, a basis other than clinical expertise) on which nurses could otherwise have validly questioned 'acceptable' medical and hospital practices. It is contended that by denying the moral authority and professional ethics of nurses, the courts have effectively preserved the legitimated subordination of nursing, and, not least, have made it extremely difficult for nurses to practice their profession in a morally autonomous, responsible and accountable manner.

Finally, chapter 10 draws together the threads of the arguments presented in the preceding chapters and makes some further suggestions about what the nursing profession can and should do to improve its legal, social and moral position. Brief consideration is given to the radical change in thinking and approach that nurses must take if they are to succeed in bringing about the kinds of legal reforms the nursing profession desires, and which clearly are required not only for the sake of nurses, but for the sake of those requiring and/or receiving nursing care. The conclusion of this chapter — and of this book — is that it is possible to effect positive change, and to make the law and legal institutions more responsive to the realities of nursing practice and to the lived experiences of nurses struggling to practise their profession in a safe, competent, ethical and effective way. In order to achieve these important goals, however, nurses will need to be better informed (for example, through formal education) about the genderisation of law and its 'real' impact on nursing, and to make their experiences of the law more public. Nurses will also need to lobby actively for law reform in areas where existing legal regulations are not conducive to the safe, effective and ethical practice of nursing. This will involve lobbying not just for the reform of Acts and Statutes relevant to the profession and practice of nursing (and ones which, for example, have tended to treat nurses in a dismissive and/or discriminatory way), but also for the reform of traditional legal processes and procedures themselves — including the 'masculinist' and male dominated processes and procedures of law making, law reform, law enforcement, and so on. The real problem facing nurses, however, is determining how best to achieve these goals (see Olsen — cited in Menkle-Meadow 1988, pp. 74–76; Rhode 1988, p. 44).

It should perhaps be pointed out here that an underlying assumption of this book is that improving the legal position of nurses involves moral critique. This is because the questions of nursing justice, freedom, autonomy, 'best interests', 'professional interests', 'public good' and the like, as considered in this book, are all value questions and 'depend on moral choice' (Dahl 1987, p. 85; Minow 1987, p. 92). This book also assumes that there is a 'better' legal position which nurses could occupy, and further that nurses ought, in the strict moral sense of the term, to occupy this 'better' position.

ENDNOTES

1   As a point of interest, the International Council of Nurses also antedates by many years the international hospital and medical associations (Kelly 1985, p. 629).

2   See, for example: Ardener 1975; Yates 1975; Rich 1979; Midgley 1980; Richards 1980; O'Brien 1981, 1989; McMillan 1982; Spender 1982, 1985; Frye 1983; Jaggar 1983; Midgley and Hughes 1983; Eisenstein 1984; Lloyd 1984; Matthews 1984; Burton 1985, 1991; Lerner 1986; Mitchell and Oakley 1986; Pascall 1986; Pateman and Gross 1986; Burton et al. 1987; Connell 1987; Cott 1987; Dubois et al. 1987; Harding 1987; Caine et al. 1988; Pateman 1988, 1989; Rowland 1988; Waring 1988; Brittan 1989; Franzway et al. 1989; Fraser 1989; Graddol and Swann 1989; Cameron, D. 1990.

CHAPTER ONE

The Political Threat of Early Nursing Reforms

INTRODUCTION

HISTORICALLY, INDEPENDENT WOMEN HEALERS have posed a major threat to the cultural hegemony of men — in particular men of the church, the state and the 'masculinised' medical profession (Ehrenreich and English 1973a, 1979; Corea 1977; Walsh 1977; Achterberg 1991). The degree to which women healers have been perceived as a threat by the ruling male establishment can be measured, at least partially, by the extraordinary lengths to which male professionals (priests, doctors, and politicians among them) have gone in order to control and eradicate women's knowledge and practice of the healing arts. From the fourteenth to the seventeenth centuries, for example, the suppression of women healers saw many women (estimates range from 'less than a thousand' to 'millions') legally executed by live burnings at the stake for alleged witchcraft (Ehrenreich and English 1973a, p. 7, 1979, pp. 31–35; Corea 1977, p. 23; Daly 1978, pp. 178–222; Achterberg 1991, p. 85; Hester 1992, pp. 128–130). During the nineteenth and early twentieth centuries, women healers were likewise legitimately suppressed, although not by live burnings at the stake (society had become more civilised, and both science and law had rejected the rationality — and the reality — of the 'witch accusations' (Achterberg 1991; Ehrenreich and English 1979)). Rather, as will be discussed more fully later this book, they were suppressed by being denied legal status as persons, the legal right to a tertiary education, and the legal right to practice a profession of their own choosing. Where women did manage to 'legitimately' participate in the healing arts, this participation was 'swiftly downgraded to one of service only' and, in essence, emerged as being little more than 'bondage to a male-dominated system of health care' (Achterberg 1991, pp. 18, 52).

Among the many casualties of the legitimated suppression of contemporary women healers (midwives among them (see Ehrenreich and English 1979, pp. 84–88; Starr 1982; Kitzinger 1988; Willis 1989; Achterberg 1991, pp. 118–132)) were nurses. A primary reason for the legitimated suppression of nurses was that they posed a major threat not just to medical men (and their monopoly of medical diagnosis and prescription), but to the credibility of medicine itself as a healing art. The questions remain, however, of why nursing was able to pose the threat to medicine that it did, and what was done in order to contain it? It is to answering these questions that this chapter will now briefly turn.

The threat posed by Nightingale's nursing reforms

The transformation of nursing in the nineteenth century from a 'domestic service' to a 'health care practice' profoundly threatened the existing patriarchal political order (namely, male dominated relationships of 'power, rule and authority' (adapted from Dahl 1984, pp. 9–10, 12; see also Pateman 1989, p. 92)) of the developing public health care system. Before 1860,

> the relationship between doctor and nurse was unequivocal: the nurse was the skilled servant who operated 'in strict obedience to the physician's or surgeon's power'.
> (Morrow 1986, p. 217)

Following the 'Nightingalean' reforms of the 1860s and thereafter, however, the master–servant relationship between doctors and nurses changed significantly and in a way that seriously threatened the cultural hegemony of medical men[1] both in health care and in the broader community.

Undoubtedly, one of the most notable and major challenges to the cultural hegemony of medical men came in the form of the spectacular success of Florence Nightingale's hygienic nursing experiment in the Crimean campaign (Woodham-Smith 1964, p. 228). Nightingale's much opposed nursing reforms in the military hospital at Scutari saw the mortality rate among injured and ill soldiers drop from 42 per cent to just two per cent in less than six months (Dolan et al. 1983, p. 161; Achterberg 1991, p. 150). The success of Nightingale's nursing experiment proved two significant things:

- the unequivocal worth of the 'trained nurse' and organised hospital nursing;
- that medical treatments alone could not be effective without skilled and quality-controlled nursing care.

The medical establishment could not, and ultimately did not, ignore these points. In fact, after the medical establishment's initial resistance to the 'intrusion of women' into the masculine domain of orthodox medical care, medical men came to recognise fully the importance of the trained nurse. As one American physician later acknowledged: 'much depends on the proper organization of one's corps of nurses' (Simpson 1909, p. 1175). And as another eminent physician conceded:

> From a medical man's point of view the nurse is absolutely essential for the care of patients seriously ill, confined to bed, or in need of skilled watching or attention of various kinds.
> (Bart 1929, p. 119)

The medical establishment was also very much aware that 'trained nurses and their use of aseptic techniques ... were major factors in making hospitals more safe' (Ashley 1976a — cited in Aaronson 1989, p. 275). This factor enabled doctors to promote hospital care as a 'superior' alternative to home care, and thereby secure the hospital as 'the workshop of the physician' (Rosen 1963, p. 29).

Historically, competent nursing has always made an exceptional contribution to healing, and probably a greater contribution than medicine — even with all its gadgetry, for example, 'lancets, pills, saws and pincers' (Achterberg 1991, pp. 52, 149). Ashley (1973, p. 639) notes, for example, that at the turn of the century 'diet, rest, and "fever sponges" saved more patients with typhoid fever than the medical therapies then available. She makes the additional and important point that

> in lowering mortality rates, nurses were not performing the discarded functions of physicians; they were practicing their own profession and, in so doing, preserving life.
> (Ashley 1973, p. 639)

In her book *The hidden malpractice*, Corea (1977, p. 57) argues along similar lines, pointing out that

> the ill probably recovered faster by having nurses massage their bodies, change their bed linen, and hold their hands than having doctors place leeches on their bodies to suck out their blood.

Smoyak (1987, p. 35), writing from a North American context, makes the additional important point that in 1900, 75 per cent of all health practitioners were 'either doctors or nurses, and they were almost equal in number and in level of skill'. However, unlike nursing, the 'standard of medical care was very uneven and, in many instances, life-threatening' (ibid.). The largely experimental use of anaesthesia during this time was a particularly life-threatening medical procedure, with the large number of associated injuries and deaths of patients universally being 'explained' (read 'dismissed') as 'medical accidents' (see, in particular, Keys' (1978) text *The history of surgical anesthesia*).

Other literature sources also suggest that in many instances the 'cures' offered by the 'regular doctors', as they were known, were often 'either fatal or more injurious than the original disease', and that a major ingredient in 'healing' was *caring*, not 'scientific' medicine per se (Ehrenreich and English 1973a, p. 23; Carlson 1975, p. 19; McKeown 1979; Broad and Wade 1982; Valenstein 1986; Achterberg 1991). Even today, it is well recognised that 'without nurses, people would hurt, become infected and remain ill', and that nurses are essential to the health care system (Dean 1982, p. 326). The nursing profession, meanwhile, has always been aware of its role in promoting patients' health and healing processes, and the importance and centrality of 'care' in the promotion of health and healing (see in particular: Benner 1984; Watson 1985a, 1985b; Roach 1987; Leininger 1988a, 1988b, 1988c; Wolf 1988; Benner and Wrubel 1989; Bevis and Watson 1989; Carson 1989; Marriner-Tomey 1989; Leininger and Watson 1990; Bishop and Scudder 1991; Chinn 1991; Gaut and Leininger 1991; Gaut 1992; Brown et al. 1992).

When nursing was primarily a 'domestic service' performed in the 'private sphere' of the home, it could be controlled with relative ease. But when it became 'professionalised' and primarily carried out in the 'public sphere' of the community and the hospital, it was not so easily controlled. As is discussed more fully in chapter 3 of this text, when nursing first emerged as an organised and professionalised force, there was no statutory authority regulating its affairs. The law had not kept pace with the professional development of nursing, and as a result both the state and the medical profession were (unusually!) relatively powerless to stop trained nurses entering the public sphere and practising the art of healing for gain which their formal training as nurses enabled them to do.

Gamarnikow (1991) argues persuasively that nursing reforms threatened medicine in at least three specific ways:

1. The control of hospital (ward) nursing was taken away from doctors and placed in the hands of qualified nurses.
2. Nurse education reforms introduced nurses to the medical curriculum and hence medical knowledge.
3. Although doctors had the legitimated authority to give instructions, nurses were nevertheless left to make 'autonomous translation of medical instructions into nursing tasks' — something which, in the ultimate analysis, made it difficult if not impossible to state 'at which point doctoring ended and nursing began' (ibid., p. 116). This, in turn, made it very difficult to prove and sustain the popularly recognised division of labour between nursing and medicine (ibid., p. 122).

The traditional division of labour between nursing and medicine was strained further by the inescapable fact that 'supervising' doctors were mostly absent from their patients, making it almost impossible for them to have and maintain a monopoly of diagnosis and prescription (Gamarnikow

1991, p. 120; Ashley 1975c, p. 1466). The nurse, however, 'who was constantly present', and who was left to interpret, alter if necessary, and implement standing medical instructions (including those pertaining to drug administration) could not be prevented from diagnosing and prescribing (Gamarnikow 1991, p. 120). An important and politically threatening end result of this situation, as Gamarnikow (1991, p. 125), I think, correctly concludes, was that:

> medical rights to diagnose and prescribe [could] no longer be justified purely on the grounds of superior knowledge and skills.

It should perhaps be added that the constant presence of nurses in caring for the sick also made it extremely difficult for doctors to claim sole credit for the 'cures' they achieved — something which threatened further the alleged 'uniqueness' and 'superiority' of medical knowledge and skill.

Trained nurses had reached a position from which they could validly claim recognition for their contribution toward the therapeutic successes generally attributed to the 'scientific' practice of 'great' medical men. Indeed, as will be discussed later in this text (see the section entitled 'Opposition to the state registration of English nurses' in chapter 3) trained nurses (particularly district nurses) had become a credible force of health care practitioners in their own right as nurses — a development which posed a serious threat to medical dominance in the emerging public health care system. The threat that trained nurses posed becomes even more significant when it is considered that, contrary to popular rhetoric, medicine (the practice of which was seen to consist primarily of three things: diagnosis, prognosis and the prescription of drugs (*Journal of the American Medical Association (JAMA)* 1906b, p. 438; Harris 1911, p. 1319; King 1991)) was not at that time a science. In fact, the early modern medical establishment was generally very resistant to 'scientific innovations from both without and within' (Broad and Wade 1982, p. 136), and as late as 1906 was still struggling to define the practice of medicine as a 'science' (see Hemmeter 1906, pp. 243–248; *JAMA* 1906a, pp. 40–41).

In light of these considerations as well as the conspicuous absence of firm scientific data proving medicine's social worth[2] and its supposed superiority to nursing, there is small doubt that the medical establishment had cause for concern about the rise of nurses as a major competitor in health care. It needs to be clarified, however, that what the medical and nursing professions were competing for was not the 'same body of knowledge and skill', as some have argued (see, for example, Aaronson 1989, p. 274), but for the right to practise and to gain a monopoly over their own respective distinct genderised modes of 'healing' — medicine being the prototype of a masculine (high-tech, aggressive 'cut and thrust') mode of healing, and nursing being the prototype of a feminine (high-touch, gentle 'care and nurture') mode of healing — both of which aimed to restore the patient to health, in other words, to cure (Masson 1985, p. 71; Symanski 1990, p. 138).

Medical reaction to the 'nurse threat'

Early articles published in both the medical and nursing press provide some striking examples of just how seriously members of the medical profession viewed the 'nurse threat,' and how deeply they feared that nurses (mere women) could and would encroach upon and 'take over' their territory of medical practice. For instance, in an article entitled 'Nurses' schools and illegal practice of medicine', published in a 1906 issue of the *Journal of the American Medical Association*, doctors are warned of 'the danger of putting power to practice medicine into the hands of those who will use it wrongly' (*JAMA* 1906c, p. 1835). After briefly voicing the concern that 'some physicians . . . do not seem to learn this lesson', the article quotes in full the following four unanimously adopted resolutions supporting the suppression of illegal medical practice by nurses:

> 1. Every attempt at initiative on the part of nurses, attendants, orderlies, etc., should be reproved by the physicians and by the hospital administration. 2. The program of nursing schools and the manuals employed should be limited strictly to the indispensable matters of instruction for those in their position, without going extensively into purely medical matters which might give them a false notion as to their duties and lead them to substitute themselves for the physician. 3. The professional instruction of orderlies and nurses *should be intrusted exclusively to the physician, who only can judge what is necessary for them to know*. 4. The physicians charged with this instruction should never forget, in the course of their lectures, to insist on the possible dangers of the initiative on the part of orderly and nurse and on the serious responsibility that would be incurred in case of accident by the persons thus *inconsiderately stepping out from their proper sphere* [emphasis added].

The article concludes its support for the suppression of nurses by arguing that it is a matter of 'simple justice' for medical practitioners to refrain from encouraging nurses 'to take steps that are not in her province' (ibid.).

Five years after the publication of the *JAMA* article, an article by the *British Medical Journal* (*BMJ*), published in the *Australasian Nurses Journal*, expressed similar concerns. It warned that there was a real risk of the establishment of 'a new form of unqualified [medical] practice', namely, the independent practice of trained nurses (*BMJ* 1911, pp. 185–187). Upon condemning independent nursing practice as a 'dangerous outgrowth' of the 'universally approved' system of medicine (it is apparent that the medical establishment did not recognise or wish to acknowledge that nursing was distinct from medicine, or that nursing practice required different (nursing) knowledge and skill), the *BMJ* further warned that encouraging a nurse 'to aspire to [a] position of independence' risked undermining her 'definite and honourable, if subordinate, status' (presumably as the idealised archetype of the proverbial obedient, loyal and morally pure, if inferior, 'good woman') (*BMJ* 1911, pp. 185–187). The *BMJ* then reminded medical practitioners that the nurse was primarily trained to be 'the *assistant* of the medical man, not his *independent professional equal*', and that the '*legitimate* work of the nurse [was] to act under medical instruction' [emphasis added] (ibid.). The *BMJ* concluded its criticism of the independent practice of nurses by offering the rather draconian warning that any medical practitioners supporting independent nursing practice 'will render themselves liable to have their names struck off the Medical Register' (ibid., p. 186).

The threat to deregister medical practitioners who supported independent nurse practitioners was, however, only a 'bandaid' solution to the 'nurse threat', and was obviously inadequate for the purposes of constraining the general professional development and practice of organised nursing. The main problem for the medical establishment at this time was, therefore, how to control nursing without annihilating it (the practice of medicine had become far too dependent on nursing to do away with it altogether), and equally important, how to reassert medical dominance vis-à-vis its monopoly of diagnosis, prognosis and prescription in health care?

Gamarnikow (1991, p. 123) argues that the only remaining option available to medical men was to exploit gender and to use it 'as a means of reconstructing threatened power relations within health care'. She writes:

> Medical professional power was not sufficiently secure because of the ambiguities created by medical absence and conditional orders.[3] Therefore, by defining medical power as an instance of male power and nursing subordination as a form of female subordination, doctors drew on patriarchal gender relations to reformulate the division of labour . . . Thus, the nurse's skill and abilities were collapsed into female obedience to the male doctor.
> (Gamarnikow 1991, pp. 124, 127)

Gamarnikow explains that since women were regarded as being 'naturally' subordinate to men, and since most nurses were women, it was a relatively short step to construct (and it should be added, to legitimate via law) an image of nursing as being 'naturally' subordinate to medicine, and of nurses being 'naturally' subordinate to and dependent on medical men. As the examples given throughout the following chapters show, the medical establishment was highly successful in constructing the subordination of nursing and in ensuring that the profession and practice of nursing was firmly defined and controlled by doctors, not nurses.

CONCLUSION

The medical establishment's exemplary success in constructing the subordination of nursing was due in part to its success in exploiting gender and constructing and enforcing a gender division of labour between nurses (women) and doctors (men). It would, however, be a mistake to attribute medicine's success in subordinating nursing solely to its exploitation of gender. The medical establishment's success in this instance was also largely owing to the legitimisation of nursing's subordination, most notably through the exploitation of the well ordered legalistic procedures of law to structure and reinforce cultural–stereotypical views about women (nurses), the 'correctness' of traditional patriarchal gender relations between nursing (the healing practice of women) and medicine (the healing practice of men), and to structure and reinforce generally the cultural hegemony of medicine. Indeed, as this book ultimately aims to show, much of the medical profession's strength — including its power to subordinate and suppress nursing — has a firm legal basis in so far as it has been, and continues to be, supported by the law (its substance and procedures) and the (predominantly male) agents upholding and reinforcing law's central role in adjudicating human affairs. These claims will be examined in more depth in the following chapters.

ENDNOTES

1   It should be noted that women at this time did not have the legal right to attend university to train as doctors, or to practise orthodox medicine.

2   McKeown (1979) argues that medicine's contribution to personal and public health has been misrepresented and distorted to reinforce the myth of medicine's scientific worth and hence its power. He points out that medicine's apparent contribution to the 'prevention of sickness, disability and premature death was taken essentially at its own evaluation' and not on the basis of sound scientific evidence (ibid., p. xi). As a point of interest, Florence Nightingale herself was significantly hampered in researching and producing an accurate statistical analysis of the morbidity and mortality rates in English hospitals because she was unable 'to obtain hospital records fit for any purposes of comparison' (Nightingale 1858, 1968, p. 176). It can be deduced from this that the medical profession had not scientifically researched or 'proved' either the effectiveness or ineffectiveness of its hospital practices (see also Granshaw and Porter 1989).

3   Although nurses were not permitted to prescribe drugs, they were nevertheless permitted to make 'intelligent variations' to a physician's drug orders — especially during the night — if required to meet a patient's changing health needs (Gamarnikow 1991, p. 121).

CHAPTER TWO

The Precarious Relationship Between Nursing and the Law

INTRODUCTION

HISTORICALLY, THE LEGAL POSITION of the nurse and the nursing profession's relationship to the law has been of a precarious nature. Although the nursing profession has worked hard to change this, the status quo has been preserved. As stated in the introduction to this book, despite the nursing profession's historical struggle for improved legal status, nurses still do not have legitimated status and authority as autonomous professionals, and are still not legally recognised as having sovereignty in their own realm of practice.

In seeking to free itself from its subordinate position in the legitimated hierarchy of the health professions, and the many difficulties associated with being in such a position, the nursing profession world-wide has consistently looked to the law and legal processes as a primary means of securing its professional emancipation and improving its status and authority as a profession. Indeed, the view that nurses need to know and use the law in order to advance and enhance their professional goals has gained widespread currency in nursing discourse generally, and in what is now a substantial body of literature on the topic of 'nursing and the law' in particular.

Using the law to advance the professional goals of nursing

In the preface to *The professional nurse and the law*, Rothman and Rothman (1977, p. vii) state:

> The nursing profession will never achieve the status it deserves unless nurses are willing to assume the responsibility for guiding its growth through progressive legislation and role change. For this task it is essential that nurses know their legal rights and obligations.

More recently, in the introduction and opening chapter to her book, *Legal issues in nursing: a source book for practice*, Guido (1988, pp. xiii, 3) writes:

> No longer can nurses feign a working ignorance of the law and legal doctrines; today's professional practitioner must know, understand, and apply legal decisions and doctrines to his or her everyday nursing practice . . . It is believed that if a professional nurse truly understands legal issues and incorporates them into active, everyday practice, that instead of fearing the law, the nurse will both respect the law and will be able to enhance nursing's goals through the application of legal principles.

In the introductory chapter to the widely used Australian text *Nursing and the law*, Staunton and Whyburn (1993, p. 1) write:

> A knowledge of the law as an adjunct to a primary area of activity such as nursing requires that, in the first instance, the nurse has a rudimentary understanding of what the law is, where it comes from and how it operates. Such an understanding is essential if a nurse is to be able to extract from a seemingly complex system sufficient practical information to be of benefit to her in her professional activities.

The nursing legal literature also supports the view that the law can actually 'improve' nursing practice. For example, in the foreword to her text *Nursing and the law*, Cazalas (1978, p. viii), an American nurse attorney, comments:

> Once I was told by a judge that my law had ruined my nursing because it instilled in me fear of a law suit for malpractice. I say that law has improved my nursing, for it makes me aware of the value of continuing education, and of the necessity for extreme care in practising the art of both my professions.

In a more recent text entitled *Legal accountability in the nursing process*, Murchison et al. (1982, p. 46) write:

> Nursing can draw from law to broaden its theoretical base and strengthen its operation as a socially orientated discipline.
>
> Law makes a contribution to professional nursing by defining rules of conduct that brings logic and authority to the decision-making process. As with other disciplines related to nursing . . . law must also be synthesized into nursing science before it can be utilized to enhance the quality of nursing care.

And in the preface to CCH Health et al. (1990, p. vi), an Australian text on law for the nursing profession, Suzie Laufer, an assistant professor of law at Bond University, states:

The law plays an ever-increasing role in virtually every aspect of clinical practice, commencing even at the point of registration and entitlement to practice. A clear understanding of the law is, therefore, an essential ingredient in a nurse's armoury. It enables competent decision-making at all levels of practice.

The above and similar views have had a significant influence in shaping the way nurses perceive and respond to the law, and in shaping nurses' expectations of what the law can achieve for them at a professional level. Much attention has been given in the nursing jurisprudential literature, as well as in educational and other forums, to describing and explaining to nurses what the law is, how it operates, and what nurses can do in order to avoid 'ending up in court' (see Northrop 1989a). As a result of this, nurses have gained an improved and necessary understanding of the legal dimensions and associated legal risks of their professional nursing practice (see also Cushing 1988, p. vi). Furthermore, nurses have been able to use their rudimentary knowledge and understanding of the law to avoid the many legal risks that are associated with their practice. Nurses have continually and optimistically looked to the law as a means of improving their social and professional status. At a superficial level at least, it would appear that the law has, at times, proved to be a useful mechanism for advancing these and other important nursing goals.

For all of this, it is nevertheless open to serious question whether nurses do, in fact, 'need' the law in order to advance their professional goals and to 'improve' their nursing practice or whether the law is just one instrument of legitimation among others that nurses could use. It is also open to serious question whether the law, in its present form, can be relied upon to achieve these important ends. Related to this is the additional question of whether nursing jurisprudence in its current form has been adequate in its treatment of the so-called 'nurse question', and whether it has gone far enough in questioning the nature of law and its modus operandi in the specific field of nursing.

An examination of the history of the nursing profession's experience under the law demonstrates quite convincingly that the law has never been particularly sympathetic to the advancement of the professional goals of nursing. As will be demonstrated shortly, it is evident that in fact the law has been an important influence in obstructing the professional development of nursing, and in supporting and maintaining generally the oppression of nurses as a group. Neither has the law been instrumental in 'improving' either the profession or practice of nursing. In fact, as examples to be considered later in this book will show, the law has, in several respects, worked more to undermine rather than to improve the practise of nursing, and has served more to constrain rather than enhance the ability of nurses to practise their profession in a safe, competent, effective and ethical manner. Where improvements in the practice and profession of nursing have been achieved, this has been primarily because of the nursing profession's own self-imposed standards of conduct and nurse education programs (which, incidentally, have generally been of a higher standard than that otherwise required by law), not because of the influences of law per se.

In light of these and other considerations, it is evident, in response to the question raised above, that nursing jurisprudence in its present form has not adequately addressed the 'nurse question'. As will be shown in the following chapters, there is much to suggest that the nursing jurisprudence debate up until now has failed nurses in a number of important ways. Although nursing jurisprudential scholarship has been correct to give attention to describing and explaining the legal doctrines, rules, principles, and so on that are relevant to nursing practice, and to describing and explaining the workings of the legal system, its failure to give attention to the real impact of the law on nurses and nursing practice, and to the question of whether the law has been adequate and fair in its treatment of nurses, has been to nursing's serious disadvantage for reasons which this book hopes to make clear.

An underlying assumption of this discussion and this book is that while there certainly exists a distinctive branch of law which is primarily concerned with the profession and practice of nursing (that is, nursing jurisprudence), there still does not exist what can be appropriately described as a substantive nursing jurisprudence. The notion of a 'substantive nursing jurisprudence', as used in this instance, borrows heavily from feminist jurisprudential scholarship[1] and is taken here to mean a jurisprudence which has as its central focus the distinctive experiences and viewpoints of nurses, and which takes these experiences and viewpoints as a 'methodological starting point' — at both empirical and theoretical levels — from which to examine the law and its relationship to and treatment of nurses (adapted from Wishik 1986, p. 68; Fineman 1990, p. xiii). The experiences and viewpoints of nurses are also taken as a methodological starting point from which to critique the law and its practices, with a view toward achieving social reform and improving the social position of the nursing profession. Evidence for the need for a substantive nursing jurisprudence to be developed can be found in the fact that the nursing profession still has not achieved ultimate professional status, and that nurses are still carrying intolerable burdens on account of not having the legal authority to match their responsibilities as health care professionals. Support can also be found in the fact that even where nursing law reforms have been achieved, this has worked more to reinforce than to challenge the status quo, as cases to be analysed in the following chapters will show (adapted from Thornton 1986, 1990; see also Scutt 1981, p. 17; Smart 1984, pp. 4–5; Gregory 1987; Minow 1987, p. 83; O'Donovan and Szyszczak 1988, pp. 43–44; Fineman and Thomadsen 1991).

An international report on the legal regulation of nursing

The international nursing community has always been aware of the many and various difficulties faced by nurses in their endeavours to practise nursing in a safe, competent, responsible, and morally accountable way. The International Council of Nurses (ICN), which is based in Geneva, has been particularly proactive in monitoring and supporting the professional development of nursing around the world, and in coordinating initiatives aimed at strengthening the profession and practice of nursing at both national and international levels. Of the many activities undertaken by the ICN, perhaps one of its most important initiatives to date has been its inquiry into the legal regulation of nursing in countries around the world, and its subsequent world wide dissemination of 'regulation guidelines' for member associations engaged in nursing law reviews and reforms (see also the ICN's 'Principles of professional regulation', in ICN (1986a, pp. 43–47)).

In 1983–1984, on behalf of the ICN, Dr Margaretta Styles, an American professor of nursing, undertook what is described by the ICN as probably 'the most comprehensive review and analysis to date of national nursing laws' (Holleran 1986, p. 3). In commissioning this report, the ICN (1986a, p. 15) fully recognised that

> historical debates on nursing governance contain recurring themes, particularly in relation to elements of statutory regulation. How much state control is necessary and/or desirable, for instance? What is its purpose: to protect the public or practitioners or both? Should its powers be to restrict the right to practise to qualified individuals (mandatory) or merely to confer titles (permissive)? How many levels or categories of nurses should be recognised? Should auxiliaries and basic and post-basic specialists be regulated and protected by law? What educational standards should be enforced? Can the goal of quality care and the urgency of staffing needs be reconciled in setting standards?
>
> How can practising nurses who do not meet newly established standards be fairly treated without compromising professional goals and the public interest? What procedures are appropriate for the credentialing of foreign trained nurses? What definition of nursing is most congruent with educational standards and health care needs? What is the proper relationship of the practice of nursing to the practice of medicine? How should nursing and other interests be represented in the regulatory processes? What is the role of government in providing for the social and economic welfare of nurses and how does this relate to its role in protecting the public?

The ICN's overall purpose in commissioning the report was to 'discover to what extent these issues [outlined above] persist and deserve to be addressed in ICN policy and guidelines' (ICN 1986a, p. 15).

Despite a number of acknowledged limitations, the findings of the report provided a 'worldwide and probably representative overview of standards and processes of the regulation of nursing education and practice' (ibid., p. 17). Interestingly, the findings focused mainly on legal forms of regulation, and made only small reference to 'self, professional, institutional, and voluntary governance' (ibid.), further illustrating the extent to which the nursing profession esteems the law as an instrument of reform. Significantly, the overall finding of Styles' report was that the regulation of nursing throughout the world is

> ill-defined and diverse, educational requirements and legal definitions of nursing are generally inadequate for the complexity and expansion of the nursing role as it is emerging in response to health care needs; and the goals and standards of the profession worldwide are less apparent than one-half century ago.
> (ICN 1986a, p. 43)

At the time of writing this book, six years after the release of the ICN (1986a) report, national nursing laws around the world are still ill-defined and diverse, and quite inadequate to the task of providing for or dealing with the realities and complexities of nursing care delivery (see also Morrow 1986, p. 220). Furthermore, despite the ICN developing and circulating a formal position paper stating, among other things, that 'nursing is a profession in its own right', and that 'nurses are responsible and accountable for the nursing services they provide for people, sick and well', nurses still lack legitimated authority as autonomous health professionals and still do not have ultimate control over their own affairs — including education, practice, research and administration (ICN 1986b; WHO 1986, p. 5). Despite the ICN's well known concern about the 'trend in many countries to erode nursing functions and to undermine the quality of nursing care' (ICN 1986c), the role and function of the nurse — and indeed the education of nurses — continue to be eroded and usurped by non-nurses, making it increasingly difficult for individual nurses as well as ICN member associations to 'protect standards of nursing care given to the public' (see also ICN 1986d; Uren 1988, p. 5; Birkholz 1989).

The findings of the ICN report, and the apparent failure of nurses world wide to improve their legal status, raise at least four important questions which urgently need to be addressed, namely:

1. Why has the nursing profession not succeeded in improving its legal status?

2. Why do nurses still not have the legal authority to match their responsibilities?
3. To what extent have nurses (and, it should be added, their patients) suffered on account of their (nurses) not having the full legal authority to match their responsibilities?
4. What, if anything, can the nursing profession do to improve the status quo (for example, should it perhaps be looking to mechanisms outside law for improving its social, moral and legal position)?

It is a primary aim of this book to seek answers to these questions.

The failure of law in the realm of nursing

Historically, individual nurses and the nursing profession as a whole have not fared well under the law. In several respects, as the legal cases and anecdotal experiences to be examined in the following chapters will show, it is evident that the law (as stated earlier, interpreted here as 'a core doctrine, as a system and as an approach to the social world' (Naffine 1990, p. 1), and as 'a dominant discourse' (Eisenstein 1988, pp. 43–47; Fineman 1990, p. xii; Smart 1990a)) has failed nursing in a number of important and morally unacceptable ways.

The law's treatment of nurses (as already mentioned, over 90 per cent of whom are women) is, in almost every respect, paradigmatic of its treatment of women. And in the case of male nurses (commonly viewed as 'emasculated males' or 'not real men' (see, for example, Hase 1977, p. 52; Taylor et al. 1983, p. 62; Salvage 1985, p. 23; Savage 1987, p. 76; Delamothe 1988e, p. 345, 1988f, p. 407; Williams 1989, pp. 107, 120–123)), the law's response has tended to be characteristic of its treatment of 'failed males', that is, men who do not demonstrate what one writer terms 'emphasised masculinity' (Connell 1987) — namely, a white middle-class style of masculinity (the characteristics of which include being 'assertive, articulate, independent, calculating, competitive and competent' (Naffine 1990, pp. 22, 124)). This is particularly so of male nurses working as clinical or 'bedside' nurses.

Just as the law has been influential in upholding and reinforcing 'traditional notions of what is appropriate behaviour for a woman' (Naffine 1990, p. 144; see also Smart 1984; Heidensohn 1985), so too has it been influential in upholding and reinforcing traditional (and stereotypical) notions of what is appropriate behaviour and indeed 'the proper role' for a nurse. In the main, just as 'the law treats as axiomatic the subordination of women to men' (Naffine 1990, p. 8; see also MacKinnon 1989, p. 248), so too the law treats as axiomatic the subordination of nurses to doctors (and, it should be added, to hospital administrators). From a legal perspective of the health care arena, nurses are generally expected to be the unquestioning, obedient, loyal, faithful, loving and altruistic servants of their 'masters' — the majority of whom are male doctors and/or male hospital administrators. Those nurses who have been 'bad' (for example, those who have dared to 'overstep their authority' as (subordinate) health care providers, or who have had the 'audacity' and 'impudence' to question the legal (and medical) view of their 'proper role') have invariably found themselves 'justly punished' not only in the name of law, but, to borrow from Ashe (1987, p. 1172), in the name of 'nature and practical necessity'!

An examination of the nursing profession's experience under the law reveals that, historically, the world views, knowledges, and experiences of nurses have frequently been marginalised, trivialised and, in some cases, disqualified by the law, or, more to the point, by those whose dominant interests are represented in and protected by the law. An examination of nursing's experience also shows that in the case of nurses, as in the well theorised and exemplified case of women[2] the law has failed to adhere to its own rhetoric of being an impartial, fair, objective, rational and value-neutral system of social control and arbiter of social disputes. Although the law has worked to the advantage of nurses in some areas, its treatment of them has in the main been harmfully discriminatory, unjust, subjective, and value-laden. Some morally undesirable consequences of this have been that instead of being protected by the law, nurses have sometimes been made more vulnerable by it; and instead of being enabled by the law, nurses have often been unjustly disabled by it; rather than be emancipated by the law, nurses have very often been oppressed by it; and rather than benefiting from the law, nurses have sometimes suffered irrevocable harms because of it.

Despite the general and specific harms that individual nurses and the nursing profession as a whole have suffered within the legally constructed world, there still has not been an adequate investigation of the nature and adequacy of the law and legal processes affecting nurses, nursing practice, and the professionalisation of nursing. The nursing legal literature (which, as mentioned earlier, tends to be descriptive and explanatory in nature, rather than critical) has been conspicuously silent on such issues as the nature and adequacy of traditionally accepted legal doctrines and concepts, legal rules and principles, legal processes, the way the law operates in the specific field of nursing, and the role the law has played not only in obstructing the professional development of nursing but also in supporting and maintaining nursing's continued subordination to the (male dominated) medical profession. While the nursing legal literature (at least in Australia, the United Kingdom, and the United States of America) has given attention to subjects such as the history of Anglo-American/Anglo-Australian law, the process of law making, the functioning of the courts, the role of judges and lawyers and the relationship between the law and the state, little, if any, attention has been given to the politics of law (see, for example, Kairys 1982), or to the serious professional implications of legal politics for nursing. The authority and acceptability of law as a 'neutral arbiter' of social disputes has been accepted without question, as has the supposed 'justice' of judicial decisions — even in cases which have unfairly gone against nurses (as occurred in the famous Somera case, discussed in chapter 6 of this book). Ironically, some authors (such as Grennan (1930), the author of the article entitled 'The Somera case') have even applauded the rise of litigation cases against nurses as a sign that nursing is 'at last' receiving the legal recognition that it has fought so hard to achieve. Greig (1977, p. 51) comments, for example, that the increased legal vulnerability of nurses, together with an increasing willingness of members of the community to assert their legal rights, are developments which

> are not necessarily harmful to the nurse, because they may provide the necessary impetus to make her see herself as a member of a profession in her own right and not an angel of charity dependent in turn upon the charity of the community.

Karen Rea (1987a, p. 536), a practising barrister and a registered nurse in the United Kingdom, goes a step further, arguing controversially:

> Until the day when a nurse is named on her own on the pleadings in litigation, and is thus expected to be truly accountable for her act or omission, nursing cannot be called wholly and properly professional.

And in her book entitled *The law and liability: a guide for nurses*, Janine Fiesta (1988, pp. 15, 27) writes:

> It appears that during the past 10 years, an increase in the number of malpractice cases in which nurses have been named as defendants has occurred. This is a reflection of the evolving independent status of the professional nurse . . . As the legal profession becomes increasingly aware of the education and experience of the professional nurse, as well as the unique role a nurse plays in the health care delivery system, it is anticipated that nurses will become more legally accountable for their actions. This is in keeping with the development of nursing as a profession . . . The increased accountability of the nurse is an indication of the increased recognition of the professional status of nursing.

What is often overlooked by those applauding these and other trends in nursing jurisprudence, however, is that many notable court decisions involving nurse defendants have been morally unjust (for example, nurses have sometimes been left to carry an unfair burden of punishment, while others equally and sometimes more deserving of punishment have been exonerated), and have seriously undermined both the practice and the professional development of nursing. Also overlooked is the troubling reality that in many instances nurses have found themselves the subject of litigation not because of their own actions and omissions, but because of the actions and omissions of others (the Somera case being a case in point). Perhaps what is even more disturbing is that those writing on the question of nurses and the law seem to forget that nurses have always been held 'truly' accountable for their actions (as the history of professional disciplinary action and litigation cases against nurses makes plain), and that testing this accountability in the law courts has worked more to undermine than to enhance the status and authority of nursing in terms of it being 'wholly and properly professional', as examples to be considered in the following chapters will show.

Given that, historically, the nursing profession has had a rather ambivalent and precarious relationship with the law, it is curious that nurses — and in particular nurse lawyers, nurse ethicists and nurse academics — have not been more critical of and have not more forcefully challenged given legal doctrines and concepts, legal rules and principles, legal processes and court decisions that have discriminated against individual nurses, nursing knowledge and experience, nursing practice and the nursing profession as a group. There are, however, a number of possible explanations for this. For example, it may be that, like other members of the broader community, these nurses have been so socialised into accepting the 'hegemony and authority of law' (adapted from Polan 1982; Greer 1982), and 'the power that law arrogates to itself by making [its] claim to Truth, or ultimate correctness' (Smart 1990b, p. 2), that they have never really felt any need or inclination to question it or the role it has been given to regulate and adjudicate nursing's affairs. Another explanation can be found in what Zillah Eisenstein (1988, p. 45) describes as the

> organization of law itself — its categories, its reasoning, its rhetoric —
> [that] sets many of the limits in which people think and imagine their daily
> lives.

Or, it may be, that the law

> establishes regulations, thoughts, and behaviour, and institutes expectations
> of what is legitimate and illegitimate behaviour, what is acceptable and
> unacceptable, what is criminal and legal, what is rational and irrational,
> what is natural and unnatural.
> (Eisenstein 1988, p. 43)

Either way, it has been genuinely difficult for nurses to find a position from which to effectively critique the law, and to examine and challenge its treatment of them (see also Trubek 1972; Foucault 1977, 1978).

Whatever the reasons for nursing's failure to be more critical of the law, the problem remains that by not questioning or challenging the nature and authority of law, or indeed legal discourse generally (adapted from Eisenstein 1988; Smart 1990a, 1990b), nurses risk becoming accomplices to their own continued oppression and subordination (see Ashley 1975c, p. 1466; Melosh 1982, p. 29). Nurses also risk failing to achieve the important professional and political goal of having the full socially legitimated authority they need to match their responsibilities as health care professionals.

In *Feminism and the power of law*, Carol Smart (1989), a leading scholar in the field of feminist jurisprudence, recommends that detailed consideration should be given to 'how the law operates in different fields and to analyse it in its specificity rather than generality' (p. 164). In an article entitled 'Feminist reason: getting it and losing it', Martha Minow (1988), a professor of law at Harvard University, argues that it is crucial to feminist (jurisprudential) theory and practice that there is a 'concerted and persistent search for excluded points of view', and an 'acceptance of their challenges', (p. 60). If this is not done, Minow argues, 'feminists will join the ranks of reformers who have failed to do more than impose their own point of view' (ibid.; see also Jaggar 1983, p. 386).

As noted earlier, the issue of how the law operates in the specific field of nursing has not been fully addressed either in the nursing jurisprudential or feminist jurisprudential literature. An in-depth inquiry into this issue is long overdue. In her celebrated book entitled *Hospitals, paternalism and the role of the nurse* (see in particular pp. 115–119, 129), the late American nurse scholar and feminist, Dr Jo Anne Ashley (1976a), briefly considers questions about the patriarchal nature of law, the role the law has played in organising and legitimating the oppression of nurses, the extent to which the law has 'served to protect the commercial interests of a privileged few', the failure of law to protect the interests of nurses and the public, and the role the law has played in institutionalising 'inequality between nurses and physicians'. In a small but important article entitled 'Nurses and the meaning of law and order', Ashley (1976b) calls upon nurses 'to challenge the laws of the land' and to work hard to replace 'medical sexism and despotism' with 'a form of participatory democracy in which we, as nurses, share freely and equally with other professionals of similar qualifications and expertise' (p. 25). Unfortunately, Ashley's consideration of nursing's experience of the law is incomplete, and a much deeper investigation and analysis of the issues she raises is still required. Nevertheless, her comments remain pertinent to the present day situation and to some extent provide a starting point for the inquiry being undertaken here.

Nurses' experiences as a methodological starting point in nursing jurisprudence inquiry

It is generally accepted within the feminist jurisprudential literature that analyses of law should be guided by 'women's experience of the law and legal practice' (Lahey 1985; Smart and Brophy 1985; Scales 1986; Thornton 1986; Wishik 1986; MacKinnon 1989; Smart 1989; Fineman and Thomadsen 1991). In the introductory chapter to *Women in law: explorations in law, family and sexuality*, for example, Smart and Brophy (1985, p. 3) contend:

> It is from experience that our analyses of law should be drawn and upon which political practice should be based. In this way we are prevented from simply reading law as if it were composed of legal statutes rather than the actions of legal agents (i.e. police, lawyers, judges). Experience tells us, for example, that whilst statutes might not differentiate or discriminate between women and men, legal practice certainly does. Experience also tells us that . . . structurally, women are in a disadvantaged place vis-à-vis men.

Here the point is made that women's experience is a far more reliable starting point for feminist jurisprudential inquiry than are the abstract notions of law, justice, equity, and the like, since it is the experience of women

> that has alerted us (for generations) to the impact of law. No parliamentary statute, legal text book, jurisprudential treatise on justice or equity, or Law Commission paper has that value.
> (Smart and Brophy 1985, pp. 3–4).

In an article entitled 'To question everything: the inquiries of feminist jurisprudence', Heather Wishik (1986) makes a similar claim, arguing that feminist jurisprudential inquiry is 'methodologically and substantively, inquiry from the point of view of women's experiences'. Drawing on Catherine MacKinnon's (1983) work, Wishik (1986, p. 68) makes the additional point that the value of feminist jurisprudential inquiry is its criticism and subversion of 'patriarchal assumptions about law, including patriarchal attempts to present law without a gendered "point of view"'. The value of this approach for nursing jurisprudential inquiry is obvious: like feminist scholars, nurses also need to use their experiences as a methodological starting point for analysing the law, and, more particularly, for criticising and subverting the patriarchal assumptions about (and of) law, and, more to the point, the law's patriarchal assumptions about nurses and nursing practice.

The failure of modern law in the realm of women's lived experiences

Feminist scholars have long recognised that men have had a 'material stake in resisting the emancipation of women' (Sachs and Wilson 1978, p. 11) and have set out, sometimes quite deliberately, to prevent women from achieving an autonomous, authoritative and self-determining position in the world (see, for example, Johnston and Knapp 1971; Corea 1977; Walsh 1977; Sachs and Wilson 1978; Strachey 1978; Backhouse 1985; Wortman 1985; Mossman 1988; Scutt 1990). Feminist scholars have also long recognised that one of the most influential and powerful mechanisms available to men for ensuring that their cultural hegemony has been maintained, and that women have been kept in their 'proper place' (that is, subordinate to men) has been — and continues to be — the law (see Smart 1984; Heidensohn 1985; Thornton 1990). Tove Stang Dahl (1987, pp. 13–14) explains:

> Law is an important part of the cultural hegemony that men have in our type of society, and a cultural hegemony means that a ruling group's special way of viewing social reality is accepted as normal and as part of the natural order of things, even by those who are in fact subordinated by it. In this way law contributes to maintaining the ruling group's position . . . Law as an institution to a large degree contributes to the maintenance of the traditional male hegemony in society.

It is not, of course, the law per se which has supported and maintained the hegemony of men and the subordination of women. Rather it has been those formally charged with the responsibility of making, interpreting and applying the law who have done so. For instance, as Jocelynne Scutt (1990, p. 1) points out, the writings and actions of many common law judges and noted jurisprudential figures 'were deliberately or unconsciously designed to prevent women from operating autonomously in the world' and, it should be added, designed to protect male supremacy. An important example of this can be found in the words of Justice Tuck (*In re French* 1905, at 361, 2), who, in defending his decision to rule against allowing women the right to become lawyers, explained:

> If I dare express my own views I would say that I have no sympathy with the opinion that women should in all branches of life come in competition with men. Better let them attend to their own legitimate business.

The legal position of women has improved significantly since the days when women were regarded as 'non-persons' or as 'civilly dead' in law and by the courts.[3] Nevertheless, the law and legal processes remain inherently 'phallocentric' (male centred) (Smart 1990a, p. 201, 1990b, pp. 7–13), and continue to 'advance a traditional view of women: as the antithesis of the man of law' (Naffine 1990, p. 137). Furthermore, despite the so-called 'feminisation of law' over recent years (as manifest by the steady progression of women into law; the proliferation of feminist legal writings; the teaching of discrete 'women and the law' courses; and the establishment, in some universities, of women's law as an academic discipline in its own right), the law continues to be made, applied, and dominated by men (Johnston and Knapp 1971; Weisberg 1982b; Bentzon 1986; Dahl 1986; Menkel-Meadow 1987, 1988; Dalton 1988; Mossman 1988, 1990; Shalleck 1988; Graycar 1990; Graycar and Morgan 1990; Olsen 1990; Scutt 1990; Thornton 1990; Smart 1991). The law also continues to be largely unresponsive to the lives and special needs of women. More than this, as Karen DeCrow (1974, p. 4) points out:

> Women have fared miserably under the law, not only in the decisions which went against us, but even in the cases that went 'for' us; and we are deluding ourselves if we think that women can get justice in the courts. The record of court decisions, statutes, state constitutions, and legislative interpretations — all of these were written by men. And until they begin to be written by feminist women and feminist men, women will never achieve equity in our legal system.

Over the past two decades, feminist jurisprudential research has conclusively shown that the law:

- remains oppressive and inequitable in its treatment of women (see Smart 1984, pp. 3–23);
- operates with only a 'partial or incorrect vision of the reality of women's lives' (Smart 1990a, p. 199);
- continues to apply legal standards and categories which are 'articulated from the male point of view' (Eisenstein 1988, p. 63) and do not 'fit' the realities of women's lived experiences (Freedman 1983; O'Donovan and Szyszczak 1988; Mossman 1990; Graycar and Morgan 1990);
- continues to limit and obstruct the aims and aspirations of women;
- perpetuates generally the subordination of women in order to maintain the status quo: male dominance in both the public and private spheres of life (see also: Johnston and Knapp 1971; DeCrow 1974; Sachs and Wilson 1978; Atkins and Hoggett 1984; Brophy and Smart 1985; Chesler 1986; Dahl 1987; MacKinnon 1987; Naffine 1987, 1990; Smart 1989; Graycar 1990; Scutt 1990; Thornton 1990).

Feminist jurisprudential scholarship also shows that the law remains supremely influential in reinforcing its (male-constructed) view of 'the good woman' (the ideal counterpart to 'the man of law') and of what her 'proper role' in the world should be (see Eisenstein 1988, pp. 52–53). Describing this legal prototype of 'the good woman', Naffine (1990, p. 137) explains:

> She is the woman who manifests a form of emphasised femininity: she is loyal and loving, compliant and altruistic . . . The good woman is a faithful wife and mother whose sphere is the home, not the competitive marketplace.

An examination of women's experience of the law further shows that women who dare to deviate from the legally sanctioned ideal of 'the good woman', or who resist the oppression it brings, risk not only being coerced by the penal system (Eaton 1986, p. 9) but, contrary to the popularly held chivalry thesis (that socially deviant women are treated more leniently by the courts), also risk being treated more harshly than their male counterparts (Scutt 1976; Smart 1976; Armstrong 1977; Chesney-Lind 1977; Mackinolty and Radi 1979; Feyerherm 1981; Shelden 1981; Windschuttle 1981; Leonard 1982; Carlen 1983, 1985; Edwards 1985; Heidensohn 1985; Naffine 1987, 1990; Worrall 1990; Easteal 1993).

Significantly, while the law extols the virtues of 'the good woman', it has nevertheless failed to improve her status. As Rhode (1986, pp. 153–154) points out, although legal ideology has 'celebrated woman's domestic realm, it [has] declined to grant her sovereignty within it'. By denying women sovereignty in the domestic realm, the law has ensured that even within the 'feminine domain', a woman is kept in her 'proper place'; that is, subordinate to her husband and 'captive' in 'the prison-house of home' (Gavron 1966; Oakley 1981, p. 173; Heidensohn 1985, p. 176).

Nursing parallels to women's experience of law

The parallels which can be drawn between women's experience of law (as revealed by feminist jurisprudential inquiry) and nursing's experience of law (as will be partially revealed in the following chapters of this book) are substantial. As stated in the preface to this book, the law's treatment of nurses has, in almost every respect, been paradigmatic of its treatment of women. Like their sisters in other cultures and historical periods (see, for example: Johnston and Knapp 1971; Hoegrefe 1972; Strachey 1978; Sachs and Wilson 1978; MacLean 1980; Pateman 1988; Anderson and Zinsser 1988; Sealey 1990; Scutt 1990; Helfield 1990), nurses have been subject to the legally enforced principles of 'female legal incompetence, female subordination, and the establishment of male guardianship' (adapted from Anderson and Zinsser 1988, p. 337). As the following chapters will show, this has resulted in nurses being denied full recognition as legally competent professionals, made subordinate to their (mostly male) superiors (doctors and lay hospital administrators), and kept subject to the 'protective' guardianship of men. This has, among other things, seen nurses:

- disqualified from having full professional status;
- denied sovereignty in their own realm of practice;
- forced (that is, by verbal threat of dismissal, deregistration, and so on) to obey uncritically the orders of their predominantly male superiors;
- allowed to practice only under the 'supervision' of medical practitioners; and when seeking more authority as independent practitioners, they have been forcefully reminded that if granted professional autonomy they would lose the 'benefits and protection' that are otherwise afforded by doctors assuming total control of, and responsibility for, patient care.

For all of this, in what stands as a classic example of legal double standards, the law has nevertheless regarded nurses as having sufficient personhood and sufficient professional autonomy to be held independently responsible and accountable for their actions and omissions (even when these have been in direct response to a 'superior's orders') and has punished them accordingly.

CONCLUSION

To understand better why the law has been so resistant to (and has even denied) the concerns of nurses, it is evident that much more is required than mere compensatory scholarship — that is, an 'add-on-nurses-and-stir' approach to correcting what legal scholars have left out (an approach which was characteristic of first phase feminist jurisprudential inquiry (Wishik 1986, p. 67)). Neither is it enough merely to focus on 'recovering that which has been silenced', namely, nursing's experience of law from the point of view of nurses — although this is, of course, a necessary and important prerequisite to any inquiry into nursing and the law (see also Turkel 1990). And neither is it sufficient just to criticise the law, legal scholarship, and society for the failure to address nursing concerns or for the apparent readiness to use 'patriarchically based assumptions' to sustain nurses' oppression (Wishik 1986, p. 67) — although 'critique is a prerequisite for the formulation of an alternative perspective' (Smart 1976, p. xv). Like feminist jurisprudential scholarship, nursing jurisprudential scholarship needs also to engage in 'a positive project of constructing and developing alternative models, methods, procedures [and] discourses' (Gross 1986, p. 195), and indeed of 'decentering law in the hierarchy of discourses' (Smart 1989; see also Thornton 1986, 1990; Turkel 1990; Fineman and Thomadsen 1991).

It is self-evident that in order to achieve the above and other important tasks, nursing jurisprudential inquiry will need to follow closely in the footsteps of its sister discipline, feminist jurisprudence. In so doing, nursing jurisprudence might succeed in challenging nurses to accept and engage in not just 'a new way of thinking' about the law, but also 'thinking about new things' (MacKinnon 1987, p. 9). If nurses meet this challenge, they will be in a better position to overcome the powerful and dominant patriarchal forces which have, up until now, constrained and oppressed their identity, existence, and activities in the male-dominated world, and which in turn have effectively prevented them, as health care professionals, from fulfilling their very real moral responsibilities toward the community at large.

ENDNOTES

1 See, for example: DeCrow 1974; Taub and Schneider 1982; Weisberg 1982a, 1982b; MacKinnon 1983, 1987; Brophy and Smart 1985; Lahey 1985; Dahl 1986, 1987; Erika 1986; Mossman 1986; Scales 1986; Stubbs 1986; Thornton 1986, 1989, 1990, 1991; Wishik 1986; Ashe 1987; Menkel-Meadow 1987, 1988; Minow 1987, 1988; Morgan 1987/1988, 1989; Eisenstein 1988; Lacey 1989; Smart 1989, 1990a, 1990b, 1991; Graycar 1990; Graycar and Morgan 1990; Naffine 1990; Olsen 1990; Scutt 1990; Young 1990; Fineman and Thomadsen 1991.

2 See, for example: Kanowitz 1969; Johnston and Knapp 1971; DeCrow 1974; Sachs and Wilson 1978; Mackinolty and Radi 1979; Mukherjee and Scutt 1981; Taub and Schneider 1982; Weisberg 1982a, 1982b; Freedman 1983; Atkins and Hoggett 1984; Brophy and Smart 1985; Edwards 1985; Lahey 1985; Wortman 1985; Chesler 1986; Eaton 1986; Rhode 1986, 1988, 1989; Dahl 1987; MacKinnon 1987; Menkel-Meadow 1987, 1988; Morris 1987; Naffine 1987, 1990; Eisenstein 1988; Minow 1988; Mossman 1988, 1990; O'Donovan and Szyszczak 1988; Gillespie 1989; Smart 1989, 1991; Graycar 1990; Graycar and Morgan 1990; Olsen 1990; Scutt 1990; Thornton 1990; Worrall 1990; Fineman and Thomadsen 1991; Kennedy 1992; Robson 1992.

3 The question of whether or not a woman could in law be regarded as 'a person' became the subject of intense legal debate and deliberation for six decades between the mid-eighteen hundreds until the early nineteen hundreds. Regardless of whether women addressed the courts themselves, or were represented by distinguished male lawyers, their cases seeking recognition as 'persons' were always unsuccessful (Sachs and Wilson 1978, p. 34). The judiciary persistently and consistently regarded the notion of 'women being persons' as utterly 'incomprehensible' and 'manifestly absurd' (ibid., pp. 6, 30). Changing social attitudes toward women eventually forced a change in judicial attitudes, however, and after the famous case of *Edwards v Attorney-General of Canada* (1929), in which the Judicial Committee of the Privy Council held women to be 'persons' in

the eyes of the law, women made their formal debut as persons in the United Kingdom. Incredibly, the decision saw six decades of precedents stating that women could not be included in the term 'person' . . . swept aside by the simple proposition: 'The word "person" may include members of both sexes, and to those who ask why the word should include females, the obvious answer is, why not?' (Sachs and Wilson 1978, p. 41).

CHAPTER **THREE**

The Nursing Profession's Quest for Legal Status: A Brief Historical Overview

INTRODUCTION

IN ADVANCING THIS INQUIRY into the nursing profession's relationship to and experience of the law, it is important to consider first some of the factors which motivated the early modern nursing leaders to look to the law as a means of improving the professional status of nursing. It is also important to identify some of the forces (for example, the male dominated processes of law making, and the general male resistance to women achieving personal and professional independence in the public sphere) which were influential in preventing the nursing profession obtaining the kind of legal status it fought for and which, to this day, it still has not obtained.

'The status quo is quite good enough'

In 1904, the chairman of London Hospital, the Honourable Sydney Holland, publicly opposed the state registration of nurses, declaiming: 'The status quo is quite good enough' (Holland 1904, p. 37). As far as the nursing profession was concerned, however, the status quo was — and had long been — far from 'quite good enough', and its response was to fight even harder to achieve recognition of the nurse 'as an individual of some importance to the State' (Hobbs 1904, p. 75).

The history of the early modern nurses' struggle for legal status is a history of radical determination 'to establish control of their own profession' (Minchin 1977, p. 2). Their vision, moulded and guided by the powerful influence of Florence Nightingale, was to see the development of nursing as a profession *of* women, *for* women (of all backgrounds), and to be totally controlled by women. Indeed, Dock and Stewart (1938, p. 127) point out that the 'specially revolutionary feature' of Florence Nightingale's original plan for the professionalisation of nursing (a feature commonly overlooked by the critics of nursing, including some feminists) was

> the positive mandate that the entire control of a nursing staff, as to discipline and teaching, must be taken out of the hands of men, and lodged in those of a woman, who must herself be a trained and competent nurse.

At a time when few woman 'could make any claim to having an "occupation", let alone a "profession"' (Trembath and Hellier 1987, p. 4), nurses succeeded in establishing their own schools of education and unofficial registering authorities, and in doing so also succeeded in establishing their identity and status as 'qualified nurses' (see: Cook 1913a, 1913b; Breay and Fenwick 1931; Dock and Stewart 1938; Abel-Smith 1960; Bridges 1967; Bendall and Raybould 1969; Hector 1973; Ashley 1976a; Minchin 1977; Kalisch and Kalisch 1978; Melosh 1982; Dolan et al. 1983; Maggs 1983; Kelly 1985; Reverby 1987; Trembath and Hellier 1987; Russell 1990). Through their determination, hard work and commitment, these nurses also succeeded in gaining public respectability for their growing profession (Trembath and Hellier 1987, p. 4). What is particularly remarkable about these accomplishments is that they were achieved in the face of overwhelming odds — including fierce opposition from the powerful and well-organised (male dominated) medical profession, not to mention the opposition from influential (all male) politicians (the law makers) who, like the Honourable Sydney Holland, also felt the status quo was 'quite good enough'.

What is perhaps even more remarkable about the nurses' achievements, however, is that they established and developed nursing as a profession at a time when women, married or single, had no legal right 'to engage in any lawful occupation of their choosing' (Hill 1979, p. 250) — a point sometimes overlooked by those writing on the history of nursing. As already briefly mentioned in the previous chapter, up until the early 1900s the very idea of a woman choosing a lawful profession was regarded as being 'counter to the common law tradition' (ibid.). Placed in historical context, it is, then, small wonder that nurses experienced the enormous difficulties they did in trying to obtain state registration. In several respects, the situation was quite hopeless, since to grant nurses state registration would have been tantamount to recognising that women had the right to engage in a lawful profession of their own choosing — a truly unacceptable and undesirable outcome for those (professional men) vehemently opposed to women 'operating autonomously in the world' (Scutt 1990, p. 1; see also *Bradwell v State of Illinois* (1873); *United States v Anthony* (1873); *In re French* (1905); *Edwards v Attorney-General for Canada* (1929); Walsh 1977; Sachs and Wilson 1978; Wortman 1985; Mossman 1990).

Contrary to popular thought (see, for example, Ashley 1976a, p. 116), the early modern nurses were very aware of the difficulties they faced as women in trying to obtain legal status. (As a point of interest, the International Council of Nurses (ICN), an influential international nursing organisation still in existence today, was in fact inspired by and established shortly after the 1899 London meeting of the International Council of Women (Breay and Fenwick 1931, p. 60). Furthermore it is known that the founders of the ICN were greatly encouraged in their efforts by the woman's suffrage movement at that time (Dock and Stewart 1938; Breay and Fenwick 1931)). Nursing leaders were, however, also aware that without legal status, the nurse had 'no rights, and no protection': she would be merely a 'lady with a vocation', not a professional with rights of self-determination (*Una* 1917, p. 390; Godden 1989a, p. 14). The early modern nurses further realised that unless nurses obtained legal status (such as that offered by state registration) they would be unacceptably vulnerable to abuse and exploitation as a source of cheap labour by doctors and lay hospital administrators, as in fact they already were.

In examining nursing's quest for legitimated professional status, it is important to keep in mind that, historically, the legal status of nurses was, to a very large extent, inextricably linked to and dependent on the legal status of women (see also Bullough and Bullough 1969; Christy 1972; Heide 1973; Brand and Glass 1975; Dachelet 1978; Gunning 1983; Meredith 1987). Evidence of this can be found in the fact that, with the notable exception of some American states (for example, North Carolina, New Jersey, New York, and Virginia, in all of which, state registration was achieved for nurses in 1903 (Shannon 1975, p. 1327)), the state registration of nurses was not generally achieved until after women were enfranchised, the significance of which did not go unnoticed by some of the early modern nurse leaders (see, for example, Brand and Glass 1975). One such leader was Lavinia Dock, a distinguished American nurse and the first Honorary Secretary of the International Council of Nurses. Commenting on the comparatively early passage in 1901 of the *New Zealand Trained Nurses Registration Act* (the first discrete Nurses Act to be passed in the world), Dock[1] (1906, p. 9), a passionate supporter of women's suffrage, explained:

> I have a strong conviction that one great reason why the New Zealand work is so good is that every woman there has full suffrage just as men have. They are thus placed on an equality with men in sharing public duties and responsibilities.

She continued (ibid.):

> Although the New Zealand Act does not make registration by the State compulsory, it was very soon found by nurses that such registration was greatly to their advantage, and gave them a professional status hitherto lacking.

The position of the New Zealand nurses was further strengthened by the remarkable fact that the statutorily empowered Assistant Inspector of Hospitals and the Registrar[2] of Nurses (being two posts held by the same person in this instance) was a nurse — and, as Dock (1906, p. 9) was quick to point out, 'a quiet, capable and efficient woman' as well! It was this fact, argued Dock (1906), that was the very 'strong point of the New Zealand law'.

The situation of nurses in other countries was not so encouraging, however. Without the legal right to vote and to elect their own legislators, nurses around the world faced an uphill battle in their attempts to obtain legitimated status as professionals (see Fickeissen 1986, p. 12). In the case of English nurses, this uphill battle developed into full-scale war, the details of which will be given later in this chapter. As in other countries, the legal position of English nurses was not to change until women in England were given the vote. Compelling evidence for this can be found in a 1919 House of Lords debate on the state registration of nurses, during which the legal status of nurses was inextricably linked to the enfranchisement of English women. In debating the merits of a proposed nurses registration Bill, Earl Russell (1919, p. 846) forcefully reminded his fellow Lords in the House:

> Women now have the vote; they have to be considered more than they used to be. It is not easy to say, 'I do not like the registration of nurses'. Women are now likely to get what they insist on having, and . . . they must have registration.

Earl Russell was not alone in his views. There was a mounting fear among some politicians that unless the status of nursing was significantly improved (that is, given statutory recognition), 'suitable women' would no longer find nursing attractive as a profession and would be diverted into other occupations which, owing to various social and legal reforms (not least female emancipation), had become more accessible to women. In a House of Commons debate on the 1919 Nurses Registration Bill, for example, Mr Briant MP (1919, pp. 778–779), argued:

> I am more and more convinced that, unless some steps be taken to give nurses the status which they have a right to demand, and which they have deserved, then in the future, when nurses will be required more than ever before, we shall find there is a scarcity . . . And unless the nursing profession has some security that it will have a definite status in the nation, and be protected from being possibly misunderstood and misrepresented as belonging to that large class of people who pose as nurses without any efficiency and without any real training, then we shall lose that better class of nurse which is so important, and indeed essential, for the health of the nation . . .

I want to point out that increased avenues of employment are open to women. Women during the last few years have had opportunities for employment at comparatively high rates of wages which were not open to them many years ago, and, unless the position of the nurse is improved, not only by legal status, but by conditions of service and pay, the women of the class which is required will be diverted into other occupations, and the health of this country will undoubtedly suffer.

The quotation above illustrates the increasing public and political recognition of the fact that qualified nurses were essential to the promotion of public health and to improving generally the nation's health services. Doctors, for example, declared 'we cannot do our work properly without good nurses' (Molson 1919, p. 787); and politicians conceded, 'nursing is an absolute essential to the health activities of the country' (Watson Cheyne 1919, p. 800). Politicians also recognised that the success of the Ministry of Health itself had become utterly dependent on the improved status and efficiency of the nursing profession (Astor 1919, p. 813). The state registration of nurses thus could no longer be dismissed as a trivial women's issue: it was now a major political issue, and one demanding immediate political attention and action.

In examining the question of the professionalisation of nursing and the nursing profession's historical appeal to the law to protect both its own and the public's interests, it is important to first consider some of the major factors which prompted the early modern nurse leaders to seek state registration as a means of enhancing nursing's professional status. An examination of these factors will, in turn, help to expose some of the patriarchal forces which were influential in preventing nurses achieving the legal status they desired and needed, and which, to this day, have continued to be influential in preventing nurses achieving the legitimated authority and autonomy they need in order to practise their profession in a safe, competent, effective, ethical, and publicly accountable manner.

For the purposes of this chapter, attention will focus primarily on the nursing struggles which occurred in England, the United States of America and Australia. These three countries have been chosen for four main reasons:

1. Each initially adopted the Nightingale model of nursing, and therefore shares a common philosophy and approach to the practice and profession of nursing (Dock and Stewart 1938, p. 193).
2. Each has been either directly or indirectly subjected to the influences of the common law — including its legal structures and processes.
3. Each has experienced similar problems in obtaining legal recognition of the practice of nursing and the validity of nursing knowledge and experience.

4. Taken together, the historical happenings in each of these countries highlight the contemporary need for a radical new direction in thinking about the law as an instrument for improving the status of nursing, and the kinds of strategies which the nursing profession worldwide should adopt if it is to succeed in achieving its professional, political and moral ends.

The abuse of pupil nurses

During the late 1800s and early 1900s, 'nurses' (most were in fact only pupil or student nurses) were used — or more to the point, abused — as a source of free or cheap labour by both small and large hospitals. The conditions that these early 'nurses' endured were appalling and in retrospect serve as a poignant modern-day reminder of how vulnerable women (and, it should perhaps be added, girls[3]) are as workers. Long hours, poor or no pay, an inadequate diet, high morbidity and mortality rates, severe staff shortages, rigid discipline, and a short career span became the dominant characteristics of the emerging modern nursing profession. Significantly, these characteristics were not unique to any one country and indeed typified nursing in common law countries around the world. Although the deplorable work conditions caused great hardship and personal suffering for the early 'nurses', little was done to change the status quo. In fact, those who had vested material interests in the exploitation of cheap pupil nurse labour wholeheartedly defended the situation of 'long hours and poor pay' on grounds that it was 'beneficial' to the nurses concerned, and in the 'public interest'. As one commentator put it:

> The student nurse, if we would join in her fairmindedness and honour, must understand from the beginning that her relation with the hospital is a perfectly dignified, well-balanced business arrangement whereby she gives three years of service in return for technical training that lifts her forever from the ranks of unskilled labor.
> (Flash 1915, p. 442)

Nurses who were brave enough to complain about their plight were portrayed as 'failed women' (selfish, disloyal, disobedient, and uncaring), and thus deserving of reprimand, scorn and rejection. The low view held of 'complaining nurses' was made clear by the statement of one matron (MacLean 1903, p. 34) who warned nurses:

> One thing I do most heartily deprecate is the habit many hospital nurses have of grumbling — never satisfied, work too hard, hours too long, food not all that they desire . . . Loyalty to their own training schools is, I am afraid, lacking in many nurses, and yet what happier time have we had than

when eagerly learning all that is to be learned in theory, and doing all that can be done in practice for the relief of those suffering ones under our care, without anxiety or responsibility when off duty, busy and perhaps hard worked when on duty . . . Beware of that captious spirit of finding wrong everywhere.

As mentioned above, and as the following discussion will attempt to show, the harsh conditions of the early nurses were not unique to any one country and typified nursing in other common law countries. Neither was the rhetoric defending these conditions unique to any one country, and in fact many of the public statements made by dominant interest groups defending the exploitative work conditions the early nurses were forced to endure were remarkably similar regardless of the country, the time period, or the socio-cultural context in which they were uttered.

In an attempt to ensure that an accurate account is given of the rhetoric used against nurses during this historic period, and of the nursing profession's response to it, published comments relevant to this inquiry will be quoted in full. Many of the comments quoted will also provide important examples of the extent to which medical men and lay (male) hospital administrators used their legitimated positions of power and authority to marginalise, trivialise, discredit and disqualify nursing discourse. Equally important to this inquiry, the lengthy quotations cited will also serve to show how the very processes of law making and law reform (including, in this instance, government select committees of inquiry, political lobbying, parliamentary debate, petitioning and consciousness raising) were themselves overwhelmingly biased in favour of, and structured to ensure, the cultural hegemony of men (in this instance doctors, lay hospital administrators and politicians) and the subordination of women (nurses). For example, the politicians involved in formulating and debating the early state registration laws for nurses were all men, as were the members of the English government select committees of inquiry into nursing registration during 1904 and 1905. Other select committees of inquiry into the work conditions of nurses were also dominated by men. Although nurses (women) were called as witnesses to present evidence to these select committees, they were always outnumbered by male witnesses (most of whom were prominent physicians or lay hospital administrators). Under such conditions, the nursing profession's only hope of success in achieving its professional goals was almost entirely dependent on securing the support of benevolent influential men, which is precisely what many nursing leaders did (including, and not least, Florence Nightingale (see, for example, Cook 1913a, 1913b; Cope 1958; Woodham-Smith 1964; Shannon 1975; Fickeissen 1986)).

Nursing conditions in England

During the 1890s, early 1900s, and beyond, the conditions in most English hospitals were deplorable. Nurses worked 12 to 14 hours per day, and in some instances up to 87 hours per week, and were poorly paid (Lyons 1912, p. 241; Gordon 1920, pp. 93–94; Abel-Smith, 1960, pp. 55–56; Maggs 1983, p. 96, 1987, pp. 176–189). Living like prisoners, these nurses worked without a break except at meal time, often slept on the wards in which they worked, were not allowed visitors, were denied the opportunity to attend chapel, and were granted only one late pass (that is, after 10 p.m.) a year (*Report from the Select Committee on the Registration of Nurses* 1904, 1905; Abel-Smith 1960, pp. 58–59). Being generally 'over-tired and over-worked', the nurses 'suffered very much in health' (Yatman 1890, p. 294); morbidity and mortality rates were culpably high (Minchin 1977, p. 3).

Of those working in the general hospital, 75 per cent were pupil nurses, and only 25 per cent were qualified or trained (Maggs 1983, p. 9). Pupil nurses were 'preferred because they were the cheapest form of labour for hospitals which faced the constant problem of under-financing' (ibid., p. 14). Maggs (1983, p. 88) explains:

> As far as the hospitals were concerned, the need was for the cheapest form of workforce, women who could work for little material reward but would also do so for a considerable period of time.

Hospitals also unashamedly earned money and made considerable profits by selling the services of second-year pupil nurses who were effectively contracted out to the unsuspecting public as 'qualified' private duty nurses. Pupil nurses so contracted out were expected to pay a commission of varying rates from 5 to 7.5 per cent, 15 to 25 per cent, and 25 to 40 per cent of their earnings to the contracting agencies (Kent 1905, p. 181; Dingwall et al. 1988, p. 80). The 'sweating' of nurses was big business, but not just for hospitals. 'Ex men-servants and managers of registry offices' also made good business out of this practice (Kent 1905, p. 181). It is estimated that up until as late as 1914, almost 70 per cent of the nursing labour force was employed in private duty nursing (Maggs, 1983, p. 131).

Further evidence of the appalling conditions under which the early pupil nurses worked can be found in the *Report from the Select Committee of the House of Lords on Metropolitan Hospitals* (1890). The report found that the pupil nurses were poorly fed, poorly housed, given responsibility which far exceeded their level of training, and were generally overworked. Evidence was given that ill-health frequently meant dismissal, and so rather than seek sick leave when ill, many nurses worked until they 'dropped', sometimes dying as a result (Raymond 1890, p. 308; Valentine 1890, pp. 317, 329; Fenwick 1890, p. 551). One nurse witness claimed:

I know of a nurse who went on working until she was quite unfit; she was
so ill that she could hardly breathe, and then she excused herself from
supper; the home sister went to her room, found that she had high fever; and
sent for the house physician, who ordered her at once to be warded; 10 days
after that she was dead.
(Raymond 1890, p. 308)

In support of this evidence, another witness quoted the following comments
of a policeman who had been a patient:

It is a cruel way in which these women are worked; they are simply
murdering that nurse that works so hard for us.
(Valentine 1890, p. 331)

The seriousness of the conditions being endured by the pupil nurses did
not escape the attention of the early modern nursing leaders. In 1892,
Nursing Record, an official British nursing periodical, declaimed that nurses
were

the white slaves of hospitals — overworked, underpaid, often more than
half-starved inside their walls, or sweated as private outside nurses to
produce larger profits for the hospitals and then, when their health was
broken down under the strain, discharged — tossed aside like old worn-out
things.
(*Nursing Record* 1892, pp. 350–351)

Hospital management remained unsympathetic, however, and even as
late as 1930, nurses were still working a 57 hour week (Abel-Smith 1960, p.
137). Not surprisingly, nurses had only a brief working life, and attrition
rates were high (research suggests that less than 65 per cent of entrants to
general nursing training between 1908 and 1921 stayed for more than one
year (Maggs 1981a, p. 100)). Rather than attributing high attrition rates to
overwork and exhaustion, the medical profession argued they were because
of the 'slightly morbid motive' of those entering the profession (Minchin
1977, p. 102). These 'slightly morbid motives' were described in the *British
Medical Journal* (1880) in the following terms:

They [nurses] are disappointed in love, or they want something to kill
ennui, or they have religious convictions on the subject; none of which
sentiments, we may venture to say, are (sic) likely to produce good staying
workers.
(cited in Minchin, 1977, p. 102)

In the main, however, those leaving 'the system' were generally considered
to be:

either emotionally inadequate ('too neurotic'); morally unsound ('inclined to flirt with male patients'); or educationally backward ('too lazy to study').
(Maggs 1981a, p. 100)

In 1947, attrition rates were still high at an estimated 54 per cent (Sheehan 1985, p. 18). Hopes of improving nurses' work conditions and of reducing the numbers of nurses fleeing the profession remained low, however. As one commentator (Mavor 1943, p. 248) lamented in the *British Medical Journal*:

Nurses have little hope from their seniors, their 'employers', or the medical profession, who are much too worried about the future of their own sixpences and guineas to devote much time to the rights of their sister profession. The truth is that nursing is the only indispensable profession in the modern world . . . Yet she [the nurse] is treated at best like an irresponsible school girl and at the worst like a Czech in a German labour camp.

Nursing conditions in the United States of America

Conditions in the United States of America were similarly appalling. As in the case of English pupil nurses, American pupil nurses also worked long hours and were unashamedly exploited by profit-seeking lay hospital administrators and doctors.

As in England, the bulk of hospital labour was carried out by pupil nurses. The so-called 'education' of these students consisted of '95 percent service and less than 5 percent instruction in theory' (Kalisch and Kalisch 1975, p. 233). Even this 'education' was considered 'too much' by doctors who complained that nurses were being 'overtrained'. Shifts ranged from between 12 to 24 hours per day, and an incredible 84 to a 168 hour week, conditions which were considered the norm right up until the late 1920s (Reverby 1987, p. 100). The extent to which nurses worked these long hours was revealed by a 1926 survey which found that

80 percent of the private duty nurses worked a twelve-hour day, 18 percent worked a twenty-four-hour day, and 2 percent worked a different schedule.
(Bullough and Bullough 1969, p. 166)

Like their English counterparts, American pupil nurses were hired out as 'qualified' private duty nurses, a practice which was widely recommended in the hospital literature 'as a legitimate means of bringing in added income to the hospital' (Ashley 1976a, p. 26). Hospitals would solicit private cases for their students by placing advertisements in the public press. All remuneration for student services sold was paid directly to the hospitals (ibid., pp. 25–26). The use of this sweated labour enabled many hospitals (small and large alike) to become established and to stay in business (Ashley 1976a, p. 6; Kelly 1985, p. 42; Reverby 1987, p. 61). But the major factor which enabled the hospital industry to grow was its exploitation of the apprenticeship nurse training system and the ready source of cheap labour it supplied which enabled hospitals to keep their running costs artificially low (Kalisch and Kalisch 1975; Ashley 1976a; Christy 1980; Reverby 1987). By 1904, there were 1484 hospitals throughout the United States of America. Of these, 867 (over 50 per cent) had schools of nursing with a total enrolment of 21 844 students (Kalisch and Kalisch 1975, p. 227). Despite the proliferation of nursing schools (the 1901 United States Bureau of Education Annual Report estimated that nursing increased 706 per cent compared with medicine at only 79 per cent), career prospects for the graduate nurse remained poor (Kalisch and Kalisch 1975, p. 227). The constant supply of pupil nurses militated against the need to employ graduate nurses which would have certainly increased the hospitals' overall operating budget. Kalisch and Kalisch (1975, p. 226) note that

> even in the late 1920s it was estimated that not a single graduate nurse was employed as a general staff, or general duty nurse in 73 percent of hospitals with nursing schools.

Unemployment among graduate nurses thus emerged as a major professional problem.

The unabashed exploitation of the pupil nurses' free labour and time, predictably took its toll. As in England, morbidity and mortality rates among pupil nurses were high. Nurses suffered severe exhaustion, and many developed typhoid fever, scarlet fever, pneumonia, diphtheria, influenza, and tuberculosis (Reverby 1987, p. 64). The incidence of tuberculosis among student nurses was particularly high. Although having a negative tuberculosis test upon entering a school of nursing, most nurses tested positive by the time they finished their training program (Kalisch and Kalisch 1975, pp. 230–231). Indeed, it was common knowledge that in

> the average general hospital with a tuberculosis service, approximately 80 percent of the student group graduated with positive tuberculosis.
> (Kalisch and Kalisch 1975, p. 230)

In one school of nurses '91 per cent tested positive to tuberculosis' (Harrington et al. 1935, p. 1871). One study also found that student nurses in three general hospitals in Minnesota had a tuberculosis infection rate five times greater than other women who were attending a college of education in the same community (Harrington et al. 1935; Kalisch and Kalisch 1975, p. 231).

In 1893, physicians became so alarmed by the illness rates among students, that they strongly advised 'only very healthy women should be admitted into training programs' (Reverby 1987, p. 64). This was because only the 'fit and healthy' would be able to do the strenuous work that was required of them at that time (Kalisch and Kalisch 1975, p. 230). At no time did either doctors (most of whom owned the private hospitals in which the students laboured) or hospital administrators suggest that the pupil nurses should have their hours of work cut or their work load lightened (Reverby 1987, p. 64).

Although nursing superintendents worried about their students suffering exhaustion. it was not for humanitarian reasons that they did so, but for reasons of etiquette and sustaining a 'good business relationship' with 'clients' (private patients). The main concern seemed to be not that pupil nurses might 'drop dead' from exhaustion, but that their exhaustion may result in 'moral laxity' and/or the collapse of their 'moral purity'. The moral purity being referred to here had nothing to do with the student nurses keeping their physical virginity as might be expected (many of the students privately cared for single men in hotels and were subjected to their advances; the students were also vulnerable when caring for married female patients in private homes where they sometimes found themselves subject to the advances of their female patient's husbands). Rather, it was to do with the (feminine) moral purity of remaining gentle, humane, sympathetic and, above all, tactful after working long and stressful hours (Reverby 1987, p. 97; see also Parsons 1916; Gladwin 1930; Aikens 1943).

As well as enduring harsh physical working conditions, nurses had to endure fragile terms of employment. Nurses could be and were dismissed without reason and without notice (Kalisch and Kalisch 1975; Ashley 1976a; Kelly 1985; Reverby 1987). Grounds for dismissal were often trivial and included:

- having a 'determined manner';
- not wearing a cap;
- not acquiescing to a head nurse's whims (Reverby 1987, p. 68);
- talking with other nurses in their rooms after duty;
- 'complaining' about not having enough food to eat (Kalisch and Kalisch 1975, p. 231);
- questioning hospital rules;
- questioning a doctor's orders (Ashley 1976a, p. 27).

Without exception, all of these things were regarded as constituting 'professional misconduct'; the latter two reasons for dismissal (that is, questioning hospital rules and questioning a doctor's orders) are to this day sometimes cited as grounds for upholding charges of professional misconduct, as will be shown later in this book.

Private duty nurses also suffered dismissals. These nurses would suddenly lose their case work for no apparent reason. The most likely reason, however, was an arbitrary use — or rather abuse — of power by influential lay hospital administrators, doctors and nursing superintendents who were more interested in protecting the whims of the upper-class families and individuals who employed private duty nurses, than they were in protecting the interests of the overworked private duty nurses (see in particular, Reverby 1987, p. 98).

It might be asked at this point why women flocked to enrol in nurse training programs if the conditions of nursing were so appalling? (Some of the more famous hospitals received anywhere between 100 and 1000 applications each year (Kelly 1985, p. 43)). The short answer is that, at that time, nursing provided untrained women with the *only* occupational alternative to factory work, domestic service, keeping boarders, working in almshouses, and prostitution (ibid.; Wortman 1985, pp. 213–266, 332–355; Reverby 1987, p. 16). However, that the option of nursing-training quickly proved to be no real option at all is evidenced by the 75 per cent attrition rate in hospitals around the United States of America (Kelly 1985, p. 43).

Nursing organisations and conscientious physicians in the United States of America were concerned about the exploitation of pupil nurses as early as 1897. In 1918, for example, a physician from Virginia wrote in a letter to a staff member of the Division of Nursing Education at Teachers College in New York City:

> Our government has regulated the hours of service for stalwart men to eight hours. I don't know of any railroad men or government service men who have as tiresome, nerve-racking work as the pupil nurse.
>
> I think it next to criminal to require a young girl to go at breakneck speed over hard floors for ten consecutive hours . . . then some training schools require twelve hours when on night duty for weeks. The idea of a special[4] serving sixteen hours! Horrors of horrors — shades of the Spanish Inquisition.
>
> (Baker to Stewart, 20 June 1918 — cited in Ashley 1976a, p. 38)

Despite these and other outcries, change was slow in coming, and the exploitation of pupil nurse labour continued. Although the practice of using pupil nurses as sweated labour eventually died out, this was not for humanitarian reasons or because of successful lobbying by the nursing profession and sympathetic physicians. Rather it was because the public began increasingly to use hospital facilities and as a result the need for home care drastically declined (Ashley 1976a, p. 27). Despite improvements in hospital facilities, however, the value and importance of nursing work was still not formally recognised and continued to be exploited. Nursing work was (and is) regarded as 'non-work' (Lowery-Palmer 1982, p. 197) and subsidised the entire health structure 'through wages unreceived and benefits unobtained' (Gunning 1983, p. 118). Well into the 1980s nursing costs were not itemised on hospital accounts and tended to be subsumed under the daily room rate thereby masking the variability and complexity of nursing care delivered to patients (Lowery-Palmer 1982, p. 197; *American Journal of Nursing* 1983, pp. 1251, 1262; Gunning 1983, p. 117; see also Gaston unpub.). This situation remains unchanged in several American states, as well as in some other countries. In Australia, for example, nursing costs are sometimes included as 'hotel costs' (meals, room, laundry, and so on) in the hospital budget (Cuthbert 1987, p. 15).

Nursing conditions in Australia

Nursing conditions in Australia (described by one nurse as 'white slavery' ('A' 1911, pp. 153–154)) paralleled those in England and the United States of America. As was the case in those countries, pupil nurses endured intolerable living conditions, worked excessively long hours, undertook strenuous tasks and were used as sweated labour by the hospitals (Edwards 1911; *Australasian Nurses Journal* 1920, pp. 181–183; Minchin 1977; Godden 1989a, 1989b; Trembath and Hellier 1987; Gregory 1988; Russell 1990). It has been suggested that nurses were in fact 'amongst the most sweated people in the community' (Trembath and Hellier 1987, p. 37). Trainees typically worked up to 12 to 15 hours a day, six days a week, for 49 weeks of the year (Russell, 1990, p. 27; Trembath and Hellier 1987, pp. 35–36, 81, 96–97). Some worked 24 to 48 hours at a stretch (Templeton 1969, p. 120). Nurse–patient ratios were dangerously low. It was estimated, for example, that in Melbourne the ratio of nurses to patients was one-third less than the numbers employed in English hospitals (Norman 1890, p. 154). As a general rule, pupil nurses were paid nothing and more often than not were required to pay a premium to the training hospitals for the 'education' they were receiving. The trainees' educational needs, however, were always secondary and subservient to the service needs of the hospital (Russell 1990, p. 38).

As in other countries, this exploitation of nursing labour was rationalised and defended on grounds that 'the public benefited, the hospital benefited financially, and the nurse herself benefited by gaining experience' (Templeton 1969, p. 118). For example, at the 1890 Victorian Royal Commission of Charitable Institutions, evidence was given that although the hours worked by nurses were 'probably too long', the hours were nevertheless 'absolutely essential if the sick [were] to be attended to, unless you duplicate your staff, and then the expense would be beyond the means of the institutions' (Williams 1890, p. 130). It was further claimed that as a general rule the nurses were a 'remarkably healthy looking lot of women' and that only the 'weakly' broke down or got injured (ibid.).

In reality, morbidity and mortality rates among nurses were unacceptably high and, significantly, higher than 'among other professions' (Templeton

1969, p. 135). In fact, so notorious was the bad health of nurses they were generally considered to be a 'bad insurance risk' (ibid.). The Colonial Mutual Life Assurance Society of Melbourne was one company that considered nurses to be a bad insurance risk. 'Perceptively', the company attributed the bad health of nurses to the fact that 'they were worked too hard and were not given enough to eat' (ibid.).

Nurses suffered from exhaustion and were vulnerable to cross-infection from their patients (Fitzgerald 1890, p. 237; Gardiner 1968, p. 65). As was the case in the United States of America, the incidence of tuberculosis among pupil nurses was particularly high (Sleeman 1939; Cowan 1946; Hambridge 1950; Roche 1953). One study conducted from 1924 to 1936 found that of the pupil nurses who were initially uninfected at the time of entering a nurse training school, 41.3 per cent annually contracted primary infection — which was 'five times as many [as] under ordinary conditions' (Sleeman 1939, p. 44). Despite these appalling statistics, it was not until 1946 that positive steps were taken by the nursing profession to try and protect its members against acquiring occupational infection of the disease. In February of that year, the Federal Council of the Australian Nursing Federation passed a resolution which stated that

> no trained nurse or student nurse shall be required to nurse a case of tuberculosis in any hospital or institution until her chest has been x-rayed and she has been tested as to her immunity to tuberculosis.
> (Australian Nursing Federation 1946, p. 57)

The health of nurses was further compromised by poor living conditions and bad diet. Nurse accommodation facilities were typically overcrowded, and the food supplied to nurses was often inedible. In one report (Templeton 1969, p. 131) it was claimed that

> mutton supplied to the nurses' table one day contained a large tubercular ulcer and the meat from which the nurses' and patients' soup was made was found to be fly blown. Another sample of meat was full of hydatids.

In this particular instance, the hospital board responsible for the nurses 'could see no reason for complaint' and dismissed the whole affair as a fabrication sparked by a disgruntled resident who was 'resentful because his wife was not permitted to live in the institution' (ibid.).

Unlike their American counterparts, Australian trained nurses were generally employed for one to two years after graduation. However, their rates of pay were much lower than they should have been and their general working conditions were poor. Even as late as 1918, the market rate for private nurses was less than the average wage paid to a cook (Minchin 1977, p. 7) or an unskilled forewoman of a laundry (Russell 1990, p. 28); wages were certainly much less than those paid to an unskilled male labourer who could earn between £A135 and £A168 per year compared with a trained nurse's wage of just £A90 per year (ibid.).

Although the 1890 Royal Commission on Charitable Institutions noted the deplorable conditions under which nurses worked, and made a number of recommendations on how these might be improved, little was done for much the same reasons that prevented reforms in England and the United States of America. Nurses continued to be talked of as 'ministering angels' and continued to be treated as 'willing horses' (*Una* 1918, p. 3). In one instance, a move to prevent nurses working more than 52 hours a week in the State of Victoria was met with open hostility and was rejected by the hospital committees of two major city hospitals as being 'inconvenient, expensive and altogether unnecessary' (Minchin 1977, p. 6). For the time being, nurses were to be kept firmly in their 'womanly place' and to continue performing their 'multiple duties' and 'strenuous physical work' without complaint (Gregory 1988, p. 44). A few years later, a newspaper report commented that 'the woman who enters the profession [of nursing] knows what she is doing, and abides by it' (*The Argus* 1904, p. 78). Not surprisingly, the average professional life of a trained nurse during this early period was estimated to be only 15 years, primarily because she became 'more or less broken in health' (*Australasian Nurses Journal* 1911b, p. 270).

The 'thirty-year war' for state registration

The next logical step in this history of nurse-abuse by lay hospital administrators and doctors was for nurses to protest and to fight for nursing self-determination. To this end the early nurse leaders reasoned that the only way to free nurses from the tyranny of lay hospital administrators and doctors was to put the control of nursing firmly in the hands of nurses (Breay and Fenwick 1931; Dock and Stewart 1938; Bendall and Raybound 1969; Minchin 1977; Kelly 1985). This, they believed, could only be achieved by self-regulation via state examination and registration, with the state as the regulating authority for nurses (Dock 1913; Dock and Stewart 1938; Minchin 1977; International Council of Nurses 1986a; Kelly 1985, p. 50). This belief was to be formalised at the first International Council of Nurses Congress in 1901, held in Buffalo, NY, when the ICN President, Mrs Bedford Fenwick (one of the first 'to challenge the received wisdom of Florence Nightingale's teaching' (Hector 1973, p. vii)) presented the final paper of the day. Entitled 'The organisation and registration of trained nurses', this paper was well received and was followed by unanimous acceptance of the following resolution:

> Whereas, the nursing of the sick is a matter closely affecting all classes of the community in every land; whereas, to be efficient workers nurses

should be carefully educated in the important duties which are now allotted to them; whereas, at the present time there is no generally accepted term or standard of training, nor system of education, nor examination for nurses in any country; whereas, there is no method (except in South Africa[5]) of enabling the public to discriminate easily between trained nurses and ignorant persons who assume that title, it is the opinion of this International Congress of Nurses in General meeting assembled, that it is the duty of the nursing profession of every country to work for suitable legislative enactment, regulating the education of nurses and protection of the interests of the public by securing state examination and public registration with the proper penalties for not enforcing same.

(quoted in Bridges 1967, p. 20)

Following the acceptance of this resolution, nursing associations around the world became chiefly occupied with securing 'legal protection for professional standards of nursing practice and education' (Dock and Stewart 1938, p. 169). It was thought that legal regulation would ensure:

- protection of the public from being cared for by 'nurses' not qualified to nurse (including pupil nurses);
- protection of the nursing profession's interests and status (Minchin 1977; Ellis and Hartley 1984; International Council of Nurses 1986a; Kelly 1985).

Thus, as already mentioned in the introduction to this chapter, the state registration of nurses came to be advocated on grounds that it would:

- safeguard the public;
- safeguard trained nurses themselves;
- raise the status of the nursing profession (Kent 1905, p. 181).

The task remained, however, to convince the state, the public (who had been kept largely ignorant of the fact that nursing care was mostly given by students), and even nurses themselves, of the value of state registration for nurses (Dock and Stewart 1938; Ellis and Hartley 1984; International Council of Nurses 1986a). This was not to be an easy task and, in retrospect, it is probably fair to say that the early nurse leaders grossly underestimated the (patriarchal) forces which were pitted against them. The struggle for registration was long and desperate with the notable exception of New Zealand which, as already mentioned, achieved state registration relatively early (in 1901) and, interestingly, an eight-hour working day by 1909 (Dock and Stewart 1938, p. 260; Trembath and Hellier 1987, p. 97). For English nurses, the struggle was so intense that they dubbed it the 'thirty-year war' (Dock and Stewart 1938, p. 257; see also the Report from the Select Committee on the Registration of Nurses 1904, 1905).

The debate on whether nursing should be a regulated profession was essentially argued from three different positions:

1. Those who wanted state registration.
2. Those who were opposed to state registration of any kind (although some nurses belonged to this faction, it was mostly doctors and lay hospital administrators who were opposed to state registration).
3. Those who wanted to occupy some 'middle ground' (that is, opt for voluntary registration only).

(Dock 1904b, pp. 139–143; *The Lancet* 1904, p. 946; Report from the Select Committee on the Registration of Nurses 1904, 1905; *Medical Times and Hospital Gazette* 1904, pp. 75–76; *Australasian Nurses Journal* 1909, pp. 257–259; 1910b, pp. 130–131; 1917, pp. 136–137; *Una* 1919, pp. 145–149; Birnbach 1985).

Nurses supporting the push for registration argued that statutory regulation would establish uniform qualifications for nursing and simultaneously safeguard the interests of the public and the profession (International Council of Nurses 1986a). Other nurses, including Florence Nightingale, were not so convinced (Abel-Smith 1960; Bullough 1975, p. 10; Minchin 1977, p. 11; Birnbach 1985, pp. 15–17; International Council of Nurses 1986a, p. 13). Some argued that 'any system of State Registration would be detrimental to the public and harmful to the nurses themselves' (*The Lancet* 1904, p. 946). Nightingale feared, and not without some cause it might be added, that statutory regulation would undermine the very nature of nursing and the authority and independence of the nurse to practise it. One of her chief concerns was that 'character training' and the acquisition of 'moral qualifications', which she considered as important as technical skill, could not be accounted for or tested by public examination (Woodham-Smith 1964, p. 412). These qualities could only be accounted for and tested by 'direct supervision', and by the matron of the nurse's training hospital who

> was able to guarantee by personal knowledge that her pupil possessed the qualities of character as well as the degree of technical skill which were essential to the calling of a nurse. Devotion, gentleness, sympathy, qualities of overwhelming importance in a nurse, could never be ascertained by public examination.
> (Woodham-Smith 1964, p. 412)

Nightingale was also gravely concerned that

> standards would be levelled down by state licensing and that nurses would deteriorate if released from the control and supervision of their schools and given permanent status as registered nurses.
> (cited in LaSor and Elliot 1977, p. 164)

Nursing was still in its infancy and, wrote Nightingale, 'still too unorganised, and contained divergences too great, for a single standard to be applied' (Woodham-Smith 1964, p. 412). Although Nightingale had a profound respect for rules and the order they could import, she was very aware that rules could be 'very stupid' and restrictive, and that regulations 'were generally made by men, who were incapable . . . of devising suitable regulations for women' (Cook 1913b, p. 194). On one occasion, for example, when trying to settle a hospital quarrel over 'bad regulations', Nightingale is alleged to have exclaimed: 'Oh, how I wish there were no men!' (ibid., p. 195). Furthermore, it is evident that Nightingale was under no illusion about the masculinist nature of law, the extent to which laws protected male interests and 'disabled' women, and the dubious value of law reform for its own sake[6] (Cook 1913b, pp. 194–195, 332–333; Woodham-Smith 1964, 308–309; Smith 1982, pp. 190, 193). In light of these and other considerations, Woodham-Smith (1964) is probably quite correct in her interpretation that Nightingale was not against registration per se, but against the kind of registration that was, at that time, being proposed (see also Howse 1989). Even so, Nightingale's opposition to state registration (it was in fact her main public preoccupation during 1891 and 1892 (Cook 1913b, p. 356)) caused a terrible split in the nursing world and, as an examination of early literature on the subject shows, provided medical men and lay hospital administrators who were opposed to improving the legal status of nursing with the very arguments they needed to reject nurses' demands for statutory recognition (see in particular, evidence given by medical witnesses in the *Report from the Select Committee on the Registration of Nurses* 1904, 1905).

Other groups of people opposed to the registration movement included doctors, lay hospital administrators, and interestingly, editors of the lay press. In the case of the lay editors, it is perhaps worth noting here that from the 1890s, the press succeeded in obstructing the professional development of nursing for almost 30 years by either failing to cover important nursing issues or else presenting them in a trivial or negative manner (Fenwick 1904, p. 93; Bridges 1968; Jones, A.H. 1988). The press obstruction was eventually overcome to some extent when, in 1923, the International Council of Nurses established an international nursing journal — to be controlled by nurses, and to reflect nursing opinion and nursing issues (Bridges 1968, p. 10). At the 1923 ICN Executive Committee meeting at which the proposal to establish an international nursing journal was originally considered, one of the delegates present gave a solemn warning that the lay press publications were a 'very serious peril to personal and professional liberty' (cited in Bridges, 1968, p. 10), a warning which finds relevance even today.

The reasons for the non-nursing groups' opposition were, predictably, quite different to those advanced by the nurse-opponents. Doctors and lay hospital administrators had long since realised they were dependent on nurses to ensure both the survival of the hospital industry and, perhaps more importantly, to enhance the reputation of treating doctors working within the hospital system[7] (Ashley 1976a, pp. 19, 23). The implications of this were that doctors and hospital administrators wanted total control of nursing staff and education, and were not about to relinquish their self-appointed sovereign rights easily.

As the registration debate gained momentum, doctors and hospital administrators increasingly feared 'loss of control over nurses and the "unmerited" granting of professional status to nursing' (International Council of Nurses 1986a, p. 13). Some doctors argued that the whole idea of state registration for nurses was 'dangerous' and positively against the 'public good' (Minchin 1977, p. 12). Politicians also feared the consequences of granting nurses state registration. An Australian member of parliament, for example, objected that

> it would possibly create a close burrow on the part of nurses, and that there would be comparatively few nurses to do the work, and that it would be almost impossible for the poorer classes to obtain a nurse.
>
> (*Una* 1914, p. 110)

Opposition to the state registration of English nurses

In England the main 'danger' seemed to derive from the 'volatile situation' that many of the new nurse trainees were educated women from the upper social classes. Since a large number of the doctors working in the same hospitals as these trainees were from lower social classes, they feared that 'these educated women would undermine their authority, however much the nurses protested that they were there to carry out the doctor's instruction' (Abel-Smith 1960, p. 27).

One influential figure who was particularly concerned about the state registration of nurses was the chairman of London Hospital, the Honourable Sydney Holland. In his evidence to the 1904 Select Committee on the Registration of Nurses, Holland not only argued against the state registration of nurses, but sought to discredit those who supported it. For example, with regards to the nurse-proponents of state registration, he argued (Holland 1904, p. 29) (in what stands as a classic example of a dominant discourse marginalising, discrediting and disqualifying a weaker discourse):

I do not wish to say anything disrespectful of those who are in favour of registration, because I am perfectly certain that they, equally with ourselves, are advocating what they think is best for nursing . . . but I suggest to you that you should satisfy yourselves as to the experience and position of those who are supporting registration. May I warn you against accepting the verdict of the Matrons' Council as bearing, we will say, very great weight. I only say this because people are apt to think when they see an opinion given by the Matrons' Council that the Matrons' Council represents all the matrons, whereas . . . that Matron's Council is a self-elected body, and in no way represents the matrons of England, Scotland and Ireland.

Holland sought to further discredit the Matrons' Council by speculating that 'very few [were] actually engaged in work' (in making this criticism, Holland appears to have conveniently overlooked the fact that he was himself a 'self-elected' spokesperson for the nursing profession, and furthermore one who had had no practical work experience as a nurse). As to the state registration of nurses itself, Holland (1904, p. 29) objected:

If registration were to pass it would lead nurses to consider themselves as belonging to what is called a 'Profession'. The tendency would be to think themselves much more the colleagues of the doctors instead of simply carriers out of the orders of the doctors; in fact they would be a sort of *pseudo-scientific person* [emphasis added]. That is an argument very largely felt by doctors in the profession, and perhaps concerns them more than me.

When challenged by the Chairman of the Select Committee to consider that medical opposition to the state registration of nurses was at least partially motivated by a fear among doctors that their authority would be 'infringed upon by the nurses', Holland (1904, p. 36) replied:

If that is the reason that has moved their minds it is an uncommonly good one because it is a very great danger when a nurse thinks herself an amateur doctor . . . [All] those who advocate registration are always holding me and others up as slave drivers and all the rest of it because we oppose the line of nursing being considered a profession like doctors.

He concluded this point by arguing that his main concern, and the concern of his respected medical colleagues, was primarily

to stop nurses thinking themselves anything more than they are, namely, the faithful carriers out of the doctor's orders. The other side are always talking about nursing being a profession and 'graduates' in nursing, just as they do in America . . . A woman who wants to become a nurse will become a nurse because she *loves nursing* and not because she is going to have a

professional status. *There is absolutely nothing in it* [emphasis added].
(Holland 1904, pp. 37, 39)

Another influential entity opposed to the state registration of nurses was the Society of Apothecaries. The clerk and solicitor of this society argued before the 1905 Select Committee that the state registration of nurses was wholly 'unnecessary' since

> the nurse at the present time holds the position which she ought to hold, and that, as I say, according to the view of the Society, without offence to the nurses in any sense, is a position which should be entirely subordinate to the medical practitioner in the treatment of medical cases . . . We think the tendency of giving the Nurse a State registration would be to enable her to a greater extent to break loose from the Institutions with which, as a rule, she is connected at the present time, and set up for herself, and she would be called in independently of the medical man . . . With a Register, and with a Council presiding over her . . . I think the tendency would be very much for her to assert an *undesirable independence* [emphasis added].
> (Upton 1905, p. 46)

Upton (1905, p. 47) expressed the additional concern that the 'undesirable independence' of the nurse, if given, would enable her to 'set herself up in this curious position of antagonism, or at any rate competition, with the doctor'. Upton's view exposed the crux of the matter, and the real basis of the Society's (and the medical profession's) opposition to the state registration of nurses, namely: a profound fear that 'mere women' would enter into economic competition with men, and, in so doing, would also challenge 'societal notions of male superiority' (Thornton 1984, p. 11).

During the Select Committee's inquiry, opposition to the state registration of nurses was to be manifested in another unexpected form. In at least one known instance, for example, there was a blatant manipulation of the evidence brought before the Select Committee. The person whose evidence was manipulated was none other than the internationally reputed American nurse, Lavinia Dock. Dock (1905, p. 61) promptly complained to the Select Committee:

> I would like to make a correction to the Minutes. Two questions have been inserted in my testimony which were not put to me at all, and answers which I did not give. The questions are quite preposterous, and the answers given, give an impression which is highly erroneous, and calculated to give an entirely incorrect idea of what I said, and to injure the Registration movement.

Dock's request to have the offending sections (No's 831 and 832) 'struck out' was granted, and these are missing from the final *Report of the Select Committee on the Registration of Nurses* (1905, p. 44).

Although many of those who opposed the state registration of nurses were medical practitioners, it should be noted that the British Medical Association (BMA) had formally approved the principle of the registration of nurses as early as 1895 (Horsley 1905, pp. 62–63). Furthermore the BMA was firmly opposed to voluntary registration, as was being advocated by some camps, on grounds that is was 'not sufficiently thorough' (Balfour 1905, p. 71). It needs to be clarified, however, that a primary reason for this position was not a bona fide support of the professionalisation of nursing, but a desire to gain ultimate and legitimated control of nurses and nursing practice. For example, when questioned about the work of district nurses in the community, and their alleged tendency to 'tread on the corns of the general practitioner' (district nurses were viewed as a kind of 'general practitioner' in their own right), Sir Victor Horsley (1905, p. 73), a representative of the BMA giving evidence to the Select Committee on the Registration of Nurses, replied:

> That is exactly one of the principal reasons in favour of registration in my opinion, because, until we get a Central Nursing Council, a disciplinary body before whom complaints can properly be laid and action taken accordingly, we are perfectly powerless. These district nurses sometimes are a source of the greatest trouble to the medical profession, but *we cannot control them until we have a Central Nursing Council. It is quite impossible to do anything at the present time.* I think that is the strongest argument in favour of registration [emphasis added].

(The apparent need to control female nurses and to keep them firmly out of competition with male medical men was to find considerable political support, as will be shown shortly).

Proponents of state registration responded with equal force. One such proponent was Mrs Ethel Fenwick, as already mentioned, a distinguished English nurse and the first president of the International Council of Nurses. Addressing the 1905 Select Committee on the Registration of Nurses, Mrs Fenwick responded (p. 32):

> I should like to emphasise the fact that the question of justice to nurses as a class should also receive due consideration. Only those who, like myself, have been intimately connected with nursing work for nearly thirty years can estimate at their true value the reforms effected, sometimes under very discouraging circumstances, by the thousands of women who have taken part in raising the moral tone, and the practical efficiency, of the care of the sick in the wards of hospitals and infirmaries during that period. The sum total of self-sacrifice, devotion to duty, and powers of organisation which have been expended in this great social reform are inestimable, and leave the State under a debt of obligation to our nurses which it can only

discharge by doing all in its power to organise their education and work, so that they may be qualified in the best manner for the performance of their duties. An efficient nursing service is a valuable national asset, and one which it is important should be appreciated at its true value as a factor in the well-being of the people. I might here strongly dissent from the opinion expressed by a former witness that a systematic knowledge of the principles of nursing would produce pseudo-scientific workers, eager to assume the responsibilities of the medical faculty. Such a suggestion is exceedingly mischievous, and not founded on fact . . . It is always the semi-trained and thoroughly untrustworthy woman who attempts to cloak her ignorance with pseudo-scientific pretensions.

This and similar views were eventually given some political support. For example, in a House of Lords debate on a proposed nurses registration Bill, Lord Ampthill (1919, pp. 823, 834), an influential supporter of the nursing cause, argued that state registration

was necessary as a protection to the public, as an act of justice to women in general and to nurses in particular, and one which was required to advance the noble profession . . . Nurses for a long time have been grossly and scandalously underpaid, and have been subject to a great deal of tyranny and oppression. Now is the time to remedy that.

Interestingly, Lord Ampthill went on to oppose an early draft of the 1919 Nurses Registration Bill brought before the House of Lords on grounds that it was 'not a registration Bill proper', and that if passed it would 'put nurses more into the hands of the lay managers of hospitals than they are now'[8] (ibid.) (see also Kent 1918, p. 144; Marquess of Dufferin and Ava 1919, p. 843). Nevertheless, the English Nurses Registration Bill was eventually passed without division on 1 November 1919.

As a point of clarification, it should be noted that it was not so much the lobbying by nursing leaders or influential (pro-nurse) men that eventually persuaded English politicians to acquiesce to the nursing profession's demands for legal status. Rather it was a combination of factors which prompted political action including, as already mentioned, the enfranchisement of women and the removal of legal barriers to women entering into a profession of their own choosing. Another equally significant factor was the threat of industrial agitation. Female membership of unions had risen from 183 000 in 1910 to an incredible 1 086 000 by 1918 (Dingwall et al. 1988, p. 86). Although nurses were not actively engaged in the trade union movement (and in fact, up until relatively recently, have passionately resisted using trade union tactics to advance their cause (see Clay 1987, p. 37)) English nursing activists at the time, unlike their American counterparts, quickly recognised the advantages of using trade union strategies (including the language of unionisation) for furthering the nursing profession's interests. Nurse leaders argued that passing a registration Bill would have a 'pacifying effect' and would 'do much to allay nursing unrest' (Fenwick 1919). In a House of Lords debate on the state registration of nurses, for example, Lord Ampthill (1919, pp. 826–827) warned his fellow Lords that if there was a delay in granting nurses registration:

> You will force nurses into trade unions. It is what is already happening. You have seen it in the case of the Asylum Workers Association and you will force nurses to form trade unions in order to secure what they regard and rightly regard as a right to them, you will simply throw them into the arms of the Labour Party. Is that a desirable thing to do at the present time?

The Labour Party, meanwhile, had already made an issue of the poor wages and conditions experienced by nurses and had accepted that 'sweated labour in the noble profession of nursing' should be eliminated (Roberts 1919, p. 796). The presiding government was thus forced to act: it either had to grant nurses state registration, or risk political defeat at the hands of the opposition Labour party. The Lords assented to the passage of the 1919 Registration Bill, and thereby effectively put an end to the 'thirty-year war' for state registration.

Opposition to the state registration of American nurses

In the United States of America, protests against legitimated educational and professional reforms in nursing were equally strong, with the result that all of the proposed Bills for state registration during this time were, as Sophie Palmer (1902), editor of the *American Journal of Nursing*, observed 'torn to pieces by the legislators' (cited in Fickeissen 1986, p. 4). One physician complained that the trained nurse was 'often conceited and too unconscious of the due subordination she owes to the medical profession, of which she is a sort of useful parasite' (*Journal of the American Medical Association* 1901, p. 33). Kelly (1985, p. 51) notes 'some physicians did not see the necessity for any fancy standards and worried about overeducation of nurses'. She goes on (ibid.) to cite the comments of one troubled physician who advised:

> Nursing is not, strictly speaking, a profession. Only intelligent, not necessarily educated, women can in a short time acquire the skill to carry out with explicit obedience the physician's directions.

Like their English colleagues, many American doctors feared that nurses would 'out do' them — educationally, professionally and, perhaps more to the point, economically (Ashley 1976a, pp. 81–83; see also Christy 1975, 1980). Male medical students were already having to compete with female nursing students for learning experiences in the hospitals (a problem which was also experienced in Australia (Minchin 1977; Willis 1989)). And the increasing fees being paid to practising nurses caused many physicians to fear 'economic competition from women' (Ashley 1976a, p. 81). Ashley (1976a, p. 83) even goes so far as to suggest that one of the major reasons doctors and lay hospital administrators opposed the growth of the nursing profession was precisely 'a fear of competing with women'. An equally if not more plausible explanation, however, is that cheap pupil nurse labour had become the economic salvation of most hospitals (Beard 1913, p. 2151), and that many doctors and hospital administrators feared losing the student nurse work force upon which they had become so dependent for commercial gain (Reverby 1987, p. 121).

As in England and Australia, disparaging rhetoric was used in an attempt to discredit those (mostly nurses) pushing for positive nursing reforms. One physician (Satterthwaite 1910, pp. 108, 110) complained:

> The modern nurse is sometimes apt to err in her appreciation of the relative position of patient and physician. This is largely due to the idea which prevails to some extent among nurses that nursing is a 'profession' like that of medicine, law, or theology . . . The main fault with the present system is not chargeable to the ordinary graduate nurse, but to a comparatively small number of women, possessed, I am sorry to say, of inordinate ambition, and having improper conceptions of the relative position they hold to physicians on the one hand and to patients on the other. They have injected into nurses' associations ideas that are erroneous and full of danger to the nursing community. Unfortunately, complaisant legislators have been found to frame some of these notions into statutes, while we as physicians have failed to recognize the grave consequences of the movement.

Opposition to the state registration of Australian nurses

Efforts to obtain state registration for nurses in Australia closely paralleled those in England and the United States of America; and, as in those countries, involved a long and determined battle against prejudiced opposition from nurses as well as non-nurses (Bowe 1961, p. 92). In Victoria, for example, the Victorian Trained Nurses Association (VTNA) — a medically dominated[9] professional nurse organisation which was established in 1901 and which became the Royal VTNA after gaining a Royal prefix in 1904 — initially opted for face-to-face negotiations with hospital administrators and making 'private agreements' at the expense of pushing for statutory regulation. Minchin (1977, p. 10) suggests that for the most part 'the association was quite happy to ignore the question of State

Registration'. Indeed it was not until 1915, well over a decade after its establishment as a professional organisation, that the RVTNA committed itself to a policy of 'campaigning for the immediate introduction of State registration of general nurses' (Trembath and Hellier 1987, p. 69). Before this, it seems most nurses viewed government control 'as unnecessary interference in work which was already well managed' (ibid.). Although the idea of state registration was first espoused as early as 1904, the nursing press gives the impression that many nurses were hostile or indifferent to the idea (ibid.). Caution should be exercised in accepting this impression, however, since during the early years of the state registration debate, *Una*, the official journal of the RVTNA, was edited by doctors (ibid., p. 52), raising the very real possibility of editorial bias in the publication of nursing views on the matter. Doctors, meanwhile, apparently feared — as they had in the case of the statutory regulation of midwifery — that the state registration of nurses would give 'a legal hall-mark to an imperfectly educated class' (see *Australian Medical Gazette* 1898, p. 480; Trembath and Hellier 1987, p. 40).

One of the biggest problems facing the nursing profession, however, was public and political ignorance about what was required in a nurse (many considered nursing to be merely a natural extension of the role of the proverbial 'good woman' and therefore not requiring legitimated standards of entry into practice), and ensuring that any draft Bills accurately and adequately reflected a high standard of nursing practice. On at least one occasion, the *Australasian Nurses Journal* (1907, pp. 360–361) warned members of the Australasian Trained Nurses Association in New South Wales that

> it is of vital interest to them all to have a satisfactory Bill passed. A Bill allowing a low standard of training to be sufficient for registration will do incalculable damage to the Nursing profession as well as the public. Better to go on as we are than to have incompetent women given the protection of State registration.

Unfortunately, as will be shown in the next chapter, the early nurse registration bills in Australia were 'less than satisfactory', and when passed were profoundly to the detriment of both the public and the nursing profession as a whole.

The International Council of Nurses' position

The ICN remained undaunted by the widespread opposition to the state registration of trained nurses and at the Second Quinquennial Meeting of the

International Council of Nurses held in London in 1909, it reaffirmed its commitment to obtaining the legal regulation of nursing practice in all countries. The first resolution on the agenda was as follows:

> The International Council of Nurses desires again to record its earnest conviction that it is desirable, both in the interests of the professional status of trained nurses and of the public whom they serve, that provision should be made for their registration by the State, that such registration should be under the supervision of a Central Professional Authority, and that admission to the Register of those who have fulfilled the prescribed conditions as to training should be by the single portal of a State Examination. The International Council of Nurses offers its most cordial congratulations to all trained nurses so registered.
> (Breay and Fenwick 1931, p. 53)

Even though the ICN's position was widely supported by its member associations, only slow progress was made toward achieving registration by the state. Nurses in England did not obtain state registration until 1919, 18 years after New Zealand and 10 years after the second ICN resolution on the issue. Although a number of American states had obtained nursing licensure laws in 1903 (Shannon 1975), it was not until 1923, 14 years after the 1909 ICN resolution, that all 48 American states had enacted nursing licensure laws (Ellis and Hartley 1984, p. 112). In Australia, although nurses were first registered in the State of Queensland under the *Health Act 1911*, it was not until 1933 — 24 years after the 1909 ICN resolution — that all Australian states and territories had passed laws and/or ordinances providing specifically for the registration of nurses.[10]

Other attempts to improve the working conditions of nurses

As the struggle for registration continued, other attempts were made to reduce the hours worked by nurses and to improve their working conditions. Notable among these, were attempts to introduce various labour laws into nursing and hospital affairs. Of interest to this inquiry, is:

- the attempt, in 1912, to include student nurses under the 'Eight-Hour Law for Women' passed by the California Legislature in 1911;
- the attempt in 1930 by a British Labour backbencher to introduce a private member's Bill to restrict the working hours of English nurses;
- the introduction in 1916 of legislation in the State of Victoria which improved the working conditions of hospital domestics, but not nurses.

What is interesting about these examples is:

- the apparent dim view nurses themselves held of the attempts to introduce labour laws into their affairs, and why they rejected these attempts;
- the extraordinary lengths those outside nursing (for example, doctors, lay hospital administrators, and politicians) were prepared to go (in the Californian case, as far as the Supreme Court) in order to prevent nurses from being granted a shorter working week.

Before considering these examples, however, there is a small but important matter which requires brief comment. Nurses have sometimes been criticised for their apparent 'professional snobbery' with regard to their 'not wanting' to be brought under early protective legislation affecting women working in factories and other areas (see, for example, Ryan and Conlon 1975, p. 46). This criticism is, however, unfair for a number of reasons. In the first instance, protective labour laws never covered all women workers (Hill 1979; Erickson 1982) and, as the examples given below will show, tended to intentionally and explicitly exclude graduate and pupil nurses. In such instances nurses did not even have the opportunity to 'choose' whether or not they 'wanted' protective legislation, and thus it is misleading to suggest that nurses generally 'did not want' to be brought under such legislation: many were simply not given the opportunity to decline protective labour laws in the first place. Secondly, it is incorrect to imply that because nurses were suspicious of outside attempts to introduce labour laws into their affairs, they 'did not want' to improve their working conditions. The nursing profession's quest for state registration (a form of protective legislation) was itself partially inspired by a desire to improve the working conditions of nurses and to prevent their exploitation by their employers as a cheap source of labour. Thirdly, although it is true that some nurses were opposed to pupil and graduate nurses being included under protective labour laws, as the following discussion will show, in the main it was doctors, lay hospital administrators and politicians who were most vehemently opposed to nurses having shorter working hours and better pay.

The exclusion of nurses — and in particular pupil nurses — from early protective legislation was clearly not accidental. The emerging modern hospital system was utterly dependent on cheap (pupil) nurse labour and thus there was no need to have laws to 'keep nurses out of jobs'. Instead, the need was to keep (pupil) nurses on the job for as long and as cheaply as possible — regardless of the consequences to their health and lives. This perhaps helps to explain why it was that the most vehement opposition to including pupil nurses under protective legislation came not from nurses, but from those outside nursing — as already mentioned, doctors, lay hospital administrators and politicians — all of whom had major vested economic interests in keeping nurses, and in particular pupil nurses, exempt from proposed protective labour laws.

In view of these considerations, there is considerable scope to argue that it was not protective legislation per se that nurses were opposed to accepting, but the kind of legislation that was being proposed. As examples soon to be given in this chapter will demonstrate, nurses were cognisant of the fact that so-called 'protective' labour laws were paternalistic in nature and, despite their apparent benevolence, did not always reflect nursing needs and interests. Feminist research has since shown that so-called 'protective legislation' was not necessarily concerned with protecting women's needs and interests either. Rather it was concerned with '"protecting" one class of workers (men) from competition from another class (women)' (Hill 1979, p. 259). Hill (1979, p. 260) points out that 'protective' labour laws for women were often 'turned upside down and applied to keep women out of jobs, rather than to protect them on the job'.

The Californian 'Eight-Hour Law for Women'

In 1911, the California legislature passed a Bill that was known as the 'Eight-Hour Law for Women'. The intent of this Bill, which eventually became law, was to limit the working hours of women

> employed in any mercantile, mechanical, or manufacturing establishment, laundry, hotel, or restaurant, or telegraph or telephone establishment or office, to eight hours a day for six days in the week.
> (Williamson 1914, p. 257)

The Bill was introduced as an attempt to minimise the exploitation of the working population that had been occurring. However, the law bypassed the hospitals, and thus was powerless to protect student nurses who, as has already been mentioned, were working between 10 hours and 24 hours a day, seven days a week. It was not until sometime later, in 1912, that attempts were made to amend the law to include nurses, resulting in the controversial enactment, in 1913, of two laws concerning nurses, namely 'The Nurses Registration Act and the extension of the eight hour law for women to include student nurses' (Jamme 1915, p. 124).

Not unexpectedly, these attempts to restrict the working hours of student nurses met with stiff opposition from the commercial hospitals and the doctors running them. Hospital administrators argued that the law was preposterous since it would make the availability of private-duty nursing cost-prohibitive to the average family (a claim that actually had no basis). They argued that if the working hours of nurses were decreased to just eight hours a day, then instead of needing only one private-duty nurse, families would have to employ three circulating nurses, which was unacceptable. This, in turn, would create enormous gaps in the hospital work force, gaps which could only be filled by the more expensive graduate nurses. The overall consequences of this, it was argued, would be disastrous for the hospitals in so far as they would lose a lucrative source of revenue (notably the sweated labour of the pupil nurses), and they would have to pay a higher wage bill and thereby increase the hospitals' overall operating costs (Williamson 1915, p. 132; Jamme 1915, p. 129). This in turn would decrease the amount of charity work hospitals could offer, increase expenditure for patients and indeed the tax payer, and would decrease the dividends of commercial hospitals (Kalisch and Kalisch 1978, p. 284).

Desperate to get the Bill scuttled, the state hospital association sent delegates to the governor requesting him not to endorse the Bill. In pressing their claims they argued that the Bill was not supported by nurses themselves, as was 'apparent' by their failure to defend the Bill (Williamson 1914, p. 260). When it was pointed out to the governor, however, that the young women supporting the law were tied up 'caring for the sick' and could not get away from the hospitals to present their claims, he signed and the Bill became law (Kalisch and Kalisch 1978, p. 283). Unremarkably enough, opposition to the law did not end there, and was fought right through to the Supreme Court. In the Supreme Court case in question, it was argued (in terms reminiscent of those used in the noted 1895 case *Ritchie v People*[11]) that the amended 'Eight-Hour Law' was unconstitutional since it violated the student nurse's 'freedom of contract' (cited in Ashley 1976a, pp. 40–44). Others, meanwhile, argued that the law was not only contrary to the principles of the American Constitution but contrary 'to all principles of humanity'. Notable among those supporting this and like views was Dr H.T. Summersgill (1915, p. 91), Superintendent of the University of California Hospital, and President of the American Hospital Association, who argued:

> Some legislators are prone to enact laws with only a single thought to the cause and none to the effect, and it should be one of the duties of [the American Hospital Association] to see, in so far as those bills affecting hospitals are concerned, that the hospital's side of the case should be fairly and fully presented.
>
> Much has been said and written pro and con on the eight hour law for nurses. The constitutionality of this law was passed on by the Supreme Court of the United States ... On its face it appears to be contrary to the principles of not only the American Constitution but to all principles of humanity. For we all recognize the impossibility of strictly limiting the hours of attendants, nurses and others engaged in taking care of the sick.

The Californian Supreme Court was not moved by these and similar entreaties, however, and in February 1915, rendered its decision that

> restriction as to the hours of employment of student nurses in hospitals is not an unconstitutional violation of the freedom of contract, as these

persons, upon whom rests the burden of immediate attendance upon and nursing of the patients in hospitals, are also pupils engaged in a course of study, and the propriety of legislative protection of women undergoing such a discipline is not open to question.
(cited in Jamme 1915, p. 130)

Although this decision appears to reflect a 'sympathetic' view of the student nurses' plight, a brief examination of the courts' history in deciding so-called 'liberty of contract' cases yields a different explanation. In the decade prior to this decision, the courts had been severely criticised for their reasoning in a number of 'liberty of contract' cases. In those cases, the courts had, on supposed constitutional grounds upholding liberty of contract provisions, tended to favour employer interests over the interests of exploited workers. The consequences of these decisions for the workers involved were so severe that the courts were accused of 'siding against the aspirations of the common man for social justice' and of 'turning the Constitution into an instrument of class warfare' (Friedman 1965, p. 489). Roscoe Pound (1909, p. 482), writing in the *Yale Law Journal*, was even more scathing. In voicing his criticisms, Pound argued against the courts that

the great majority of the decisions are simply wrong, not only in constitutional law, but from the standpoint of the common law, and even from that of sane individualism.

Friedman (1965, p. 488) points out that the result of these decisions 'was to injure the reputation of the courts themselves'. In particular, the decisions caused the working classes to distrust profoundly the integrity of the courts, an observation which prompted Pound (1909, p. 487) to warn: 'The evil of those cases will live after them in impaired authority of the courts long after the decisions themselves are forgotten'. In light of this, one can speculate that it would have been a very brave judge indeed who decided against the interests of the student nurses in this case. The court was thus perhaps acting more to protect and strengthen its own reputation and to avoid further criticism of its integrity, than to protect the interests of the student nurses per se.

Another possible reason the court had no difficulty in reaching its decision was that a legal precedent (see *Muller v State of Oregon* (1908)) had already been established whereby 'women's working hours could be restricted by law even in employment that was not generally considered especially hazardous to health' (Erickson 1982, p. 155). Given this, what is perhaps surprising about the Californian Supreme Court case is not that it succeeded, but that it applied only to pupil nurses and thus had no bearing on the hours worked by graduate nurses — the majority of whom were women.

Tactics used in trying to defeat the Bill and later to obstruct its enforcement after it became law were not only directed at the law-makers. They were also directed squarely at nurses themselves. Hospital physicians cleverly argued that if nurses accepted the eight-hour labour law they would effectively be allowing their profession to become 'tainted' with trade unionism — an argument which continues to find popular usage even today (Dock 1913; Kalisch and Kalisch 1978, p. 282; Johnstone 1989, pp. 344–348). In an editorial published in the 15 January 1908 issue of the *National Hospital Record* (p. 3), for example, it was argued that hospitals do not operate in the same manner as factories or department stores and therefore 'could not be confined to an eight-hour day'. The editorial further contended:

> Hospital life is full of emergencies, its needs can never all be catalogued, and any form of legislation that would hinder it in its lifesaving work would surely come sooner or later under the ban of public disapproval. How could such legislation be enforced even if it were secured.

As if threatening nurses with the 'taint' of trade unionism was not enough, still others sought to warn nurses that accepting the eight-hour law would be tantamount to a kind of 'religious heresy' in so far as it would amount to an abandonment of their 'womanly duty to care' and their religious duty to be 'self-sacrificing' (see Reverby 1987). One physician (Young 1913, p. 270) sought to remind nurses that service was 'the greatest [duty] of all' and that

> the element of sacrifice is always present in true service. The service that costs no pang, no sacrifice, is of course without virtue. And generally without value.

Another physician, an Associate Professor of Physiology at the University of Minnesota (Beard 1913, p. 2150), wrote:

> The instinct of the eternal feminine for sacrificial service has been her [the nurse's] sole saving grace, the guiding light of her star of undoubted destiny, leading her on to the realisation of her important social function.

These and similar views accorded with the more general stereotypical view that 'self sacrifice' was inherent in nursing (womanhood), and that nurses would receive 'heavenly rather than earthly rewards' for their labours (Passau-Buck 1982, p. 207). It also reinforced the more pervasive medical view that

> nurses, because they are women and tainted by their continued ties to nature are required to redeem themselves through 'sacrificial service'.
> (Lovell 1982, p. 216)

Despite the deceitfulness of the rhetoric used by doctors and hospital administrators (see also Lovell 1986), it had the desired effect, and nurses (including the state nursing association) began to voice their opposition to the Bill and later the law. When the Bill was first introduced, for example, the representative of the State Nurses Association passed the following resolution:

> Resolved, That the California State Nurses' Association do not endorse a bill including nurses under the Eight-Hour Law for Women.
> (Williamson 1914, p. 258)

Some nurses also began to reinforce and support the rhetoric of 'sacrificial duty'. For example, a superintendent of nurses at one California hospital (Williamson 1914, pp. 263, 265) wrote:

> Young women enter the training school with the understanding that it is hard work, and they know it is a life of self-sacrifice, but anything worthwhile comes hard ... Nursing is a profession which belongs exclusively to women ... It calls for the highest character and education, and it cannot succeed without perseverance, determination, and self-sacrifice. But how can we [hospital schools] instil those principles into the minds of our pupils when the first lesson we must teach is the self-centered eight-hour law?
>
> How can we at the command of the law turn against those first principles that our patient's comfort is first, our own second?
>
> Real nursing, self-sacrificing service, can not be timed by the clock. It never has been, it never will be. Soldiers going into battle are not called to retreat because time is passing, neither should those soldiers who are fighting disease and death be told to lay down their arms and steal away because a certain hour has arrived.

One year later, this same superintendent of nurses (Williamson 1915, p. 137) argued:

> Nurses should be made of sterner stuff than those who must work by the clock ... Without self-sacrifice, without trials and hardships now and then, the profession of nursing will lose its attraction to those who are enthusiastically in earnest. The standard of nursing being lowered, the personnel of the profession will be lowered.

The distinguished American nurse leader and feminist, Lavinia Dock, was one of the few who was not moved by these misguided attempts by nurses to be seen as being 'professional' and the unscrupulous methods used by doctors and lay hospital administrators to undermine the nursing profession's efforts to improve the situation of its members (see, for example, Dock 1904a). She pleaded in the *Trained Nurses and Hospital Review* (1914, p. 38):

I think nurses should stand together solidly and resist the dictation of the medical profession in this as in all other things. Many M.D.'s have a purely commercial spirit toward nurses (have private hospitals of their own, etc.) and would readily overwork them ... If necessary, do not hesitate to make alliances with the labor vote, for organized labor has quite as much of an 'ideal' as the M.D.'s have, if not more.

Adelaide Nutting, another distinguished American nurse leader and feminist, was of a similar view. She argued (ibid., p. 37):

It is time for labor to step in and control the matter. I see no real loss of dignity in so doing, yet I know you all feel that in some way the dignity of our profession will be impaired and the status of nursing lowered, and I wish it were possible to secure righteous conditions for our workers in other ways.

Dock's and Nutting's pleas were largely ignored, however. Nurses continued to object to the eight-hour law primarily because they perceived it as classing them as 'trade labourers' (Ashley 1976a, p. 41). They were not even moved by arguments which pointed out that if nursing schools were really schools, 'it would not be possible for them to be under any labour laws' (Ashley 1976a, p. 49). Having succumbed to nursing's historical desire to be recognised 'as women training for a profession', student nurses were not about to allow themselves to be classified as trade labourers — something which, as Ashley (1976a, p. 43) correctly points out, 'would hardly aid their acquisition of professional status'. Additionally

for nursing to be classified with labor as a trade provided another basis for those arguing against elevating educational standards. Laborers did not require a higher education, let alone professional preparation.
(Ashley 1976a, p. 45)

An editorial in the *Trained Nurses and Hospital Review* (1914, p. 37) further argued:

If we put our hospital training schools under labor control, it will not be a question of impairing the dignity of the profession, but the absolute doing away of nursing as a profession. Let no nurse deceive herself into thinking that she can be a trade-union apprentice during training and then blossom out as a professional woman after graduation ... We see very grave danger in the entrance of labor laws into nursing and hospital affairs, for when once the wedge is entered who can tell how far it will go.

The editorial concluded, 'the idea of labor control in hospital training schools is a very repugnant one to us' (ibid.).

Unfortunately, although the nurses' aspirations were understandable, they were unrealistic and failed to deal with the fact that hospitals were exploiting the labor of pupil nurses. Ironically, it was nursing's claim to 'professional status' which 'protected' it from being subjected to the careful scrutiny and social investigations that every other kind of women's employment was subject to (Reverby 1987, p. 129). Thus, the Women's Bureau in the United States of America, which had been issuing reports on women's employment since 1918, did not formally investigate the conditions of nurses until as late as 1943 (ibid.). Equally ironic is that although the original Bill including nurses under the Eight-Hour Law for Women made provision for all nurses, graduates were excluded on the false grounds that 'the graduate nurse had the same status as a physician, and that to put her under the law would be both a hardship and an injustice' (Williamson 1914, p. 259).

Even after the Bill became law, the consensus of nursing opinion was against it (*Trained Nurses and Hospital Review* 1914, p. 37; Bullough and Bullough 1969, pp. 166–167). One superintendent of nurses ('Duty' 1914, p. 75) wrote:

> The eight-hour law is still a heavy burden, really the most cruel thing they have ever done in the nursing profession; I don't know when it is going to end. Patients are complaining, head nurses work day and night doing the student nurses' work, while the latter are constantly grumbling and in a state of discontent at not getting all the experience they should have; that is, the conscientious ones while the others are running round, attending picture shows, theatres, etc., tiring themselves out before they begin their work. One shift of nurses does not put in an appearance till 3:30 p.m. daily, so you can imagine how much experience they lose. They come on duty tired out with being out all day, and not fit for work. I am trying to arrange some rule whereby I can keep them all in for two hours of their time each day to study, but as they are all off at different hours it is almost impossible to arrange unless I give up my whole time, and I cannot devote that to looking after the nurse off duty, when those on duty require so much attention. I worked out a system of instruction — it worked beautifully, but the eight-hour law has smashed it all up, crippled us, for every time a head nurse wants to teach a student anything she is off duty, and I have to form classes at night to give instruction that should be learned in the wards. The patients also complain of the constant changes of nurses — the Doctors also, as orders are frequently overlooked or not properly attended to. We cannot keep a nurse on half-an-hour longer to-day and make it up to her to-morrow, even if it is in the middle of an operation or Obstetric case she must drop everything and go. The eight hours has compelled us to increase the number of nurses three fold, which also means more Head Nurses, maids, cooks, waiters, etc., etc.

The eight-hour law was to stay, however, and was to have a lasting impact on shift and staffing patterns in hospitals around the world (see also Kaplan

1933). To this day, staffing patterns are commonly based on three eight-hour shifts commencing, respectively, in the morning, afternoon and evening; although some countries operate on a model involving 12 hour shifts for four days a week — with the extra hours worked (that is, above a 36 or 40 hour per week limit) later claimed as an accrued day off (ADO).

Even after all the furore, the eight-hour law had little effect in terms of improving the status or working conditions of nurses. Instead of hiring graduate nurses to fill the gaps created by student nurses finishing work after eight hours, hospitals simply increased the student intake into their apprenticeship programs. Ashley (1976a, p. 51) writes:

> Thus, shorter hours in that state [California] meant greater numbers of students, rather than an increase in the number of graduate nurses employed. Clearly an eight-hour system in the schools did not alter the fact that pupil nurses carried the workload in the hospital. Hours were arranged and numbers increased so that students still provided the nursing care.

As there were no numerical limitations on the numbers of students a hospital could admit to its apprenticeship program, it was virtually free to meet its own needs regardless of the effect this stood to have on the broader community and indeed on individual graduate nurses (ibid.).

The eight-hour law, then, as Reverby (1987, p. 128) correctly points out, 'did not achieve much of the legal protection accorded either professional or other women'. Neither did the law legitimate 'the professional nursing association's right to regulate nursing or facilitate the creation of a united occupation' (ibid.). Even when state registration laws were eventually enacted, these did little to improve the status quo for the nursing profession, as will be discussed in the next chapter.

The 1930 Brockway Bill

As was the case in the United States of America, English hospitals were likewise excluded from law reforms regulating the hours and conditions of industrial workers (Dingwall et al. 1988, p. 100). Attempts to legitimately reduce the working week and improve the working conditions of nurses were similarly met with criticism, and condemned as being 'impractical' and 'inappropriate for professionals' (ibid., p. 102). It has been suggested that the English nurses themselves did not formally discuss the eight-hour day as a professional nursing issue until at least 1921 (Maggs 1983, p. 95).

Despite the introduction of the 10-hour day for women and young people as early as 1847 (Warner 1930, p. 295) and the introduction of a 56½ -hour week in 1874 (Pelling 1963, p. 77), by as late as 1930 nurses in English hospitals were still working more than 56 hours a week; and in some hospitals were working an 84 hour week made up of 14-hour shifts

(Brockway 1930, p. 418). An attempt to rectify this situation (and to improve nurses' extremely low rates of pay) came in the form of a private member's Bill introduced by Mr Fenner Brockway, a backbench Labour member of parliament. The intent of this Bill was 'to lay down minimum wages and maximum working hours for the nursing profession' (Nursing Profession (Wages and Hours) Bill 1930). Had the Bill been successful, it would have established a maximum 44 hour week, and imposed higher rates of pay (Dingwall et al. 1988, p. 101).

Brockway's Bill received no support from either the voluntary hospitals (who quickly perceived and were appalled by the cost implications) or the government (who just as quickly recognised the substantial implications for public expenditure) (ibid.). Nurses also opposed Brockway's Bill. Part of their opposition was in response to the unfortunate move by Brockway to introduce his Bill without first consulting with the country's professional nursing organisations (MacDonald 1931, p. 72). An editorial in the *British Journal of Nursing* (incorporating the *Nursing Record*) (1931, p. 1) responded indignantly:

> How different are the methods employed by our law makers when legislating for the Working Man; with them, quite rightly, they must confer before Bills affecting their lives are drafted, but apparently this precaution is considered superfluous when attempting to control the highly skilled profession of the Registered Nurse, who may have her work and salary and even her meals arranged for her, without her knowledge much less her approval.

Another major concern was the threat the Bill posed to the working opportunities for registered (qualified) nurses. Since the Bill applied only to 'registered' nurses, its likely effect would have been to hand over the bulk of private case work to 'unqualified' nurses (ibid.).

A more major concern for nurses, however, was that if the Bill became law, it would effectively erode their much fought for professional status. Like their Californian colleagues, English nurses worried that by allowing labour laws to intrude into their affairs, they would be perceived as 'labourers', rather than 'professionals'. This, they feared, would undermine their attempts to gain full professional recognition. The *Nursing Times* (1931, p. 219), a British nursing periodical, responded by arguing:

> Can the ideals of nursing grow and flourish under such hard-and-fast regulations? Would doctors, artists, professors or university students call in the law to regulate their hours of study and service? Would they not rather evolve a code for themselves, and from within, as all professions have done before them?

The article concluded (*Nursing Times* 1931, p. 220) by asking all nurses

> to explain to their members of Parliament that, well-meaning as this Bill
> may be, it does not interpret our real needs, and that, however moving an
> appeal on such lines may sound in the House, the principles embodied in
> the Bill are not the principles for which we stand, nor are its ideals the
> ideals with which we should have to be associated.

Brockway's Bill was quickly dismissed in the House of Commons,
however, on grounds that there was no demand for it among the nursing
profession, and that it was merely 'a political stunt of the Labour Party'
(Fremantle 1930, p. 2188). Fenner Brockway lost his seat in the 1931
general election, and his Bill was extinguished almost without being noticed
(Dingwall et al. 1988, p. 101).

The 1916 Peacock Bill

The Californian and English labour law experiences were to be parallelled in
Australia, and nurses were once again targeted to be the exceptions to the
standard industrial rule. In 1910, an editorial in the *Australasian Nurses
Journal* (p. 1) pondered:

> Eight hours work, eight hours play, eight hours sleep has long been the
> strongest platform of unionism, but it also is the cry of the rationalist. As
> such one wonders why its application to the nursing profession has only of
> late met with any serious consideration. Is it because the labours of a Nurse
> are so light and easy that she is well content with the present conditions of
> work, or is it that her loyalty and forbearance prevent complaint and so the
> inevitable is accepted?

Up until 1914, the Labor party in Victoria directed its attention to
improve the working conditions of hospital domestics and hospital
attendants (Trembath and Hellier 1987, p. 122). And in 1916, Sir
Alexander Peacock, the Liberal Premier of Victoria and Minister of
Labour, successfully introduced legislation to reduce the working hours
and increase the wages of those workers. Hospital nurses were not,
however, included under the new legislation which left them in the
invidious position of working longer hours and earning less money than
a hospital domestic. Ironically, in supporting the cause of the hospital
domestics, politicians 'sometimes painted a fictitious contrast with the
satisfactory conditions enjoyed by nurses' (ibid., p. 97). For example, one
member of parliament remarked, unfairly, that nurses were 'in a better
position because, as soon as they have had the necessary instruction and
experience, they can go out privately and earn fairly good wages' (Solly
1915, p. 2424).

Arguments raised against reducing the working hours of hospital nurses were almost identical to those raised in the United States of America and England. For example, in 1911, the Inspector of Charities, H.C. Malcolm, declaimed that:

> In almost every case a decrease in hours would necessitate an increase in staff, and . . . an increase in staff necessitates increased accommodation.
> (cited in Trembath and Hellier 1987, p. 98)

As in the United States of America and England, the bottom line was that reduced hours would 'mean an extra burden on the perennially strained finances of Victoria's [hospital] charities' (ibid.). And, as was the case overseas, the doctors' and hospital administrators' financial interests prevented them from giving support to improving the working conditions of nurses (Godden 1989a, p. 17). Despite the fact that a 'long working day invariably meant a short working life' (Trembath and Hellier 1987, p. 78) many nurses had long been suspicious of 'outside attempts to improve their conditions' (Godden 1989b, p. 26) and, like their overseas colleagues, were very slow to embrace the eight-hour day as a professional issue. In 1903, for example, the matron of Melbourne's Women's Hospital objected:

> I consider if any fixed limit is set to our working hours it will be at the greatest sacrifice of the dignity of our profession, bringing it down to the level of a trade. I hope nurses will never allow such an interference with their rightful liberty, to give as much of themselves as they wish to the cause of relieving the sufferings of others.
> (MacLean 1903, p. 34)

In 1904, a prominent private nurse voiced similar objections, arguing:

> Trained nurses do not need any political influence used on their behalf, simply because the long hours and hard work inseparable from private nursing is their willing and cheerful contribution to the cause of suffering humanity, and is not in any sense exacted from them. The Trades Hall spirit of measuring out so many hours and so much exertion to each day, regardless of the public need, has so far found no favour among our nurses, and it will be an evil day for profession and public when it does so . . . Nursing must mean to some extent self-renunciation, and anyone intending to 'Scorn delight and live laborious days', not to mention the nights, should not grumble about the apprenticeship.
> (Jones 1904, p. 64)

Victorian nurses, like their American and English colleagues, were, however, unable to present their own claims to the relevant authorities investigating the working conditions of nurses. This was primarily because when the opportunity to do so arose, the nurses were working or were simply too exhausted to do anything else but go to bed after being on duty. On one occasion, rather than perceiving the situation for what it was, an inspector of charities concluded that nurses were 'indifferent' to their own well-being and had little 'feeling' or 'interest' in their own affairs (Trembath and Hellier 1987, p. 99). The position of nurses was also hardly helped by the medically dominated RVTNA who preferred not to comment on the working conditions of hospital nurses. Trembath and Hellier (ibid.), note that if the RVTNA's official opinion was sought, its reply was always the same:

> The council of the Association state that they do not at any time interfere with the inner workings of hospitals.

Demands for a shorter working week for nurses in other Australian states received much the same response as they did in Victoria (see Beattie 1950). Even as late as 1934, views were being expressed that

> it was not desirable in the public interest that [nurses] should be included in the general declaration of standard hours of 44 hours week for the following, amongst other, reasons, namely, (1) that 44 hours week would be detrimental to a nurse in training, in that she would not have sufficient time with her patients to gain necessary experience, (2) that such a working week would not be in the best interests of the patients, inasmuch as it would be necessary to change attendant nurses too frequently, (3) that an increased staff would be required if reduction in hours were ordered, and that the financial position of the hospitals was such that it would be impossible to increase the staff or to provide necessary accommodation therefor.
> (*In re Standard Hours — Nursing Staff in Hospitals* 1934, p. 318)

In a Queensland case (McCawley 1921, p. 218), it was likewise argued that

> it would be impracticable to establish a forty-eight hour week at present, as the requisite number of nurses is not available, nor could the requisite accommodation be provided.

Although Australian nursing organisations rejected early protective legislation aimed at regulating the working conditions of factory hands or shop girls (Ryan and Conlon 1975, p. 46), the majority of nurses did support a shorter working week (Trembath and Hellier 1987, p. 115). In fact, many nurses were highly critical of their colleagues (including the medically dominated executive of the RVTNA) who opposed moves to improve the working conditions of nurses. One nurse complained:

> It [nursing] is work of a highly responsible character, often involving very hard work and great self sacrifice. Of course we all know that the public speaks reverentially of nurses as 'those noble and self-sacrificing women', also that it regards nobility and self sacrifice as its own reward, bread and

butter and frocks being a superfluity, but one does not expect to find such sentiments among our own members.
(R.D.K.L 1904, p. 79)

Almost a decade later, another nurse complained:

We have done with the foolish old pedestal of the past years; people are still willing to use it, it's much cheaper to put nurses on it by high-sounding terms of praise than it is to give either consideration, shorter hours, or higher pay. We want common sense ideas, common sense treatment; we are practical women, we give skilled and valuable service, we have no time for grovellers or time-servers that play to the gallery.
(E.S. 1912, p. 165)

As was the case with their English and American nursing colleagues, the Australian nurses' quest for improved working conditions was, in almost every respect, doomed to fail. On the one hand they were viewed as 'unskilled employees', and therefore not deserving of the remuneration or status comparable to that of other 'true professionals' (see Burton et al. 1987; Burton 1991). And yet, on the other hand, when it suited the powers that be, they were viewed as 'professionals' and thus vulnerable to severe criticism for allowing their aspirations and activities to become 'tainted' with trade unionism (see, for example, *Medical Journal of Australia* 1921b, p. 48). Perhaps even worse was the problem that because they were women, these nurses were not taken seriously. With the majority of nurses being women, it was relatively easy for medical men to marginalise, trivialise, discredit and disqualify nursing views and activities aimed at improving the status and working conditions of nurses. A poignant example of this can be found in the case of an editorial which appeared in the *Medical Journal of Australia*, the official journal of the Australian Medical Association. The author of this editorial was clearly enraged by the attempts of a group of Queensland nurses to secure registration as a trade union, and proceeded to dismiss the group involved as being nothing more than a 'misguided body of foolish virgins' (*Medical Journal of Australia* 1921b, p. 48). In another commentary in the *Medical Journal of Australia*, this same group of nurses was accused of suffering from 'hare-brained delusions' (*Medical Journal of Australia* 1921a, p. 302).

Although emotionally upsetting, these and like ad hominem arguments did little to stop the eventual unionisation of nurses. Medical discourse did, however, ensure that even with unionisation, the power of nurses did not significantly improve and, as the following chapters of this book will attempt to show, ensured that any economic or political threat that nurses posed to medical men was totally — and legitimately — contained.

CONCLUSION

The early modern nurses were forced to endure exploitative work conditions characterised by employer demands to perform arduous duties, coupled with low pay, poor living conditions, long hours, and rigid discipline. Attempts to improve the working conditions of these nurses (for example, to shorten their working hours and to increase their pay) met with stiff opposition from, and were systematically rejected by, employer groups (doctors, lay hospital administrators and politicians) on grounds that work reforms would not be 'in the public interest' or 'beneficial to the nurses themselves'. Nurses who dared to complain about the conditions they were working under or their low professional status were severely criticised and portrayed as 'failed women' (selfish, uncaring, disobedient and disloyal).

When nursing leaders sought to improve the status of nursing and the conditions under which nurses were working, medical men and lay hospital administrators used their legitimate positions of power to trivialise, discredit, marginalise and, in some instances, disqualify the views and arguments these nursing leaders attempted to advance. Since the very processes of law making and law reform were themselves overwhelmingly biased in favour of, and structured to ensure, the cultural hegemony of men and the subordination of women, it was virtually impossible for the early modern nursing leaders to ensure that any law reforms that were achieved in nursing's 'favour' fully reflected the needs, aspirations and lived experiences of nurses whose lives and practice were at issue. Given the gender biases of the law (its processes and structure) it is not surprising that when state registration was eventually achieved it did not bring the remedies and benefits that the early nurses had hoped and fought for. It is also small wonder that rather than ending the historic 'thirty-year war' for nursing's legitimated status as an autonomous profession, the passage of state registration laws merely marked the beginning of a greater war for 'real' status — a war which, as the next and following chapters will show, has still not been won.

ENDNOTES

1 Lavinia Dock has the distinction of being one of the few nursing leaders who gained the great satisfaction of going to jail three times for women's suffrage (Brand and Glass 1975, p. 168). In 1910, Lavinia Dock, along with two other great nursing leaders, Isabel Stewart and M. Adelaide Nutting, 'joined the ranks of women who marched down 5th Avenue in New York City in support of suffrage' (ibid., p. 169).

2 'Registrar' was defined in section 2 of the Act as the 'Inspector-General of Hospitals in New Zealand'.

3   Prior to 1901, girls as young as 10 to 15 years of age 'nursed for gain' (Fenwick 1904, p. 4)

4   A 'special' is a nurse who is assigned to remain constantly with and exclusively care for a patient who cannot be left alone. Patients typically assigned a 'special' nurse (even today) included those who were seriously ill and who required constant observations, monitoring and intensive nursing care, or those who were a danger either to themselves or to others.

5   The earliest measure to secure state recognition of professional standards of nursing was put into effect by Cape Colony, South Africa. It should be noted, however, that it was not 'a complete and separate act, but only a section of the Medical and Pharmacy Act of 1891' (Dock 1904b; Dock 1906; Dock and Stewart 1938, p. 259). The first country to bring into effect a discrete Nurses' Registration Act was New Zealand (Dock 1904b; Dock 1906; Dock and Stewart 1938, p. 260). This Act was passed by the New Zealand Parliament in September 1901, and came into operation on 1st January 1902 (Dock 1904b, p. 140).

6   Nightingale generally believed that legislative reforms in themselves were worth 'no more than the public opinion and individual effort which they express or inspire' (Cook 1913b, pp. 332–333). And she seriously doubted the ability of law reforms to secure true 'love and justice' and 'freedom and progress' for women (see in particular Nightingale's (1852, 1979 edn) little known essay 'Cassandra'). Her opinion of the politicians responsible for initiating and overseeing law reform was even less complimentary. In her view, very few politicians had any real ability to effect meaningful and useful law reform. As for the political parties of the day, Nightingale considered they existed primarily 'to register popular feelings, to satisfy popular ignorance, to make a scene in effect before the pit', and that they frequently abandoned 'solid practical administrative things' in favour of mere 'glittering politics' (Smith 1982, p. 190).

7   It is interesting to note that as recently as 1988, an American study found that almost 87 per cent of the 10 000 doctors surveyed by a professional research consultancy group, cited 'the quality of a hospital's *nursing staff* as being '*the* most important factor when admitting patients to hospital' [emphasis added] (*Nursing 88* 1988, p. 12). Only around 78 per cent of those surveyed said 'the quality of medical staff was equally important'. This kind of survey reflects the historical irony that often patients are not admitted to hospitals unless they require nursing care, and that the care which is so necessary is so 'invisible' to the public eye (see Vance et al. 1985, p. 283).

8   At this time, there were, in fact, two Bills before the House; namely, the Nurses Registration Bill, and the Royal College of Nursing Bill. Lord Ampthill was particularly opposed to the latter Bill on grounds that its 'primary object [was] not the State registration of nurses', but 'to secure the incorporation of a private company known as The College of Nursing, Limited, and, of course, to secure for that company financial support under the aegis of State authority (Ampthill 1919, pp. 823–824).

9   The RVTNA continually had doctors as its president until as late as 1932, when the legendary Jane Bell, Lady Superintendent of the Royal Melbourne Hospital, became president (Williams and Goodman 1988, p. 112).

10   As a point of interest, the federal Australian Nursing Federation is currently fighting for a national register of nurses — something which was first proposed in 1951 (Beaumont 1990, p. 9; Vidovich 1990, p. 21).

11   The Ritchie case declared unconstitutional an Act limiting women to an eight-hour work day and a 48-hour week in all factories and workshops (see also Friedman 1965, p. 487).

CHAPTER **FOUR**

The Pyrrhic Victory of State Registration

INTRODUCTION

THE NURSING PROFESSION'S QUEST for legitimated status as an autonomous health care profession has been long and hard, and, as shown in the previous chapter, seriously hampered by those who had competing economic interests. Nevertheless, 'success' was eventually achieved. England obtained state registration in 1919; all 48 American states had enacted nursing licensure laws by 1923; and in Australia, registration laws[1] were passed in all states and territories by 1933. Contrary to popular impression, however, this major law reform was not to nursing's advantage, and to this day stands as a classic example, to borrow from DeCrow (1974, p. 4), of a law reform going 'for' nurses (women) also going 'against' them. Instead of challenging and improving the status quo, state registration laws merely reinforced and legitimated it: the public interest was not protected (unqualified people could still 'nurse' for gain), and the status of nursing was not improved (statutory regulation merely reinforced and legitimated the cultural hegemony of medical men, legitimated the subordination of nurses (women) to medical men, and provided medical men with a powerful mechanism for keeping nurses in their 'proper sphere'). Equally disturbing was the fact that state registration failed to protect nurses from exploitation by unscrupulous employers — including and especially the state. Rather than free nurses to operate autonomously in the 'public sphere', state registration worked more to isolate nurses in the 'private sphere' (behind the secluded walls of the hospital–castle) already dominated and controlled by medical men. To borrow from Taub and Schneider (1982, p. 122) writing on the legal plight of women generally, state registration thereby contributed directly to the nurses' (as women)

> inferior status by denying them the legal relief that they [had sought] to improve their situation and by sanctioning conduct of the men who [controlled] their lives.

Thus, while obtaining state registration appears at first glance to have been a major political coup for the nursing profession, in reality it was, at best, only a Pyrrhic victory; and at worst a legitimation of medical supremacy, control and oppression of nursing, as this chapter will show.

The failure of state registration to give 'real' status to nurses

During a 1919 House of Lords debate on the question of state registration for English nurses (to be distinguished here from Scottish and Irish nurses who were subject to separate Registration Acts (see Bendall and Raybould 1969, p. 27)), Lord Buckmaster (1919, pp. 848–849) argued:

> Registration by itself is nothing but the compiling of a dictionary. There are registered plumbers; there are registered auctioneers, and all kinds of people are registered, and registration by itself conveys neither authority, nor skill, nor character of any kind, nothing but the compilation of a book. If you want to make registration real you must associate with it something that will establish the status and improve the position of the people who register.

Despite frequent parliamentary debate (a nurses registration Bill was placed before parliament each year from 1904 to 1914 (Abel-Smith 1960, p. 81)) and strict adherence to the state's formal law-making processes, the state registration that was eventually granted to English nurses in 1919 was not 'real' in so far as it did not establish the status of nurses, and it failed to improve significantly the position of the nurses who registered. State registration was also 'not real' because nurses as a whole lacked both the political power and the financial resources necessary to ensure that registration laws would be formulated, interpreted and applied in a way that would achieve the ultimate ends that the nursing profession had long been fighting for. Thus, as Susan Reverby (1987, p. 166) — writing from an American context — concludes:

> Legitimation of professional goals, without the funds or political power to implement them, became nursing's Pyrrhic victory.

This situation was equally true of the state registration granted to nurses in other common law countries including, as already noted above, the United States of America (1903–1923), and Australia (1911–1933).

Although nurses' registration Acts did everything to protect the title 'Registered Nurse', they did nothing to protect nurses or the practice of nursing. As a result, nurses continued to be abused and exploited, and the public continued to receive nursing care from those not qualified to nurse.

Equally disturbing was the problem that even if a nurse was struck off the register there was nothing to stop her continuing to perform nursing duties for financial gain, provided she did not claim the title 'Registered Nurse'. Another disappointing feature of the new state registration laws was that rather than freeing the nursing profession from its traditional 'masters' (doctors and lay hospital administrators or managers), the new registration laws ensured that nursing remained subordinate to and controlled by them. For example, the statutorily prescribed composition of the registration boards ensured medical governance and legitimated the authority of doctors (and, it should be pointed out, the state) to ultimately decide and prescribe the standards of nursing education and practice. This, in effect, served to legitimately bind nurses and nursing practice to the authority of doctors (and the state), rather than to free them from it. In particular, it served to reinforce and sanction the image of the nurse 'as one who merely aids the physician in his work or hospitals in their work' — an image which has remained constant to this day (Ashley 1976a, p. 74). And, more importantly, it served to ensure that doctors 'had a great deal of control over what nurses learned, who passed the exams and who registered after graduation' (Keddy et al. 1986, p. 747). In short, it ensured that nurses did not gain professional autonomy.

It can be seen, then, that instead of having its deeply felt historical desires transformed into enforceable legal rights, what the nursing profession inherited were more oppressive (male dominated) forms of regulation, greater surveillance and greater demands for conformity to new (masculinist) regulations — problems which women have had to deal with in the broader realms of human activity (see, for example, Sevenhuijsen 1986; Wishik 1986; Zipper and Sevenhuijsen 1987; Smart 1989). The nursing profession also inherited a form of legislation that deprived it of any real ability to determine its own affairs including restricting the entry of unqualified others into nursing practice — something which, as the remainder of this chapter will show, has risked (and is risking) not just the de-professionalisation of nursing as we know it today, but also its demise.

The American experience

The first registration laws adopted in America were 'permissive' laws only. What this meant was that people who satisfied the legal standards were permitted to register and use the title 'Registered Nurse' (Ellis and Hartley 1984, p. 11). These permissive laws, however, were virtually useless since they were powerless to restrict people 'nursing' for gain. Students who failed the licensing examinations were merely referred to as graduate nurses and continued on in gainful employment (*ibid.*, p. 113). Since these nurses were not claiming to be 'Registered Nurses', they were not, strictly speaking, breaking the law and therefore could not be either prosecuted or restricted from practising.

Nursing schools were also able to avoid meeting the legal guidelines set down in the permissive licensure laws. Where schools lacked the resources to upgrade their programs, they often chose to forego the legal requirements (Reverby 1987, p. 127). As registration was not compulsory, this did not pose any serious problems for the hospitals, since they could still rely on their graduates rather than the more expensive registered nurses as a source of labour. In some states, the lack of money and human resources meant that many nursing schools were accredited without ever having been formally inspected by the state's nursing board (*ibid.*). Hospital management justified their implicit support of 'low entrance requirements' into nursing practice, and the accreditation of sub-standard nursing schools, on grounds that it was in the 'public interest' (Ashley 1976a, p. 114).

The laws also did little to improve the general working conditions of nurses. By 1933, only 2.3 per cent of the nation's hospitals had eight-hour days in effect (Reverby 1987, p. 187). Well into the 1940s, nurses were still expected to 'work split shifts and long hours, to move from ward to ward when needed, and to live and take meals within hospital walls' (*ibid.*, p. 192). Staff turnover remained high and wages remained low (a registered nurse could expect to earn less than a typist). Nurses continued to be dismissed at short notice 'when cheaper workers became available' (*ibid.*). Unemployment and an oversupply of qualified nurses continued to plague the American nursing profession, and the willingness of nurses to deal seriously with these problems reached an all-time low.

During the 1930s the possibility of unionisation was considered. In June of 1937, however, the American Nurses' Association (ANA) voted against nurse membership in labour unions, explaining:

> We have spent many years in an effort to have our work designated a profession. Can it continue to be a profession if we join the labor unions?
> (Susan Francis, ANA Advisory Council Minutes 24 April 1938, p. 99 — cited in Reverby 1987, p. 197)

In 1938 resistance to the organising efforts by unions was reiterated when an ANA state representative argued that the nurses' best defense against the unions was to align themselves with medical groups. She explained:

> We have felt our greatest strength was in our close working with the medical groups . . . I think when we tie ourselves up definitely to these professional groups, that is the best defense we have against anything of that kind.
> (Susan Francis, ANA Advisory Council Minutes 24 April 1938, p. 99 — cited in Reverby, 1987, p. 197)

It is evident that these nurses really expected the medical profession to help them and did not entertain any thought of the possibility that their medical colleagues might betray them which, ultimately, they did — not only in the United States of America but also in England and Australia (see also Dock and Stewart 1938, p. 255; Minchin 1977; Williams and Goodman 1988, p. 117).

Gradually nurses began to realise that the state's permissive registration laws had done little to protect either their own or the public's interests, and they responded by demanding that mandatory licensing laws be enacted. Such laws would require all people who wished to practise nursing for gain to meet established education and practice standards (Ellis and Hartley 1984, p. 113). The first mandatory nurse practice Act was passed in New York in 1938, but did not come into effect until 1947 (Kelly 1985, p. 450). Moreover, it was not until recently (in 1985) that all states had mandatory laws for professional nurses (Kelly 1985, p. 450), although critics argue that some Acts are 'loose' in their interpretation of 'mandatory' and as a result it is still possible for almost anyone to 'nurse' provided they are 'supervised' (ibid., p. 451) — the implications of which will be considered more fully later in this chapter.

The English experience

England's nurse registration laws, like those in the United States of America and Australia, were also only 'permissive'. Even if nurses were deregistered, it was, technically speaking, still possible for them to continue nursing (Pyne 1981, p. 27). This anomaly existed in England up until 1925, six years after the passage of the *Nurses' Registration Act 1919*. Thus, although the title 'Registered Nurse' was protected, the *Nurses' Registration Act 1919* was powerless to make registration a pre-condition of entry into practice (Dingwall et al. 1988, p. 88). What this effectively meant was that, like their counterparts in the United States of America and Australia, hospital employers were virtually free to employ whoever they wanted — so long as those who were 'nursing' did not claim to be 'registered' nurses. The implications of this were not formally raised at a political level until as late as 1943, when, in a House of Lords debate on a proposed revision of the 1919 Act, the then Minister of Health, Mr Ernest Brown (1943, p. 1649), admitted:

> There is nothing in the Nurses Registration Act, 1919, to prevent a person from calling herself a nurse or practising nursing without training or qualification. The result of that is that the public and the patients may be, and indeed are, misled. There are many thousands of nurses who are called assistant nurses at the present time, but the phrase 'assistant nurse' has no

accepted meaning whatever. It describes a great variety of people, some with training, some without, some capable, some not capable.

The minister went on to point out that 'a large number of assistant nurses with small qualifications' were being employed by unscrupulous private nursing agencies and sent out to care for patients 'at high fees without any indications that they were not qualified to give expert attention' (*ibid.*). Rather than strengthening the 1919 *Nurses' Registration Act* and outlawing the employment of 'assistant nurses with small qualifications', the parliament amended the Act to legitimate the role of assistant 'nurses' caring for the sick, and thereby created a less qualified 'second level' of nurse, namely, the state enrolled nurse (SEN) (see *Nurses Act 1943*). What this ensured was not the protection of the public against being 'nursed' by unqualified people, but the supply of a cheaper 'qualified' nursing force for the nation's hospitals.

Equally disappointing, however, was the Act's failure to grant the nursing profession the autonomy and authority it had been seeking to determine its own affairs. It soon became clear that the English government had no intention of granting the nurses professional autonomy, indeed quite the reverse. For example, the General Nursing Council (GNC), set up under the Act to work out detailed regulations for governing nursing education and practice, was not to be controlled by nurses. Instead, it was to be controlled by the minister of health. The minister assumed the power to nominate members of the council, to approve (or disapprove) all regulations drafted by the council, to veto any council decision to deny accreditation to training schools and, significantly, to control the council's financial resources — its political life-line (Bendall and Raybould 1969, p. 29; Dingwall et al. 1988, p. 88).

Although nurse activists lobbied the minister for health to have a nurse appointed as the first chairperson of the GNC, the minister appointed a barrister and justice of the peace to the position (Bendall and Raybould 1969, p. 29). This controversial appointment was later challenged in parliament, where the minister was asked whether he was 'aware that the Chairman had neither the experience nor knowledge of *medical* matters sufficient to enable him to understand and guide the General Nursing Council in its deliberation on professional subjects [emphasis added]?' (ibid., p. 40). The minister replied simply that he was 'under no obligation to consult the Council [or nurses, it seems] and there was no suggestion that it had been hampered in its work' (ibid.). He dismissed all criticism of the chairman's appointment on grounds that it had been fuelled by 'foolish gossip which had nothing to do with the matter' (ibid.). Although the first registrar was a nurse, it was not until six years after the first GNC meeting, that a nurse was elected chairperson of the council (ibid., pp. 40, 86). Nurses have been elected to these positions ever since.

The minister's power over the GNC's actions was, however, total, and he used it in a way that ensured that the council was quite unable to engage in any independent action. For example, the minister 'refused to enforce the recommended syllabus of training' drawn up by the council, thereby effectively preventing the nursing profession from setting its standards as high as it wished (Abel-Smith 1960, p. 113; Bendall and Raybould 1969, p. 59). The minister's readiness to intervene also meant that parliament was able to preserve the 'rights' of unqualified nurses which, as was the case in the United States of America, had the undesirable effect of exacerbating the 'shortage' (read 'unemployment') of trained nurses — a problem which was to persist for the next 30 years (Abel-Smith 1960, p. 113). Thus, under the guise of 'parliamentary democracy' and of 'protecting the liberties of the under-privileged' (namely, the untrained 'nurse'), the government was able to create a legal loophole through which it could legitimately secure and sustain its use of unqualified staff as a cheap source of labour (ibid., p. 111; Bendall and Raybould 1969, pp. 71–73).

Historical research has since shown that the GNC 'willingly or unwillingly, was, in effect, an agent of the Ministry of Health and assisted in a process of deskilling nurses' (White 1985, p. 584). White (ibid.) argues persuasively that after the coming of the National Health Service (NHS), the GNC

> was not so much concerned with improving the quality of nurse training as it was with recruiting the highest number of trainees and that, in order to achieve this, they had to depress the standard of entry and, therefore, of course, the standards of their qualifying examinations.

Thus, in this instance, it can be seen that rather than improve and legally enforce the standards of nursing care, state registration laws — through being vulnerable to political manipulation — actually eroded and undermined the enforcement of professional nursing standards, a problem which persists to this day.

The English *Nurses Registration Act 1919* was to fail and be less than 'real' for the nursing profession in yet another way. Of the first 30 'professional misconduct' cases to come before the GNC, 26 resulted in deregistration. What is significant about this figure is not only that it is relatively high, but that most of the nurses were deregistered for reasons which had little or nothing to do with their professional practice (Pyne 1981, p. 21). It would appear that those enforcing the Act were more concerned with reinforcing and maintaining traditional notions of what was 'appropriate behaviour' for the proverbial 'good women' making up the nursing profession, than they were with enforcing and maintaining professional standards of nursing care. For example, of the first 30 nurses to come before the General Nurses' Council on disciplinary charges, most related to things like 'shoplifting' and theft (something which was in itself a reflection of the economic plight of nurses), and 'personal conduct' (Pyne 1981). The 'personal conduct' cases are interesting in so far as they clearly reflect a marked gender bias against female nurses and the parochial moral values used to censure their conduct. For example, in one 1934 case, a nurse was struck off for 'staying in a hotel with a married man' (Bendall and Raybould 1969, p. 114). In another case which occurred during the same year, a nurse (the matron of a hospital) was struck off for the 'professional misconduct' of giving birth to an illegitimate child (the nurse later married the child's father) (ibid.). It is probably no coincidence that of the first 30 professional misconduct cases listed, one of the few nurses to escape punishment was a male nurse who was brought before the council for 'deserting his wife' (Pyne 1981, p. 20). A number of the early 'personal conduct' cases are cited in Reginald Pyne's book *Professional discipline in nursing* (1981, p. 20), and, for the sake of interest, are outlined below:

CHARGE	DECISION
Betting in a public house	Warned about behaviour
Desertion of his wife	No action taken
Bore two illegitimate children	Removed from the register
Living in adultery	Removed from the register
Misconduct with a man in a hotel	Removed from the register
Convicted of making an unauthorised street collection for a good cause	Warned about behaviour (This lady could be regarded as being singularly unfortunate, in that she rattled her collecting box at the chairman of the local Watch Committee, who then prosecuted her!)
Drunk and disorderly in a public place	Removed from the register

It was not until the thirtieth case, in 1931, that the council dealt with an offence involving a serious deviation from acceptable professional standards of care. The case in question involved the misappropriation of drugs and is described in the council's records as 'Taking and unlawfully possessing Morphine' (cited in Pyne 1981, p. 21). Theft from shops and drug related offences continue to make up a significant number of the disciplinary cases involving nurses heard today (ibid.; Young 1991). The majority of other cases involve nurses who have succumbed to intolerable work-related pressures, a point formally noted by the (now defunct[2]) General Nursing Council. In fact, in its annual reports for 1978–1979 and 1979–1980, the GNC for England and Wales publicly expressed and placed on record their concern that

> such a significant number of cases appearing before the Disciplinary Committee are a consequence of excessive and unacceptable pressures in working situations.
> (Pyne 1981, p. 78)

In regard to the 'illegal' practice of nursing, it was not until 1930, 11 years after the passage of the 1919 *Nurses' Registration Act*, that the first prosecution was brought against an unqualified person who had falsely represented herself as a 'State Registered' nurse. After appearing in court, she was fined £3.00 (Bendall and Raybould 1969, p. 114). Only 10 similar cases occurred over the next two years.

The Australian experience

Australia's registration laws were also to fail the nursing profession. As was the case in the United States of America and England, Australia's registration laws were 'permissive' and thus powerless to prevent unqualified 'nurses' practising for gain. This meant, as it did in the United States of America and England, that a person could only be prosecuted for performing 'nursing duties' if she called herself a 'Registered Nurse'. In a paper presented at the ICN's 1937 Quadrennial Congress of Nurses in London, Jane Bell, Lady Superintendent of the Royal Melbourne Hospital and a passionate supporter of the professionalisation of Australian nursing, complained: 'unskilled freelancers are allowed to do as they like and are subject to none but the ordinary forces of law' (Bell 1937, p. 160; see also Williams and Goodman 1988). Recognising that this was a matter which could only be remedied by law, she argued further that

> the need for reform in this matter becomes increasingly evident, and it is most desirable that legislation should be introduced making it compulsory that those engaged in the responsible work of nursing involving, as it does, the issues of life and death, to say nothing of the prolonged or permanent disability which may be the result of unskilled nursing, should be nurses who are registered by the state.
> (Bell 1937, p. 160))

Not unexpectedly, Bell's calls went unheeded by the government of the day, and the situation which she lamented remained legitimated until as late as 1958 (Minchin 1977, p. 13). In reality, however, the situation persisted well after state registration became mandatory, and even now unqualified people are able to perform nursing duties for financial gain without being registered nurses.

The new registration laws failed the nursing profession in another and perhaps more important way, by legitimating medical control and dominance of both nurses and nursing practice. For example, people wanting to enter 'the calling of nursing' — as it was described in two Acts the *Nurses Registration Act 1927* (Tasmania) and the *Nurses and Masseurs Registration Act 1928* (Queensland) — were legally required to have a medical certificate of health. While this was generally seen to be justified on grounds that it was necessary to ensure that prospective nurses were 'healthy' (and therefore could be relied upon as workers) and did not carry diseases which could be cross-infected to patients, it should be noted that this provision also ensured a significant degree of legitimated medical control over who should be permitted to train and become a nurse.

Medical men were also given considerable control over disciplinary proceedings. In the Northern Territory *Nurses and Midwives Registration Ordinance 1928–1957*, for example, authority to investigate 'any charge of malpractice, negligence or misconduct on the part of any nurse or midwife' was invested not in a nursing or midwifery peer, but in the chief medical officer (see section 21(3)). This control was even more stringent in New South Wales, the Northern Territory and South Australia, where registration laws explicitly cited 'insanity' or 'lunacy' as grounds for deregistration — a provision which, once again, allowed the medical profession an extraordinary degree of power over nurses. When it is considered, for example, that mere nonconformity to social norms of 'acceptable' feminine behaviour was once regarded by doctors as a manifestation of 'female insanity' and 'female invalidism' (see, for example, Chesler 1972; Szasz 1972; Ehrenreich and English 1973a, 1973b, 1979; Hutter and Williams 1981; Matthews 1984), it can be seen that the 'insanity' provision in effect provided the medical profession with a powerful (and draconian) instrument for ensuring nurses stayed firmly within their 'proper sphere' and conformed fully to feminine norms of behaviour (that is, remained obedient, submissive, loyal, altruistic, and so on).

State registration legitimated medical dominance in nurse education as well. Pupil nurses were, for example, specifically required to receive instruction from a 'legally qualified medical practitioner' as well as from a 'matron'. In one state, people wishing to register as nurses were also required to submit certificates of competence (proficiency) from two legally qualified medical practitioners (see the NSW *Nurses' Registration Act 1924*, s 10(2)). The legitimated participation of medical men in nurse education ensured that doctors remained the guardians of 'nursing' knowledge, could set the limits on how much nurses 'needed' to know, and ensured that nurses remained dependent on doctors for information and knowledge.

A particularly interesting feature of the Australian nurse registration laws is the emphasis they gave (and, it should be added, continue to give) to empowering registration boards to prescribe and regulate the wearing of traditional nursing garb — such as the nurse's badge and uniform. The emphasis given to regulating and prescribing nursing garb is significant and stands as a very good example of the inadequate manner in which the law has tended to view nurses. That is, as women whose status is best defined or described not by what they do or by their educational achievements, but by what they wear (see also Mundinger 1980, pp. 12, 88).

The legitimation of traditional nursing garb should not be dismissed as a mere coincidence. The uniform is a powerful symbol of conformity (Savage 1987, p. 77), and, in the case of the traditional nurse's white uniform, a symbol of conformity to a quasi-religious life of 'humility, service and obedience' (Szasz 1982, p. 397; see also Holden 1991, p. 70). Interestingly, registration laws in all states made it an offence for unregistered people to wear traditional nursing garb, notably the nurse's badge and uniform. Victorian (1923), Tasmanian (1927), and Queensland (1964) registration laws also made it an offence for unregistered people to wear a 'distinctive head-dress' (a particularly significant piece of traditional nursing garb and one which is exclusively female). The 1927 Tasmanian *Nurses Registration Act*, for example, states 'No person who is not registered shall . . . wear or use any badge or distinctive head-dress prescribed for the use of registered nurses' (see also Tasmanian *Nurses Registration Act 1952*, s 18(1c)). The Victorian *Nurses Registration Act 1923* is even more explicit, stating:

15. On application to the Board in the prescribed form every person who has been registered as a nurse shall be entitled to receive a prescribed badge and a *written authority* [emphasis added] to wear a prescribed distinctive head-dress . . .
18. (1) After the commencement of this Act no person . . .
(b) shall wear or use any prescribed badge or any prescribed distinctive head-dress — unless such person is registered as a nurse under this Act.

The most comprehensive statement concerning the wearing of a nurse's distinctive head-dress is to be found in the amended Queensland *Nurses and Masseurs Registration Act 1928–1933* (assented to 24 November 1938), in the subsequent revised (first discrete) Queensland *Nurses Act 1964* and the revised *Queensland Nurses Act 1976*. Section 32 of the 1964 Queensland Act regulating the wearing of the nurse's distinctive head-dress is unique, and, for the purposes of this discussion, worth quoting in full. It states:

32. Wearing of nurse's veil. (1) Any person not being a person registered under this Act who wears a nurse's veil shall be guilty of an offence against this Act.

(2) The provisions shall not apply to —

(a) a member of a religious order wearing a habit conforming with the requirements of customs of that order, or any persons taking part in a religious rite wearing any raiment customary or necessary therefor;

(b) any person taking part in any theatrical performance wearing a nurse's veil;

(c) any person under the age of sixteen years being a junior member of the Australian Red Cross (Queensland Division).

(3) For the purposes of this section the term 'nurse's veil' means a veil of the design commonly worn by registered nurses.

The Queensland provision is particularly significant when considered in relation to the religious origins of the veil. The requirement for a woman to cover her head (particularly when in the presence of a man) has a firm religious basis. In 1 Corinthians 11:4 of the Bible, for example, it is stated that if a man covers his head when praying or prophesying, his head will be 'dishonoured'. This, we are told, is because man 'is the image and glory of God' and therefore he 'ought not to cover his head' (1 Corinthians 11:7). Woman, on the other hand, must cover her head when either praying or prophesying, since to do these things with her head uncovered would be to dishonour her head and bring shame (1 Corinthians 11:5). Corinthians (1 Corinthians 11:5–6) further instructs:

> Every woman who prays or prophesies with her head uncovered dishonours her head, for that is one and the same thing as if her head were shaved. For if a woman is not covered, let her also be shorn. But if it is shameful for a woman to be shorn or shaved, let her be covered.

Since woman was 'of man' and 'created for the man', and lacked the authority of being in the image and glory of God (man), it was necessary for her to 'have a symbol of authority on her head' — a head covering (1 Corinthians 11:10). A woman's 'long hair' was regarded as being a God given 'natural' covering, and therefore 'a glory to her' (1 Corinthians 11:14–15). This explains why a woman's shaved head was such a dishonourable and shameful thing, since it meant she no longer reflected God's (man's) glory.

The development of the nurse's uniform complete with its distinctive veil/cap has been strongly influenced by these religious values, and indeed is widely recognised as having originated in the dress of convent nuns. In a short but excellent article entitled 'The tyranny of uniforms', Shermalayne Szasz (1982, p. 397) explains:

> The cap originally included an attached veil, which was symbolic of humility, service, and obedience — a custom that has been retained by most Catholic orders and by many marriage ceremonies. The meaning of nurses'

caps is usually considered a remnant of this custom, the cap being a symbol of humility and service to humanity.

Why the Victorian, Tasmanian, and Queensland state legislators felt the need to make such explicit reference to the 'distinctive head-dress' is unclear. The reference is even more interesting when one considers that other Acts have not specifically regulated the wearing of a 'distinctive head-dress'. Even the comparatively conservative English *Nurses Registration Act 1919*, which originally declined to include male nurses on the general part of the register — listing them instead on a supplementary part[3] (see sections 2(b) and 4 of the Act) — is not so specific. Although the English Act (see sections 8(1a) and 8(1b) of the Act), like most other nurse registration Acts, makes reference to the registered nurse's distinctive and identifying 'uniform'[4] and 'badge' (both powerful symbols of servitude — even for men), it does not make mention of a 'distinctive head-dress'. One possible explanation is that the Australian legislators were strongly influenced by powerful cultural–stereotypical images of the nurse (the archetypal 'good woman') which were popular at that time (and which remain popular among the laity), including the image of her being a 'humble and obedient servant' as was symbolised by the wearing of a veil, and later a cap.

By legally prescribing the wearing of a 'distinctive head-dress', the Australian Acts effectively reinforced and legitimated the stereotypical image of the nurse as a 'humble and obedient good woman' and, it should be added, one who was in total submission to men (doctors and lay hospital administrators). In so doing, these registration laws managed to avoid legitimating the emerging image of the nurse as a financially independent professional woman with 'real' status and authority. Significantly, nurses who engaged in 'improper conduct' risked not only losing their legal right to be registered under the Act, but also their legal right to wear the distinctive and very public hallmark of the proverbial 'good woman' — the veil/cap. Given the religious origins and significance of the nurse's veil, it can be seen that this legal punishment was far from trivial. By denying a registered nurse the legal right to wear a 'distinctive head-dress', the law was effectively 'uncovering her head' and thereby stripping her of her 'symbol of authority'. This symbolic 'uncovering' of the nurse's head (an act which has its parallel in the shaving of a woman's head) had the additional effect of punishing the offending nurse by 'dishonouring' and 'shaming' her.

It should be noted that although male registered nurses were called 'Sister' for many years, they were not required to wear either a veil or a cap. The wearing of the distinctive head-dress was gender specific to female registered nurses. While it might be objected that it would be ridiculous to expect male nurses to wear a veil or a cap, it is not so ridiculous to consider that a distinctive 'male' head-dress, similar to that worn by junior army personnel for example, could have been developed and worn by male nurses. As we know, a distinctive male head-dress was never designed for, nor worn by, male nurses. One explanation for this is that the primary function of the veil/cap was to tie the identity of the (female) nurse to symbolic and traditional garments (rather than educational status, for instance). This in turn served as a constant psychological reminder that the 'proper role' of the (female) nurse (the 'good woman') was one of 'obedience, servitude, and humility' (Szasz 1982) — characteristics which were not generally considered as fitting the stereotypical image of the male nurse (who, at that time, was considered an 'asset' to nursing because of his physical strength (see, for example, Anderson 1908, p. 122)). Another possible explanation is that the religious values which so obviously influenced the dress code of (female) nurses simply did not apply to male nurses. As the biblical position cited earlier makes clear, 'every man ... having his head covered, dishonours his head' (1 Corinthians 11:4). From this viewpoint, expecting male nurses to wear a head covering would have been tantamount to 'dishonouring' them and worse, undermining their 'natural' (God given) authority as men.

It should perhaps be clarified that it was not just in relation to prescribing and regulating nursing garb — or indeed to legitimating medical control of entry into nursing practice, nurse education, and disciplinary action — that state registration failed nurses. It failed nurses in an overall and more serious way; by legitimating medical dominance of the newly established registration boards. Medical men and politicians opposed to nurses having any form of professional power vehemently opposed the significant representation of nurses on the newly proposed nurses' registration boards. Some did not want any nurse representation on these boards at all. In one state, a member of the Legislative Assembly even objected to board membership by nurses on grounds that they 'did not have the qualifications necessary to determine the extent of knowledge a nurse required' (Russell 1990, pp. 21–23). The opposition mounted was largely successful, and statutory nursing registration boards around Australia became dominated by non-nurses, notably 'benchmark'[5] men (Thornton 1990, p. 1) with backgrounds in either medicine, law or general education. In Victoria, for example, nurses were given a significant but not majority representation on the board. The first chairperson of the nurses' registration board was a male medical doctor. Subsequent chairmen came with backgrounds in law and general education. Just why Victorian nurses 'allowed' (if indeed they did allow) themselves to be dominated by non-nurses (in particular by medical doctors) is a matter for speculation. Williams and Goodman (1988, p. 112) suggest that the RVTNA (itself medically dominated):

simply accepted that neither hospitals nor doctors would accept policies made by nurses . . . or that they were so trained to 'know their place' that self-determination was unthinkable.

Another equally plausible explanation is that medical men worked behind the scenes to sabotage the nursing profession's attempts to gain control of and majority nurse representation on the board. It should perhaps be pointed out that it would not have been difficult for members of the medical profession to have their interests protected by the government of the day. For instance, during the time the Nurses' Registration Bill was being debated in parliament (it was eventually passed on 18 December 1923), the chief secretary of the Legislative Assembly (and later Victorian premier) was a medical doctor, Dr S. Argyle (RVTNA 1923, p. 167). Dr Argyle's commitment to the medical profession and to championing medical interests can be assumed by the fact that in 1925 he was also the president of the Victorian branch of the British Medical Association (Pensabene 1980, p. 131). Pensabene (ibid.) argues that in fact Dr Argyle's political position 'gave the medical profession an important voice in Parliament' and ensured the speedy passage of legislation which was in the interests of the medical profession (ibid.). When Dr Argyle was Premier, for example, he introduced a Bill amending the *Medical Act*. Commenting on the relatively speedy passage of the Bill, Pensabene (ibid.) writes:

> it was one of the shortest debated Medical Bills in Victorian legislative history and there was little opposition or modification to the amendment.

Dr Argyle's support of medical legislation should not be interpreted as implying his support of nursing legislation. Although he appears to have supported the Nurses' Registration Bill, there is little to suggest that his political position gave the nursing profession an important voice in parliament. Dr Argyle could have done a lot more than he did for the nursing profession, not least, making state registration mandatory and ensuring that nurses were given control of and majority representation on the new Nurses' Registration Board. Even though the RVTNA (1923, p. 167) gives the distinct impression that it viewed Dr Argyle as a champion of the nursing cause (in an editorial in *Una* (1923), for example, it praised Dr Argyle's 'thorough grasp of the principles of the issue, and of the necessity for registration and his solicitude for the welfare of Nurses as a whole'), it should be remembered that the executive positions of the RVTNA were and had long been dominated by 'benchmark' medical men (Trembath and Hellier 1987, pp. 46–47; Williams and Goodman 1988, p. 112). If Dr Argyle had a 'thorough grasp of the principles of the issue'(RVTNA 1923, p. 167), they were not the principles of professional autonomy for nurses. Rather, they were the principles of ensuring that nurses and nursing remained under the control of the medical profession, and, as was the case in England, subject to the overriding authority of the minister of health. It was not until late 1989, that the first nurse was appointed as chairperson of the Victorian Nursing Council (*Australian Nurses Journal* 1990, p. 19). Meanwhile, the Victorian Nursing Council (VNC) remains subject to the overriding authority of the minister for health.

The first Victorian nurses Act, the *Nurses Registration Act 1923*, is a particularly good example of state registration not being made 'real' (to borrow from Lord Buckmaster (1919, pp. 848–849) cited in the introduction to this chapter) in so far as it lacked the power either to establish or improve the status of the nurses who registered. This is reflected to a large extent by two noticeable occurrences:

1. The extraordinarily large number of names removed from the register shortly after it had been established.
2. The relatively few prosecutions under the Act after it was first passed. For example, between 1924 and 1933, hundreds of names (possibly close to a thousand) were removed from the newly established nurses register. These names were removed not because of 'professional misconduct', but because the nurses had either:
   - failed to pay their registration fees;
   - requested to have their names removed on grounds that they were 'discontinuing their practice' (possible reasons for this include getting married or moving to another town or state); or
   - died.

If state registration had conferred 'real' status, it is possible that the nurses discontinuing their practice might not have been so keen to 'give it away' by requesting that their names be removed from the register (which, incidentally, they were not legally required to do).

As for unqualified people practising in contravention of the *Nurses Act 1928*, it appears that the VNC did not initiate proceedings to censure someone under the Act until as late as October 1939. The VNC minutes of that period mention a 'Matron' of a country benevolent home who was observed to have committed an offence under the Act for a 13 month period between August 1938 and September 1939. Her 'offence', in this instance, was not that she had called herself a 'registered nurse' while practising nursing for gain, but that she had worn a legally prescribed 'distinctive headdress while not a registered nurse' (VNC unpub., p. 219). Proceedings were initiated against the matron presumably under sections 19(1b) and 19(3) of the amended *Nurses Act 1931*, which state:

19. (1) No person —
(b) shall wear or use any prescribed badge or any *prescribed distinctive*

head-dress, unless such person is registered as a nurse under this Act or the corresponding previous enactment.

(3) Every person who knowingly takes or uses any such name or title or addition or description or wears or uses any such badge or special badge or *prescribed distinctive head-dress* in contravention of this section shall be liable to a penalty of not more than Twenty pounds [emphasis added].

The first case of a general nurse (to be distinguished here from a registered midwife) being removed from the register for professional misconduct appears not to have occurred until late 1933, some nine years after the *Nurses Registration Act 1923* came into effect (VNC unpub., p. 14). The nurse concerned was deregistered under sections 21(1) and 21(3a) of the *Nurses Act Registration 1923*, following a conviction for a civil offence in a Melbourne district court.[6] After some debate among council members about the nurse's conduct, disciplinary proceedings were commenced by the VNC following information received from the chief commissioner of police. The nurse's name was restored to the register 12 months later on grounds that there was 'no further evidence of misbehaviour'.

Victorian state registration was not unique in its failure to be 'real'. State registration laws in other Australian states also failed to give nurses 'status' and, like the Victorian legislation, served more to disempower nurses and to legitimate medical control of nursing, than to give nurses the right to professional self-determination.

When the New South Wales Act was eventually passed in 1924, for example, registered nurses did not have the power to elect the Nurses' Registration Board. New South Wales nurses worked hard to rectify this situation, and to get 'a large elected nurse majority' on the board (*Australian Nurses' Journal* 1954, p. 175). Their attempts were unsuccessful, however. In 1953, after long deliberations with the minister for health, the nurses succeeded in persuading the government to allow nurses a majority of one on the board. The minister reneged on his agreement, however; and, without consultation with the nursing profession, suddenly announced that he 'intended to amend the Act to allow himself another nomination' (ibid.). An editorial in the *Australian Nurses' Journal* (ibid.) lamented:

> The proposed new amendment will eliminate even that majority of one, so that the longed for, worked for Nurses' Board will not be conducted by nurses themselves. We feel it is time governments realized that the community expects the nursing profession to manage its own affairs. The Nurses' Committee, which has delegates from each nursing body in the State, has appealed to the Minister, and the ATNA has made a separate appeal to ask that for every additional person selected by the Minister there be a nurse elected by the nurses themselves, but without success; the Minister will not receive a deputation to discuss it. The present Act

provides for seven nurses elected by the nurses and six nominations, all of whom are medical men.

Registered nurses were not granted the legitimated power to elect the NSW Registration Board until as late as 1955 (*Australian Nurses Journal* 1955, p. 1).

In Queensland (the first Australian state to provide for the state registration of nurses[7]), nurses also faced enormous difficulties in trying to secure professional self-determination. They were confronted, however, with a particularly frustrating problem, and one which had all the dimensions of a 'catch-22' situation. Nurses were not eligible to either elect representatives to, or to be elected to, the newly formed nurses' registration board unless they were registered nurses. The problem was that they could not become registered nurses until after the statutorily empowered state registration board was formally established to confer state registration. In a letter to the editor of the *Australasian Nurses' Journal*, Jane Bell (1912, p. 247) fumed:

> One naturally wonders how it has come about that, in the State of Queensland, where women are enfranchised, and where Nurses have been organised for the past ten years with the direct object of obtaining recognition by the State, when an Act is passed no Trained Nurses are appointed to the Board which is to administer its affairs. Three medical men are already appointed, and when Nurses are registered they are to have the privilege of electing to represent them the remaining two out of the five members constituting the Board.

Bell (ibid.) went on to lament the control of medical men of the board:

> It is true that, of the three medical members appointed, one has held the position of President of the Trained Nurses' Association in Queensland, and another that of joint Honorary Secretary . . . While no one would question the great indebtedness of Nurses to medical men for their generous help on the Association Councils, it is quite a different matter to have the State Registration of Nurses handed over entirely to the control of medical men. There is no need at the present day to demonstrate that the work of trained Nurses is a valuable asset to the State. If their work is important enough to be regulated by legislation the very least they may expect is to be given a just proportion of control of their own affairs.

Although the ATNA had already anticipated the problems which Bell had correctly identified, and had suggested an amendment to the Queensland nurses registration Bill before its passage to allow for the appointment of two nurses to the nurses' board, the 'suggestion was rejected by the Upper House, and the Act was passed allowing only registered nurses to elect the two representatives' (*Australasian Nurses Journal* 1912b, p. 247). A major and important consequence of this was that by the time nurses could be and were formally elected to the board, a large portion of the board's work had already been completed — without nursing input (ibid.).

The de-professionalisation of contemporary nursing

To this day the original stated aims of state registration have not been achieved by statutory regulation. These are:

- to safeguard the public interest;
- to safeguard qualified nurses;
- to improve the status of nursing.

Evidence of this can be found in countries around the world, including the United States of America, England and Australia. A particularly poignant example of the failure of state registration to achieve its early stated aims can be found in England. Since the situation in that country yields important lessons for other common law countries, it will be considered at some length here. On considering what has happened in England over the past decade, one has a profound sense of déjà vu: the picture that emerges is not one of nurses advancing their professional cause, but one of nurses once again having to expend their valuable energy fighting the same battles.

Nursing under siege in the United Kingdom

In the early 1980s, at a time when increasing numbers of nurses were facing dismissal, redundancy, and unemployment (see Fineman 1982; Hicks 1982; Gaze 1983; *Nursing Times* 1983i, p. 17; *Nursing Times* 1983a, p. 18), a post-registration student nurse wrote a letter to the *Nursing Times* (a British nursing periodical) complaining:

> I have just completed a night duty at a university hospital psychiatric unit. Recently, a nursing assistant was assigned to the ward. It was her very first night and she had not been in a psychiatric ward before. As the unit was busy and very short staffed, within 10 minutes of her arrival she was assigned to special an acutely disturbed young patient.
>
> I fail to see how somebody who has just walked in off the street can administer special nursing care and observation, although this situation is widespread in all types of hospitals throughout the country. I could supply many other examples from my own experience including one at my previous hospital where I was shocked to observe nursing auxiliaries carrying out neurological observations and changing drips on unconscious patients with severe head injuries. This is an abuse of nursing assistants,

patients, nurses and the profession as a whole . . .
(Post-registration student nurse 1983, p. 6)

The student concludes (ibid.) by urging the relevant authorities to

stop recruiting staff who do not hold a statutory qualification or who are not
beginning training for one, while an increasing number of nurses are
unemployed and many nursing students face the grim prospect of joining
them upon qualifying.

Five years later, an editorial in the *Nursing Times* (1988o) warned:

Nursing is under siege at the moment, seeing its professional standards and
ideals threatened by a whole range of people who do not have statutory
qualifications.

The editorial went on to estimate that the use of unqualified staff stood to save
the National Health Service (NHS) up to £Sterling 50 million per year (ibid.).

Unemployment among qualified nurses

During 1989, the British Government spent £Sterling 4 million on an
advertising campaign to 'boost recruitment to schools and colleges of
nursing' at a time when ever increasing numbers of qualified nurses were
facing unemployment (Friend 1990a; Thompson 1990; *Nursing Times*
1990j). Despite extremely low staffing levels in some areas (in one case 72
acutely ill elderly patients were left to the care of just three people, only one
of whom was a qualified nurse (Turner 1990c)), and the widespread closure
of hospital wards and other health services because of an alleged 'shortage
of nurses',[8] both newly graduated and experienced nurses found it extremely
difficult to get jobs (*Nursing Times* 1990d, 1990f, 1990g, 1990j; Turner
1990b, 1990d; see also *Nursing Times* 1988b). Those who were employed
faced redundancy or redeployment in areas outside of their clinical expertise
(Carter 1990; Carlisle 1990f; Friend 1990a; *Nursing Times* 1990a, 1990h;
Thompson 1990; Turner 1990d). Exasperated by the crisis of unemployment
among qualified nurses, Judith Carter (1990, p. 19), national officer of the
Confederation of Health Service Employees (COHSE), declaimed:

Nurses are being forced into the dole queues at a time when hospitals are
closing wards owing to a shortage of nurses. Has the world gone mad?

Criticising the government, Carter (ibid.) explained that the primary cause of
the crisis was that the

government [had] consistently underfunded pay awards for healthcare staff,
making it more and more difficult for health authorities to maintain existing
services and staffing levels, let alone expand to meet increasing demand.

Delamothe (1988b, p. 121), writing in the *British Medical Journal*, argued further that the 'nursing crisis' could have been avoided since the underfunding of hospitals had been 'by political choice rather than economic necessity'.

Nurses were to be burdened not just with unemployment, however. In 1988 a scheme was introduced to help 'hard-pressed' health authorities contain costs and subsidise their budgets. This 'contribution related to adjusted salary scheme' (deservedly given the acronym CRASS) empowered health authorities 'to deduct at source up to 5% of a nurse's monthly salary to help make up their shortfall' (*Nursing Times* 1988d, pp. 2–3). Arguments used to defend the scheme were reminiscent of those used in the late 1890s and early 1900s to defend hospital and state decisions not to shorten the hours or increase the wages of nurses. One notable example of the type of argument used involves a spokesman for the Department of Health and Social Security (DHSS). In his defence of CRASS he argued:

> We believe nurses will be attracted by this appeal to their spirit of altruism and self sacrifice, and will be keen to make this contribution to patient care. (quoted in *Nursing Times* 1988d, pp. 22–3)

It was further clarified that

> if the scheme was successful, the department would consider applying a similar levy on doctors' and administrators' salaries. *Obviously, they would be subjected to a smaller percentage because they carried so much more* [emphasis added].
> (ibid., p. 22)

Not surprisingly, any thought that doctors and administrators could probably have afforded to pay the levy, or that because of being poorly paid[9] most nurses probably could not afford to pay the levy, appears not to have been considered.

It has since been revealed that nurses are not only working for low wages, but in some cases are regularly working for no wages at all (see Delamothe 1988b, p. 122). Staff shortages and increased work loads have created a predictable need for nurses to work overtime. Yet, in 1986, figures showed that increased earnings related to overtime increased by less than two per cent. This low statistic is accounted for by the fact that nurses are mostly offered 'time in lieu' rather than overtime pay, by their employers (ibid., p. 123). Most time in lieu is rarely taken, however, and those who try to claim overtime rates can expect to be censured in some way (for example, have their time sheets 'doctored', or be denied a work rostering request (personal observation)).

More disturbing than the unemployment and wage problems, however, has been the state supported erosion of the traditional role and function of the nurse (a problem which is of international importance, and one which seriously challenges the nursing profession's historical and misplaced faith in the state as a just and beneficent regulator of its affairs).

The Griffiths Report

In February 1983, Mr Roy Griffiths (now Sir Roy), the deputy chairman and managing director of Sainsbury's, a major British food store chain, was invited by the Secretary of State to chair an inquiry into the 'effective use and management of manpower and related resources in the NHS [National Health Service]' (Social Services Committee 1984, para. 1). Upon the completion of the inquiry, Griffiths wrote a 24 page letter to the Secretary of State for Social Services, proposing radical changes to the managerial structure of the NHS. Despite being 'consciously impressionistic' and lacking supportive evidence and investigation, the Griffiths letter (referred to as the Griffiths Report (1983)) was accepted (Social Service Committee 1984, para. 5), and 'set in train potentially the most important internal reorganisation of the NHS since its creation in 1948' — the effects of which were eventually felt at every level in the NHS, 'from the Department of Health right down to ward and community level' (Owens and Glennerster 1990, pp. 3–4, 159).

For nurses, governmental acceptance and implementation of the Griffiths report was a serious blow not just to their already faltering morale, but more importantly to their very professional status and to what little professional independence they had in the NHS (Clay 1987, pp. 1–2). Before the Griffiths inquiry, nurse managers had done 'exceptionally well in reinforcing their position as leaders in health care' (ibid., p. 61). After the Griffiths report was implemented, however, all nursing gains were lost despite vigorous campaigning by representative nursing groups[10] which tried to salvage something out of the situation for the nursing profession. The radical reorganisation of general management saw nurses 'stripped off' the hospital hierarchy and replaced by mostly male non-nurse managers who, despite not having any clinical knowledge, were 'placed in a position to influence decisions about patient care, whether for better or worse' (Newberry 1985; Owens and Glennerster 1990, pp. 55, 83, 87; see also *Nursing Times* 1985b; Jarrold 1986; Crabbe 1989, p. 18; Slack 1986). The exclusion of nurse management was later described by a Social Services Committee (1984) set up to inquire into the Griffiths report as 'unfortunate' (s 62).

Right from the outset, the Griffiths report marginalised and disqualified nurses. Trevor Clay (1987, p. 57), General Secretary of the RCN, writes:

> Nurses were deemed monumentally unimportant — barely mentioned in the report itself except for a whimsical reference to Florence Nightingale — and only briefly mentioned in the associated notes.

When nurses voiced their concerns, Griffiths quickly offered the false and somewhat patronising reassurance that

> the proposals don't threaten nurses at all. The nurses are doing a good job and the changes that are being talked about aren't designed to affect them, *except beneficially* [emphasis added].
> (quoted in Delamothe 1988d, p. 273)

Nevertheless, Griffiths stopped short of allowing the nursing voice to be heard. Indeed, the health services advisory board proposed by the Griffiths report — and described as the 'right-hand man of the Secretary of State' — omitted to include the chief nursing officer among its members for the first year of its existence (Social Services Committee 1984, s 10; Delamothe 1988d, p. 274). Not surprisingly, this was interpreted by nurses 'as a snub and symbolic of just how far their stock had fallen' (Delamothe 1988d, p. 274; see also Social Services Committee 1984, s 14).

Regardless of the publicly stated reassurances that Griffiths gave to nurses, it is quite apparent that the restructuring proposed in his report was fully intended to set in place a male dominated (non-nurse) general management capable of making all the 'right' (read 'rational' and 'economically aggressive') decisions that 'needed' to be made. There is substantial statistical support for this observation. In 1987, for example, it was estimated that 82 per cent of unit general managers (UGMs) were male (Owens and Glennerster 1990, p. 65). Of these, most had come from administrative backgrounds (cited in Owens and Glennerster 1990, p. 65). Men had an even higher representation in the acute units, where almost 90 per cent were male (ibid.). Most of those serving as district general managers (DGMs) — a higher level of manager — were ex-NHS (male) administrators (ibid., p. 80).

Female (nurse) representation, by comparison, was (and remains) marginal. Although some nurses applied for DGM and UGM positions, they were said 'to fare less well in the selection process because their training was considered *too narrow* [emphasis added]' (ibid., p. 66). Delamothe (1988d, p. 274) points out, however, that 'since its early nadir [the Griffiths restructuring of the NHS] there has been a steady improvement in the representation of nurses at all levels [of management]'. Although Delamothe is correct in his observations, the level of 'improvement' he refers to does not offer the nursing profession much ground for optimism. A 1988 survey showed, for example, that of the 14 serving regional level general managers, only one was a nurse; of the 192 DGM positions, only five were filled by nurses; and of the 650 UGM positions, only 80 were filled by nurses (ibid.).

Following Griffiths' restructuring, the only 'genuine' career opportunity available to nurses was in middle management as 'service managers' (SMs). The role of the SM was, however, surrounded by ambiguity and was (is) in reality little more than a 'hybrid role' (Owens and Glennerster 1990, p. 130). Although the SM position was (is) supposed to give nurses in this post 'greater power and responsibility', in reality male dominated institutional structures and philosophy have prevented this. One study found, for example, that 82 per cent of nurses in SM positions had no control over their budget, making it difficult if not impossible for them to establish staffing patterns according to service need (ibid., p. 134). Clay (1987, p. 126) adds that 'many nurse managers [have] found themselves placed in advisory roles [only] with no control over the deployment of nurses'.

Another major problem has been the refusal by doctors to accept nurses (in this instance, 75 per cent of whom are female) in middle-management roles (Owens and Glennerster 1990, p. 126). Owens and Glennerster (ibid.) found that in some cases doctors have simply flatly refused to acknowledge nurses in SM positions — at times to the detriment of patient care. It seems then that the SM position is little more than another paradigmatic example of nurses being given more responsibility, but no 'real' authority.

Doctors have, of course, also been affected by the implementation of the Griffiths report. Nevertheless, they have not fared as badly as nurses. From the outset, the Griffiths report made it very clear that doctors were 'clinically autonomous' and 'not responsible to any "top doctor"' (Owens and Glennerster 1990, p. 15). As for resource allocation, the report merely stated the 'expectation' that general managers would engage in 'regular discussion with [medical] consultants about the use of resources' (ibid.). The report made no mention of any 'expectation' that general managers would also engage in 'regular discussions with nurses about the use of resources'. It seems, then, that in the Griffiths scheme of things, as in the general male dominated health care scheme of things, nurses — like women workers generally — effectively 'count for nothing' (see Waring 1988).

A case of 'nursing without nurses'

In a paper presented at the 1985 Trades Union Congress (TUC) conference entitled 'Health 2000', Lady Margaret McCarthy, fellow in employee relations at King's Fund College, argued: 'nurses are too well trained and too expensive to work in the community with elderly and mentally handicapped patients' (quoted in Vousden 1985, p. 9). Ignoring the fact that these groups of people often suffer multiple health problems and require highly skilled nursing care in order to meet even their most fundamental health needs, she went on to argue that 'people trained in simple skills would be much more appropriate to deal with the elderly and mentally handicapped in the community'. Lady McCarthy defended her controversial views by arguing further: 'I am not talking about deskilling the skilled ... but about improving the skills of the unskilled' (ibid.).

Although Lady McCarthy's views did not accurately reflect either the needs of or the complexity of the type of care required by the elderly and intellectually disabled, they appear to have gained some currency among those who are committed to radically reducing the cost of health care. In 1990, for example, a pilot scheme in 'continuing care' involving the establishment of 'a ward without nurses', was implemented at a hospital for the elderly in Hertfordshire (Dopson 1990). The ward is staffed by nursing auxiliaries and is managed by a non-nurse who previously worked as a manager in Marks and Spencer, a leading British department store chain. The ward manager is described as not being 'daunted by the prospect of running a ward without being a qualified nurse' (Dopson 1990, p. 48). She is quoted as arguing (ibid.):

> If I was caring for someone at home, I would not rush out and get a nurse. I would learn how to cope with the nursing needs, and to do that I would seek advice. That is how we are going to do it. We are not abandoning nursing care. And we are trying to provide all the needs of the residents, which include intellectual needs.

The deputy ward manager, whose previous position was with the British Army, defended the pilot scheme arguing 'we are not putting untrained people to care for old people . . . We are training them in special skills' (ibid., p. 47).

The scheme has also met with approval from members of the medical profession. A consultant geriatrician is quoted as being 'strongly behind' the scheme (Dopson 1990, p. 48)

> even though local GPs were worried initially that 'untrained' staff would not act as a filter, like nurses, and would always be consulting them.

The usurpation of nursing functions by other allied health workers

As well as being under threat by unskilled workers, the role of the nurse is being eroded by rival allied health professional groups, such as social workers. In 1988, for example, a government-commissioned review recommended that by 1993, all heads of residential care homes for the elderly 'must have a recognised social work qualification', in other words, they must be social workers (Campbell 1988, pp. 16–17). The report also recommended that nurses 'working in residential homes should take an in-service conversion course in social work' (Campbell 1988, p. 16) — this is quite ironic given that social work had its origins in early nursing (see, for example, Dolan et al. 1983, p. 139; Kelly 1985, p. 177).

The erosion of the role and function of the nurse has occurred not only in the aged and mental health care areas, however. Theatre nurses are also under threat, and are already being replaced by 'operating department assistants' (ODAs) (Chudley 1988a; Roberts 1989). Curiously, while assistants are regarded as being 'interchangeable with the nurse', the nurse is not regarded as being 'interchangeable with the ODA' (Ogilvie 1988, p. 13). Qualified nurses working in acute care areas are also under threat. At one top London hospital, for example, less qualified and less experienced state enrolled nurses[11] (a second level trained nurse) were used to replace and function (illegally) as registered nurses (*Nursing Times* 1987a, p. 7). Private nursing agencies, meanwhile, have admitted to using 'unskilled staff' as a cheaper alternative to qualified nurses (see Patrick 1988, p. 12).

It was estimated recently that approximately 50 per cent of all nursing care delivered in the country's hospitals (particularly in the intellectual disability and elderly care areas) is given by unqualified and unregistered 'nurses' who have little or no training or experience (Owens and Glennerster 1990, p. 36). What is particularly disturbing about this statistic is that the nursing profession appears to lack not only the legal, but also the social and political power to stop the entry of unqualified people into professional nursing practice. To highlight the extent to which this is so, it is worth reflecting on why there has not been a public outcry (by either the lay community, human rights or social welfare groups, or even allied health workers) against what amounts to a discriminatory erosion of quality care for some of society's most disadvantaged and vulnerable members — the elderly and the intellectually disabled (see also Johnstone 1990).

If medical care rather than nursing care was at issue, and if, for example, Lady McCarthy (whose views were cited earlier) had suggested that doctors rather than nurses were 'too well trained and too expensive to work in the community with elderly and mentally handicapped patients', it is likely that the nation would have witnessed a deafening public outcry. Undoubtedly the medical profession would not have tolerated criticism of either the qualifications of its members or the cost of employing doctors to treat the elderly and intellectually disabled. Furthermore, it is highly unlikely that the medical profession would tolerate even one instance — let alone 50 per cent — of medical treatment being given by people who are not legally qualified medical practitioners — even though much of what is considered 'medical care' could be provided more cheaply, and in some instances more competently, by others (for example, nurses, pharmacists, dieticians and physiotherapists). Yet nurses are expected to passively and uncritically accept that they have become 'too well trained and too expensive' to care for those abandoned at the bottom of the social ladder, and to tolerate unqualified and inexperienced people gaining what has become virtually unrestricted entry into nursing practice. Even worse, is the cavalier way the state expects nurses to train and supervise unskilled health workers, and thereby effectively engineer their own de-professionalisation and occupational demise. One important political 'benefit' of this, is that it helps the government to escape criticism and to place any blame for the nursing profession's demise firmly on nurses themselves. Indeed, it has become common both within and outside of nursing circles to hear the comment that 'nurses have brought many of their problems on themselves'.

The marginalisation of nurse educators

It is not just 'hands on' nurses whose role is being eroded. Nurse educators are also under threat and are being increasingly marginalised as 'more qualified' non-nurses become involved in teaching nursing students, thus reducing further the nursing profession's ability to determine its own fate (Dingwall et al. 1988, p. 224). Nurse academics who have embraced uncritically the rhetoric and practice of cross-disciplinary teaching have, unfortunately, also embraced the exploitation of their nursing students by other non-nurse departments struggling to maintain their student numbers and needing a solution to the problem of having 'surplus staff' requiring employment (ibid.). As a result, increasing proportions of the nursing curriculum are now controlled by 'life scientists or social scientists' (ibid.) — and, it should perhaps be added, moral philosophers and lawyers who are becoming more involved in the teaching of nursing law and ethics courses (see also Clay 1987, p. 76; Chudley 1988b, pp. 16–17). This is also a problem in Australia. For example, 'progressive' educational reforms involving the transfer of nurse education into the tertiary education sector has, in some cases, seen up to 40 per cent of the nursing curriculum (if electives are included) lost to the control (and dominance) of non-nurses (mostly male lecturers in the biological and social sciences) who have insisted on their 'right' to 'service teach' in nursing courses. Their outbursts over territorial rights (read monopoly of knowledge) have seen important and necessary nursing curriculum reforms perverted and obstructed, with nursing content being sacrificed in a bid to keep the peace and/or to ensure that a given revised curriculum is approved in time for its scheduled implementation.

'Project 2000' and the rise of the 'professional' support worker

One of the most disturbing developments to affect the nursing profession in recent years is undoubtedly the government's outright support of the development and role of a new health occupation, namely, the professional support worker. The rise of this new occupational group threatens to turn the metaphorical 'nursing clock' back at least one hundred years, not just in England, but in other countries as well — particularly where overseas 'reformers' (that is, economic rationalisers) of health care look to the English example to help guide the development of new policies on restructuring health care in their respective countries.

In 1986, the position of English nursing (already compromised by the implementation of the Griffiths report) was to deteriorate even further. In May of that year the United Kingdom Central Council for Nursing, Midwifery and Health Visiting (UKCC) tabled its report on *Project 2000: A New Preparation for Practice*. The overall aim of Project 2000 was to 'improve standards of care by training and educating more effective nurses' (Clay 1987, p. 63). To this end, the report on the project proposed:

- A single level of registered practitioners (the registered general nurse) and the end of enrolled nurse training (nursing leaders sought this change in an attempt to curb the abuse of SENs who were often required to 'take on responsibilities which exceed[ed] the limitations of their training' (see also Fardell 1989a, p. 30)).
- The establishment of a common foundation program (that is, involving the establishment and use of one curriculum and thereby setting one minimum nursing qualification for entry into practice).
- Five branches for specialisation (it was envisaged that registered nurses would be the main care givers, a position defended on grounds that the public were entitled to be cared for by qualified nurse practitioners; nurses could progress up the career ladder by becoming specialist practitioners after undertaking further courses (Clay 1987, p. 63)).
- Students should be granted supernumerary status (ibid., p. 158).

The project also proposed the introduction of a crucial 'new helper grade' to whom nurse practitioners would assign work. It was envisaged that before taking up their roles, the new helper (for whom the title 'aide' was proposed) would receive

in-service instruction over a period of *three months*, arranged by the employing authority based on guidelines from the National Boards [emphasis added].
(Clay 1987, p. 105)

Nursing leaders promoting the aims of Project 2000 sought and obtained government support for the nursing profession's requested move toward its proposed one grade/level of nurse. Initial enthusiasm among nurse proponents of the proposal declined rapidly, however, when DHSS press briefings 'stressed the importance of the helper grades as a *channel of recruitment*' [emphasis added] (something which the nursing profession had not intended) and as offering the very means by which a smaller profession of registered nurses supported by a less qualified worker could be achieved (Dingwall et al. 1988, p. 235; *Nursing Times* 1988j; see also *Nursing Times* 1988i; Carlisle 1989; Fardell 1989a; Johnston 1989; Laurent 1989; Chapman 1990). Thus, what initially had all the markings of being a progressive step toward achieving a larger, stronger and more qualified profession, was in effect perverted by political manipulation into a retrograde step forcing nurses into 'an aimless drift towards a smaller profession supported by a larger number of [unqualified and cheaper] helpers (*Nursing Times* 1988f). Regrettably, the nursing profession's misplaced faith in the government's initial support of its proposals has cost it dearly. Among other things, it has paved the way for the demise and de-professionalisation of nursing (Fardell 1989b, p. 20).

Equally regrettable is that an important opportunity to control the damage caused by the political manipulation of Project 2000's proposals was lost to the nursing profession when statutory bodies declined the responsibility of defining the role of the new helper (Fardell 1989a, p. 30). It should be noted, however, that the primary reason the statutory bodies declined this task was not so much because they were 'uninterested' as could appear to be the case, but because they were totally (and perhaps inappropriately) preoccupied with 'preparing the way for Project 2000 curricula within an unrealistic timescale set by the government to get the first pilot schemes up and running' (ibid.). There can be small doubt that the decision to decline the responsibility to define the role of the new helper is one which the nursing profession in the United Kingdom will long regret.

Initially, reassurances were given by government promoters of the new health supporter proposal that there was no way 'the support worker would in any way replace or overlap the role of the professional nurses' (Laurent 1989, p. 28). Later developments, however, have suggested that this is precisely what the government had in mind, and that representatives of the nursing profession were, in fact, seriously mislead about the government's ultimate intentions and were deceived into accepting the government's initial support (see Gaze 1990c; Malby 1990).

Raising serious questions about the government's integrity with regards to the entire support workers scheme, Jill Fardell (1989a, p. 30), writing in the *Nursing Times*, cites a report (of what she describes as a 'high-powered Department of Health workshop') in which was envisaged 'a future for support workers quite out of line with all previous thinking'. She reminds nurses that originally it was thought that the new support workers would receive only three months training to prepare them for their role. The workshop report, however, proposed a two-year course (ibid.; see also Clay 1987, p. 79). Furthermore, it was made clear that the government expected registered nurses to 'take a lead in conducting training and assessing the competencies of the new assistants' (see *Nursing Times* 1990b). As well as this, the report envisaged that support workers with five years experience could undertake a 'shortened' nursing course, further undermining the profession's attempt to improve its educational status (Fardell 1989a, p. 30). Incensed with the government's apparent about-turn on the health support worker proposal, Fardell (1989a, p. 31) challenged: 'It is surely stretching credibility to believe these ideas were simply plucked out of the air'.

Promoting work opportunities for women, the unemployed and 'ethnic minorities'

In retrospect, it is quite apparent that the government had its own political agenda and reasons for endorsing the new support worker scheme — and, in fact, appears to have had very little regard for the professional aspirations of the promoters of Project 2000. The government envisaged, for example, that the new 'helpers' would be tapped from 'new sources of recruits such as the unemployed and mature women' and 'ethnic minorities' (*Nursing Times* 1988f; Laurent 1989, p. 29). 'Mature women' (described as being between the ages of 35 and 55 years old) were thought to be a particularly attractive source of recruits since it was believed that a woman in this age group was 'unlikely to have qualifications or to want to take up formal training under NCVQ [National Council for Vocational Qualifications]'. It was also thought that a woman from this age group would 'certainly bring valuable life experience to the job' — skills which, it was argued, 'must be recognised and credited' (Johnston 1989, p. 27).

It was further argued that tapping the unemployed provided a 'useful' outlet for the Youth Training Scheme (YTS) which would be encouraged to give 'increasing emphasis . . . to training young people as support workers' (*Nursing Times* 1988g, 1989d). The development of the support workers was further defended on grounds that it would provide a needed 'opportunity for personal development to unskilled staff' (Malby 1990, p. 33).

Not everyone accepted the postulated 'merits' of the support worker proposal, however. For example, Gary Nash, a union shop steward, argued:

> I'm suspicious of the support worker idea. All the government is trying to do is to bring in more YTS people and bring down the unemployment because the figures will look better.
> (quoted in *Nursing Times* 1989c, p. 33)

Other grounds for suspicion included the government's apparent desire to see the de-professionalisation and demise of nursing, and to reduce the nursing profession's political power to challenge the status quo (Fardell 1989b, p. 20; Owens and Glennerster 1990, p. 21).

The return to an exploitative apprenticeship system

It does not take a great deal of imagination to perceive the serious flaws in the government's version of the support worker proposal. While ostensibly creating opportunities for the unemployed, mature women and ethnic 'minorities'[12] to develop as skilled workers, the proposal is in reality a return to an exploitative apprenticeship system in which the 'unskilled learner' slaves for the benefit of her or his 'masters' (the employers). Furthermore, as was the case in the days when hospitals were staffed by 'pupil nurses' supervised by a small core of qualified staff, the unsuspecting public is once again facing the prospect of being cared for by (unqualified and inexperienced) trainees (see *Nursing Times* 1984). One question which arises here is that if the government was really interested in improving occupational opportunities for the unemployed, married women and ethnic 'minorities', why did it not also propose the development of support worker schemes involving other more 'prestigious' professions, such as medicine and law — including the provision that after five years of service, support workers could undertake a shortened course in either medicine or law?

The government's targeting of nursing for the support worker scheme is, among other things, reflective of the state's cultural–stereotypical (male constructed) view that 'nurses are born, and not made' and that virtually any 'good woman' can walk in off the street and be a nurse. What is particularly cynical about the support workers scheme, however, is that the government has chosen nursing (a profession which historically has had a low status compared with other professions) as the focus of its efforts to give status to those whose lives and experiences have historically been undervalued — women, the unemployed, and ethnic 'minorities'. By attracting these already devalued and essentially disempowered classes of people into nursing, the net effect will probably be one of further devaluing and disempowering nursing as a profession. It is extremely probable that this will happen, given the Griffiths restructuring (mentioned earlier) and its introduction of a male dominated general management in the NHS which has

> dislodged and in many places destroyed the nursing hierarchies, has knocked many female nursing managers out of the scene and created a NHS management with an overwhelming male ethos.
> (Clay 1987, p. 111)

This 'overwhelming male ethos', has, in turn, brought with it a 'narrow economic rationality' which, to borrow from Margaret Thornton writing in another context, is discriminatory against nurses (women), in so far as it undervalues nurses' (and other women's) work. It also pays nurses (women workers) less than they are worth, refuses to deem nurses (women) fit for authority, and expects them to play only a passive ancillary role to men (Thornton 1990, p. 5; see also White 1985, p. 589; Gaze 1990c; Owens and Glennerster 1990, pp. 18, 138, 154).

Even more alarming, however, has been the cost to patient care and the public interest, since 'cheapness ousting quality' seems to have become the main criteria of staff employment (see Delamothe 1988c, p. 183). Since the era of health care rationalisation began in 1983, nursing journal reports have detailed deplorable cases of patient injury and even death because of a lack of — or, more to the point, a failure to employ — qualified nursing staff (see, for example, *Nursing Times* 1983e, 1983g, 1987b, 1987c, 1988a,

1988c, 1990g). However, nursing reports attempting to link patient injury and death to nursing staff shortages have been systematically dismissed by the DHSS on grounds that the link 'is almost impossible to prove' (see, for example, *Nursing Times* 1988c).

The current position of nursing in the United States of America and in Australia

The position of nursing in the United States of America and in Australia is, in several respects, similar to its position in England. In the 1990s, American and Australian nurses, like their English colleagues, are also having to expend energy 'refighting the same old battles' to promote and protect not just their own interests, but the interests of the public. Owens and Glennerster (1990, p. 25) observe, for example, that financial pressures in the United States of America have produced similar tensions to those experienced in Britain, with hospital managers also looking for cheaper workers to perform nursing duties. As in the United Kingdom, the rhetoric of 'nursing shortages' is being used to justify the development of a new tier of health workers. In one scheme, developed by the American Medical Association (AMA), a new support worker called a 'registered care technologist' (RCT) (described by the AMA as a 'bed side care giver') has been proposed (*Nursing Times* 1988m, 1988n). It is envisaged that the RCT's scope of practice will involve 'executing medical protocols at the bedside with a specific emphasis on technical skill' (Palmer 1989, p. 28). Although the nursing profession has protested strongly against the AMA proposal, the RCT program (regarded by the AMA as an 'innovative solution' to the nursing shortage in the United States of America), has nevertheless been referred to the AMA Board of Trustees for implementation (ibid., pp. 28–29). The proposal has been slammed by nursing critics as 'an insult to nursing as a profession' and as a blatant attempt by the AMA to interfere with and to control nursing (ibid., p. 28).

Another type of support worker, the 'physician assistant', has also threatened to erode the role and authority of the nurse.[13] Although the care offered by this type of worker is 'cheaper', it is far from ideal because it is relatively unsupervised. In a 1982 court case (*Polischek v United States* (1982), p. 1262), for example, it was revealed that approximately 50 to 65 per cent of accident and emergency patients were seen by physician assistants 'without physician involvement either during the patient visit or even retrospectively' (*Regan Report on Nursing Law* 1982b).

The significant rise of the new support worker has not gone unnoticed by health service commentators. The *Regan Report on Nursing Law* (1982c) comments for example:

The personnel impact of technicians, paramedicals, physician assistants and the like threatens to engulf nursing or at least to stifle the professional growth of nursing. Hospital economics dictates the plain fact that many traditional nursing functions can be done just as well and a lot more inexpensively by unlicensed employees.

Not all would agree that many traditional nursing functions can be performed 'just as well by unlicensed employees'. Trinosky-Lind (1988), for example, shows that patients can and do suffer many negative effects because there is insufficient qualified nursing staff to care for them. Included among the negative effects she lists are the problems of: patients not being monitored adequately, nursing cares not being completed, call bells not being answered promptly, delays in the administration of needed medications, medication errors being made, inadequate psychological support being given owing to a lack of time, and a general breakdown in the standards of patient safety (ibid., p. 35).

The role and function of the clinical nurse in Australia is also under threat by 'cheaper' and less qualified or unqualified health workers. Evidence of this can be found in the increasing use of so-called 'nursing attendants' and 'personal carers' or 'personal care attendants' in special accommodation and residential care homes (Cameron unpub.; RCNA (Victorian Chapter) unpub.; Talbot 1991a, 1991b). Nursing attendants or personal care attendants can literally 'walk in off the street'; they receive no training, are unqualified, and are cheaper to employ than registered or enrolled nurses. State governments have implicitly endorsed and even facilitated the use of this cheaper and unqualified labour force by deregistering special purpose nursing homes and placing them under the jurisdiction of state disability service Acts. This means that these homes are no longer subject to private hospital health regulations or nursing home regulations and thus can escape the scrutiny they might otherwise be subjected to under those regulations. It is known that in the deregistered special purpose nursing homes, unqualified staff are performing registered nurse duties, including drug administration and oropharyngeal/tracheal suctioning (Sellers unpub.; *"On the Record"* 1990a). Allegations have also been made that residents of these homes have suffered increased morbidity and mortality rates because they did not receive the quality of care they would have received had they been cared for by qualified nurses (Sellers unpub.; *"On the Record"* 1990b). Other 'cheaper' and less qualified health workers eroding the role of the nurse include: home health aides ('home helps'), pathology technicians, child care workers and anaesthetic technicians (Morieson 1987; Uren 1988; Cameron unpub.; Schwartz 1991).

Many traditional nursing functions are also being taken over by allied health professionals, including: occupational therapists, physiotherapists, speech therapists, dieticians and pharmacists (Uren 1988). The involvement of these non-nursing personnel in the management of the patient has resulted in patient care being unacceptably fragmented which, at times, has meant the patient's health needs have not always been met adequately.

Equally problematic is the erosion of nursing lines of authority; with nurse managers, like their English counterparts, being 'stripped off' the hospital hierarchy and replaced by non-nurse (mostly male) managers (ibid.). In an editorial in the *Australian Nurses' Journal*, for example, Robyn Parkes (1991), ANF Federal Nurse Advisor, warns that the positions of the director of nursing (DON) and assistant director of nursing (ADON) — posts which are essential to the strength and efficiency of any nursing service and department — are at risk of being 'restructured' into annihilation (and, in fact, at the time of writing this book, is already beginning to happen). Alerting nurses to the powerful external forces working against the nursing profession at this time, Parkes (1991, p. 7) challenges:

> Are key strategic positions targeted for annihilation? Has your nursing department been invaded yet? Use this 'reconnaissance quiz' to check:
> - has a management consultancy firm been in your hospital lately?
> - are people talking about devolution, divisionalisation, restructuring, regionalisation?
> - has the Director of Nursing position been vacant for some time, or been given a new title?
> - is money allocated to the nursing staff budget spent on other than nursing division requirements?
> - when nursing resources are down, does the hospital continue to admit to full capacity?
>
> If you don't know the answers find them out now.

She goes on to warn that in all states and territories 'proposals and reviews are being directed towards organisation restructuring' (ibid.). And while 'on paper' proposals give in-principle support for nurses to be included in management restructuring, Parkes warns that in reality this is unlikely to happen. She asks (Parkes 1991, p. 7):

> In practice what happens?
> - Nurses compete with doctors for senior positions which have control over both nursing and medical staff. Nurses can be, and have been, appointed to such positions, but only rarely.
> - Is shared divisional management between doctors and nurses possible?
> - Who would have the final say on budget decisions?
> - Who would spend the most time in the units?
> - Who would take responsibility for standards, adherence to policy, performance appraisal?

- Would both persons receive the same pay?
- Can a hospital Director of Nursing ensure professional standards when she/he has no control over divisional staffing levels, procedure guidelines, staff performance, etc.?
- What power would nurses have to over-rule decisions which allocate money to new diagnostic equipment in preference to nursing staff positions?

If the United Kingdom experience is a reliable indicator, then answers to the above questions must be overwhelmingly in the negative.

Despite the commonwealth government's stated recognition that nurses are the linchpin of any health system (see Hawke 1988; National Health and Medical Research Council 1991), the Australian nursing profession still appears to lack the legal, political and social power necessary to champion its own cause fully. The indications are that, like the British government (see *Nursing Times* 1988f), the Australian government (supported by some sectors of the nursing profession) is also opting for the development of a smaller profession supported by a larger number of unqualified or less qualified, and cheaper helpers (see, for example, Grigg 1987; Morieson 1987; Price 1987).

In Victoria, for example, a 1987 Health Department Victoria report canvassed increasing the role of SENs, substantially increasing the intake to college based training (it should be noted that when undertaking learning in the clinical area, tertiary sector nursing students are effectively a 'free' source of labour for the hospitals), introducing 'fast tracking' in nurse training, and using fewer registered nurses for administration and replacing them with professional (non-nurse) managers (Health Department Victoria 1987; Grigg 1987). Although the report also canvassed 'increasing the workforce participation rate of qualified general nurses', there is room to suggest that in real terms this has not happened (given that even where nursing numbers have increased, work loads may still be high, particularly in high dependency units).

In 1993, Victorian college and university nursing graduates were finding it extremely difficult to get jobs. An explanation for this fact, drawn from informal criticism, is that the colleges and/or universities are taking in too many nursing students. Another possible explanation — and one which is reminiscent of the past — is that unqualified and/or 'cheaper' and less qualified workers (for example, personal care attendants and SENs) are being employed in preference to, and at the expense of, graduate/registered nurses (this information is based on personal observation/communication; see also Johnson 1991, p. 1). Meanwhile, it has been informally alleged that because they are unable to secure permanent hospital positions, new graduates are being forced to work for private nursing agencies (although job opportunities through this outlet are also limited) (personal communication/observation). In many instances, because of a 'shortage' of experienced nurses, these new graduates are finding themselves being assigned to a ward or unit and 'thrown in the deep end' — that is, placed 'in charge' and expected to function at a level above their education and experience. Although it is not publicly acknowledged (and the idea itself is rejected by some entities), hospitals may sometimes employ agency staff in preference to permanent staff because, in the long term, it is cheaper for them to do so. For instance, by employing agency staff, a hospital is spared the extra expense of having to pay for a worker's superannuation, sick leave, maternity leave, annual leave and other worker entitlements (see also Delamothe 1988b, p. 123; *The Lamp* 1990, p. 26). A similar situation exists in other Australian states. In New South Wales in 1992, for example (less than a year after the state government's $A475 000 nurse recruitment campaign), 2000 graduates had to compete for only 1200 vacancies (Johnson 1991, p. 1).

The professional status of nursing and its link with the economy

In many respects, the present position of nursing heralds a return to the past. As in the early days of the profession after statutory recognition was first given to trained nurses, and as just mentioned above, graduates are facing a serious professional crisis of unemployment. Those who have found work are working under extremely stressful conditions (they are understaffed and overworked). Also reminiscent of the past, is the rhetoric being used to defend this situation. The public is told that nurses 'won't mind these hardships', that nurses' 'spirit of altruism and self sacrifice' will see them 'keen to make their contribution to personal care' (see, for example, *Nursing Times* 1988d; Delamothe 1988f, p. 406), and that the employment of unqualified 'nurses' is in the 'public interest' (read 'in the needs of the capitalist economy'). And, as in the past, while nurses are cajoled into making their self-sacrificing service to the public, the state and the medical profession are left free 'to serve God's rich and to make a handsome profit at nursing's expense' (Lovell 1982, p. 216; see also Milburn 1989, p. 17; Johnstone 1990; Heath 1991, p. 3; Johnson 1991; Staunton 1991a, p. 3, 1991b, p. 3).

Of equal cause for despair is that when nurses find themselves sick and disabled, they will be, like their predecessors over 100 years ago, 'tossed aside like worn out things' (*Nursing Record* 1892), or, as Friend (1990b, p. 18) points out 'counselled [read 'cancelled'] out'. Others will simply turn to alcohol or drugs (see Blatch et al. 1979; Pyne 1981; *Nursing Times* 1983h;

Pavitt 1985, p. 8; Clay 1987; Gelfand et al. 1990; *"On the Record"* 1990c; Owens and Glennerster 1990, pp. 123–124; Sullivan et al. 1990), or will resign out of fear that their stress will cause them 'to do something wrong' (*Nursing Mirror* 1985; see also Pavitt 1985, p. 8; *Nursing Times* 1986, 1988e).

The current nursing situation poignantly reminds nurses that their professional status and entry into practice (the public sphere) are not — and never have been — contingent on state registration. Rather, these things have been contingent on 'the needs of the economy' (see Thornton 1990, p. 254; Swendson unpub.) and the vested political interests served by the economy. What this in turn tells us is that, contrary to popular impression, the nursing profession does not have — and never has had — 'real' state registration. If it did, it would probably be in quite a different (for example, a more stable and more powerful) position than it is now.

Had nurse registration Acts paid more attention to making minimum standards of entry into practice mandatory, and given less attention to prescribing the wearing of 'badges' and 'distinctive head-dresses', the nursing profession today would almost certainly be in a better position to control the entry of unqualified workers into practice (recognised as an important hallmark of 'real' professional status (Freidson 1970, 1973, 1988)), something which, historically, it has never really been able to do.[14] Instead, the nursing profession's status and strength has been — and remains — dependent on the fluctuating economic needs of capitalism, and hence on the whims of those whose vested material interests are at stake (see Thornton 1984, pp. 13–14, 1990, p. 71; Waring 1988; Fraser 1989; Swendson unpub.). Evidence of this can be found in the nursing profession's historical struggle to gain self-determination. Its successes and failures in this struggle have almost without exception been tied to the economy of the day (recall that the main opposition to nurse registration was on grounds that it would not be 'in the public interest' — that is, it would not be 'economically viable' and would cause employing hospitals acute 'financial embarrassment').

CONCLUSION

It has been argued in this chapter that state registration failed to give nurses the legal relief they sought in their quest for professional status and autonomy, and in so doing also failed to maximise the public interest. Instead of improving the status of nurses and giving them 'real' authority as independent professional women, state registration merely reinforced the cultural hegemony of medical men, legitimated stereotypical views of nurses as 'good women' (that is, as the obedient and humble servants of medical men), and, not least, legitimated the role of medical men as the 'gatekeepers' to nursing. State registration also provided medical men with a legitimate means of controlling nursing practice itself and ensuring that it did not encroach on the practise of medicine — sometimes to the detriment of patient care, as examples to be given in the following chapters will show.

Although state registration stands as an important example of the failure of law (its processes and structures) to respond adequately to the needs of nurses (and it should be added, to the needs of those requiring nursing care), it would be a mistake to conclude that state registration has been the only legal factor which has contributed to the nursing profession's failure to obtain 'real' status and authority as a self-determining socially accountable health professional group. Indeed, the question of state registration represents only a part — albeit an important one — of the overall picture of nursing's precarious relationship to and experience of the law. There are other legal factors which have also been influential in obstructing the professional development of nursing, and which have been instrumental in legitimating nursing's subordination to the medical profession and to the state. In order to create a more complete picture of nursing's relationship to and experience of the law (and the state), these other legal factors will be identified and examined in the following chapters.

ENDNOTES

1   See the *Health Act 1911* (Queensland), and the *Nurses and Masseurs Registration Act 1928* (Queensland), assented to 27 October 1928; *Nurses Registration Act 1920* (South Australia), assented to 9 December 1920; Nurses Registration Act, 1921 (Western Australia), assented to 31 January 1922; *Nurses Registration Act 1923* (Victoria), assented to 18 December 1923; *Nurses' Registration Act 1924* (New South Wales), assented to 17 December 1924; *Nurses Registration Act 1927* (Tasmania); *Nurses and Midwives Registration Ordinance 1928–1957* (Northern Territory), commenced 1 October 1929; and *Nurses Registration Ordinance 1933* (Australian Capital Territory), assented to 6 February, 1933.

2   The GNC has been replaced by the United Kingdom Central Council (UKCC), a new statutory nursing authority established under the *Nurses, Midwives and Health Visitors Act 1979*.

3   Male nurses were originally excluded from the main register because they underwent a 'different' training program from female nurses (male nurses were not taught 'women's subjects' such as gynaecology). Other nurses (for example, mental nurses, children's nurses, and the like) were likewise put on a supplementary register on grounds that they, like male nurses, had had 'a different training altogether, and must be put on a supplementary register' (see Barnett 1919, pp. 774–775). There is room to suggest, however, that the main reason why men were not permitted to have their names entered in the general register was a fear by the medical and political establishments that 'male recruitment to nursing

would have threatened nursing's subordinate role in the medical division of labour in a way that the recruitment of women did not' (Austin 1977a, p. 116). Male and female registers were not combined until 1949, partly in response to the shortage of qualified nurses that was plaguing the government at that time (Savage 1987, p. 67).

4 Parliamentary debate on the proposed 1919 Nurses Registration Bill reveals a widespread concern about the problem of unqualified people masquerading as 'true nurses' (see, for example, Lyle 1919, pp. 788–789; Molson 1919, pp. 786–787). There was also the problem of tricksters dressing up in a nurse's uniform and appealing for money for bogus charities (Briant 1919, p. 779). The nurse's uniform was seen to be as 'honourable' as the uniform worn by those in the armed forces and thus worthy of protection. Suggestions included hospitals 'copyrighting' their own uniforms, or, alternatively, following the armed services' example and making it an indictable offence for unqualified people to wear a nurse's uniform when not a registered nurse (see Roundell 1919, p. 788; Loseby 1919, p. 808). The latter option was accepted, and remains in force to this day.

5 To borrow from Margaret Thornton (1990, p. 1) the 'benchmark' figure is likely to be 'a white, Anglo-Celtic, heterosexual male who falls within acceptable parameters of physical and intellectual normalcy, who supports, at least nominally, mainstream Christian beliefs, and who fits within the middle-to-the-right of the political spectrum'. Thornton explains that anyone not conforming to this norm is regarded as 'other' and therefore inferior (see also Johnston and Knapp 1971, pp. 738–739; Minow 1987; Naffine 1990).

6 Unfortunately, owing to a lack of records, it has not been possible to discover what the nurse's offence was.

7 Queensland is generally credited with being the first state to obtain state registration for nurses. It should be noted, however, that nurses were first registered under the *Health Act 1911*, and not under a discrete nurses registration Act per se. A specific Act providing for the state registration of nurses was not passed in Queensland until 1928. This Act was not, however, exclusive to nurses since it also provided for the registration of Masseurs (see the *Nurses and Masseurs Registration Act 1928*). In fact, Queensland did not have a discrete and exclusive nurses registration Act until 1964 (see the *Nurses Act 1964*).

8 A 1987 study of nursing vacancies revealed that 3.5 per cent of funded positions had been vacant for more than three months (cited in Owens and Glennerster 1990, p. 23). Inner London, however, was reported to have an exceptionally high vacancy rate of 20–25 per cent (Delamothe 1988a, p. 26; see also *Nursing Times* 1990e, p. 6). Factors influencing this high vacancy rate were identified as including: cuts in the NHS, staff shortages, a bad atmosphere at work, stress, low pay (the average gross earnings of registered nurses working in inner London were estimated to be '16 per cent below the regional average wage for female non-manual earnings'), low status, long hours/shift work, and a change in management structure (Delamothe 1988a, p. 26; Owens and Glennerster 1990,

p. 23). Some vacancies had arisen because of 'poaching' by the private sector (Delamothe 1988a, p. 28).

9   A 1988 report revealed that 40 per cent of nurses earned less than the national Low Pay Unit's threshold of a meagre £132.27 per week (Delamothe 1988b, p. 120). It has also been revealed that one in five nurses are having to take extra jobs (mostly agency nursing) in order to supplement their incomes. Despite 70 per cent of nurses wages making up 40 per cent or more of the total household income, in a 'good' year, nurses can expect to earn only 60 per cent of what men do (Delamothe 1988b, p. 120, 1988e, p. 345).

10   The Royal College of Nursing (RCN), for example, launched a vigorous advertising campaign costing £250 000 in an attempt to combat the report and to inform the broader public of the ramifications of its implementation for the NHS generally (Clay 1987, pp. 114, 133).

11   During and following the Second World War, the demand for qualified nurses increased substantially. This demand lead to the passage of the *Nurses Act 1943*. Despite vigorous opposition from many nursing leaders of the day, the *Nurses Act 1943*, as already pointed out in this chapter, created a second grade of nurse, the State Enrolled Nurse (SEN). To this day, the existence and role of the second grade of nurse (the SEN) remains a source of internal division in nursing not just in England, but also in Australia and New Zealand (see Abel-Smith 1960).

12   Note the inverted commas around the word 'minorities'. These have been inserted because, although it is a widely accepted and used notion, it is nevertheless problematic in that it perpetuates discrimination. As Martha Minow (1987, p. 10) points out '"minority" itself is a relative term; people of color [sic] are numerically a majority in the world. Only in relation to white Westerners are they minorities'.

13   Although physician assistants receive only one year of classroom instruction followed by one year of clinical rotation in a hospital alongside medical students, they are able to take and record medical histories, investigate patients' health complaints, perform physical examinations, request diagnostic tests (including blood counts), render medical diagnoses, and prescribe routine medication (see *Polischeck v United States* (1982)). Furthermore, because they are legally recognised as the agents of 'supervising' physicians, physician assistants have the legitimated authority to order nurses to perform certain tasks, such as administering drugs which they (the physician assistants) have prescribed (see, for example, *Washington State Nurses Association v Board of Medical Examiners* (1980)).

14   It should be clarified that while historically the nursing profession has fought to control the entry of unqualified workers into professional nursing, this has not been motivated strongly by 'usurpationary and exclusionary aims' as has been suggested elsewhere (see Witz 1992, p. 128). As argued in chapter 3 of this book, the main bases upon which the early modern nurse leaders advocated state registration for nurses and the professional autonomy it was hoped this would bring, were:

- To safeguard the public interest (that is, against receiving substandard and dangerous care).
- To free nurses from the tyranny of and exploitation by lay hospital administrators and medical doctors.
- To raise the status of nursing as a profession for women. Significantly, even today nurses have not achieved these important aims, and there is mounting evidence that the public's interest in receiving nursing care that is safe and therapeutically effective has been compromised as a result (see also the section entitled 'The return to an exploitative apprenticeship system' in this chapter).

It should also be noted that the question of whether nursing is a 'profession', or indeed whether nursing ought to be or could ever be a profession has not been unproblematic (Ashley 1975a, 1975b, 1980; Cohen 1981; Melosh 1982; Styles 1982; Oakley 1986, p. 193). One reason for this, as suggested by Cohen (1981, p. 113), is that 'nursing researchers and educators have fallen into the trap of defining professionalism in the framework of male professionalism'. It is not surprising, then, that the notion of a 'profession' has not served either the public or nursing well (Styles 1982, pp. 40, 55, 74). Styles (1982) argues, however, that this need not be taken as cause for nurses to abandon their quest for professionalisation. To the contrary. What is required, she suggests, is not the abandonment of the ideal of 'profession', but to make the ideal more responsive to the social realities and needs it has been culturally constructed to deal with. In the case of nursing, Styles (1982, pp. 60, 76) suggests that this can be achieved by the nursing profession 'reinstating the service ideal' of professionalism and by nurses giving more concerted attention to developing and upholding 'a set of internal beliefs about nursing than a set of external criteria about professions'. This should include the view that it is people (not some abstract idealistic criteria about professions) that are 'the central phenomenon of nursing concern' (ibid, p. 92).

While it is acknowledged that traditional conceptions of 'profession' have tended to embrace patriarchal values (something which, incidentally, has long been problematic for feminism (Cott 1987, pp. 217–239)), this should not preclude the development of new definitions of 'profession' — and ones which not only 'reinstate the service ideal', but which also remind us of the important cultural role that the notion of 'profession' plays in legitimating certain behaviours — in this case, caring behaviours by nurses which would otherwise only be permitted by lay carers (such as close family members and intimate friends). Were nurses to be denied this legitimation (that is, the authority 'to nurse'), in the event of lay carers not being able to care for their loved ones (as frequently happens in the case of serious illness, health crises, or lack of personal resources), the outcome for those requiring skillful nursing care would quickly deteriorate into a situation of 'care-neglect' and a level of human suffering that could otherwise have been avoided (Lawler 1991; Brown et al. 1992). In light of these considerations, to view nursing's quest for professional status solely in the patriarchal terms of 'occupational usurpation and exclusion' is to not only misrepresent nursing's history, but to do violence to nursing's integrity as a (female dominated) profession that is committed to giving a social service that is caring as well as safe, therapeutically effective, culturally appropriate and morally accountable.

CHAPTER **FIVE**

The Medical Construction of Nurse Subordination

INTRODUCTION

IN COMMON LAW COUNTRIES around the world nurses have been led to believe that they have achieved legitimated status as autonomous health professionals. This belief has been encouraged, at least partially, by the nursing profession's own history in relation to:

- its relatively early success in establishing itself as a distinct women's profession (as stated earlier, this was achieved even before women gained the legal right to enter into a profession of their own choosing);
- its relatively early 'success' in obtaining statutory recognition (state registration);
- ongoing 'progressive' law reforms relevant to the profession and practice of nursing;
- the significant (and deceptive) changes in the language commonly used to describe the nurse's position both in law and society.

In actual practice, however, and contrary to popular rhetoric, it is evident that nurses have not achieved legitimated status as autonomous professionals at all (Ashley 1976b, p. 24). Nurses are not — and never have been — 'free' to use their knowledge and skills autonomously and independently to promote patient welfare (Ashley 1973, p. 638; Maas 1973, p. 238; Lee 1979; Lyon 1990, p. 269). In short, to borrow from Maas (1973, p. 238), 'nurses are not free to nurse' — and never have been.

The problem for nurses has been not only their lack of legitimated freedom to use their professional knowledge and skill autonomously. Another problem for nurses (both in the past and in the present) is that they have had no control over when and if they would accept responsibility for the results of their own professional judgments and actions (Maas 1973, p. 238; Lyon 1990, p. 269). Historically, others (namely, doctors, employers, and the courts) have 'benevolently' decided these things. Furthermore, contrary to superficial appearances (such as the existence of statutory nursing authorities and legally recognised representative professional nursing organisations), the nursing profession does not have — and never has had — ultimate power to shape and control 'what nurses are required, permitted and prohibited to do' (Murphy 1990a, p. 32). Instead, the ultimate power to decide these things has rested primarily with the law, and with those outside of nursing (for example, doctors and employers) whose patriarchal authority and dominant interests are both represented in and protected by the law.

Historically, the law has tended to view the nurse as being quintessentially the 'natural' subordinate of and as having a primary duty of obedience to the medical practitioner. Although some nursing and legal commentators argue that the law is increasingly recognising the nurse as an 'autonomous professional', and that 'the role of the professional nurse has changed, in a pragmatic sense, from one of legal dependency to one of legal accountability' (Murchison et al. 1982, pp. 1–2; see also Campazzi 1980, p. 1; *Regan Report on Nursing Law* 1980e; Kiefer 1983; Fiesta 1988, pp. 15, 27), it is evident that the 'real' legal status of the nurse has changed very little over the past 130 years. Indeed, despite so-called 'progressive' law reforms relevant to the profession and practice of nursing, and despite apparent improvements in the social and legal status of nurses and women generally, it is evident that the nurse is still viewed not as an autonomous health professional, but as a subordinate whose primary duty is to follow (read 'obey') the instructions (read 'orders') of the medical man (read 'the master').

In furthering this inquiry into the legal status of the nurse and the role the law has historically played in legitimating nursing's subordination to medicine, it would be useful to examine first the medical construction of nurse subordination (to be distinguished here from the closely related legal construction of nurse subordination), and to identify some of the influential patriarchal assumptions that medical men have made about nurses and nursing practice in order to justify and obtain political support for the legitimated medical control and dominance of nurses and nursing practice.

The medical construction of nurse incompetence

In an important paper read at the annual meeting of the Massachusetts State League of Nursing Education, held in Boston in 1921, Isabel Stewart, a distinguished American nurse, warned:

> The soundest reasoning will make slow headway against a deeply rooted conviction or prejudice which is sanctioned by age or which conflicts with vested interests. The suffragists had their hardest task in breaking down the age-old tradition that men are naturally superior to women, that women

exist mainly to serve the comforts and purposes of men, whether in politics or education or domestic life.

I am not sure that this feeling is entirely eradicated yet, in spite of the recent political emancipation of our sex. I am inclined to think it is still pretty strongly intrenched [sic] in the rank and file of the medical profession, and that it tends to color most of the discussions which we have been hearing recently about the function and the education of nurses. (Stewart 1921, pp. 424–425)

Isabel Stewart's views in this instance were and remain demonstrably correct. An examination of the early medical and nursing literature reveals that the medical profession fully accepted the 'age-old tradition that men are naturally superior to women' and the view that women existed primarily 'to serve the purposes of men'. More importantly, it is evident that the medical profession actively exploited these and other cultural–stereotypical views about women as part of its attempt to structure and gain legal support for its own cultural hegemony in the health care system, and to secure, reinforce and maintain the legitimated subordination of the nursing profession — its major competitor.

Historically, medical men have declined to recognise nurses qua women as being fully competent 'persons'. Concomitantly, medical men have tended to reject outright that:

- nurses are capable of exercising independent professional judgment;
- nurses are capable of functioning as independent health professionals.

Instead, doctors have tended to regard nurses qua women as being only 'semi-persons', or, to borrow from Aristotle, as 'children who never grow up' (Aristotle 1957, 1259b18–1260b24; see also Sealey 1990, p. 49) — in other words, as entities who lack complete (read 'adult male') rational competence, and thus as requiring the 'benevolent' and 'protective' supervision and guardianship of men, in particular, medical men.

From the very inception of modern nursing, medical men and their (mostly male) supporters have portrayed the nurse as suffering from a 'deficiency in judgment' and as 'lacking a judicial mind', and hence as needing to defer to the 'rational wisdom' of their male superiors, notably, medical men. For example, in a letter to the editor of the *British Medical Journal* (*BMJ*), published in February 1880, a medical practitioner expressed his outrage about the 'tyranny' of power being invested in the 'hands of one woman', namely the lady-superintendent of the hospital at which he had a position. In explaining why he was 'concerned', the doctor argued:

I think, as a rule, that women are more strong in their likes and dislikes than men are, consequently that they are more apt to be swayed by prejudice —

thus they lack the 'judicial mind' which should distinguish the ruler over a large establishment.
(A former House-Surgeon of Guy's 1880, p. 272)

The doctor argued further that the only way the lady-superintendent's central system of hospital management would work would be for the lady-superintendent herself

to work under the control of a select committee, on which there shall be at least two members of the professional [medical] staff.
(ibid.)

A week later, in reply to the above letter, another correspondent to the editor of the *BMJ* complained:

Considering how important in the treatment of disease nursing is now considered, I fail entirely to understand how such a valuable means of treatment should not have been retained in the hands of the hospital medical staff instead of being handed over to the management and control of an *irresponsible* person like the matron or lady-superintendent ... I feel satisfied that no hospital administration can possibly be permanently successful where the medical staff has not the control of the nursing staff, matron, or housekeeper [emphasis added].
('Gamma' 1880, p. 389)

The next week, another correspondent to the *BMJ* replied:

I fully endorse the proposal that the lady-superintendent should be directly under the control of a subcommittee containing a *proper proportion* of the honorary medical staff [emphasis added].
(L.R.C.P.L 1880, p. 425)

It should be noted that it was not only the matron or lady-superintendent who was regarded by the medical establishment as 'lacking a judicious mind' and thus as being 'irresponsible'. Nurses were likewise viewed as lacking certain necessary 'qualities of mind' and hence as needing to be controlled by 'benevolent' medical men.

In an early article published in the *Australasian Nurses Journal* (*ANJ*), for example, women qua nurses are described as having a 'deficiency in judgment' and thus as lacking the qualities that are 'especially necessary in those women who take up worldly professions' (Kyogle 1908, p. 417). By comparison, men qua doctors are described as being endowed with

natural faculties [which] have adapted them to frame and accept certain codes of professional law and etiquette not so easily recognised by the frailer sex.
(Kyogle 1908, p. 417)

Portraying the doctor as being by nature 'more suited' than the nurse to engage in professional activities, the article goes on to contend that

> a clever doctor is consistent and logical, his professional knowledge is built upon accepted facts and careful deductions, the treatment of his [sic] patients is based upon well-conceived theories, the result of wide experience. But with women it is different; their method of calculation is not the same; they fly to results without weighing evidence. To make up for this *deficiency in judgment,* Nature has endowed her daughters with a strong power of intuition and a swift perception of the drift of vague ideas. These are most valuable attributes in a Nurse, *but they do not comprise that other quality [the capacity to judge fairly and rightly] which makes men more suited for business habits and professional concerns* [emphasis added].
> (Kyogle 1908, p. 417)

In another early article written by a professor of medicine, nurses are again portrayed as being 'naturally' deficient in the ability to exercise rational judgments. In this article, nurses are informed that 'a capacity for original thought is rarer apparently in women than in men', and that any attempt 'to force nurses into more independent and more scientific activity' would probably be 'less fruitful' than in the case of medical men (Pirquet 1927, p. 344). The author goes on to state that in his clinic 'it [was] chiefly the kitchen', rather than 'the field of scientific activity', that had in the past offered nurses the greatest opportunity to develop their independent and 'scientific' thinking.

Similar views were expressed in the American medical and nursing literature. Stewart (1921, p. 426), for example, cites an American report in which it was conclusively stated:

> The nature of a nurse's work as ordinarily understood does not call for much initiative or independent judgment; on the contrary, she must learn to carry out instructions. There are certain inhibitions which must become a part of her professional consciousness and behaviour if she is to prove successful in her bedside work.

Citing other fallacious 'assumptions and statements which medical men are still circulating', and clearly perturbed by the noticeable damage that the medical profession's 'same old lies' were doing to the reputation of nursing as an acceptable and respectable career option for 'numbers of splendid women', Stewart (ibid.) goes on to retort:

> Is it true that nurses do not need to know or to think, only to tread a routine path which is laid out for them by someone else? If so, we do not need to look much farther for an explanation of our present scarcity of candidates.

> High grade morons would do quite as well as high school graduates, and we
> ought to make it perfectly plain to any intelligent young woman who
> wishes to enter the nursing field that her hands and feet will be needed and
> the lower centers of her brain and spinal cord, but the rest of her brain might
> as well be put in cold storage.

By portraying the nurse as being by 'nature' moronic and intuitive,[1] rather
than rational, and by portraying the nurse's work as not involving or calling
for 'much initiative or independent judgment', the medical establishment
was able to construct and publicly reinforce an image of the nurse as being
less rationally competent than the medical man, and therefore as being
'naturally' inferior (professionally speaking) and subordinate to the medical
man.

There is much to suggest that these patriarchal views about the nurse's
'natural' subordinate position to the medical man were supremely
influential. They were widely reinforced not just by hospital rules and
etiquette, but by the nursing literature and, perhaps more significantly, by
nursing codes of conduct as well. For example, in one early Canadian
hospital code of ethics (reprinted in the English periodical the *Nursing Times*
in 1907 and in the Australian periodical the *Australasian Nurses Journal* in
1908), it was plainly stated: 'A Nurse should always accord to a physician
the proper amount of respect and consideration *due to his higher
professional position* [emphasis added]' (*Australasian Nurses Journal* 1908,
p. 65). In an early article published by the English periodical the *Nursing
Mirror* (1909, p. 142), and reprinted in *Una*, it was succinctly stated:

> Socially a nurse ranks beneath a doctor, no matter what her position in life
> may really be, and she best upholds her position who allows him to see
> during her professional intercourse with him that she is ready at all times to
> *treat him with the deference and respect which in view of his professional
> rank he has a right to demand* [emphasis added].

The medical construction of nurse subordination did not end with the
mere portrayal of the nurse as being 'rationally incompetent' (moronic),
'irresponsible' and professionally 'inferior' however. Another crucial part of
the medical construction of nurse subordination was to portray nurses as
'needing' (for moral reasons) to be under the 'benevolent protection' and
'benevolent guardianship' (read 'control') of medical men. This was
portrayed as being 'necessary', not just for the sake of nurses (because of
their incapacity, nurses might act contrary to their own best interests) or for
the sake of patients (an 'unsupervised' incompetent and irresponsible nurse
might recklessly cause harm to patients), but for the sake of the 'public good'
(it would be against the public interest to have incompetent and irresponsible
nurses 'let loose on the world' to freely practise their profession). In actual

practice, however, nurses did not need the 'benevolent protection' or 'benevolent guardianship' of medical men at all, as Nightingale's nursing reforms had already long demonstrated. Indeed, there is room to suggest that the real reason the medical establishment considered that nursing needed to be controlled had, in fact, very little to do with protecting the genuine interests of either nurses, patients, or the general public (as already argued, nursing had become well organised without the help of medical men; furthermore, it was evident that nursing care was often more effective than medical treatment in achieving successful therapeutic outcomes). Rather, the control of nursing was necessary in order to protect the threatened interests of the medical profession and, to this end, for ensuring, among other things, that nurses were kept firmly in their 'proper sphere' (that is, out of professional and economic competition with medical men).

It was not difficult for the medical establishment to construct an image of the nurse as 'needing' to be controlled by medical men. By exploiting its own legitimated position of power and authority, and by exploiting prevailing dominant and legitimated cutural–stereotypical views at that time concerning the 'natural incapacity' or 'natural disorder' of women — and the perceived 'threat' that women posed to the existing political order (see Jagger 1983; Lloyd 1984; Pateman 1989) — the medical establishment was very successful in promoting and gaining support for its fallacious patriarchal view that 'since' nurses were by nature 'rationally incompetent' and hence 'irresponsible', they needed to be controlled — and, in particular, controlled by medical men. A good example of the kind of rhetoric used by the medical profession supporting this and similar views can be found in a short commentary published in the *New York Medical Journal* and later reprinted in the *Journal of the American Medical Association* (*JAMA*). In this commentary, it was simply stated:

> The medical profession should define emphatically and clearly the limitations of the nurse's sphere of work and study. Physicians connected with institutions fostering training schools should insist on representation on their boards of school management, not merely in an advisory but in a governmental capacity.
> (Thompson 1906, p. 1476)

After constructing an image of the nurse as 'needing' to be controlled by medical men, it was a relatively short step to construct and reinforce an image of the nurse as owing a correlative 'duty of obedience' to the medical man, which in turn was reinforced by portraying as 'dangerous' any nurse who failed to fulfil this duty faithfully and loyally. It is to demonstrating the medical construction of nurse obedience that this discussion will now turn.

The medical construction of the nurse's 'duty to obey'

During the late 1800s and early 1900s, the view that the nurse's duty was 'not to reason why', but to 'loyally carry out the doctor's instructions' was widely canvassed, and appears to have been accepted not just by the medical profession, but by the nursing profession as well (see, for example, *Australasian Nurses Journal* 1908, p. 65; Barclay 1912, p. 230; Symonds 1914, p. 112; Morgan 1918, pp. 100–101; *The Trained Nurse* 1921, pp. 200–202; Karll 1926; Farquharson 1929, p. 340; Gladwin 1930, p. 166). More importantly, as will be shown in the next chapter, it appears to be during this period that the nurse's medically constructed 'duty to obey' was also legitimated and reinforced by the law.

In 1890, a witness giving evidence to the Royal Commission on Charitable Institutions in Melbourne, argued:

> There was some prejudice among medical men against trained nurses, whose knowledge they seemed to fear would make them less inclined to obey orders and more ready to act as if their training placed them on a level with the doctor. It ought to be well understood, therefore, that the strictest obedience is one of the principles which is most strongly enforced upon those who are being trained for the nursing profession. In some of the religious nursing sisterhoods obedience is taught in a fashion which might almost be thought too severe, though it is right to acknowledge that *it is perhaps the most important factor in a nurse's career. A nurse who cannot be trusted to obey is dangerous* [emphasis added].
> (Morris 1892, p. 472)

Nursing journals (some of which, it will be recalled, were edited by medical men) also reinforced medically constructed views about the nurse's 'natural' duty to obey. Lena (1903), for example, writing in the medically edited nursing journal *Una*, reminded nurses that the doctor's position in a hospital was one of 'absolute command' and, as such, was a position which called for 'absolute loyalty' and 'obedience' on the part of the nurse. An early Canadian 'code of ethics' developed *for* (note not *by*) nurses asserted a similar view, prescribing as follows:

> A Nurse should strictly carry out the orders of the physician under whom she is working.
> (*Australasian Nurses Journal* 1908, p. 65)

A year later, the English periodical the *Nursing Mirror* (1909, p. 142) published an article entitled 'The relationship between nurse and medical officer' in which nurses were instructed:

A nurse's duty is solely to carry out [the doctor's] instructions, to keep him constantly informed concerning the condition of his patient, to put before him any points she has observed which, owing to her more constant intercourse with the patient, have been more obvious to her than to him, to assist him as far as possible in his treatment of the patient, and to uphold him loyally.

The article also reminded nurses that they are 'not by any means qualified to act as a doctor', and that they 'can only work under medical instruction' (ibid.).

McNeil (1910, p. 194), writing in the *Australasian Nurses Journal*, articulated a similar view, stating that 'one of the first requirements a physician exacts of a Nurse is obedience'. And in an early English article published by the *Nursing Times* (1913), nurses were instructed that

obedience implies the immediate compliance not only with those directions which commend themselves to the good judgment or convenience of the staff, but with all orders, even though in the private opinion of the nurse others better might be issued . . . If a nurse, or any subordinate, if it comes to that, finds she can set an order aside which does not commend itself to her, then good-bye to authority, discipline, and responsibility.

Two years later, in a 1914 'prize winning essay' written by a trainee nurse at the Training School, Children's Hospital, Melbourne, and published in *Una*, nurses were similarly reminded of their primary duty to the medical officer. The author of this award winning essay instructed:

It is necessary to remember that a nurse's *first duty is to obey*, and that promptly; and when receiving orders to do so with attention, and to see that such orders are carried out thoroughly and conscientiously, if not by herself, by those working under her [emphasis added].
(Symonds 1914, p. 112)

Meanwhile, in an article published in the *Australasian Nurses Journal*, Dr Agnes Morgan (1918, pp. 100–101), an American Assistant Professor of Household Science, argued:

Every nurse knows well her duty to her patient, to her commanding officers, the physician, to the hospital . . . She knows without ever putting it into definite words that she must obey the physician's orders unquestioningly, cheerfully, accurately.

Dr Morgan (1918, p. 101) made the further controversial claim that 'in many places the *sole purpose* of the nurse's training was to fit her for the faithful execution of the physician's orders in the care of sick people [emphasis added]'.

In another early nursing journal article entitled: 'The ethics of nursing', nurses were similarly instructed on their primary duty of obedience to the medical man. In this article, nurses were plainly told: 'To the physician who has charge of the case you owe allegiance and unfaltering obedience' (*The Trained Nurse* 1921, p. 201). Perhaps one of the most important examples of how seriously the nurse's duty of obedience had come to be viewed can be found in what appears to be a 'code' of nursing ethics (possibly an Australian first) written by Martha Farquharson (1929), an English-born Australian nurse and matron (Trembath and Hellier 1987, p. 28) who had also been a member of the provisional council of the International Council of Nurses in 1900 (Russell 1990, p. 17). Section 9 of Farquharson's code states:

> Obedience is better than sacrifice. Obedience. — It is necessary for peace that we should all learn obedience. There are two kinds, loyal and disloyal, but whichever it is, no hospital can be carried on without it. Loyal, willing obedience brings happiness with it. Unwilling obedience the reverse. (Farquharson 1929, p. 340)

The obedience clause in the Farquharson code is important for a number of reasons:

- It shows how successfully the medically constructed notion of nurse obedience had been translated from an authoritative medical statement into both a 'moral virtue' and a fully fledged professional moral duty.
- It seems to suggest that if and when obedience was 'burdensome' (for example, when it required the nurse to 'sacrifice' her own independent professional judgment concerning what might be a better course of action), it was nevertheless morally obligatory 'to obey' in order to preserve the 'peace' (read the 'patriarchal political order') of the hospital (read 'the dominance of hospital administrators and doctors').
- The statement itself would have provided a firm basis upon which a disobedient nurse could be 'justly' punished for her deviant behaviour.
- The statement seems to suggest that 'disobedience' could take several different forms — for example, it could include acts of 'disloyalty' (translate as 'questioning or failing to loyally carry out a superior's orders'), or acts which 'disturbed the peace' (also translate as 'questioning or failing to loyally carry out a superior's orders').

Significantly, the nurse's duty to obey the doctor's orders was later enshrined in the International Council of Nurses' first *International code of nursing ethics* which was adopted by the Grand Council of the ICN in 1953 (among other things, this enshrinement stands as a significant measure of the success of medical discourse in influencing the nursing profession's perceptions of the 'proper role' of the nurse). The relevant section of this code (*International code of nursing ethics* 1953, clause 7) reads:

The nurse is under an obligation to carry out the physician's orders intelligently and loyally.

The International Council of Nurses' *International nurses' pledge* (nd, p. 79) also required nurses to commit themselves to obey doctors' orders faithfully and loyally. The relevant section of the pledge (which, in several respects, reads like a marriage vow!) states:

I promise to carry out intelligently and loyally medical instructions given to me.

The *International code of nursing ethics* was eventually revised — once in 1965 and once in 1973. It was not until the 1973 revision, however, that clause 7 — which clearly 'abrogated the nurse's judgment and personal responsibility and showed dependency on physicians' (Kelly 1985, p. 207) — was deleted from the code, and from other nursing codes around the world which had been based upon it. It should be noted that the revision of the 1965 code was prompted not by a group of 'visionary' nursing leaders, as might be assumed, but by a group of Canadian nursing students who objected to statements in the code which supported nursing subservience to medicine (Bergman 1973, p. 140). The 1973 code has recently been reaffirmed without alteration.

The medical construction of the nurse's 'duty to be loyal'

An important step in the medical construction of nurse subordination was to portray the nurse as owing a strict 'duty of loyalty' to the medical man which, among other things, required the nurse not only to be 'obedient', but also never to 'stand in judgment' of an attending doctor's actions — and certainly never to discuss her judgments with others, especially not the patient or the patient's relatives.

The normative force of the 'duty to be loyal' helped to ensure that nurses were kept in their 'proper sphere', and, more importantly, to ensure that the nature and outcomes (especially the negative ones) of medical actions were kept 'strictly private' and hence protected from (potentially damaging) public scrutiny. In short, the nurse's medically constructed 'duty to be loyal' helped to ensure the silence of nurses, whose intimate knowledge of the failures as well as the successes of medical practice had the potential, if publicly disclosed, to seriously damage not just the doctor–patient relationship, but more seriously, medicine's growing reputation as a 'successful' and 'infallible' therapeutic science (see also *Nursing Mirror* 1909, p. 143; Sandroff 1981; Masson 1985; Fagin and Diers 1987, p. 116; Gamarnikow 1991, pp. 117–118). A good example of the kind of threat a nurse could pose to the reputation of an individual doctor and/or to the doctor–patient relationship, and of the consequences to the nurse who behaved in a 'disloyal' manner (for example, by disclosing 'privileged information'), can be found in an early anecdotal case published by the English periodical the *Nursing Mirror* (1909, p. 143). Outlining the relevant details of the case, the unidentified author writes:

> A doctor once told me of a nurse who had lately been working with him, but whom he never wished to work with again. Outside the bedroom door of her patient she asked him, 'What is really the matter with Mrs. So-and-So? I can make nothing of her.' He answered her quickly, without stopping to think, 'Neither can I. Hysteria, rank hysteria; at least, that is all the diagnosis I can make of her.' The nurse went straight back to her patient's room and told her. The next day the doctor received a polite little note informing him that his services would no longer be required.

The unidentified author goes on to admonish nurses as follows (ibid.):

> The incident speaks for itself. Honour, commonsense, discretion, and tact are generally acknowledged to be peculiar to women. Then nurses should endeavour to acquire a double portion of these qualities, for, indeed, they need them.

Another example of the perceived threat nurses posed to the 'good' reputation of medicine and medical men can be found in the controversy that ensued when a nurse wrote to the *Nursing Mirror* in 1907 criticising doctors for 'rush[ing] to the knife instead of to medicine or other treatment' (H.W. 1907, p. 192 — cited in Gamarnikow 1991, p. 117). The nurse in this case was attacked for 'expressing doubts about particular diagnoses and prescriptions, and for publicly criticising and questioning medical decisions' (ibid., p. 118). What is particularly interesting about the attacks directed against H.W. is the emphasis given to her apparent lack of 'loyalty' and the 'disgust' this engendered in her colleagues. For example, one correspondent to the journal responded by reminding H.W. that it was a doctor's prerogative to diagnose and treat disease, and that it was the nurse's duty 'to be loyal to her doctor' (N.C. 1908, p. 221 — cited in Gamarnikow 1991, p. 117). Another correspondent, outraged by H.W's views, was more scathing and expressed 'disgust' at the nurse's statement on grounds that nurses had no right 'to sit in judgement upon our surgeons' (Gee-Wiz 1908, p. 268 — cited in Gamarnikow 1991, p. 118). Other letters to the editor of the *Nursing Mirror* indicate that the nurse was viewed as having 'clearly overstepped the bounds of acceptable behaviour in nursing' (Gamarnikow 1991, p. 118). The fact that H.W. received the reprobation of her professional peers for criticising medical work demonstrates just how powerful — and effective — the 'duty to be loyal' was as an action guiding/behaviour controlling norm.

The nurse's 'duty to be loyal', like her 'duty to obey', was formally taught and reinforced through nursing codes of conduct, nurse education, nursing literature, and hospital rules of etiquette. For example, the 1893 *Florence Nightingale pledge for nurses* (prepared by a special committee appointed by the Farrand Training School Committee of Harper Hospital, Detroit), required nurses to pledge before God — 'With loyalty will I endeavour to aid the physician in his work'. And in the Canadian hospital code of ethics cited earlier, it was prescribed that a nurse 'should never discuss or criticise a physician with her patient or with her patient's friends' (*Australasian Nurses Journal* 1908, p. 65). A few years later in a prize winning essay on 'Nursing etiquette, in hospital and private work', it was argued that the nurse

> should inspire the patients with confidence in the doctor, never criticise his treatment or compare it with that of other medical men. She should not discuss one doctor's treatment of a patient with another medical man, or with friends or relations of patients.
> (Symonds 1914, p. 112)

Several years later, in an article entitled 'The ethics of nursing' (*The Trained Nurse* 1921, p. 201), nurses were similarly instructed on their 'moral' duty to be loyal to the medical man. The unidentified author of this article instructed:

> To stand in judgment on your physician's acts implies a larger knowledge of medicine than is his own ... In the name of the noble profession which you honour refrain from criticism to others of whatever the physician does. You must, at least, give him credit for honesty of purpose; if he falls short in execution of judgment let the mantle of sweet charity fall upon him. More than this we are fellow soldiers in the battle with disease, and lack of fealty or loyalty comes like a sword thrust from the hand of a friend.

In a series of short commentaries on professional ethics and etiquette published by the *Nursing Mirror* and *Una* respectively, nurses were again reminded that 'there is no more serious breach of etiquette than the nurse's criticism of the doctor to the patient' (Gullan 1925, p. 260), and that the nurse must be 'absolutely discreet and loyal' to the doctor (Wiles 1925, p. 262). The eminent and authoritative Sir Humphrey Rolleston Bart, K.C.B., Regius Professor of Physics at Cambridge University, asserted a similar view. In an address to members of the Cambridge branch of the College of Nursing, Bart (1929, p. 122) argued that the doctor 'rightly expects and receives the loyal support of the nurse' and that the nurse, although 'tempted to mention her more modern knowledge', must not even 'think of discussing, with the patient, the doctor or his treatment, or of recommending the name of a second medical man to come into consultation'. Bart explained that an important reason for the nurse to be loyal was that 'disloyalty' (which seemed to include giving patients 'privileged information') could 'unconsciously or unintentionally reflect on the competency of the doctor' (ibid.).

Perhaps one of the most compelling examples of the normative importance and force of the nurse's medically constructed duty to be loyal can be found in an early article (also written anonymously), published in the American nursing periodical the *Pacific Coast Journal*. In this article, loyalty is described in rather extraordinary legalistic terms, and as being essential to the effective performance (read, patriarchal political order) of the hospital. Loyalty is also portrayed as being a 'rational' moral duty, and as such as something which ought to be upheld — especially by subordinate nurses. The relevant section of the article is quoted in full below:

> Loyalty is an absolute necessity in the life of every thinking individual. The imbecile is the only being who can afford to exist without loyalty. In civil life we must be faithful to the laws that are laid down by our superiors for us to follow. Each court in each State is loyal to the supreme court of the land and every human being who wishes for the exercise of the personal liberty which is afforded him as a human being must needs be loyal to the courts of justice. He must be upright in his dealings with his fellow man in order to escape the anger of the courts and so enjoy to the full this liberty. In no place should this loyalty be more in evidence than in an organization such as a hospital. Here we have our superintendent and our management, our court and our supreme court, to whom we should rightly show all the loyalty due them as superiors, and whose laws and wishes should be obeyed without question. If we have loyalty within an organization we will have no friction, and friction means a dividing of attention and this is not conducive to the performance of the exacting, painstaking work that is demanded and must be forthcoming in a nurse's life. Loyalty to her school, her superintendent, and her management will establish within the nurse such ideals and standards as to work and conduct as will maintain the principles of good, justice and charity . . . If a nurse is loyal to her superintendent and to the management of her hospital and gives them the honor due there will be no doubt or question of her OBEDIENCE.
> (*Pacific Coast Journal* 1920, pp. 384–385)

What is particularly interesting and significant about the above excerpt is:

- the deference it gives to the rule of law;
- the way it analogises the rule of the hospital hierarchy to the rule of law (something which, incidentally, stands as a paradigmatic example of the way the law can and does structure people's thinking about the world and how they should operate in it);
- the deference it gives to the rule of the hospital hierarchy;

- the special emphasis it gives to the importance and 'necessity' of nurse obedience.

The position expressed in the above article is unequivocal: the law (of state and hospital alike) must be obeyed — and, more particularly, obeyed by nurses. Failure to obey is to be disloyal. More importantly, failure to obey is to threaten 'order' (in this case, the patriarchal political order of the hospital) and ipso facto to cause chaos. The stringent and specific requirement for nurse loyalty and obedience is not merely incidental, but is representative of the kind of discourse typically used to ensure that nurses as women were kept in their 'proper sphere'. Indeed, there is room to suggest that just as women generally were perceived as being a 'subversive force within the political order'[2] and thus as a profound threat to the patriarchal state (Pateman 1989, p. 17), so too were nurses perceived as a 'subversive force within the hospital order' and hence as a threat to the patriarchal hospital 'state' (institution). An effective means of controlling this perceived threat was to demand nurse obedience and loyalty — a demand that was relatively easy to promote and enforce, given prevailing cultural–stereotypical views at the time about the 'rightful' subordination of women to men. In support of these points, it is highly significant that there is no comparable discourse to be found arguing that doctors ought to be 'obedient' and 'loyal' to the hospital hierarchy[3] (probably because doctors were and are at the top of the hierarchy, and it was and is they who must be obeyed). This suggests that it was primarily nurses (women) who were perceived as a threat to the patriarchal political order of the hospital, and hence it was primarily nurses (women) who needed to be controlled.

Today, the rhetoric of 'loyalty' is not so commonly used — at least, not in Australia (it is still sometimes used in the United States of America (see, for example, Greenlaw 1982, p. 71)). Nevertheless, it is evident that nurses are still expected to exhibit 'allegiance' to their hospitals, doctors and superiors. Hospital cultural norms continue to make it extremely difficult for nurses to exercise independent judgment, to evaluate standard medical practice, to criticise medical errors or bad hospital/employer practices, to advise patients to seek a second medical opinion or alternative health therapies, and even to protect their own moral interests (see, for example, *Lampe v Presbyterian Medical Center* (1979); *In re Parkes District Hospital and the NSW Nurses' Association* (1979); *Tuma v Board of Nursing of the State of Idaho* (1979); *Misericordia Hospital v NLRB* (1980); *NLRB v Mount Desert Island Hospital* (1983); *Jones v Memorial Hospital System* (1984); *Wrighten v Metropolitan Hospitals* (1984); *Warthen v Toms River Community Memorial Hospital* (1985); *Sides v Duke Hospital* (1985); *Francis v Memorial General Hospital* (1986); *Free v Holy Cross Hospital* (1987); *Johnsen v Independent School District* (1989); *Seery v Yale-New Haven Hospital* (1989)). Nurses who do these things are portrayed as being 'unethical' (read 'disloyal') and as therefore deserving severe professional censure. In the ultimate analysis, as the cases to be discussed in the following chapters will show, although the language of 'loyalty' is no longer used, its normative power remains very much in force in guiding 'acceptable' nurse behaviours.

CONCLUSION

There are many other examples in the early medical and nursing literature which demonstrate the influential role that medical discourse has played in constructing the subordination of nursing. Although the examples given here are by no means exhaustive, they (together with the many other examples given in the preceding chapters in this text) are nevertheless sufficient to illustrate that (female) nurses have tended to be viewed by the medical establishment as lacking full rational competence, as lacking the ability to exercise sound professional judgment, as being by nature inferior to medical men, and as needing to be under the 'benevolent' guardianship and supervision of the more 'judicially minded' medical men. The examples given have also been sufficient to demonstrate that the assumed (it was, in fact, never shown) 'natural incapacity' of nurses was used as a basis for constructing the nurse's 'moral' duty of obedience to her superiors, and for portraying as 'dangerous' any nurse who failed to fulfil this duty 'loyally and faithfully'.

The extent of the medical establishment's success in constructing the subordination of nursing can be measured, at least partially, by the fact that nurse subordination and its corollaries obedience and loyalty came to be viewed as 'moral virtues'. Equally important, these emerged as the accepted hallmarks (of what can now be seen as being in essence a patriarchal medically constructed view) of the proverbial 'good nurse' (see also Gamarnikow 1991). More importantly, subordination, obedience and loyalty also emerged as the 'accepted' characteristics of — and, ironically, the legitimated standard measurement of — a patriarchal legally constructed view of what constituted a 'reasonable and prudent' nurse. Indeed, it is evident that 'obedience' came to be viewed by the courts (as it was viewed by the medical profession) as being a nurse's primary duty; and, in a perverted deontological sense, as therefore constituting a reasonable act. Conversely, 'disobedience' came to be viewed by the courts, as it had been viewed by the medical profession — as being an 'unreasonable' and/or 'imprudent', and hence negligent act — the 'unreasonableness' or 'imprudence' of which, incidentally, was (and continues to be) interpreted by the expert testimonies of 'reasonable and prudent' medical men[4] — or those, including some nurses, who are supportive of the cultural hegemony of medical men. Significantly, 'disobedience' (which included the exercise of independent professional nursing judgments — also regarded as a 'disloyal' act) likewise tended to be characterised in law (as it had been characterised in medical discourse), as a 'threat' to the political order of health care and hence to the 'public interest'. Chapters 6 and 7 will examine these claims further and will demonstrate more fully the nature of nursing's medically constructed and legally reinforced subordinate position.

ENDNOTES

1   It should be noted here that intuition (which was associated with nature and irrationality (see Olsen 1990)) was generally regarded as being less scientific and thus less reliable and less valuable than rationality and reason. Although the nurse's 'sixth sense' (intuition) was recognised (by doctors as well as nurses) as playing an important and reliable role in guiding a nurse's clinical judgment, for example, that 'something is not quite right with a patient', it was nevertheless characterised as having less authority than reason, and, in particular, as having less authority than the reasoning of medical men. Even today intuition is recognised as playing an important and reliable, although not an exclusive role in guiding a nurse's clinical judgment (see, for example, Benner 1984, p. 37; Wolf 1988, p. 37). However, because it cannot be 'scientifically measured', it tends to be undervalued, trivialised, marginalised and sometimes even scorned. Wolf (ibid.), for example, cites the recent case of a nurse who had a 'sense that something wasn't right' with a patient. She informed the doctor of her feelings, adding that 'he would probably think she was crazy'. The doctor agreed, and asked, 'What do you want me to do?'. The nurse replied, 'I don't know'. Forty-five minutes later the patient suffered a cardiac arrest. The doctor is reported to have later told the nurse that 'she [the nurse] was a witch' (ibid.).

2   Women were generally regarded as lacking 'the capacities necessary for political life' — that is, the capacities of rational competency, the ability to use reason to 'sublimate their passions, a sense of justice, and the ability to develop a political morality' (Pateman 1989, p. 4). For this reason, men popularly regarded women as a threat to the (patriarchal) political order of the state. The 'disorder of women' as Pateman (1989) describes it, was effectively cited by men as justifying women's exclusion from the public (male) world and from participating in public affairs.

3.   It is acknowledged that during the nineteenth century, voluntary hospitals (unlike the specialist hospitals that were being founded and controlled by doctors) were administered by lay governors or lay hospital managers who 'had in theory complete authority over everything that happened in their hospitals' (Abel-Smith 1964, p. 33; see also Starr 1982, pp. 162–169; Granshaw and Porter 1989, p. 9). Abel-Smith (1964, p. 33) points out, however, that in practice the lay governors' authority over professional medical men was limited. Explaining this apparent inconsistency, Abel-Smith (1964, p. 33) writes that the lay governors

were careful not to question the clinical judgement or examine the quality of the work of *any* [emphasis added] of the doctors in the hospital unless they were forced to do so. Except where matters of finance were concerned, the doctors were left to run the medical side of the hospital.

It should also be noted that doctors 'formed themselves into medical committees to co-ordinate their activities, to prepare advice for the lay governors and to ensure that their collective interests were properly represented in the management of the hospital' (Abel-Smith 1964, p. 33; see also Starr 1982; Turner 1987; Freidson 1988; Granshaw and Porter 1989).

4   As is discussed more fully in chapter 8 of this book, female doctors have not featured very prominently as expert witnesses in legal cases involving nurses.

CHAPTER SIX

The Legal Construction and Reinforcement of Nurse Subordination

INTRODUCTION

HISTORICALLY, THE LAW HAS played a powerful (although not exclusive) role in structuring and maintaining nursing's subordinate and subservient relationship to medicine; and, as has already been shown, in obstructing the development of nursing as an autonomous profession. As argued in chapter 2 of this book, the law's role in this instance has been wholly compatible with the role it has played historically in reinforcing the traditional principles of 'female incompetence, female subordination, and the establishment of male guardianship' (Anderson and Zinsser 1988, p. 337). In the case of nursing, these 'parent' principles have readily translated into the derivative principles of nurse incompetence, nurse subordination, and the establishment of medical guardianship and supervision. The remaining chapters of this book will demonstrate more fully the law's reinforcement of the above principles, and show how this reinforcement has undermined both the profession and practice of nursing.

In this chapter a number of real life examples and legal cases will be used to demonstrate the law's reinforcement of the above principles and to show how this reinforcement has served to obstruct and undermine the professional development and status of nursing as an autonomous profession, and, more specifically, has legitimated nursing's subordination to medicine. Although the examples and cases used are by no means exhaustive, they are nevertheless sufficient for the purposes just stated, and also to demonstrate a number of key patriarchal assumptions the law makes about nurses and nursing practice. These are:

- that nurses lack full rational competence, and thus lack the capacity to be full professionals and to exercise sound independent and responsible professional judgment;

- that nurses are the 'natural' subordinates of doctors and as such have a 'natural' duty of obedience to doctors;
- that because of their 'natural incapacity', nurses ought to be controlled and supervised by doctors.

Before proceeding, it should be noted that owing to a paucity of reported Australian and English cases involving nurses (an issue which will be addressed near the end of chapter 7) most of the legal cases used in the following discussion are from the United States of America. Although the cases considered are not binding on (and should not be generalised to hold for) other common law countries, the points they illustrate and the arguments they support are nevertheless of relevance to nurses around the world. One of the main reasons for this is that — given the socio-cultural and historical similarities between the profession and practice of nursing in common law countries — the cases considered offer important and valuable insights into the kinds of patriarchal assumptions that 'the law' can and does make about nurses and nursing practice, and the extent to which these assumptions can and have influenced nursing's relationship to and experience of the law in North America. In countries such as Australia where there is a paucity of reported legal cases and exemplars involving nurses and nursing practice, the lessons offered by North American cases concerning the patriarchal nature of law (and more to the point, law's patriarchal assumptions about nursing) might otherwise be missed. This may leave the nursing profession in a disadvantaged position vis-à-vis being informed better about the nature of law and being able to dismantle its legally constructed and reinforced subordination to medicine and, more importantly, the state. Furthermore, while it is true that the North American cases do not have universal application, it is nevertheless apparent that the patriarchal assumptions they express certainly do. This is borne out, if not by reported legal cases, then by anecdotal experience — and, not least, by nursing's continued (and universal) lack of control over its own affairs.

What status the nurse — autonomous professional or dependent servant?

From the earliest parliamentary and legal debates on the nurse question, nursing has consistently been referred to as a 'profession'. Nevertheless, in everyday practice and in law, nurses have been regarded historically as 'servants', not as (autonomous) professionals; and, as such, as having a primary 'duty of obedience' to their 'masters' — that is, to doctors and employers (hospitals). Doctors and employers, by contrast, have traditionally been viewed as 'masters' — both in life and in law — and, as such, as having the ultimate right to direct and control their servants (nurses). Although this has not been problematic for doctors and employers (among other things, it has been instrumental in ensuring their dominance and control of nurses, nursing practice, and the nurse–patient relationship), it has been so for nurses. Not least because the master/servant relationship (the common law conceptualisation of the employment relationship) is the very antithesis of the (autonomous) professional relationship that nurses have aspired to achieve with their patients, co-workers and employers.

Today the terminology 'master/servant' tends not to be used to describe the relationship between nurses and doctors/employers (Staunton and Whyburn 1993, p. 77). Instead the more 'democratic' terms of *doctor/nurse relationship* and *employer/employee relationship* are used. However, it should be noted that although master/servant terminology is not so widely used in day-to-day discourse, the hegemonic ideology it connotes remains very much in force.[1] Despite apparent 'improvements' in the legal status of nursing, it is evident that nurses are still viewed as being quintessentially the 'servants' of doctors and employers, and doctors and employers are still viewed as being the 'masters' of nurses.

Historically, the question of whether nurses are skilled professionals or dependent servants has not been without legal controversy (see in particular the New Zealand Supreme Court case *Logan v Waitaki Hospital Board* [1935]). There has been a diversity of judicial opinion on the matter, raising early speculation that either 'the rules of law are unsatisfactory, or that their application depends upon some other factor which does not appear in the text-book rules' (Wright 1936, p. 701).

During the early 1900s, for instance, arguments were advanced to support the view that because the trained nurse was expected to exercise professional skill, then, strictly speaking, she was not a servant and therefore the hospital was exonerated of liability for her actions (Goodhart 1938, p. 553). In *Halsbury's Laws of England* (2nd edn), for example, the section on 'Medicine and pharmacy' states:

> Nor is a public or voluntary hospital, which has fulfilled its duty to employ duly qualified nurses, liable for the negligence of a duly qualified nurse when performing nursing duties in which she uses professional skill, although liable for her negligence in the performance of purely ministerial or administrative duties.
>
> (s 737, pp. 358–359, cited in Goodhart 1938, p. 553)

This principle was established in law by the famous (and controversial) 1909 English Court of Appeals case *Hillyer v Governors of St Bartholomew's Hospital* (reversed three decades later by Lord Denning in the leading English case *Cassidy v Ministry of Health* (1951); see also *Gold v Essex County Council* (1942); Eddy 1956, p. 103; Denning 1979, pp. 238–241), involving a patient who suffered burns and other injuries whilst having an examination under general anaesthetic. In this case, the court held that when nurses were employed for the purposes of operations and examinations by the medical officers, they ceased to be servants of the hospital, and the hospital was not liable for their negligent actions (*Hillyer v Governors of St Bartholomew's Hospital* (1909), pp. 826, 829). The case was widely interpreted as

> establishing the principle that . . . nurses when acting professionally should not be treated as being servants, and that therefore the hospital could not be held liable for their negligence.
> (Goodhart 1938, pp. 556)

This interpretation was accepted by the nursing profession as well. For example, a barrister-at-law (1911, p. 213), writing in the *Nursing Times* warned:

> The liability of the nurse is increased by the Hillyer v. Governors of St Bartholomew's Hospital decision; for while it leaves the hospital immune, it exposes the doctors and nurses to be shot at. For it may be pointed out that if the action is not brought on the contract but on the bare fact of negligence, then in such case a nurse contributing to it would be liable; for it is a legal principle that everyone who is party to a legal wrong is liable to answer for it.

Some years later, in another noted English case *Strangeways-Lesmere v Clayton* [1936], the King's Bench division of the High Court likewise held that the hospital board should not be held liable for the negligence of nurses 'when acting professionally'. Citing Justice Swift's decision in the unreported English case *James v Probyn* (1935), Horridge J accepted that

> the duties of doctors and nurses are the duties of skilled people to be carried out by skilled people, and the actions of doctors and nurses cannot be controlled in my opinion by members of a Committee who do not for one moment pretend that they have knowledge or the ability to perform these duties themselves. They do not seem to me to be there as the servants of the Committee at all in the sense that the Committee can control their method of carrying out their work. That being so, they are not responsible for any negligence of which they may be guilty in the way in which they do carry out their work.
> (*Strangeways-Lesmere v Clayton* [1936], p. 17)

The original findings of the Hillyer case were, however, controversial, and not everyone accepted its interpretation (see Wright 1936; Goodhart 1938; Eddy 1956, pp. 89–113). Writing in the *Law Quarterly Review*, Goodhart (1938, p. 556) argued that interpretation of the Hillyer case was 'strange' and 'might more accurately be termed, *misinterpretation* [emphasis added]'. Analysing a number of court cases involving nurses in England, Scotland, Canada, New Zealand, and the United States of America (for example, *Hall v Lees* (1904); *Evans v Liverpool Corporation* [1906]; *Smith v Martin and Kingston-upon-Hull Corporation* (1911); *Logan v Waitaki Hospital Board* [1935]; *Powell and Wife v Streatham Manor Nursing Home* (1935); *Strangeways-Lesmere v Clayton* [1936]), he argued further that it was 'contrary to ordinary experience' to suggest that nurses [were] not 'servants' — that is, 'were not supervised or controlled in their work'. In support of this claim, Goodhart cited Lord-Justice Clerk's dissenting judgment in the Scottish Court of Sessions case *Lavelle v Glasgow Royal Infirmary* (1932), pp. 255–256), which states:

> The position of a physician and that of a nurse seem to me, for the purposes in hand, to be in marked contrast the one to the other. The physician exercises an uncontrolled direction in the treatment of his patient. He is not the servant of any master. He is his own master. He is subject to no interference by anyone. In short, he is independent . . . The position of the nurse is otherwise. She is not necessarily a skilled or experienced person like a surgeon . . . The nurse, differing from the doctor, is controlled at every point. She was controlled in this case by the superintendent, by the matron, by the doctors, and by the residents. *That she is a servant and has a master seems to me indubitable.* The problem is to find him [emphasis added].

Rejecting the view that when acting in a professional capacity, nurses, like doctors, cease to be servants of the hospital, Goodhart (1938) further contended (correctly in my view) that the Hillyer case interpretation was advanced and upheld 'merely to avoid the vicarious liability of charitable hospitals'[2] whose limited funds were viewed as something which

> ought to be carefully protected and that a patient, receiving gratuitous service, ought not to be awarded money which has been given in trust for the general public.
> (Goodhart 1938, p. 559)

After advancing lengthy arguments demonstrating the fallacious reasoning in the Hillyer case and other cases affirming its decision, Goodhart (1938, p. 555) contended it was an error to hold that 'because the doctor occupies a peculiar status [as a professional man] therefore the nurse must occupy a similar one'. He concluded (ibid., pp. 573–574):

> The trained nurse is *the servant* of the hospital as she is employed to *render service* and is at all times *under the general control of the hospital* officials. The fact that she is expected to exercise professional skill and is required to obey the orders of the medical staff does not affect her position [emphasis added].

Cecil Wright (1936), editor of the *Canadian Bar Review*, held a similar view. Like Goodhart, Wright contended that regardless of whether the nurse used 'professional skill', she was still controlled. Citing a number of cases from England, Scotland, New Zealand, and Canada (for example, *Evans v Liverpool Corporation* [1906]; *Hillyer v Governors of St Bartholomew's Hospital* (1909); *Lavere v Smith's Fall Public Hospital* (1915); *Nyberg v Provost Municipal Hospital Board* [1927]; *Logan v Waitaki Hospital Board* [1935]; *Strangeways-Lesmere v Clayton* [1936]; *Vuchar et al. v The Trustees of the Toronto General Hospital* [1936]), Wright argued that even when not subject to the control of the hospital board, the nurse was still subject to the paramount control of the physician. This was because, even though the hospital board was responsible for employing the nurse, and had the power to control her 'ministerial and administrative' duties, she had been employed primarily to 'assist in carrying out treatment prescribed by medical officers' (Wright 1936, p. 704).

It would be a serious mistake to conclude on the basis of the Hillyer case — and other judicial decisions affirming it — that the courts in any way recognised the nurse as having a bona fide professional status independent to that of the doctor, and thus as occupying a position from which she could legitimately and independently use her own professional discretion and skill as a nurse. One reason for this is that it is clear the primary concern of the courts during the early 1900s was not to clarify or establish the professional status of the nurse as an 'independent expert performing services for the patient' (Goodhart 1938, p. 553). It is evident that this was a non-issue, despite the ongoing battle for state registration. Rather, the primary concern of the courts was to clarify who (for example, the hospital or the doctor) had ultimate control over directing the nurse's activities, and therefore who was vicariously liable for the nurse's negligent actions under the rule of *respondeat superior* (Wright 1936, p. 702).

Where it could be proven that the nurse was performing duties that required professional skill — as distinct from the mere 'routine' and 'domestic' duties (commonly referred to as 'ministerial and administrative duties') as otherwise required by standing hospital orders — then the hospital could escape liability for a nurse's negligent actions. It should be noted, however, that the ultimate test of whether a nurse's duties required the use of 'professional skill' rested not on whether it involved the application of learned nursing knowledge or on the expert testimony of experienced qualified nurses, but on whether the nurse's duties were ordered by or performed under the direct supervision of a medical man (such as a surgeon in an operating theatre). In the leading New Zealand Supreme Court case — *Logan v Waitaki Hospital Board* [1935] — for example, Johnston J accepted that the question of whether a nurse's actions could be properly called 'professional' depended not on the nature of the acts themselves, but on whether they were carried out in response to a doctor's orders. Referring to the comments of Kennedy LJ in the Hillyer case, Johnston J argued that 'where the acts of the nurse were the acts of the doctor and under his control as though they were his own' then they could be properly referred to as being 'professional' in character (*Logan v Waitaki Hospital Board* [1935], p. 444). Interestingly, the doctors in this case testified that even a nurse's action of 'disregarding' a medical order constituted a 'professional act'. This appears to be because the act in question would nevertheless have been contingent on a medical directive as opposed to a directive from a non-medical hospital administrator. The examination of medical officers on this point is as follows:

> Q. Would a nurse handling hot-water bottles be acting professionally?
> Yes, practically everything the nurse does is professional.
> Q. In a sense everything a nurse does within the ambit of her duties is professional?
> In a wide sense, yes.
> Q. The supervision of patients has been placed in the same category as making beds; do you agree with that?
> It depends on whether the patient is on the bed or not. I would not put counsel in charge of the patient.
> Q. Supposing after an appendix operation the doctor instructed the nurse not to give the patient sausages, would her disregard of the order be professional?
> Yes. The polishing of the ward-floor would not be a professional duty, and, as conclusion from such testimony, the Court is asked to find that failure to keep close watch is a professional act.
> (*Logan v Waitaki Hospital Board* [1935], pp. 443–444).

Where it could be shown that a nurse was acting under the direct supervision and/or control of a doctor, it was generally held that the nurse 'temporarily ceased' to be a servant of the hospital, and the hospital was thus exonerated of liability for the nurse's actions. In the Hillyer case, for example, Farwell LJ said of the three nurses and the two 'carriers' (orderlies) involved in the case, that while they were servants of the hospital board for general purposes

> they [were] not so for the purposes of operations and examinations by the medical officer. If and so long as they [were] bound to obey the orders of the defendants, it may well be that they [were] their servants, but as soon as the door of the theatre or operating room closed on them for the purposes of an operation . . . they ceased to be under the orders of the defendants, and [were] at the disposal and under the sole orders of the operating surgeon until the whole operation [had] been completely finished; the surgeon [was]

for the time being supreme, and the defendants [could not] interfere with or gainsay his orders.
(*Hillyer v Governors of St Bartholomew's Hospital* (1909), p. 826)

If, on the other hand, it could be shown that the nurse was acting under the 'standing orders' and policies of the hospital, then it was the doctor who could escape vicarious liability for the nurse's negligent actions. In the Canadian Appellate division case *Lavere v Smith's Falls Public Hospital* (1915, p. 125), for example, the court held that the nurses, whose negligent actions were at issue, were

> not acting under the control and directions of the doctors, but were performing *routine duties* in their capacity as the servants or representatives of the defendants. In that view, the defendants [the hospital trustees] are liable [emphasis added].

Significantly, it appears that only rarely was it suggested — either by the courts or by jurists commenting on legal cases involving the negligence of doctors and nurses — that nurses themselves either could or should be held independently liable for their own negligent actions. At no time was it suggested that nurses could be vicariously liable for either a doctor's or a hospital's actions, further indicating the subordinate status of the nurse. Indeed, the courts positively rejected such a proposal (see, for example, *Hillyer v Governors of St Bartholomew's Hospital* (1909), p. 827; *Gold v Essex County Council* (1942), p. 313). A compelling example of this can be found in the High Court (Court of the Queen's Bench) English case *Perionowsky v Freeman* (1866), the first reported case of its kind. In this case the defence briefly suggested that 'the nurses . . . were the parties really liable' in the case at hand (ibid., p. 875). Nevertheless, the nurses in question were not called as witnesses. Counsel for the plaintiff 'urged that the nurses ought to have been called as witnesses' but it appears that the suggestion was not taken seriously.[3] Despite the fact that the plaintiff suffered severe burns as a result of the nurses' negligent actions (the nurses were alleged to have 'wrongfully placed and immersed' the patient in a bath of scalding hot water, and 'forcibly held him down' in the water despite his screams), the jury returned a verdict in favour of the defendants (two surgeons) on grounds that they were 'not near enough to be aware of [the nurses' negligence] and to prevent it' (ibid.).

There were, however, some notable — although strictly qualified — exceptions to the principle of nurses not generally being held liable for their own negligent actions. For example, in the previously mentioned English case, the court found that the two nurses involved were 'liable in this action' (*Strangeways-Lesmere v Clayton* [1936], p. 15). The case involved a patient who died after she was incorrectly administered a lethal dose of the dangerous drug paraldehyde. The original medical prescription had been for six drachms of the drug, but owing to a badly communicated order, six ounces of the drug was mistakenly given and the patient died without recovering consciousness. The court held that because the nurses' actions involved a 'skilled operation' (the administration of a dangerous drug), the hospital authorities were not liable. However, the court appears to have also accepted that because the nurses were not acting under the direct control and supervision of the doctor prescribing the drug, the doctor was not liable either. Judgment was made for the plaintiff against the nurses who were found liable for damages (*Strangeways-Lesmere v Clayton* [1936], p. 18).

Just why the prescribing doctor or the trustees of the hospital were not held vicariously liable for the nurses' negligence in this case is a matter for speculation. One explanation is that because of the seriousness of this case (it involved the death of a patient, as opposed to a mere injury), it was more difficult to 'buck pass' the liability, as tended to happen in other cases. As previously mentioned, if the hospital was sued, it could be successfully argued that the nurse was performing a 'professional duty' and therefore the hospital was not liable. Conversely, if the doctor was sued, it could be argued that the nurse was performing only a 'ministerial or administrative duty', and therefore the doctor was not liable. In this case liability was not easily avoided, since clearly there had been gross negligence in the care of the patient and someone had to be made to account. It appears, however, that neither the hospital nor the doctor were willing to accept vicarious responsibility for the patient's death. The 'solution' in this case was found by allowing the nurses to carry the full burden of both the responsibility and the liability for the incorrect and lethal drug administration.

Regardless of the findings of the Hillyer case, the Strangeways-Lesmere case and others like them, it is evident that nurses were not generally recognised as being autonomous legally responsible and skilled professionals. It is certainly clear that the courts did not in any way recognise the nurse as having the same professional status as the medical practitioner, or even as having a genuine professional role to fulfil as an 'independent expert performing services for the patient'. At best, as the New Zealand Supreme Court case *Logan v Waitaki Hospital Board* [1935] clarified, the nurse was generally seen by the courts as having only a 'vicarious' professional status vis-à-vis the medical practitioner. In so far as nursing actions were concerned, the question of whether these could or should be properly regarded as being 'professional' — as opposed to being merely 'domestic' or 'ministerial' or 'routine' — appears to have rested entirely on whether or not they were ordered by a doctor, suggesting that nursing actions also, at best, had only vicarious professional status. As a point of interest, a similar view has been expressed recently in a Supreme Court of Michigan case *Green v Berrien General Hospital Auxiliary* (1990) (see the section entitled 'The problem of "ordinary" negligence' in chapter 8).

There is little doubt that nurses were seen by the courts as having a significantly different and inferior professional status to that of the medical practitioner. Whereas doctors were seen as professional men and ipso facto 'masters', nurses were seen as being 'other' — that is, as women who, ipso facto, were not — and could not be — professional men, and thus at best could only be the 'servants' of medical men.

In the Hillyer case, for example, Farwell LJ argued that it was 'impossible to contend' that the doctors involved in the case

> were servants in the proper sense of the word; they [were] all professional men, employed by the defendants *to exercise their profession to the best of their abilities according to their own discretion*; but in exercising it they [were] in no way under the orders or bound to obey the directions of the defendants [the governors of the hospital] [emphasis added].
> (*Hillyer v Governors of St Bartholomew's Hospital* (1909), p. 825)

As for the nurses in this case, Farwell LJ held that they were 'on a somewhat different footing', namely, that 'they [were] the servants of the defendants' (*Hillyer v Governors of St Bartholomew's Hospital* (1909), p. 826). Some years later, in the English Court of Appeals case *Wardell v Kent County Council* (1938), the court likewise held that there was 'no doubt' that the nurse was — on account of being controlled at every point of her work — a servant (p. 1030).

That nurses were indeed 'on a somewhat different footing' to that of doctors, and were regarded primarily as being 'servants', can be readily shown. For instance, unlike doctors, nurses were neither expected nor permitted to use their 'own discretion'. The nurse's duty was to obey the instructions of either her employer (the hospital) or its agents (the doctors), not to exercise independent professional judgment. Even in instances where it was evident the nurse exercised or should have exercised her own discretion or 'best judgment', this tended to be characterised, at worst, as involving 'nothing special' — as being merely 'routine', not professional — and at best, as merely an act of compliance, namely, with the standing orders of either the hospital or the absent 'supervising' doctor. A good example of this can be found in the Canadian case *Lavere v Smith's Falls Public Hospital* (1915), involving a patient whose foot was severely burned by an over-heated brick which had been placed in her bed for the purpose of heating it. Relevant excerpts of the cross-examination of a nurse witness in this case are quoted in full below:

> Q. His Lordship is asking, as I understand it, in regard to the preparation of the bed; is there anything special about that?
> A. Nothing special. It is a standing order in all hospitals that a bed for a patient under an anaesthetic is well heated.

His Lordship. Now then, Miss Thomas knew when she was told that she had charge of the room where the patient was, didn't I understand you to say before that it was her duty to see that the bed was properly warmed?

A. Yes.

Q. That would not be in accordance with any doctor's orders?

A. Not in her special case. The doctor would not give her any direct order . . .

Q. Take a case where the patient is put to bed in an unconscious condition, has the nurse any discretion to exercise, has she any duty to exercise, or who exercises discretion then, about the condition?

A. I think the nurse would.

Q. Would do what?

A. Use her discretion.

Q. About what?

A. About the warming or cooling the room.

Q. But would she be subject to any order in regard to that?

A. I think the doctor would order her.

Q. That is what I was getting at, the doctor would order her?

His Lordship. That narrows it to this extent, it is the duty of the nurse in the first place to do as suggested to her, in seeing that the bed is properly warmed for the patient, and then if the doctor comes in it may be his duty to see if it is over-heated or under-heated, and give his directions in regard to that; but, in the absence of any directions in regard to that, it stands that it is the nurse's duty.

Mr Watson. Do you know if the doctor ordinarily inspects the bed, or does he not?

A. I think not . . .

Q. And then I understand you that the nurses are performing domestic duties in the way of seeing that the bed is right?

A. Yes.

(*Lavere v Smith's Falls Public Hospital* (1915), p. 125)

In another noted Canadian case, *Vuchar et al. v The Trustees of the Toronto General Hospital* [1936], the requirement for nurses to use professional discretion was similarly characterised as involving little more than 'moronic routine'. The case involved a nurse who, on the instructions of a doctor, negligently applied an electric heat cradle (comprising an elaborate system of light bulbs) for the purposes of treating a localised infection. As a result of the nurse's negligent actions, the patient suffered severe burns on both her thighs. Although application of the heat cradle clearly required the nurse to exercise professional discretion, and it was known that the treatment itself carried the risk of causing serious injury to the patient if applied incorrectly, the court rejected the idea that the task involved professional skill. Instead, the court held that the task involved merely a 'ministerial' or 'ordinary routine' service (ibid., p. 390; see also *Nyberg v Provost Municipal Hospital Board* [1927]).

The reluctance by the courts to recognise that nurses exercised or needed to exercise professional discretion in their work, or that nurses had an independent professional status to that of the doctor, is only a part (granted an important part) of the overall picture of the legal construction and reinforcement of the position of the nurse as a servant. Another important part, which up until now has not been fully considered, concerns the nurse's legal (to be distinguished here from a moral) duty to obey the orders of her superiors (doctors and hospital administrators). While it is correct that qualified nurses were not generally instructed how to perform their nursing duties (the 'how' of nursing work was a matter which was formally taught in hospital schools of nursing), nurses were nevertheless instructed on what their duties were and when they ought to be carried out (see, for example, *Logan v Waitaki Hospital Board* [1935], p. 397; *Wardell v Kent County Council* (1938), p. 1027). Furthermore, unlike doctors who, as agents of the hospital, had an overriding right to 'act' and to 'direct the actions of others' (nurses, orderlies, and so on), nurses, being merely the servants of the hospital (and its agents, the doctors) had an overriding duty to 'submit' and 'to acquiesce to the orders of a superior' (a doctor or hospital administrator). This discussion will now examine more fully the nature and implications of the nurse's legal duty to obey — and in particular, her duty to obey medical orders.

The nurse's legal 'duty to obey'

Historically, nurses have had a strict duty of obedience to medical practitioners, a legal obligation to implicitly follow their instructions. In return for her obedience, a nurse could look forward to being 'protected' from liability for her own negligent actions.

In the noted English case *Hall v Lees* (1904), for example, the Court of Appeals accepted that when caring for private patients, the nurse was 'subject to the control of the medical man attending the patient', and that it was 'her duty as a nurse, and part of her work as such, to follow the instructions of the medical man in attendance' (pp. 607–609). In this case the nurse was not held liable for her negligent actions. In the Canadian case *Lavere v Smith's Falls Public Hospital* (1915), p. 101, Riddell J stated that

> if the nurse obeyed the express order of the surgeon, she was not guilty of negligence. That is the duty of a nurse.

Some years later, in the English Court of Appeals case *Gold v Essex County Council* (1942), p. 299, Lord Greene MR argued that the nurse 'is not guilty of negligence if she carries out the orders of the surgeon or doctor, however negligent those orders may be'. In the same case Goddard LJ stated:

It is part of the nurses' duty, as servants of the hospital, to attend the surgeons and physicians and carry out their orders. If the surgeon gives a direction to the nurse and she carries it out, she is not guilty of negligence even if the direction is improper . . . It is the nurse's duty to her employers and to her patient to carry out the directions given by the surgeon or physician faithfully and carefully.
(*Gold v Essex County Council* (1942), p. 310)

The disobedient nurse, in contrast, automatically lost her protection from personal liability. Thompson (1965, p. 84) explains, if a nurse 'disobeyed the doctor's instructions' or 'failed to carry them out faithfully,' she would 'render herself liable — she would be personally liable'. A major reason for this is that disobedience was itself construed as being an unreasonable and negligent act and, as such, was regarded as being the most difficult of malpractice actions to defend — hence the disobedient nurse's forfeiture of protection (Scheffel 1931, p. 35; Sarner 1968, p. 44).

In everyday practice, the nurse's legal position was clear (or so it seemed): either she obeyed the doctor's orders, or risked being held personally liable for her own negligent actions. In short, to borrow from Sachs and Wilson (1978, p. 141), 'submission and protection were correlative. Withdraw the one, and the other is lost'.[4] As time passed, however, the nurse's apparent and stringent duty to implicitly follow a doctor's orders began to weaken and was seriously challenged by the shock findings of a 1929 Supreme Court case in the Philippines (then under American jurisdiction), involving a newly graduated registered nurse, Lorenza Somera. Since this is an important case, and one which has been widely acknowledged in the nursing literature, it is considered in detail below.

The Somera case

In May 1929 in Manila, a newly graduated registered nurse, Lorenza Somera, was found guilty of manslaughter. She was sentenced to a year and one day in prison, ordered to pay one thousand pesos in damages and to pay one-third of the court costs in connection with the death of a thirteen year old girl who died during a tonsillectomy procedure after the operating doctor ordered, verified and administered the wrong drug to her (Grennan 1930). Somera was found guilty primarily because she failed to question and uncritically followed the doctor's orders.

In the lower court case that followed, witnesses testified that Dr Favis, the operating doctor, had ordered 10 per cent cocaine and adrenalin (he meant novocaine), had verified the drug when it was handed to him in a syringe, and had administered it to the patient. Additional evidence was given that Dr Bartolome, an assisting doctor, had also handled the syringe, and had 'noticed that the patient became pale and acted as if dizzy' after Dr Favis administered a third injection of the drug (Grennan 1930, p. 326). Despite this evidence, as well as other evidence (notably, that:

- Filipina nurses were formally taught 'to carry out the orders of the doctors for drugs', and 'never question the order of a doctor for drugs except to verify it';
- Dr Favis had operated for tonsillitis only once before;
- the prosecution 'had failed to establish whether the cause of death was due to cocaine poisoning or thymus lymphaticus';
- cocaine 'was and had been used for injection by many doctors';
- 'a doctor learns the actions of drugs by administering them' and that 'the nurse's training and experience are not adequate to this knowledge'.)

Somera was found guilty of the charges brought against her (ibid., pp. 327–328). Dr Favis and Dr Bartolome, however, were both acquitted. On 7 May 1929, the following decision was rendered:

> Wherefore the Court absolves the two said accused, Gregorio Favis and Armando Bartolome, of the crime of which they are accused in this case . . . and declares Lorenza Somera guilty of the crime imputed in the complaint and in conformity with the provisions of Article 568, Section 1, of the Penal Code, without finding any modifying responsibility as none has been shown, condemns her to suffer one year and one day imprisonment, to indemnify the heirs of the deceased Anastacia Clemente in the sum of One Thousand (1,000) Pesos with subsidiary imprisonment in case of insolvency and to suffer further the accessories provided in Article 61 of said Code and to pay one-third of the costs.
> (cited in Grennan 1930, p. 328)

The lower court's decision was appealed against in the Supreme Court on grounds that its findings 'were not supported either by the evidence or by the actual facts of the situation, all of which had not been brought out' (ibid., pp. 329–330). The Supreme Court upheld the findings of the lower court, however, and on 20 December 1929, handed down the following decision:

> Wherefore, finding the decision of the Lower Court to be in accordance with the facts and law, it is confirmed in all respects with costs against the appellant.
> (cited in Grennan 1930, p. 330)

Following widespread lobbying by both local and overseas nursing groups — including the International Council of Nurses, which had been kept fully informed of the case and of the court proceedings — Somera was given a conditional pardon absolving her from her sentence. Although disappointed that she had not been fully pardoned, and despite the fact that she had merely been 'following the rules', Somera accepted the pardon on the condition that she 'should not in the future violate any of the penal laws of the Philippine Islands' (Grennan 1930, p. 330). The Philippine Nurses' Association not only accepted the 'wisdom' and authority of the courts in this case, but also decided they worked to the advantage of nursing. In an article entitled 'The Somera case', Elizabeth Grennan (1930, pp. 332–333), chairperson of a special legislative committee of nurses established to lobby for Somera's pardon, concluded:

> In reviewing this case we are casting no aspersions whatever on the Courts. We believe they were discharging their sworn duty in the application of the law. While we do not know the working of their minds in relation to the case, we would say that if their decisions were influenced by the thought that human life is precious and must be guarded at any cost, and that it can better be guarded by two responsible persons, a doctor and a nurse, rather than by one, a doctor and a less responsible person, we agree with them entirely. We not only agree with them but thank them for these decisions which lift nursing from a subservient place to one of equality in responsibility and dignity with that of the doctor . . . What at times looked like a tragedy has worked together for the good of our profession.

The Somera case was interpreted by legal and nurse commentators at the time (and since) as indicating that a nurse should not follow a doctor's orders if it was 'obvious' that doing so would endanger or cause unnecessary harm to the patient. In other words, although as a general rule nurses had a duty to obey a doctor's instructions, they also had a correlative duty to disobey in instances where the patient's interests and wellbeing were clearly at risk (Sarner 1968, p. 52). As Scheffel (1931, p. 119), author of one of the first definitive American texts on law for nurses, commented:

> [The Somera case] dramatically brings out the legal point that nurses must not carry out a doctor's order if the execution of the order carries with it probabilities of criminal negligence. It is true that under ordinary circumstances professional ethics would decree that doctors' orders be obeyed; but where the safety of the patient becomes endangered in this connection, this narrow application of ethics ceases to be applicable and the legal responsibilities of the nurse must determine her actions. In other words, she should invariably refuse to carry out any order which in her judgment endangers the life of her patient or may be construed as criminal negligence.

Scheffel (ibid.) made the additional important point that

> the Courts are inclined to assume the attitude that if a person holds herself out to the public as a graduate nurse, she is expected to possess a certain

high degree of professional knowledge, and exercise a definite degree of professional skill in the practice of her profession. Whenever she fails to exercise that knowledge and skill to the extent of endangering the life of a patient, then she may be deemed guilty of criminal negligence and suffer prosecution therefore.

It is evident that the Somera case marked the beginning of a change of attitude by the courts. In the past, the nurse had been regarded as having an unequivocal duty to obey a doctor's orders. However, the Somera case decision (and others that followed it) seemed to suggest that, under some circumstances, nurses also had a (qualified) duty to disobey a doctor's orders. For example, in the noted Supreme Court of North Carolina case, *Byrd v Marion General Hospital* (1932), p. 740, Brogden J stated that

nurses, in the discharge of their duties, must obey and diligently execute the orders of the physician or surgeon in charge of the patient, *unless*, of course, such order was so *obviously negligent* as to lead any *reasonable person* to anticipate that substantial injury would result to the patient from the execution of such order or performance of such direction [emphasis added].

To emphasise the point, Brogden J made the extraordinary[5] statement (ibid.):

Certainly, if a physician or surgeon should order a nurse to stick fire to a patient, no nurse would be protected from liability for damages for undertaking to carry out the orders of the physician.

In the English Appeal Court case *Gold v Essex County Council* (1942), p. 313, a similar position regarding the qualified nurse's 'duty to disobey' was expressed. In the conclusion of this case, Goddard LJ stated :

I can conceive that a nurse might be regarded as negligent even though she was carrying out the orders of the doctor. If a doctor in a moment of carelessness, perhaps by the use of a wrong symbol in a prescription, ordered a dose which to an experienced ward sister was obviously incorrect and dangerous, I think it might well be held to be negligence if she administered it without obtaining confirmation from the doctor or higher authority.

Several years later, in the noted Supreme Court of Illinois case, *Darling v Charleston Community Memorial Hospital* (1965) p. 256, it was clarified once again (in exactly the same terms as used by Brogden J in the case of *Byrd v Marion General Hospital* (1932), p. 740) that a nurse had a duty to obey/execute a doctor's order

unless such order is so *obviously* negligent as to lead any reasonable person to anticipate that substantial injury would result to the patient from the execution of such order [emphasis added].

In the New York Court of Appeals case *Toth v Community Hospital at Glen Cove* (1968), p. 374 s 3, the court likewise argued that the nurse had a duty to follow the doctor's orders unless 'the doctor's orders are so clearly contraindicated by normal practice that ordinary prudence requires inquiry into the correctness of the orders'. More recently in another American case, the New York Supreme Court (Appellate Division), citing *Toth v Community Hospital at Glen Cove* (1968), similarly accepted that the hospital or its servants could escape liability when following the explicit orders of the attending physician (*Killeen v Reinhardt* (1979), p. 177). Still more recently, in the American case *Poor Sisters of St Francis v Catron* (1982), p. 308, the Indiana Court of Appeals accepted that

> while in most cases the nursing staff is not negligent in following the orders given by the attending physician, an exception to this rule exists when the nurse or other hospital employees knows the doctor's orders are not in accordance with normal medical practice.

'Not free to disobey'

In theory, the nurse's legally constructed 'duty to disobey' seems relatively straightforward and uncontroversial. In actual practice, however, it has been — and continues to be — extremely difficult for a nurse to question, let alone 'wilfully disobey', a doctor's or indeed a superior's (for example, an employer's or a hospital administrator's) orders. Even when justified in questioning a doctor's/superior's instructions, a nurse can encounter a number of serious problems, including:

- The doctor/superior may simply ignore her requests to have a particular medical/administrative instruction checked or altered.
- The doctor/superior may intimidate the nurse (for example, by using verbal threats, and/or verbal or physical abuse) for 'overstepping her authority' as a subordinate, and/or may 'bully' her to comply with the order in question.
- The nurse may find herself being 'punished' in some way (for example, by being suspended or dismissed from her job) for 'insubordination'.

A more serious problem is that, contrary to legal rhetoric, the law does not recognise either the nurse's ability or authority to exercise professional discretion and/or to evaluate independently a medical judgment, action, or instruction. Although the nurse has a legally recognised duty to refrain from carrying out dubious medical instructions, the reality is, to borrow from Sarner (1968, p. 52), 'she is not in a position to be second-guessing the doctor or substituting her judgment for his'. Nurses who have 'second-guessed' doctors' judgments have risked severe punishment, including dismissal from their jobs and deregistration; raising serious questions about the real intention behind the apparent legal requirement for nurses to question dubious medical orders (an issue which is examined more fully in chapter 7). The task here, meanwhile, is to identify and examine some of the factors which sometimes make it genuinely difficult for nurses to fulfil their duty to disobey a doctor's 'manifestly incorrect' orders.

The problem of doctors ignoring a nurse's expressed concerns

Historically, the role of the nurse has been to 'observe' and 'report', but never to 'diagnose' or 'treat'. If a nurse observes that something is 'wrong', or has concerns about a given medical judgment, decision, or prescription, her duty is clear: she must report her concerns to the prescribing doctor or to a higher authority (for example, to another more senior doctor or a hospital administrator) where the matter can be re-evaluated. As a general rule, the nurse has no legitimated authority to initiate treatment or to alter a doctor's existing orders. She certainly has no authority to countermand a doctor's orders outright — and indeed can be punished for doing so.

Although the nurse has a legal duty to question a doctor's instructions, the problem remains that sometimes a doctor will ignore a nurse's requests for a given medical judgment, instruction or prescription to be checked or altered. The consequences of this are that patient safety is placed at serious risk and/or the legal vulnerability of the questioning nurse is unnecessarily increased. In a 1982 English case, for example, a state enrolled nurse (SEN) repeatedly requested a doctor to double-check a drug order for a narcotic analgesia (papaveretum) which he had prescribed for a 15-month-old boy (*Nursing Times* 1982a). Despite the SEN's queries, the doctor 'insisted the drug dosage was correct'. Unfortunately, the dose was far in excess of what it should have been, and shortly after it had been administered the toddler suffered a respiratory arrest. He remained in a coma for six months and died without recovering consciousness.

A similar case occurred in New Zealand, where a 28-year-old woman died after being given an incorrectly prescribed dose of morphine. The attending 'doctor' (she was in fact only a fifth year medical student) in this case prescribed 50 milligrams instead of the correct dose of 15 milligrams of intramuscular morphine for the patient. The charge nurse of the ward was overheard to challenge the 'doctor's' order repeatedly and 'loudly'. The 'doctor' would not listen, however, and insisted the amount was correct and 'ordered' that it be given (Johnstone 1989, pp. 42–43). The charge nurse acquiesced and administered the drug. The patient died several hours later.

One of the most instructive examples of the kinds of difficulties a nurse can face when trying to get a doctor to check or re-evaluate his instructions, but where the doctor ignores or refuses to respond to the nurse's queries, can be found in the 1987 New Jersey Superior Court (Appellate Division) case *Edwards v Our Lady of Lourdes Hospital* (1987). The case involved a baby boy born prematurely at 27 weeks gestation and weighing only 1130 grams. At the time of delivery, the baby 'had no detectable heart beat and was not breathing' (ibid., p. 243). Upon being resuscitated, he was transferred immediately to the hospital's Neonatal Intensive Care Unit (NICU) for care and treatment. Despite receiving intensive therapy, there were problems with the baby's blood circulation in his lower limbs. In order to try and improve his circulation, the baby had to receive intravenous fluids. Unfortunately, he had difficulty maintaining an intravenous line (it kept blocking or falling out), and the decision was made to perform a 'cut-down' (which is a surgical procedure 'whereby a scalpel is used to make an incision to open the skin and a small catheter is inserted into a vein to provide fluids') (ibid., p. 245). The doctor performing the cut-down, however, negligently inserted the intravenous cannula into an artery, which had the effect of further impeding circulation to the baby's right leg.

At the time of the cut-down, the doctor was assisted by a new graduate nurse who had only recently started work in the NICU. She had never observed a cut-down before. Later the court held that this nurse should have questioned the doctor's choice of location because she was 'in the best position to know about the baby', and 'had a duty to report to her supervisor that a surgical student was going to operate on the prematurely born baby' (ibid., p. 246).

At 11.00 pm the new graduate nurse went off duty and was replaced by the on-coming night nurse for the 11.00 pm — 7.00 am shift. The on-coming night nurse thought that the cut-down 'was in an artery, not a vein'. When she brought this to the attention of the operating doctor, however, he told her quite simply that 'he knew where the cut-down was' and that 'she did not know what she was talking about' (ibid.). During the night shift, the baby's leg became blanched (a sign of poor blood supply), and his overall condition deteriorated. When the nurse attempted to put some intravenous fluid up as instructed, she observed blood pulsating back into the line — a definitive sign of arterial pressure. When she informed the doctor of this, still he took no action. The nurse located the doctor again and pleaded: 'please come back and look at it [the cut-down]'. Again the doctor refused and instructed her to 'hook up the intravenous fluids to the catheter' — which included hyperalimentation fluids (also called total parental nutrition or TPN) (ibid.). The nurse then made several unsuccessful attempts to contact her nursing supervisor. At 5.00 am the doctor ordered the hyperalimentation fluids stopped. The cut-down was not removed, however, and a neutral fluid was allowed to continue being infused. At 7.30 am the baby's condition had deteriorated further. His leg had become gangrenous and it was evident that the gangrene had already spread to the abdominal wall. The right leg had to be 'amputated at the hip level including one-half of the buttocks' (*Edwards v Our Lady of Lourdes Hospital* (1987), p. 246).

It is obvious that had the doctor listened to the nurse in this case, the serious injury that was caused could have been avoided. Furthermore, all the parties involved, including the questioning nurse, could have been spared the trauma of the court action that followed. As a side issue to the one being considered here, the case also illustrates that had the nurse in question had the legitimated authority to initiate action independently, and to countermand the doctor's instructions, she could have simply removed the cut-down and thereby have prevented the baby from suffering the unnecessary harm that he did (see also *Goff v Doctors General Hospital of San Jose* (1958); *Utter v United Hospital Center, Inc.* (1977); *Cignetti v Camel* (1985)).

The abuse and intimidation of questioning nurses by doctors: the Daley case

Another equally serious problem faced by nurses when attempting to question a doctor's judgment or instructions is that the doctor may intimidate the nurse (for example, by verbal threats and/or even by verbal or physical abuse) for 'overstepping her authority' as a subordinate, and/or may 'bully' her to comply with the order in question (see Johnston 1976, p. 26; Stanley 1979; Lowery-Palmer 1982, p. 192). This can happen even when the nurse is fully justified in her actions. A good example of this can be found in the US District Court (E.D. Pennsylvania) case *Daley v St Agnes Hospital, Inc* (1980).

On 10 January 1975, Thomas Daley RN, the Director of Nursing of a small community hospital in Pennsylvania, was abruptly dismissed from his position on the recommendation of medical staff who were 'unhappy' with his persistent demands that nurses be given 'authority to match their responsibilities' (Cleary 1975, p. 43; see also Donnelly et al. 1975). After a motion favouring the dismissal of the director of nursing was passed at a medical staff meeting in mid-December, certain attending physicians and residents began intimidating nurses. Donnelly et al. (1975, p. 36) write:

> Nurses were reported to the appropriate Department Head. Intimidation and threats were tools used by some physicians against nurses at all levels in the organization. One physician threatened to 'fire' a nurse for questioning a medication order. Another physician would not explain his rationale for an unusual medication order. When questioned by the nurse concerning this order, he replied flippantly, 'It's a secret!'.

Before the dismissal of the director of nursing, nurses had complained that

their skills were not being properly utilized — that they were required to follow doctors' orders, whatever misgivings might arise from their own knowledge and training.
(Cleary 1975, p. 43)

Immediately before the dismissal of the director of nursing, there were at least three instances in which nurses at the hospital had 'refused to give drugs prescribed by physicians, on grounds of potential harm to patients' (Cleary 1975, p. 44). The nurse's judgment in each of these cases was fully supported by the pharmacological literature. The incident that ultimately led to the medical staff lobbying for Mr Daley's dismissal involved an intensive care nurse's refusal to administer an incorrect and potentially dangerous drug order to an elderly patient (ibid.). Although the prescribing physician rescinded the order after the attending nurse had advised him by telephone that she had withheld the offending drug, he nevertheless felt it necessary to make a formal complaint about the matter to Mr Daley (*American Journal of Nursing* 1975, p. 384). Mr Daley defended the intensive care nurse's actions, however, and argued in her defence that the nurse had an 'obligation to question treatment when she thinks it is detrimental [to the patient]' (ibid.).

An appeal against the dismissal, informal off-duty protest picketing (dubbed 'a nonstrike for patient care' in the nursing press), and the mass resignation of over 30 nurses (including the director of the hospital's school of nursing, half of the school of nursing's faculty, charge nurses and staff nurses) failed to see Mr Daley reinstated (Cleary 1975; Donnelly et al. 1975).

The incident was to have another cost, however. For the next three years, Mr Daley had no success in securing another position in hospital or nursing administration. Although 'he applied to more than 25 hospitals over a three year period, the only positions he was able to secure [were] teaching positions at several colleges, at a considerably lower salary' (*Daley v St Agnes Hospital, Inc* (1980), p. 1313). Believing he had been discriminated against and 'blacklisted', Mr Daley sued the St Agnes Hospital. Owing to a lack of evidence showing any 'conspiracy', however, the court found in favour of the hospital. Rejecting the 'blacklist' allegation, the US District Court (E.D. Pennsylvania) stated:

Reports of a blacklist must . . . be seen as unsubstantiated rumor, and not as raising a material factual issue . . . While we are sympathetic to Nurse Daley's plight, we are constrained in view of foregoing discussion to grant the defendant's motion for summary judgment.
(*Daley v St Agnes Hospital, Inc* (1980), p. 1316)

This case illustrates the negative attitude that some doctors have in regard to the authority and ability of nurses to exercise professional discretion in clinical matters, and the extraordinary lengths that these doctors are prepared to go to in order to ensure that nurses are 'kept in their proper place' and do not 'usurp' the authority of doctors — even in situations where a patient is at risk of being harmed. Although the behaviour of medical staff in this case might seem extraordinary, as nurses well know it was (and is) not unique. There are other examples in the nursing literature demonstrating nurses' vulnerability to intimidation by doctors. Nurses are not infrequently 'bullied' into submission — making it very difficult for them to uphold even minimum standards of nursing care, placing not only themselves but also their patients at unacceptable risk. Nurses who struggle against medical resistance to nurses exercising their professional discretion in an attempt to uphold patients' interests can meet with a variety of problems, as demonstrated below.

Other problems experienced by questioning nurses

In 1981 a registered nurse working in the casualty department of an English hospital was 'given a rollicking, for having the cheek to call in a consultant without [the attending] doctor's permission' (cited by Fleming 1981, p. 1533). In this incident, a 17-year-old youth had been admitted to a casualty department with a fractured leg and a badly lacerated nose following a motorbike accident. The casualty officer referred the teenager to a plastic surgeon for suturing. The registered nurse was, however, deeply concerned about the patient's poor vital signs (he had an abnormally low blood pressure, his pulse was weak and rapid, and he was experiencing difficulty with breathing), and called both the plastic surgeon and orthopedic surgeon to examine him further. Yet, for some inexplicable reason, neither of the surgeons considered the youth's breathing difficulties as 'their problem' and proceeded to treat only the respective injuries which they specialised in treating. The patient stopped breathing, however, and the attending plastic surgeon was forced to perform an emergency tracheotomy. Curiously, the surgeon took no further action, and it was at this point that the registered nurse called the nearest on-call thoracic surgeon to come and examine the patient. By the time the thoracic surgeon arrived, the patient was moribund, and upon bronchoscopy was found to be bleeding in both lungs. Nothing more could be done for him, and he died. A post-mortem examination revealed that the patient had ruptured his subclavian artery. Although the registered nurse was vindicated for her actions, she was nevertheless chastised for having usurped the authority of the two doctors who first attended the patient.

In another more recent English case, a second year nursing student incurred the wrath of an attending doctor when he (the nursing student) questioned the doctor's actions during a failed medical procedure. The student had protested against the doctor making 'seven attempts to insert an intravenous drip in a baby's arm' (*Nursing Times* 1989f). The *Nursing Times* reports that the student's protests 'were met with anger from the doctor and his tutors later instructed him to write a letter of regret over his actions' (ibid.). The article claimed that nursing students were 'vulnerable to being "blackmailed" into keeping quiet', and that the intimidation of nurses who expose bad practice and poor standards of care 'goes on far more than we as nurses are prepared to acknowledge' (ibid.).

Nurses in Australia have faced similar problems. In one case, for example, a nurse who refused to follow the dubious request of a gynaecologist to obtain a consent to treatment from a non–English speaking and already pre-medicated woman for a surgical procedure (a dilatation and curettage of the uterus) that was about to be performed, was subjected to intense verbal abuse by the operating gynaecologist in question (Johnstone 1989, p. 173). The nurse in this case refused to obtain the consent on grounds that the woman was 'very drowsy' from the effects of her pre-medication and thus was not in a position to give competent consent. The nurse was further concerned that the gynaecologist intended to sterilise the woman despite not having properly discussed the matter of surgical sterilisation with her. On the basis of her professional assessment of the situation, the registered nurse refused to comply with the gynaecologist's order. The gynaecologist would not accept the nurse's assessment, however, and 'became abusive and was overheard to yell at her' (ibid.).

In another little-known unreported Australian industrial relations case, a director of nursing (DON) was dismissed from her position primarily because she refused to 'agree to old customs prevailing, that ultimately proved to be illegal anyhow' (*In re Parkes District Hospital and the New South Wales Nurses' Association* (1979), p. 3). The DON appealed her dismissal on grounds that it was 'unfair'. The conciliation commissioner hearing the case found that

> some people connected with the hospital in one category or another positively set out to have her [the DON] removed, so that the old dust of comfort and mutual convenience could settle.
> (*In re Parkes District Hospital and the New South Wales Nurses' Association* (1979), p. 3)

The commissioner concluded that the (medically dominated) hospital board in question had

> got itself a matron who was too highly skilled and efficient for its old, and I might say sometimes illegal, customs, and so the lazy, comfortable equilibrium that had prevailed for years was disturbed. Thus the tiger snarled.
> (ibid., p. 4)

Another example of what can happen to a 'disobedient' (questioning) nurse can be found in the little known South Australian industrial relations case involving an anaesthetist who, upon becoming frustrated with an inexperienced operating room nurse who 'disobeyed' and 'inappropriately questioned' his instructions, physically assaulted and forcibly removed the nurse from the operating theatre (*In re Tingay and Flinders Medical Centre Incorporated* (1983) and *Flinders Medical Centre Incorporated v Tingay (Appeal) Case* (1984)). The force used by the doctor resulted in the nurse developing minor bruising on her right arm and upper left thigh. The doctor was dismissed by the hospital board, but later he successfully appealed against the dismissal on grounds that it was 'harsh, unjust and unreasonable'. The Industrial Court hearing the appeal accepted that the anaesthetist had the authority to ask the nurse to leave, and although his actions were extreme, they were nevertheless explicable. The court accepted that the doctor had been under stress and that the nurse had clearly 'provoked the incident' by her 'disobedience' (*Flinders Medical Centre Incorporated v Tingay (Appeal) Case* (1984), p. 14). The doctor was reinstated, and later paid $8000 to the nurse in an out-of-court civil damages settlement for the assault (Hunter 1984).

An equally serious case of nurse intimidation can be found in another Australian case involving operating theatre nurses working in a country hospital. The nurses in this case were deeply concerned about the practice of an incompetent anaesthetist at the hospital. In a confidential letter to the writer of 'The nurse and the law' column of the *Australian Nurses' Journal*, a nurse writing on behalf of the nurses involved disclosed that two patients had already died unnecessarily because of the anaesthetist's incompetence, and that there had been 'a lot of near misses'. She further disclosed that most of the operating theatre nurses had refused to work with the anaesthetist concerned but were informed that their actions would

> get them nowhere — other than fired — as both the Nursing Super-
> intendent and Medical Superintendent have spoken to the doctor and
> nothing more can be done.
> (cited in Langslow 1983c, p. 31)

The nurse writing the letter concluded by pleading, 'Please do not mention my name. If I had more experience [authority?] behind me I might be prepared to stand up and be counted' (ibid.). This nurse's plea reflects the feelings and concerns experienced by many nurses in similar situations, and indicates how highly aware nurses are of their precarious position when attempting to address problems involving medical negligence or incompetence. If nurses had more legitimated authority than they have, and if their professional judgment was respected more, there is room to suggest that they could not — and would not — be so easily intimidated.

The punishment for insubordination of 'questioning' nurses

Nurses questioning a doctor's or a superior's orders can face the additional problem of being accused of and/or punished for insubordination, further highlighting the difficulties a nurse can face when attempting to fulfil her duty to disobey an incorrect or negligent order. For example, in a Canadian case (*Re Mount Sinai Hospital and Ontario Nurses' Association* (1978) cited in the introduction to this text, in the section entitled 'The problem of the nursing hierarchy'), nurses questioning a medical directive to admit a patient into a grossly understaffed intensive care unit were later suspended for insubordination. In the unfair dismissal case that followed, the nurses testified that they declined to accept the patient out of fear that to do so would have exposed them 'to potential civil liability and professional discipline' because there were insufficient staff to care for the patient properly, and thus patient safety could not be guaranteed. It was tendered that 'no nurse felt capable of taking responsibility' for the patient in question (Sklar 1979a, pp. 14–15). It will be recalled that the nurses' defence was not accepted. Instead, the Canadian labour arbitration court hearing the case characterised their questioning as 'dangerous' and argued that questions concerning a nurse's 'legal responsibilities' were a matter for the courts — not nurses — to decide (*Re Mount Sinai Hospital and Ontario Nurses' Association* (1978)).

One of the most compelling examples of a nurse being dismissed for insubordination for justly questioning the instructions of a superior (in this case, not a doctor) can be found in the relatively recent Illinois Appellate Court (First District, Fourth Division) case *Free v Holy Cross Hospital* (1987). The case involves a registered nurse by the name of Frances Free who was dismissed from her employing hospital because she refused to evict a bedridden patient on grounds (later rejected by the court) that to evict the patient would have been

> in violation of her ethical duty as a registered nurse not to engage in dishonourable, unethical, or unprofessional conduct of a character likely to harm the public as mandated by the Illinois Nursing Act.
> (*Free v Holy Cross Hospital* (1987), p. 1190)

The patient in question had been arrested for possession of a hand gun and an order had been given for her to be transferred to another hospital. The police officer guarding the patient pointed out, however, that because of certain outstanding matters, the other hospital would probably not accept the patient and it was likely that she would be returned to the Holy Cross Hospital. Nurse Free communicated this information to the hospital's chief of security who responded by telling her that the patient was to be removed from the hospital 'even if removal required forcibly putting the patient in a wheelchair and leaving her in the park' (ibid., p. 1189). Although Free disagreed with removing the patient, she gave the necessary instructions for the patient's transfer to the other hospital.

As part of the process of dealing with this situation, Free contacted her own hospital's vice-president to discuss the matter with him. It is reported that the vice-president 'became agitated, shouted and used profanity in telling Free that it was he who had given the order to remove the patient' (*Free v Holy Cross Hospital* (1987), p. 1189). After this incident, Free contacted the patient's physician who stated that 'he opposed the transfer' and ordered Free 'not to touch the patient but to document his order that the patient should remain at the hospital' (ibid.). After checking the patient and 'calming her down', Free received a telephone call 'ordering her to report to the office of the hospital vice-president'. When she arrived at the vice-president's office Free was advised 'that her conduct was insubordinate and that her employment was immediately terminated' (ibid.).

In a 1981 English case a nurse was similarly suspended for refusing to transfer a patient to another ward. The nurse allegedly refused to cooperate with hospital management to transfer the patient because the patient was 'distressed and crying' and did not want to be moved (*Nursing Times* 1981a). The patient first learned of the management decision to transfer her when she returned from a visit to the X-ray department and found 'her ward was locked, with other patients and staff inside' (ibid.). The *Nursing Times* reports that the move to transfer patients was part of 'the planned rundown' of services and eventual closure of a number of acute beds in London hospitals (ibid.). Although the patient was very distressed by the harsh manner in which the transfer was being organised, and although the nurse was not 'wilfully disobeying' management's instructions, but rather was attempting to protect the patient's interests in this instance, the nurse was nevertheless suspended for insubordination. There is room to speculate here that had a doctor protested the patient's transfer in this case, quite a different outcome would probably have been achieved. It is almost certain that even if management had objected to the doctor's interference, she or he would not have been suspended from her or his position in the way that the nurse was.

The 'illegitimisation' of independent professional nursing judgment

Being threatened, intimidated, verbally and physically abused, deregistered, and the like, for questioning a doctor's dubious orders — while bad enough — are not the only or even the most serious difficulties a nurse can face in the course of her everyday practice. A more serious, although generally unacknowledged problem is that, contrary to legal rhetoric and superficial appearances, nurses simply do not have the legitimated authority to evaluate independently and question a doctor's orders. One legal commentator has even suggested, controversially (and it might be added, naively in so far as it does not reflect the realities of nursing practice), that

> it would be extremely inappropriate and highly unprofessional for a nurse to assume a general attitude of regularly challenging and questioning medical orders.
>
> (*Regan Report on Nursing Law* 1980d)

One of the main reasons why nurses lack the legitimated authority they need in order to challenge a doctor's incorrect or inappropriate orders effectively is that the law does not recognise that nurses are either capable of, need to, or should be permitted to exercise independent (translate as 'medically unauthorised') professional nursing judgments. Furthermore, the law has tended to assume that the nurse has no independent knowledge base informing her practice, and is totally dependent on the medical practitioner for her practice. In reality, this has made it extremely difficult for a nurse to question a doctor's incorrect or inappropriate orders. It is evident that nurses who dare to exercise independent professional nursing judgment — and who dare to evaluate and/or question a doctor's orders on the basis of their own independent professional nursing judgment — run the very real risk of 'trespassing' on medical territory and of being censured accordingly. To add to this difficulty, in the ultimate analysis, doctors retain the prerogative to decide whether to accept or reject a nurse's queries regarding their instructions (while it may be regarded as 'unwise' for doctors to ignore a nurse's queries, it is not generally regarded as being professionally negligent to do so). If doctors do decide to reject a nurse's queries, it can be very difficult for the nurse to take the matter further, as the examples considered above have shown. The nurse certainly has no authority to countermand a doctor's orders, and could be found guilty of professional misconduct and even negligence for doing so — even if her actions are later proven to have been justified. In light of these and other considerations to be discussed below, there is room to suggest that, contrary to medical and legal discourse on the matter, the nurse's apparent legal duty to question a doctor's orders is not a 'duty to question a doctor's orders' at all (or indeed, as it has tended to be characterised, a duty to protect patients against being injured as a result of negligent medical orders being carried out). Rather, it is a duty to 'protect' (read 'be loyal to') the doctor (that is, to 'avoid compounding the physician's original negligence') (*Regan Report on Nursing Law* 1980b) and thereby to minimise the chances of malpractice lawsuits being filed against him or her — or the hospital in which he or she is working (Sarner 1968, pp. 55–56).

The legal reinforcement of nurse incompetency

Traditionally, nurses have been legitimately constrained in exercising independent (medically unauthorised) professional judgment in matters of life and death. The primary legal justification for this has been that if a nurse exercised independent professional judgment (to be distinguished here from dependent or inter-dependent (read 'medically authorised') judgment) with regard to these matters, she would be effectively engaging in the illegal practice of medicine. This is because the medical profession has a legitimated monopoly of professional discretion in life and death matters, which in effect means that it would be a crime for a nurse to exercise independent professional judgment in this area. The position of the courts and jurists on the status of nursing judgments with regards to patient care (and with regards to matters of life and death that arise during the course of caring for patients) is unequivocal, as will now be demonstrated.

In a leading American case *Richardson v Doe* (1964), p. 880, the Supreme Court of Ohio made it clear that

> a nurse, although obviously skilled and well trained, is not in the same category as a physician who is required to exercise his independent judgment on matters which may mean the difference between life and death. A nurse is not authorised to practice medicine . . . Her primary function is to *observe and record* the symptoms and reactions of patients. A nurse is not permitted to exercise judgment in diagnosing or treating any symptoms which the patient develops. Her duty is to *report* them to the physician. Any treatment or medication must be prescribed by a licensed physician . . . A nurse *by the very nature of her occupation is prohibited from exercising an independent judgment in these areas* [emphasis added].

In the New York Court of Appeals case *Toth v Community Hospital at Glen Cove* (1968), p. 374, Keating J asserted a similar view, stating:

> Nurses are not authorised to determine for themselves what is a proper course of medical treatment. They may not invade the area of the physician's competence and authority to overrule his orders.

In 1980, the *Regan Report on Nursing Law* (published in the United States of America) carried an article which also made clear the 'limits' of a nurse's professional judgment. The article warned:

> Interposing one's judgment into the physician–patient relationship in such a way that the nurse substitutes his or her judgment for that of the physician is clearly practising medicine without a license and is a violation of any Nurse Practice Act.
> (*Regan Report on Nursing Law* 1980d)

More recently in the Supreme Court of South Dakota case *Koeniguer v Eckrich* (1988), p. 604, Henderson J stated:

A life is so often in a nurse's hands when the doctor is not in attendance. Nurses are not, however, licensed to practice medicine. They are not the ultimate decision-makers in terms of the patient's care; rather, they are the decision-implementers . . . a nurse should not be required to be a practising physician and make an independent evaluation to then question a doctor's decision.

Henderson J further stated that if nurses were required to make independent evaluations and to question a doctor's decision, it would create 'extreme professional friction, if not pandemonium, in the hospital' (ibid.).

It should perhaps be clarified at this point, that although it has long been recognised that the patient's life and wellbeing often 'hangs upon the thread of the nurse's judgment and an error may mean a fatal delay' (Kyogle 1908), as stated earlier the nurse has only ever been permitted to observe and report, not to diagnose or treat (Lesnik 1953, p. 150). Legal and medical commentators have made it quite clear that the nurse's obligation is only to make competent nursing assessments — *not* to make medical diagnoses or to implement 'medical treatments'[6], even though this may be necessary in order to save a patient's life (Horsley 1979; Gunning 1983). Even when a nurse is aware of the most effective treatment, she or he dare not voice an opinion, since this would be considered an encroachment on the doctor's territory (Keddy et al. 1986). As Gunning (1983, p. 124) explains:

Although nurses are often in the best position to identify needs and recognise change in a patient's condition, they have no authority to institute care or initiate change in the [medically] prescribed care. In many cases, the nurse who makes direct suggestions about patient care is viewed as usurping the authority of the physician.

Furthermore, it is clear that any nurse who initiates 'medically unauthorised' treatment risks being severely punished, regardless of whether it has been to the benefit of the patient. A good example of this can be found in an English case involving an experienced charge nurse who was suspended from duty 'after saving a patient's life by defibrillation' (the application of a controlled electric shock to the heart or chest wall to stop fibrillation of the heart) (*Nursing Times* 1988k). In this instance, the charge nurse was suspended from his position primarily because defibrillation was not considered to be a 'nursing role'. Although he had been trained at another hospital to use the defibrillator, and despite the fact that 'no doctor was near enough to operate resuscitation equipment', the charge nurse was still regarded by his employing hospital as having 'acted outside his role' (ibid.).

Because the patient's life had been saved, however, the nurse was able to successfully appeal his suspension. Although vindicated for his actions, the nurse nevertheless suffered enormous personal hardship (including a decline in his health) as a result of his suspension, and hospital management still believed that an 'investigation was necessary'. Defending the need to investigate the incident further, a hospital spokesperson is quoted as stating: 'We are pleased that in this case the patient lived, but it could easily have been very different' (*Nursing Times*, 1988k).

While it might be objected that this type of situation is rare, anecdotal evidence suggests otherwise. For example, in another English case, a registered nurse was summarily dismissed from her job after it was disclosed she had administered unprescribed Otrivine nasal drops (which, incidentally, can be obtained without a medical prescription outside of the hospital context) to a baby who was experiencing acute breathing difficulties related to nasal congestion (Jones 1990, pp. 93–94). Despite the fact that the nurse's quick actions probably prevented the baby from suffering a respiratory or cardiac arrest, and Otrivine nasal drops were later prescribed by the paediatric house surgeon, the 'validity' of the nurse's actions were nevertheless questioned and censured. After being dismissed from her position,[7] the nurse began a course in social work, funding her studies by 'occasional auxiliary jobs' (ibid., p. 94). In short, the incident ended her nursing career.

A striking example of how unfavourably a nurse's independent professional judgment and action might be viewed (especially if the judgment in question stands to challenge orthodox medical practice) can be found in the widely discussed Supreme Court of Idaho case *Tuma v Board of Nursing of the State of Idaho* (1979). This case concerns a registered nurse by the name of Jolene Tuma who, in her capacity as a clinical teacher of nursing, became involved in the care of a patient with terminal myelogenous leukemia. On admission to hospital, the patient had been informed by her doctor that she was 'dying' and that 'her only hope of survival was chemotherapy'. The patient was apprehensive about having the chemotherapy, however, and had only given her consent to receive it 'because her son wanted her to take it' (ibid.).

Before her admission to hospital on this occasion, the patient had successfully fought her disease for 12 years, and believed her success was due to her eating natural foods, her belief in God, and her 'faithful practice of her religion'. The patient discussed with Tuma her disease and concerns, including the possibility of receiving alternative naturopathic treatments; for example, chaparral and laetrile. The patient is reported to have 'pleaded with Tuma to return that evening to discuss an alternative treatment using natural products with the patient's family' (ibid., p. 712). Tuma agreed to the patient's request, and arranged to return at 8 pm to discuss the matter further with the patient's family.

The patient, meanwhile, asked her family not to inform the doctor because this could cause trouble for Tuma. This request was ignored, however, and the doctor was informed of the nurse's actions by the patient's daughter-in-law. The doctor asked the daughter-in-law to note the nurse's name, but, as the court report states, 'he did nothing to interfere with the scheduled meeting; nor did he take up the matter with the patient' (*Tuma v Board of Nursing of the State of Idaho* (1979), p. 713). The scheduled meeting took place, and Tuma discussed with the patient and her family

> the prescribed treatment, its side effects, and alternatives provided by natural foods and herbs, as well as the fact the patient would have difficulty getting treatment, particularly blood transfusions, if she left the hospital.
> (*Tuma v Board of Nursing of the State of Idaho* (1979), p. 713)

After a brief discussion, the parties present agreed that the patient should continue the medically prescribed chemotherapy. Nevertheless, two weeks later, despite receiving the treatment, the patient died. Shortly after this, the doctor and the hospital reported Tuma to the State Board of Nursing (Creighton 1984b, p. 14). As a result of the complaint, Tuma had her licence suspended for six months on grounds that she had 'interfered with the physician–patient relationship' and thus was guilty of 'professional misconduct'.

Tuma successfully appealed the suspension of her licence in the Supreme Court. It should be noted, however, that Tuma did not win her case on grounds of the validity of the nurse–patient relationship she had had with the deceased, and/or of legitimately meeting her patient's expressed needs and rational wishes within that relationship. Rather, she won her case on a technical point of law pertaining, among other things, to the state nursing board's failure to make explicit just what constituted an 'interference with the physician–patient relationship', and further, that interference with the physican–patient relationship constituted 'unprofessional conduct'. On this point, the court held:

> We find nothing in the statutory definition of 'unprofessional conduct' which can be said to have adequately warned Tuma of the possibility that her license would be suspended if she engaged in conversations with a patient regarding alternative procedures.
> (*Tuma v Board of Nursing of the State of Idaho* (1979), p. 717)

In its conclusion of the case, the court stated:

> Given no written guidelines as to what conduct might possibly result in a suspension of her license for unprofessionalism, Tuma very well may have surmised that she was on thin ice with the particular doctor, or the medical profession in general, in suggesting to a patient alternate procedures for the treatment of cancer. But she could not know, having not ever been forewarned against so doing.
> (ibid., p. 720)

Despite winning her case, and despite the professional support she received from around America, Tuma suffered enormous personal hardship, not least the 'emotional and economic costs of many years of litigation' (King 1985, p. 162). Tuma lost her teaching post, and, owing to the publicity given to her case, she 'felt it unwise' to resume her nursing practice (ibid.). In short, Tuma's career was left in tatters as a result of her fulfilling her duty as a professional nurse, and of caring for her patient in a way that accorded with accepted professional standards of nursing rather than of orthodox medicine.

In another widely discussed American case *Warthen v Toms River Community Memorial Hospital* (heard in the Superior Court of New Jersey, Appellate Division, 1985), a nurse exercising her professional discretion suffered a similar fate. This case involved a registered nurse who was dismissed from her employing hospital of 11 years for refusing conscientiously to dialyse a 70 year old, terminally ill, bilateral amputee patient. The nurse had dialysed the patient in question on two previous occasions. In both instances, however, dialysis had to be ceased because the patient suffered severe internal bleeding and cardiac arrest. It was after the patient's second cardiac arrest that Warthen informed her superiors that she was 'professionally and morally opposed' to performing another dialysis procedure on the patient primarily because he was 'terminally ill', and the procedure was causing him 'additional complications' (ibid., p. 240). After speaking with the patient's doctor and unsuccessfully discussing the possibility of withdrawing the treatment, Warthen asked not to be assigned to care for the patient again. Although Warthen was initially granted her request, she was later assigned the patient a third time. When Warthen refused to accept this third assignment, her superiors dismissed her. Warthen later appealed her dismissal in the Supreme Court, but was unsuccessful. In making its decision against Warthen, the court made clear its position on five key points, which, for the purposes of this discussion, are summarised below:

1. Patients must be cared for in hospitals and patients must be treated basically by doctors and *doctor's orders must be carried out* [emphasis added].

2. In the absence of an employment contract, employers or employees have been free to terminate the employment relationship with or without cause.

3. An employee should not have the right to prevent his or her employer from pursuing its business because the employee perceives that a particular business decision violates the employee's personal morals, as distinguished from the recognised code of ethics of the employee's profession[8].

4. It would be a virtual impossibility to administer a hospital if each nurse or member of the administration staff refused to carry out his or her duties based upon a personal private belief concerning the right to live.

5. The position asserted by the plaintiff serves only the individual and the nurses' [sic] profession while leaving the public to wonder when and whether they will receive nursing care.

(*Warthen v Toms River Community Memorial Hospital* (1985), pp. 231, 233–234)

Both the Tuma case and the Warthen case highlight at least three important points:

■ Regardless of a patient's interests or expressed wishes — legally a nurse is primarily regarded as a 'subordinate', not a professional, whose primary obligation is to carry out the orders of the doctor (and/or the employer) not the requests of the patient (a point that had already been made abundantly clear in an earlier Supreme Court of Pennsylvania case *Yorston v Pennell* (1959)).

■ Despite the fact that nurses have enormous responsibility when caring for patients, they are not generally permitted to play an active role in decision-making about the patient's care and treatment.

■ When a nurse exercises her own independent professional judgment and/or acts in a professionally independent way, this can be construed as 'interfering with the physician–patient relationship', which in turn can be interpreted as 'professional misconduct'[9]. In other words: 'a nurse who thinks, is a nurse who misbehaves'; more accurately, 'a nurse who thinks, is a nurse who threatens the patriarchal political order of the hospital', and must be controlled.

An effective way of controlling the 'deviant' nurse (and anyone who may follow her example) is to strip her of her legal right to practice — the ultimate sanction for being 'disloyal' to medical practitioners (that is, failing to uphold them loyally, faithfully and selflessly).

Detecting medical errors — a matter of professional nursing judgment or mere 'ordinary prudence'?

The question which arises at this point is: if nurses are not legally permitted to exercise independent professional (knowledge-based) judgments or to make independent evaluations, how then can they ascertain whether or not a medical order is 'incorrect'? Furthermore, how are nurses to know if and when they should question or refuse to carry out a doctor's orders they suspect as being dubious?

In regard to detecting a medical error, the short answer is that the courts appear to regard negligent or incorrect medical orders as being, by nature, 'obvious' (like a 'fire on a hill') and therefore as requiring only 'ordinary observation' or 'careful attention' — not professional judgment — on the part of the nurse in order to be detected (see, for example, *Byrd v Marion General Hospital* (1932); *Logan v Waitaki Hospital Board* [1935]; *Norton v Argonaut Insurance Company* (1962); *Darling v Charleston Community Memorial Hospital* (1965); *Toth v Community Hospital at Glen Cove* (1968); *Utter v United Hospital Center* (1977); *Poor Sisters of St Francis v Catron* (1982)). If her 'ordinary observation' fails her, then the nurse is expected to use her 'womanly intuition' and to 'just know' that a medical order is 'wrong' (see, for example, *Norton v Argonaut Insurance Company* (1962), p. 255). With regards to ascertaining whether or not a doctor's orders should be questioned, again the position of the courts seems to be that this does not require any 'special skill' or professional judgment on the part of the nurse. At best it requires only 'ordinary prudence', or, failing this, 'womanly intuition'.

As a general rule, nurses are certainly not expected to inspect or critique medical orders actively. Rather, the expectation is that if, in the course of her 'ordinary' observations, a nurse comes to 'suspect' that an order is wrong, her duty is not to countermand it (this is not her role), but rather to bring it to the attention of a 'higher authority' so that the order can be 'properly evaluated.' The *Regan Report on Nursing Law* (1980d) instructs, for example, that 'when it appears to a nurse that an error has been made' (note, not 'when a nurse *judges* that an error has been made'), the nurse 'MUST DELAY EXECUTING THE RELATED MEDICAL ORDER', and

> must immediately institute a process designed to correct or confirm the order. Nurses should not be expected to improvise in this respect . . . The concerned nurse who finds cause to delay executing a medical order should dutifully chart the steps taken to bring that nurse's observations and reservations about executing the medical order to *those in a position to evaluate the order*. Once charted and once the order has been *properly* confirmed, corrected or modified, as the case may be, the nurse should execute the medical order *without doubt or hesitation about patient safety or the nurse's own liability* [emphasis added].
> (*Regan Report on Nursing Law* 1980d, p. 1)

Although this was written over a decade ago, and within an American context, it is neither culturally unique nor out of date. For example, in 1989, the Department of Health in New South Wales widely circulated a code of 'ethics' (it was in fact a code of etiquette, not ethics) which the Minister for Health had approved for all staff working in the New South Wales public health care system. Under a clause entitled 'Lawful orders', the code prescribes:

> Officers and employees shall not wilfully disobey or wilfully disregard any lawful order given by any person having the authority to make or give the order.

Officers and employees who dispute the propriety of any such order may appeal to the Department Head or Chief Executive Officer against being required to carry out the order, but shall, as far as possible, comply with the order until the Department Head or Chief Executive Officer determines the appeal.
(Department of Health, New South Wales 1989, p. 2)

The code has legal force, and in its introduction employees are warned that 'any departure from any of the provisions of this Code may be grounds for disciplinary action' (ibid., p. 1). Since the majority of staff working in the New South Wales public health care system are nurses, it is obvious that the code has major ramifications for the nursing profession. For instance, given that nurses are 'employees', and that doctors and hospital administrators are 'person[s] having the authority to make or give orders', the above statement readily translates into the following prescription:

[Nurses] shall not *wilfully disobey* or wilfully disregard any lawful order given by [a doctor or hospital administrator].
   [Nurses] who dispute the propriety of any such order may appeal to the [doctor] or [hospital administrator] against being required to carry out the order, but shall, as far as possible, comply with the order until the [doctor] or [hospital administrator] determines the appeal.
(adapted from Department of Health, New South Wales 1989, p. 2)

The Department of Health, New South Wales *Code of Conduct and Ethics* (1989) has not been widely discussed by the broader nursing profession in Australia, and few nurses outside New South Wales know of its existence. At the time of writing this book, it remains in force and, to the best of my knowledge, has sparked little professional debate on its ramifications for nurses and their ability to deliver safe, competent and responsible nursing care.

CONCLUSION

In the ultimate analysis, the legal position of the nurse appears to have improved very little over the past 130 years. Despite 'progressive' social and law reforms, the nurse continues to be legitimately 'controlled at every point of her work' by her traditional superiors/masters (notably, doctors and hospital administrators) and thus is still, in essence, a subordinate/servant — in practice and in law. The nurse lacks the legitimated authority to match her responsibilities, and is still not legally permitted to exercise bona fide independent (medically unauthorised) professional nursing judgments. The law continues to promote a false and misleading view of the nurse being wholly dependent on the doctor for her practice, and as being the doctor's 'loyal servant' to whom a primary duty of obedience is owed. The law also continues to reinforce the view that a 'disobedient' (read 'independently questioning') nurse is 'dangerous' (translate as 'a threat to the political order of the hospital') and hence needs to be controlled — notably by medical practitioners and/or hospital administrators. Yet, in what appears to be a contradictory position, nurses are also expected to fulfil a 'duty to disobey' and to question 'manifestly incorrect' medical orders. In reality, however, it is very difficult for nurses to fulfil this supposed duty and to question authoritatively a doctor's incorrect orders. This difficulty is exacerbated by the fact that a court may not be sympathetic to a nurse's claim that her failure to question an incorrect medical order was largely due to her being intimidated by a superior to comply with the instructions given at the time — that is, she was acting under duress. In *Czubinsky v Doctors Hospital* (1983), for example, the court did not accept a nurse's defence that she had left an operating room at a crucial time because she was 'being yelled at' by a surgeon to come next door to assist in another operating room (see also *Lunsford v Board of Nurse Examiners* (1983); *Floyd v Willacy County Hospital District* (1986)). Even more disturbing, however, is that despite apparent improvements in the social and legal position of women generally, nurses as women remain relatively powerless to change the status quo.

For all of this, many nurses still believe that the legal status of the nurse is improving, and that the legal barriers to autonomous nursing practice are gradually being broken down, giving nurses unprecedented freedom 'to nurse'. It remains an open question, however, whether the legal status of the nurse has really improved, or whether nurses are merely under an illusion that it has done so. This question will be addressed in chapter 7.

ENDNOTES

1 Note: 'master/servant' is still used as a subject category in law reports and legal reference texts.

2 Hospitals could claim 'charitable immunity' from liability on grounds that it was in the 'common good' to keep hospitals operating, and that this was more important than compensating the injuries of one patient (Sarner 1968, p. 65).

3 The failure to call the nurses as witnesses in this case and the failure to hold them liable for their own negligent actions is perhaps not surprising given the status of women during that period. It is worth noting here that women at that time were generally thought to be 'less capable' of criminal behaviour because of their 'weaker intellect, lack of physical strength, conventionality, and passive personalities' (Helfield 1990, p. 56). As well as this, 'crimes other than murder or high treason committed by a woman in the presence of her husband were presumed to have been committed under coercion and the woman was thus guiltless' (Strachey 1978, p. 15, s 4). This legal view did not change until as late

as 1925, when the defence of marital coercion was repealed (Heidensohn 1985, pp. 31–32).

It is quite possible that similar reasoning was used in the case of negligent nurses. For example, it is plausible that the courts regarded nurses as being 'less capable' of negligent behaviour because of their apparent 'weaker intellect, lack of physical strength, conventionality, and passive personalities'. The courts certainly tended to regard nurses as being 'guiltless' in the case of negligence when obeying a doctor's orders; the presumption being that the nurse was in reality a 'controlled servant' working as directed (read 'coerced') by a superior (for example, a hospital administrator or doctor) and therefore could not justly be held responsible for her actions since 'they were not her own' so to speak. This position changed, however, after the 1929 Somera case (discussed in this chapter) which, coincidentally, occurred in the same year as *Edwards v Attorney-General for Canada* which, as mentioned earlier (see under the section entitled 'The failure of law in the realm of women's lived experiences' in chapter 2), saw 60 years of legal precedents overturned, and women given recognition as 'persons' in the eyes of the law.

4 As a point of interest, arguments are still advanced in some nursing circles that nurses 'don't want professional autonomy since this would mean they would be held independently accountable for their own actions' — the underlying assumption being that submission brings protection, whereas autonomy and the 'dissentience' it imports brings vulnerability. What exponents of this view fail to understand, however, is that the nurse is — and has always been — vulnerable to being held responsible for her own actions whether she 'desires' to be or not. The only way for the nurse to avoid this responsibility is to cease practising as a nurse.

5 Brogden's extraordinary statement in this instance seems to indicate that he did not really view nurses as having the ability (or duty) to make informed clinical judgments or to exercise the fine discretion that is often required in order to determine what is (sometimes a very fine line between) a correct and incorrect medical directive. Indeed, his statement seems to suggest that nurses should as a general rule follow a doctor's orders unless they are of a nature that any 'idiot' (including a 'common woman') would know not to do (for example, 'stick fire to a patient').

6 It is not always clear why a treatment (for example, cardiopulmonary resuscitation) is regarded as being exclusively 'medical' when entities other than doctors (for example, nurses, ambulance drivers and police) are capable of performing it competently.

7 Her dismissal was also partially based on another disclosure that she had, on the instruction of a doctor, administered intravenous additives without having a special certificate authorising her to do so.

8 Warthen's actions were fully supported by the American Nurses' Association's *Code for nurses*. The court rejected the code, however, on grounds that it was not an 'authoritative statement of public policy' (see also chapter 9 of this text).

9   This contrasts dramatically with the legitimated position of the doctor. For instance, when a doctor exercises his independent professional judgment and/or acts in a professionally independent way, this is construed as 'natural' and 'normal'. Even if the doctor's actions harmfully interfere with the nurse–patient relationship or the nurse's ability to practise her profession in a safe, competent and ethical way, this can be construed as 'standard medical practice' (see, for example, Johnstone 1989, pp. 266–269).

CHAPTER SEVEN

The Improved Legal Status of the Nurse — Illusion or Reality?

INTRODUCTION

HISTORICALLY, THE LAW HAS tended to view nurses not as autonomous professionals who are capable of exercising independent (translate as 'medically unauthorised') professional judgments about patient care, but as dependent 'servants' whose work is and ought to be 'controlled at every point' — notably by doctors and hospital administrators.[1] The law has also tended to reinforce the false and misleading view that nurses and nursing practice are wholly dependent on the medical profession, and more specifically, on 'supervising' doctors and/or the orders they give to direct patient care during their absence (Ashley 1975c, p. 1466). Despite the reality that nurses can and do function quite independently of doctors, and despite the reality that the majority of nursing functions neither require — nor are performed under — the 'supervision' of (absent) medical practitioners, nurses have found it extremely difficult to overcome the legal barriers that have historically denied them the legitimated freedom 'to nurse' and the legitimated authority they need in order to practice nursing in a safe, effective and competent manner (see Ashley 1975a, 1975c, 1980; Campazzi 1980, p. 18; Gunning 1983, pp. 120–121; Hicks 1985, p. 48; Murphy 1987a). Furthermore, although it is really the doctor who has been (and is) in a 'service role' to the nurse (Scutt 1990, p. 128), the law has tended to view — and continues to view — the nurse's function as being primarily to serve doctors and to loyally carry out their orders in accordance with the traditional sexual politics of the workplace.

Many nurse and legal commentators argue, however, that the legal status of the nurse has improved, and that over the past few decades the law has come to recognise nurses as having an 'autonomous independent function' to that of the doctor (see, for example, Bullough 1975; *Regan Report on*

Nursing Law 1980e, 1981a; Hirsh 1982; Murchison et al. 1982, pp. 1–2; Creighton 1986; Northrop and Kelly 1987; Fiesta 1988, p. 27; Guido 1988; Murphy 1990a, p. 34). Evidence of this is said to be found in legal trends in common law countries around the world which, among other things, are seeing:

- nurses being held independently responsible for failing to identify and report a doctor's negligent actions to a higher authority;
- nurses being held independently liable for their own negligent actions;
- the development of expanded role/practice laws;
- nursing judgments being identified and defined in nurse practice/registration Acts;
- 'higher' (meaning 'medical') standards of care being applied in malpractice suits involving nurses and nursing practice;
- increased recognition being given to the existence of the nurse–patient relationship.

(Bullough 1975; Creighton 1986, 1986; Campazzi 1980; *Regan Report on Nursing Law* 1980b, 1980e, 1980f, 1989; Hirsh 1982, p. 38; Murchison et al. 1982; Kiefer 1983; Regan 1983a; Dimond 1987; Murphy 1987a, 1987b, 1990a, 1990b; Northrop 1987, 1989b; Northrop and Kelly 1987; Fiesta 1988; Guido 1988; Birkholz 1989; King and Sagan 1989; Lyon 1990; *Nursing Times* 1990k). As one legal commentator puts it 'they [the courts] no longer consider nurses mere "bed pan carriers"' (Hirsh 1982, p. 37). Another legal commentator observes:

> Today nurses are recognised by the Courts from coast to coast as professionals who have the legal right and the intellectual capacity to make assessments and make judgments based on such assessments.
> (*Regan Report on Nursing Law* 1980e)

Superficially, the legal status of the nurse appears to have improved significantly. However, upon a closer examination of the realities of nursing practice, and of nursing's relationship to and experience of the law, an entirely different picture emerges. For instance, what looks like an improvement in the legal status of the nurse turns out not to be an improvement at all, but rather a disguised restructuring and reinforcement of the nurse's long-standing subordinate and subservient relationship to the medical practitioner and, not least, to the state. Furthermore, contrary to popular commentary, it is evident that if the nurse's legal position has changed, it has been more in terms of liability rather than of power and authority. In this chapter, attention will be given to answering the troubling question of whether the legal status of the nurse really has improved, or whether nursing and legal commentators are merely under the illusion that it has improved.

Increased nurse liability for failing to question a doctor's negligent orders

Nursing and legal commentators have noted that over the past two or three decades, nurses have been increasingly held negligent for failing to question or 'dutifully disobey' a doctor's 'obvious and manifestly incorrect' orders (Stanley 1979; *Regan Report on Nursing Law* 1981b; Hirsh 1982; Regan 1983a; Creighton 1984a; Dimond 1987; Fiesta 1988; Murphy 1990a). Some have interpreted this trend in litigation against nurses as merely being 'part of the "coming of age" ritual in professional nursing' and as indicating that the law is 'at last' recognising the professional autonomy of the nurse (*Regan Report on Nursing Law* 1981b). This interpretation is, however, seriously problematic on at least three accounts:

1. It overlooks the fact that, despite nurses' increased liability, there has not been a commensurate increase in their legitimated authority as autonomous professionals.
2. It fails to take into account a number of other plausible reasons explaining the rise in litigation against nurses.
3. The rhetoric of improved legal status simply does not reflect the realities of contemporary nursing practice — including nurses' continued lack of sovereignty in their own realm of practice.

In examining the issue of nurses being held independently liable for failing to question a doctor's negligent orders, two important points should be noted:

1. Generally speaking, the legal demand for nurses to question a doctor's 'obviously negligent' orders has tended to be characterised not as the duty of a 'competent and judicially minded professional', but as the duty of a 'loyal and trusted servant' vis-à-vis her or his duty to disobey any instruction that, if carried out, may result in tarnishing the 'master's' (the doctor's or hospital administrator's) reputation, or worse, may result in the master's negligence being compounded (*Regan Report on Nursing Law* 1980d).
2. In the many instances in which nurses have been found negligent for failing to question a doctor's orders, their negligence has been not that they failed to exercise professional discretion or failed to take independent action, but that they failed either to 'contact' the prescribing doctor concerned, or, equally serious, they failed to go to a higher medical or administrative authority in order to report their observations and/or to have the dubious order in question 'properly evaluated', and, if necessary, altered.

In the following American cases: *Goff v Doctors General Hospital* (1958), *Norton v Argonaut Insurance Company* (1962), *Richardson v Doe* (1964), *Darling v Charleston Community Memorial Hospital* (1965), *Utter v United Hospital Center* (1977), *Kolakowski v Voris* (1979), *Vassey v Burch* (1980), *Sanchez v Bay General Hospital* (1981), *Poor Sisters of St Francis v Catron* (1982), *Haney v Alexander* (1984), *Sheppard v Kimbrough* (1984), *Cedars of Lebanon Hospital v Silva* (1985), *Edwards v Our Lady of Lourdes Hospital* (1987), *Koeniguer v Eckrich* (1988), *Phillips v Eastern Maine Medical Center* (1989), for example, the language used to describe the nurse's professional duties, and more specifically the duties that the defendant nurses in these cases had been negligent in performing, typically included terms which have historically been used to describe the traditional and subservient role/function of the nurse. These terms include: 'to watch', 'to report', 'to observe', 'to monitor', 'to document', 'to bring to the attention of', 'to obtain adequate consultation from [the doctor]', 'to inform', 'to question', 'to call', 'to advise authority of', 'to follow hospital policy', 'to go to another authority', 'to recognise the urgency of a problem' and 'to delay'. A close examination of the above and other reported legal cases involving nurses reveals that rarely, if ever, has it been suggested that a nurse should have used her 'best judgment' and 'whatever superior knowledge, skill and intelligence [she] has' (adapted from *Toth v Community Hospital at Glen Cove* (1968), p. 372), that she should have 'taken action', or that she should have directly countermanded an incorrect medical order or decision. These more 'proactive' responses have tended to be used to describe and refer to the duties of doctors, not nurses (see, for example, *Toth v Community Hospital at Glen Cove* (1968), p. 372; *Killeen v Reinhardt* (1979), p. 177; *Edwards v Our Lady of Lourdes Hospital* (1987), p. 246). Where 'best judgment' requirements have been cited (see, for example, *Vassey v Burch* (1980)), it has been in regard to the need to judge correctly when to contact the doctor. Examples of the tendency to regard nurses as having only 'passive' duties can be found in the similar American cases of *Darling v Charleston Community Memorial Hospital* (1965) and *Utter v United Hospital Center, Inc* (1977).

The first of these cases involves an 18-year-old who broke his leg while playing football. Upon admission to hospital, his fracture was manipulated into alignment and a plaster cast was applied. Shortly after the plaster had been applied, however, the patient experienced 'great pain and his toes, which protruded from the cast, became swollen and dark in color. They eventually became cold and insensitive' (*Darling v Charleston Community Memorial Hospital* (1965), p. 255). A day later, his attending doctor put a 'notch' in the plaster cast around the toes, and on the afternoon of the following day, the doctor cut the cast 'approximately three inches up from the foot'. The next day (three days after the cast had been applied), the doctor cut the plaster cast on both sides. It is reported that upon cutting the plaster

blood and other seepage were observed by the nurses and others, and there was a stench in the room, which one witness said was the worst he had smelled since World War II.
(*Darling v Charleston Community Memorial Hospital* (1965), p. 255)

Eleven days later, the patient was transferred to another hospital for specialist treatment. An examination of his leg found 'a considerable amount of dead tissue' caused by constriction of the blood supply to the leg. Despite attempts to save the leg, it eventually had to be amputated 20 centimetres below the knee. In the supreme court case that followed, it was contended that

it was the duty of the nurses to watch the protruding toes constantly for changes in color, temperature and movement, and to check circulation every ten to twenty minutes . . . and that either the nurses were derelict in failing to report developments in the case to the hospital administrator, he was derelict in failing to report development in the case to the medical staff, or the staff was negligent in failing to take action.
(ibid., pp. 256, 258)

In reaching its decision, the Supreme Court of Illinois accepted that the nurses had not 'tested for circulation in the leg as frequently as necessary' and that they had failed to promptly recognise the 'conditions that signalled a dangerous impairment of circulation in the plaintiff's leg' (ibid., p. 258). The Supreme Court held that the jury could reasonably conclude that when the patient's condition obviously worsened,

it became the nurse's duty to *inform the attending physician*, and if he failed to act, *to advise the hospital authorities so that appropriate action might be taken* [emphasis added].
(ibid.)

Significantly, at no time did the Supreme Court consider or suggest that the nurses should have acted independently when the doctor failed to do what was necessary, and just split or cut the plaster cast themselves to relieve the constriction that it was obviously causing. In this case, the nurses' negligence was found not in their failure to split the plaster, but in their failure to 'inform the attending physician', and in their failure 'to advise hospital authorities so that appropriate action might be taken'. Plainly, there is no hint of a suggestion here that the nurses were either capable of taking — or should have taken — the 'appropriate action' themselves.

In the second case, *Utter v United Hospital Center, Inc* (1977), a similar situation occurred. This case involved a man who suffered a comminuted compound fracture of the right wrist after falling from a ladder during the course of his work. On admission to hospital, his fracture was treated, and a plaster cast 'extending from above the elbow to below the knuckles of the right hand was applied'. Forty-eight hours after the plaster cast was applied, however, the patient's condition deteriorated. Records reveal that the patient's injured arm became

> swollen, black, very edematous [sic] and that there was a foul-smelling drainage emitting therefrom; that he maintained a high temperature and was sometimes delerious.
>
> (*Utter v United Hospital Center, Inc* (1977), p. 215)

After being transferred to another hospital to receive hyperbaric oxygen treatment for gangrene, the patient had his right arm amputated at the shoulder joint.

In the case that followed, the Supreme Court of Appeals of West Virginia accepted that the nurses had a duty to 'observe the condition of the ill and infirm in their care' and to take 'positive action' if a patient showed signs of worsening (ibid., p. 216). The notion of 'positive action' was, in this instance, clarified to mean that in the event of an attending doctor failing to take action, the nurse 'shall call this to the attention of the Departmental Chairman' (ibid.). As in the case of *Darling v Charleston Community Memorial Hospital* (1965), at no time was it suggested that the nurses should have acted independently and just split the plaster cast, thereby relieving the constriction to the blood supply of the arm it was obviously causing.

Once again, in a more recent case, *Edwards v Our Lady of Lourdes Hospital* (1987) (discussed in chapter 6 in the section entitled 'The abuse and intimidation of questioning nurses by doctors: the Daley case'), there was no suggestion that the nurses involved should have acted independently when the doctor failed to take the appropriate course of action. It will be recalled that although the night-shift nurse had been concerned for a number of hours that the doctor had incorrectly placed the intravenous catheter in an artery instead of a vein, there was no suggestion that she should have simply removed the offending catheter regardless of the doctor's opinion. Indeed, the nurse in this case was exonerated because she did all that was expected of her: she documented her observations, she contacted the attending doctor, and when the doctor failed to act, she contacted a 'higher authority', namely, her nursing supervisor who in turn was found negligent for failing to go to a 'higher authority' — *another doctor* (ibid., p. 246; see also Murphy 1990a, p. 35).

In yet another instance, in the relatively recent South Dakota Supreme Court case *Koeniguer v Eckrich* (1988) (cited near the end of chapter 6), there was no suggestion that the nurses involved should have taken independent action. The expectation was clearly that the nurses concerned should have gone to a 'higher authority', and were negligent in not doing so. Although the court accepted that nurses have a duty to monitor and document a patient's vital signs, it nevertheless concluded, as quoted earlier, that a nurse 'should not be required to be a practising physician and make an independent evaluation to then question a doctor's decision' (ibid., p. 604).

In light of these and other reported legal cases, the impression which emerges — to borrow from *Darling v Charleston Community Memorial Hospital* (1965), p. 257 — is that as a general rule nurses are 'not expected to act on their *own* responsibility [emphasis added]'. Rather, they must defer to a 'higher authority' so that a 'proper' evaluation of the medical order in question can be made. Given this — while it is true that nurses can no longer assume 'that their practice is protected by physicians and hospitals' (King and Sagan 1989, p. 59), that they must question dubious medical orders, and that they are being increasingly 'named as defendants in lawsuits by patients who claim their injuries are a result of negligent medical treatment' (Kiefer 1983, p. 562) — it would be a serious mistake to conclude on the basis of these trends that the law is increasingly recognising the professional autonomy of the nurse, or, indeed, that the nurse is now seen in law as being 'more professional' (ibid., p. 563). There are at least two reasons for this:

1. Contrary to popular nursing thought, it is evident that it is not independent judgment which the courts are requiring nurses to exercise. Rather, it is dependent judgment which they are requiring. Thus, while it looks as if the law is giving increased recognition to the nurse as an autonomous and independently practising professional, it can be seen that this is not the case at all. Instead, the law is merely reinforcing the nurse's historical subordinate and subservient relationship to — and dependency on — the medical practitioner.

2. Nurses who dare to exercise independent (medically unauthorised) professional judgment still risk being charged with engaging in the illegal practice of medicine (ibid., p. 562; see also *Sermchief v Gonzales* (1983)). Furthermore, it remains the prerogative (indeed, it is commonly regarded as being 'standard medical practice'[2]) of the medical practitioner to decide whether or not to 'authorise' a nurse to use her own 'best judgment' (as epitomised by the universal *pro re nata* (meaning 'as needed' or 'as required') or 'prn' order). This was clarified in the Californian Court of Appeals (Second District, Division 4) case *Fraijo v Hartland Hospital* (1979), p. 246:

   Standard medical practice permits physicians to confer upon nurses in certain medical situations the exercise of independent judgment.

Another reason why it is fallacious to conclude (on the basis of litigation trends against nurses) that the legal status of the nurse is improving, is that there are other plausible explanations as to why nurses are increasingly becoming the targets of lawsuits for negligence. For example, it is apparent that doctors and hospitals are now less willing to accept either the financial or the professional burden that can and does come with being vicariously liable for the negligent actions of their employees (Campazzi 1980, p. 17; Kiefer 1983, pp. 563–564). Furthermore, now that nurses have improved earnings, and now that many are covered by insurance schemes, suing the nurse for damages is a viable option. In the past, one reason why nurses were not often sued for negligence was because it was thought that, owing to their relative lack of earnings, plaintiffs would probably be unsuccessful in obtaining adequate, if any, compensation. If a nurse's negligent actions resulted in injury, usually it was either the hospital or the patient's doctor who was sued for damages. This was not only because, under the doctrine of *respondeat superior*, the hospital or the doctor was vicariously liable for the nurse's actions, but because they were usually in a better financial position than the nurse to compensate an injured party. In short, suing the hospital or the doctor ensured that plaintiffs were supplied 'with a defendant with money in his pocket' (O'Sullivan 1983, p. 110). Today, although nurses remain relatively poorly paid, they are nevertheless in a better financial position than their predecessors; and thus, as argued above, suing a nurse is now a viable option.

A more controversial reason why nurses are increasingly becoming the targets of lawsuits for negligence, is that they are being used more and more as scapegoats for the negligent or unprofessional actions of others (see, for example, Cushing 1982; *Poor Sisters of St Francis v Catron* (1982); *Herman v Milwaukee Children's Hospital* (1984); *Cedars of Lebanon Hospital v Silva* (1985); Murphy 1987a, p. 15; *In re Nurses Registration Act 1953 and In re Heathcote and Nurses Registration Board* (1991)). In the *Somera Case* (1929) (cited in chapter 6), for example, it will be recalled that a registered nurse was found guilty of manslaughter, fined, sentenced to serve one year in prison, and ordered to pay one-third of the court costs in connection with the death of a tonsillectomy patient. The two doctors involved in that case were, however, fully acquitted of the charges brought against them, despite the fact that their actions contributed to a greater extent to the patient's death. Accepting the details of the case, there remains room to question why Lorenza Somera was found guilty of manslaughter, whereas the two operating doctors were acquitted. Why was Lorenza Somera left to carry a disproportionate burden of punishment for her actions in this case? While definitive answers to these questions may never be found, there is nevertheless room to speculate that Somera was made a scapegoat. In this instance, her 'expendable' interests were sacrificed for the more powerful and competing interests of the two doctors, the hospital, and possibly the state.

More recently, in an unreported Missouri case, several operating room nurses were found liable for a surgeon's professional negligence during an operation on a woman to remove a dead fetus. During the procedure, the surgeon mistakenly removed nearly 6 metres of small intestine through a perforation in the patient's uterus (Cushing 1982, p. 992; Murphy 1987a,

p. 15). It appears that the surgeon mistook the small bowel for umbilical cord. Outlining the details of the case, Cushing (1982, p. 992) explains:

> The nurses testified that initially they thought it was umbilical cord; they did not recognize it as small bowel because it was stripped from the mesentery. Then, as the substance continued to be removed, one of the nurses suggested that the material might be small bowel. When it became obvious that it was, the operation was stopped and the woman was prepared for emergency surgery by another surgeon. By this time, damage to the small bowel was beyond repair and only seven inches [18 centimetres] of small bowel remained.
>

In the unreported court case that followed, the patient's attorney successfully argued that the nurses 'should have intervened and stopped the surgeon before extensive damage had been done' (ibid.). Despite the fact that the consulting surgeon had 'more training and experience than any of the nurses', and despite the fact that the doctor had been the one who had actually harmed the woman being operated on, the nurses were found negligent (ibid.). The finding was apparently based on the testimonies of expert witnesses for the plaintiff.

In another more recent American case (*Cedars of Lebanon Hospital v Silva* heard in the District Court of Appeals of Florida, 1985), operating room nurses were again found liable for what was essentially a doctor's negligence. The case involved a patient who experienced a cardiac arrest and later died after being incorrectly intubated by the attending anaesthesiologist (called 'anaesthetist' in Australia). Qualified experts testified that the anaesthesiologist 'had improperly placed' the endotracheal tube in the patient's oesophagus, or that 'the tube had slipped' depriving the patient of oxygen, and, as a result, the patient suffered a cardiac arrest. Despite evidence that the operating surgeon 'panicked' and left the operating room, and although the assistant surgeon and anaesthesiologist remained in the operating room, the nurses present were found negligent for having 'failed to detect [the patient's] deteriorating condition and obtain expert assistance in resuscitating [the patient]' (ibid., pp. 705–706, s 8). The nurses were also found negligent for failing to call an emergency code in a 'timely manner' (ibid.). Although the anaesthesiologist was found liable for negligence, the operating and assisting surgeons were not — despite evidence that upon incision the operating surgeon had noted the patient's blood was 'abnormally dark', had recognised this as 'a sign of oxygen deprivation', and had received confirmation from the anaesthesiologist that he was having difficulty ventilating the patient (ibid., p. 705, s 8). In defence of its decision not to hold the operating surgeon liable, the court argued (ibid., p. 707, s 9):

At first blush, the jury's exoneration of [the operating surgeon] might seem inconsistent with the findings against the hospital. However, there was evidence that [the surgeon] could not see [the anaesthesiologist] or [the patient's] face while performing the surgical procedure and that she had to suture the incisions she had made before she could do anything for [the patient].

One of the most significant examples of a nurse being made a scapegoat, however, is the unreported Australian case of *In re Nurses Registration Act 1953 and In re Heathcote and Nurses Registration Board and Walton* (heard in the District Court of New South Wales, 1991), the first recorded case of its kind in Australia.[3] This case involved a registered nurse by the name of Sophia Heathcote who was deregistered for professional misconduct (to be distinguished here from professional negligence) on grounds that she failed to 'properly perform her duties in relation to a patient'. The incident leading to Heathcote's deregistration occurred in the early hours of the morning at a country hospital, where she and an 18-year-old unqualified nursing assistant were the only ones on duty. The nearest 'supervising' doctor (of the Flying Doctor Service) was 200 kilometres away. The details of this case are briefly outlined below.

On the 24 June 1987, at about 2.10 am, a young Aboriginal man was brought to the hospital by his relatives. The relatives informed the on-duty registered nurse, Sophia Heathcote, that the patient had complained of 'hearing things' and of 'being in the dings' (later confirmed to mean alcohol withdrawal). After giving Heathcote a brief history of the patient's problems, the relatives left the hospital. The nurse noted that although the patient was 'vague and confused', he had no other clinical symptoms.

A short time after his arrival at the hospital, the patient disappeared. Owing to a lack of security at the hospital, and the occurrence of 43 incidents over an eight month period — including two assaults on nursing staff — the registered nurse and her assistant always accompanied each other while performing their duties (Heathcote, personal communication; Hills 1989–1990, p. 26). On this particular occasion they had gone together to make the patient a warm drink to try and settle him down, and it was at that point that he wandered off. Concerned about the patient's safety (the hospital was only 25 metres from a river, and there was a risk that he could fall in and drown), Heathcote telephoned the local police to look for him, since neither she nor her assistant was in a position to leave the hospital and mount a search. The patient returned on his own volition, however, carrying a log of wood to 'boil the billy'. After persuading the patient to leave the wood outside, Heathcote called the police to cancel their search. The police had already left, however, and could not be contacted. Meanwhile, after being directed to the toilet, the patient disappeared a second time. At this point,

Heathcote rang the hospital's director of nursing (DON) to inform her that there was an 'uncontrollable patient' at the hospital, and that the police had been called — 'was that alright?'. The DON affirmed Heathcote's actions.

At 2.30 am, the police arrived with the patient in the back of the police paddy wagon. Heathcote then telephoned the 'on-call' doctor at the Flying Doctor Service, 'because she didn't know what to do', since 'it was something [she] had not come across before' and she 'wanted to know how to manage the patient' (*Australian Nurses' Journal* 1991, p. 13). Upon being given brief details of the situation, the doctor agreed that in the interests of patient safety, the patient should go to the police station (it should be noted that this option was taken because there were no facilities at the hospital to secure an uncontrollable patient). He further instructed the nurse to check the patient's blood sugar levels only, which she did do, and which were found to be normal. The patient was taken to the police station, where Heathcote believed he would be watched by the policemen on duty. But, as Hills (1989–1990, p. 26) reports:

> The constables wrote up their report, checked on him [the patient] at about 3 am (they phoned the hospital and told Sister [sic] Heathcote he was 'peacefully asleep'), turned off the light and went home to bed, leaving [the patient] alone in the deserted police station.

Sophia Heathcote had arranged with the police to go to the station after her night shift at 8.30 am to check the patient's blood pressure and make another assessment. However, at 8.30 am, the patient was found hanging from the metal door-flap of his cell, and was confirmed dead (ibid.).

Of the seven parties who could have been held accountable in this case (that is, the doctor, the director of nursing, the police, the hospital, the NSW Department of Health, the Flying Doctor Service, and the nurse), Heathcote was the one who ultimately carried the 'heaviest burden of blame' (ibid., p. 27). Hills reports that in the coronial inquiry that followed, the two policemen were exonerated (one had since been promoted to sergeant), the doctor moved to another town to practise (although the matter had been referred to the medical board, they declined to comment, and would confirm only that the doctor 'was free to practise medicine'), the Flying Doctor Service was advised 'to keep better notes of their telephone conversations', the hospital was advised to develop 'a protocol for dealing with alcohol withdrawal', and the Health Department was advised to improve facilities at the hospital (ibid.). As for Sophia Heathcote, however, the coroner is reported to have stated:

> It is *in (her) interests*, and the interests of the public generally that the question of her actions be determined by an appropriate body [emphasis added].
> (Hills 1989–1990, p. 27)

The 'appropriate body' in this instance was the New South Wales Nurses Registration Board which found Heathcote guilty of professional misconduct and deregistered her for a period of one year. The case has been widely condemned as 'scandalous', and there remains a consensus of opinion among nurses and others (including the staff and chief executive officer of the hospital in question) that Sophia Heathcote had been 'scapegoated' (Hills 1989–1990, pp. 26–27; see also Fitzpatrick 1990, p. 3; Shanley 1990, p. 3).

The Heathcote case stands as a paradigmatic example of how a nurse's well-intentioned actions can embroil her or him in what Staunton (1990, p. 24) aptly describes as 'a professional and legal process of unbelievable length, complexity and anguish, rolling on inexorably and taking years to reach finality'. It also stands as a paradigmatic example of how a 'mere nurse' can be sacrificed with impunity in order to protect the interests of more powerful others. (As a point of interest, Sophia Heathcote successfully appealed against her deregistration.[4])

Making nurses scapegoats — deluded 'conspiracy theory' or reality?

It may seem far-fetched to suggest that nurses have been 'deliberately' used as scapegoats. Although it has not been generally acknowledged, however, nurses have a long history of being blamed and legally punished for misdemeanours and negligent actions committed by others (in particular their superiors — including doctors).[5] Gerald Winslow (1984, p. 34), for example, cites a number of letters to the editor of the *American Journal of Nursing*, published during the year of 1910, in which debate was waged on the question of: 'Where does loyalty to the physician end?'. In one of these letters, a nurse 'reported that she was blamed in order to protect the doctor's reputation' (ibid.).

More recently, a nurse alleged that in some situations where the doctor does not respond to a nurse's reported observations concerning changes in a patient's condition, and the patient suffers an injury as a result, 'the whole thing gets turned around, and they start to look at you like if you were doing your job properly this incident might not have occurred' (Smith 1983, p. 133). A good example of this can be found in the Court of Appeals of Indiana case *Poor Sisters of St Francis v Catron* (1982). In this case, nurses working in an intensive care unit were found liable for failing to protect the patient when the doctor failed to change the patient's endotracheal tube over a five day period. As a result of this negligence the patient suffered tracheal necrosis, a known complication of prolonged intubation, and later had to have surgery to remove scar tissue. She also experienced difficulty in speaking. In an appeal case that followed, the court accepted that 'as a general rule endotracheal tubes should not be left in a patient longer than three to four days', and affirmed that the nurses were negligent in their failure to 'question and report treatment not in accord with standard medical practice' (ibid., p. 309).

Another good example of nurses carrying a disproportionate burden of responsibility and blame for the negligent actions of others can be found in a 1988 English case involving a doctor who made a fatal ten-fold error in his estimation of a drug dosage he had prescribed for a patient (Jones, I.H. 1988). The nurses assisting the doctor at the time were not familiar with the drug that had been ordered, but managed to find a small box containing eight ampoules of it which they gave to the requesting doctor. Upon receiving the box, the doctor reportedly snapped 'Oh God, is this all you have? . . . there isn't sufficient here to treat a mouse! She'll need 45 ampoules. I'll fetch some more while you draw these up' (quoted in Jones, I.H. 1988, p. 50). Although concerned that the drug order 'sounded an enormous amount' the nurses nevertheless proceeded, as instructed by the doctor, to add it to the intravenous solution for administration to the patient. The main reason why the nurses did not check the drug order further was because they were working in extremely stressful conditions (the ward was short of staff and resources, and had a large number of very dependent 'heavy, immobile and incontinent' patients requiring attention) and, upon being distracted to attend to the urgent needs of other patients, had 'foolishly accepted the doctor's estimation without question' (ibid., p. 52).

Upon his return to the ward with the extra ampoules of the drug he had prescribed, the doctor re-checked the drug order, checked the intravenous line, and left to deal with a medical emergency in the accident and emergency department. As the intravenous infusion continued, the patient's condition deteriorated. A re-examination of the drug order by nurses revealed the error. Despite efforts to treat the drug overdose, however, the patient died.

A coronial inquiry was unable to establish the precise cause of the patient's death (she had originally been admitted for treatment of a paracetamol overdose). Despite this, however, and despite the fact that the doctor had made the initial mistake — and had 'compounded it by his subsequent actions' — the nurses were the only ones to be made the subject of a complaint and accused of professional misconduct (ibid.). Although the misconduct charges against the nurses were not upheld (evidence was accepted that the nurses had previously submitted a report to the hospital management detailing their concerns — among other things, about the dangerously low staffing levels they were having to endure — and that management had ignored this report), as was noted at the time, the case stood as yet another example of where

once again, nurses had been brought before a disciplinary hearing while the doctor was not the subject of a complaint to his regulating body.
(Jones, I.H. 1988, p. 52)

There is considerable room to speculate that had the matter been taken further, it would have been the nurses — not the doctor — who would have carried the blame (and punishment) for the drug error.

The symbiosis between medicine and law

At first glance it might seem extraordinary that nurses can be — and have been — legitimately exploited and abused as scapegoats by doctors, hospitals, and the state. However, given the symbiotic relationship which has traditionally existed between medicine and law (between members of the medical fraternity and members of the legal fraternity) it is not so extraordinary (see, for example, Freidson 1970, 1973, 1988; Foucault 1972, pp. 50–55, 1973, 1975, 1977; Illich et al. 1977; McLean 1981; Inlander et al. 1988; Rice 1988; Montgomery 1989; Smart 1989; Willis 1989; Gee and Mason 1990). Furthermore, it should not be forgotten, as Carol Smart (1989, p. 92) reminds us, that

> the application of some parts of the law depends on a detailed appraisal of the body, and draws heavily on medical knowledge to establish legal issues.

Smart (1989, p. 94) further points out that medical knowledge and legal discourse have long been in an alliance 'to regulate behaviours which were injurious to public and individual health (moral and social)'. In addition, she argues that 'as medicine creates new terrains, so law extend[s] its authority' (ibid., p. 96).

Prominent jurists have made no secret of the law's 'moral duty' to protect the professional medical man. An influential exponent of this view is the Right Honourable Lord Denning, described by one author as being 'the greatest single influence in cases relating to medical negligence' (McLean 1981, p. 101). In his celebrated text *The discipline of law*, Lord Denning (1979, p. 237) explains:

> At one time the Courts held that a professional man was not liable for ordinary negligence but only for gross negligence, *Crassa Negligentia*. Later on it was said that there was no difference between negligence and gross negligence. 'It is the same thing with the addition of a vituperative epithet.' But there is a tendency today to draw the distinction again. It is done so as to protect a professional man from having his reputation unjustly besmirched. A medical man, for instance, should not be found guilty of negligence unless he has done something of which his colleagues would say: 'He really did make a mistake here. He ought not to have done it'.

The tendency to reinstate the distinction between ordinary and gross negligence, in England at least, appears to have been prompted by the findings of an English Court of Appeals case *Cassidy v Ministry of Health* (1951). Lord Denning (1979, p. 241) explains that the medical profession became so alarmed by the result of this case, that the courts — after being criticised by the medical profession through journal articles, periodicals and 'so forth' (perhaps by fraternising with members of the judiciary?) — sought 'to relieve the anxieties of the medical men' in the next Court of Appeals case of *Roe v Minister of Health* [1954]. In that case, Denning LJ argued:

> It is so easy to be wise after the event and to condemn as negligence that which was only a misadventure. We ought always to be on our guard against it, especially in cases against *hospitals and doctors*.[6] Medical science has conferred great benefits on mankind, but these benefits are attended by considerable risks. Every surgical operation is attended by risks. We cannot take the benefits without taking the risks [emphasis added].
> (*Roe v Minister of Health* [1954], p. 83)

Although Denning LJ agreed that the two patients in the case at hand had 'suffered such terrible consequences that there is a natural feeling that they should be compensated', he concluded his argument by adding that:

> We should be doing a disservice to the community at large if we were to impose liability on hospitals and doctors for everything that happens to go wrong. Doctors would be led to think more of their own safety than of the good of their patients. Initiative would be stifled and confidence shaken. A proper sense of proportion requires us to have regard to the conditions in which hospitals and doctors have to work. We must insist on due care for the patient at every point, but we must not condemn as negligence that which is only a misadventure.
> (*Roe v Minister of Health* [1954], pp. 86–87)

In another English appeal case *Hatcher v Black and Others* [1954], Denning LJ again asserted his view that the medical man should not be held responsible for 'ordinary' negligence. His comments to the jury in this case are worth quoting in full:

> Before I consider the individual facts, I ought to explain to you the law on this matter of negligence against doctors and hospitals . . . Every surgical operation involves risks. It would be wrong, and, indeed, bad law, to say that simply because a misadventure or mishap occurred, the hospital and the doctors are thereby liable. It would be disastrous to the community if it were so. It would mean that a doctor examining a patient, or a surgeon operating at a table, instead of getting on with his work, would be for ever

looking over his shoulder to see if someone was coming up with a dagger
— *for an action for negligence against a doctor is for him like unto a
dagger*. His professional reputation is as dear to him as his body, perhaps
more so, and an action for negligence can wound his reputation as severely
as a dagger can his body. You must not, therefore, find him negligent simply
because something happens to go wrong; if, for instance, one of the risks
inherent in an operation actually takes place or some complication ensues
which lessens or takes away the benefits that were hoped for, or if in a
matter of opinion he makes an error of judgment. You should only find him
guilty of negligence when he falls short of the standard of a reasonably
skilful medical man, in short, when he is deserving of censure . . . [So] far
as the law is concerned, it does not condemn the doctor when he only does
that which many a wise and good doctor so placed would do. It only
condemns him when he falls short of the accepted standards of a great
profession [emphasis added].
(cited in Denning 1979, pp. 243–244)

It is evident from this statement that Denning LJ strongly supported the
idea that 'medical practice should be interfered with as little as possible'
(McLean 1981, pp. 104, 106) and that the standards of medical practice
should be determined only by 'wise and good' doctors — not by the courts.
Furthermore, the statement seems to suggest that, in the name of the 'public
good', the courts in fact had a duty to protect and legitimate the medical
profession's authority to judge its own members (see also *Crawford v Board
of Governors, Charing Cross Hospital* [1953]; *British Medical Journal*
1959; *McCormack v Redpath Brown and Co.* [1961]; Wellwood 1961, pp.
763–764; *Hucks v Cole and Another* [1968]; and *Whitehouse v Jordan*
[1980]).

There is small doubt that the medical profession stood to benefit
considerably from Denning's support and his influential rhetoric on the need
to protect the doctor from the 'dagger at his back'. Whether it stood to
protect the public interest, however, is another matter entirely. And because
there was no esteemed Lord to protect the nurse from the 'dagger at her
back', there is room to suggest that Denning's support of the medical
profession was not in the nursing profession's interests either (something
which has perhaps contributed to the relative ease with which nurses have
been made scapegoats for negligent doctors).

Although it has been suggested that Lord Denning's influence has passed
(see Gee and Mason 1990, p. 168), it is nevertheless apparent that his views
have been extremely influential, not just in the United Kingdom but in other
common law countries as well (see, for example, Rice 1988, pp. 133–147);
and have been instrumental in making it 'extraordinarily difficult to
establish that a doctor was negligent' — despite the relative ease with which

'at least some of the basic criteria for negligence' could be established (McLean 1981, p. 107). There are, of course, a number of reasons for this.

Firstly, it has always been left exclusively to the medical profession to determine its own accepted standards of conduct (Freidson 1973, 1988; McLean 1981; Rice 1988; Montgomery 1989). Historically, only expert medical witnesses have been considered sufficiently competent to judge the acceptable standards of medical care, and/or to decide whether a doctor has been 'unwise'. Furthermore, since doctors have generally been regarded as being by nature 'reasonable' — as one commentator has argued, 'a doctor is never committing an offence when he is acting as a reasonable doctor' (Kennedy 1988, p. 76) — in practice it has been (and remains) very difficult to show that a doctor has acted in a grossly negligent manner.

Secondly, it is often very difficult to get doctors to testify against one another (Rice 1988, p. 103; Rimmer 1989, p. 22; Gee and Mason 1990, p. 173). As a Sydney solicitor and former legal secretary of the Australian Medical Association (AMA) quickly discovered upon his return to private practice, 'it is not easy to find willing witnesses' (Rice 1988, p. 124). He suggests that this is largely because of the 'closed shop' attitude among doctors toward giving evidence against a colleague (ibid.). Rimmer (1989, p. 22) argues that some doctors simply 'resent being involved in a process where other doctors are, in effect, looking over their shoulder or commenting critically upon their work'. The situation in the United Kingdom appears to be very similar. McLean (1981, p. 103) comments, for example, that most doctors are reluctant to testify since 'they feel themselves to be the potential subjects of allegations of negligence and will, therefore, be loathe to criticise a fellow professional'. Gee and Mason (1990, p. 173) contend that 'some doctors who are asked to provide expert evidence against a defendant doctor in a case of alleged negligence are unwilling to do so on grounds of professional loyalty'. In an unpublished paper entitled 'Paediatrics: a new version by a medical defence union', Dr Cary Ooi, a developmental physician and the Medical Director of Neuro-Education Incorporated Australasia (based in Sydney), makes the even more radical claim that some medical defence unions (which play a major role in providing legal advice to doctors and supplying them with expert medical witnesses when needed) have regularly supplied false and fraudulent information in order to assist doctors escape liability for their negligent actions.

Lord Denning's prescription that 'medical practice should be interfered with as little as possible' appears to have been successfully upheld. For example, in *Some doctors make you sick*, Stephen Rice (1988) estimates that in Australia alone over 70 000 patients are negligently injured by their doctors each year. Of these 70 000, only 250 patients will push their legal right to sue; and of these, only a meagre 10 per cent will take their case to court. Of this 10 per cent, most will accept a 'last-minute' out-of-court settlement. Rice (1988, p. 7) states that in an out-of-court settlement 'the money is inevitably much less than a jury might award, but better than the risk of nothing'. He further states (ibid.):

> A settlement enables the doctor to escape embarrassing publicity; it usually excludes any admission of liability; and it forbids disclosure of the amount awarded. If patients want to collect the money, they have to keep their mouths shut. Most are in no position to refuse.

Statistics in the United Kingdom indicate a similar situation. Citing a 1976 report, McLean (1981, p. 99) notes that the 'number of successful claims in negligence against the medical profession was much lower than in all other negligence cases'. More recently, a 1988 *Report of a Confidential Enquiry into Perioperative Deaths* (cited in Sadler 1988), found that 'at least 1000 patients die each year as a result of operating theatre errors by surgeons and anaesthetists' or by inadequately supervised junior surgeons and anaesthetists (ibid., p. 18). Significantly, this figure was described in the report as being 'reassuringly low'. Sadler (ibid.) further notes that no respondents to the enquiry were named, 'no doctors [were] summoned to give evidence, and professional reputations remain unscathed'. Meanwhile, Gee and Mason (1990) have observed that in 1985–1986, 70 per cent of 'relevant complaints' against doctors made to the United Kingdom General Medical Council were dismissed by the preliminary screener of the council. The main reason for dismissing the complaints seems to have been that the conduct reported was not 'regarded as disgraceful or dishonourable by a doctor's professional brethren of good repute and competency'. Of the misconduct cases that were considered, only three per cent resulted in severe disciplinary action (ibid., p. 176).

In the United States of America, which is notorious for its climate of litigation (a fact frequently cited by Lord Denning in defence of his sympathetic position towards medical men), a similar situation of non-interference with medical practice exists. For example, in a 1985 report, it was claimed that although between 136 000 and 310 000 patients a year were either 'injured or killed due to medical mistakes by their doctors', serious disciplinary action was taken against doctors in only about one out of each 252 times (Wolfe et al. 1985 — cited in Inlander et al. 1988, p. 178). Inlander et al. (ibid.) further point out that of the estimated 5–15 per cent of doctors in the United States of America who are either incompetent or dangerous, only about 1.4 per cent ever become the subject of 'serious action'. Few are disciplined by deregistration. For example, in one case it took 18 malpractice suits between 1972 and 1979 before a negligent doctor's license to practice was finally suspended for an 'indefinite period of time' (ibid., p. 177). Citing a newspaper report on one American state medical board (not surprisingly there is very little written on this topic in the mainstream medical literature), Inlander et al. (1988, p. 186) state that common rationales for exonerating an errant doctor can include:

- An accused doctor's sincere and honest confession of wrongdoing.
- A doctor's inability to make a living if he were denied his right to practice.
- The embarrassment a doctor had suffered from cases made public, or might suffer if secret proceedings leaked out.
- The belief that just being forced to come before the board is a form of treatment.

Medical negligence and the nurse's 'duty to protect' the doctor's reputation

There is considerable room to suggest that the legal system's support of doctors in the case of medical negligence has, in several respects, increased the legal vulnerability of nurses (not least, as scapegoats for negligent doctors). The position of the nurse with regards to medical negligence is further complicated by the fact that there also exists a normative expectation that the nurse will uphold 'her' doctor loyally — even when he has erred — and will do all that she can in order to protect his professional reputation.

Explaining the nurse's duty to protect the medical practitioner, Sarner (1968, p. 54) writes:

> The nurse who works under the direction and control of a physician does not have any legal liability for his negligent acts. However, she does have a legal and moral duty not to act in such manner as to encourage malpractice claims against the physician.

Sarner (1968, pp. 55–56) argues further that

> if the doctor commits some obvious act of malfeasance that results in an injury to the patient, the most the nurse can do is attempt to retain as much good will as previously existed in order to reduce the chances of legal action . . . If the doctor and his nurse are able to recapture the patient's good will after an injury has occurred, it may go a long way towards minimizing the chances of a malpractice lawsuit.

Although Sarner's views were expressed over two decades ago, and therefore could reasonably be rejected as being out of date, it is evident that nurses are still expected to act in ways to protect a negligent doctor against possible malpractice lawsuits — even to the point of committing perjury. For example, in the Court of Appeals of North Carolina case *Sides v Duke Hospital* (1985), it was revealed that a nurse anaesthetist had been dismissed from her employing hospital of eleven years in 'retaliation for her refusal to testify falsely or incompletely' in a medical malpractice trial of two physician anaesthesiologists (ibid., pp. 826–827, 830). A lawsuit had earlier been brought against the two physician anaesthesiologists by the estate of Larry Downs, who, while a patient at Duke Hospital, 'suffered permanent brain damage resulting from the negligent administration of anesthetics' by one of the physicians (ibid., p. 821). The physician in this instance had initially instructed the nurse anaesthetist to administer the anaesthetic in question to immobilise the patient. The nurse refused on grounds that it 'would harm the patient and possibly cause his death' (ibid.). The physician nevertheless personally administered the drugs and, as a consequence, the patient 'stopped breathing, went into cardiac arrest for a time, and suffered permanent brain damage'. The patient's estate sued for damages.

Before appearing in the court case that followed, the nurse was advised

> by several physicians who worked at DUMC [Duke University Medical Center] and by attorneys for Duke and other defendants in that suit that she should not tell all that she had seen relating to Mr Downs' treatment; some of the doctors warned her that if she did so she 'would be in trouble'. Pressures like that had already caused another nurse anesthetist at DUMC to withhold information at her deposition.
> (*Sides v Duke Hospital* (1985), p. 821)

In spite of these threats, the nurse anaesthetist testified fully and truthfully at the trial. Later, however, many physicians (including the two against whom the lawsuit had originally been brought) 'began to adopt hostile attitudes toward her' and some refused to work with her — making it impossible for her to perform her duties. This lead to her being advised by a nursing supervisor that

> her job performance was poor in several respects, that she had 'an abusive attitude', and that her work would be closely monitored for three months.
> (ibid.)

Harassment by the doctors continued, however, and the nurse anaesthetist's competence was successfully undermined and discredited. She was dismissed from her position, and was unable to find similar work at other hospitals. In this case, the nurse was absolutely powerless to either defend or protect herself against the legitimated power and authority of the doctors she had to work with.

Another sobering example of nurses being expected to 'loyally uphold doctors' can be found in the 1987 New Zealand Cervical Cancer Inquiry, popularly referred to as the 'unfortunate experiment' at the National Women's Hospital in Auckland (see Coney 1988; *Report of the Cervical Cancer Inquiry* 1988; Johnstone 1989, pp. 10–16). The 'unfortunate experiment' in question began in 1958, and sought to examine the invasive potential of carcinoma in situ (CIS) of the cervix. The experiment involved 948 women who were included in the project without either their knowledge or consent. These women had been divided into two groups for the purposes of the research. Those in group one (totalling 817 women) received treatment, while those in group two (totalling 131 women) received only 'limited' or no treatment. The outcome was that those in group two developed invasive carcinoma at the rate of 22 per cent, compared with only 5.5 per cent in group one; and had a significantly higher mortality rate (of 6 per cent), compared with only 0.5 per cent in group one (*Report of the Cervical Cancer Inquiry* 1988, p. 57; Coney1988, pp. 4–15). Media reports also claimed that some women experienced as many as 60 hospital admissions and over 50 vaginal examinations, but no treatment. As the *New Zealand Herald* (1987) later reported, the women 'got more and more diagnoses but not always treatment, or treatment was left too late'.

The scandal was eventually brought to the public's attention when, in 1987, *Metro* magazine published an article by Sandra Coney and Phillida Bunkle on the matter. Following the efforts of these two courageous women, and the support of some few individual newspaper journalists and radio commentators (because the story involved doctors, many media personnel had been legally advised to have nothing to do with it), the New Zealand government announced that there would be an immediate public inquiry into the allegations.

During the inquiry that followed, evidence was submitted that nurses had been intimidated into not coming forward and giving evidence before the commission. The New Zealand Nurses Association (NZNA) is reported as stating that several of its members felt pressured by the medical superintendent of the hospital involved not to cooperate with the inquiry, and that two nurses in particular felt no doubt that if they gave evidence 'their jobs would be in jeopardy' and their future career prospects would be hampered (Coney 1988, p. 224; Johnstone 1989, pp. 14–15). Although doctors did not have the direct power to 'hire and fire' nurses, they nevertheless had the power to ensure that 'disloyal' nurses were removed from their positions. As a point of interest, Dr Herbert Green, the chief researcher of the cervical cancer project, ultimately evaded disgraceful conduct charges relating to his project on grounds that he was '"unfit mentally and physically" to face charges' (*Sun Herald* 1990, p. 168). However, Professor Bonham, the head to committee which approved the original project, and who was also head of the department of obstetrics and gynaecology at the time the project was being carried out, is reported to have been found by the New Zealand Medical Council to be guilty of a 'total of six misconduct charges, including four of disgraceful conduct' (*Waikato Times* 1990, p. 3; see also Coney 1990, pp. 201–245). Significantly, none of the doctors involved in this scandal have been censured for their alleged intimidation of nurse witnesses (Coney 1990, pp. 213–242). Nurses in New Zealand also remain relatively powerless to challenge negligent medical behaviour effectively. Indeed, in the final report of the inquiry, the Commissioner expressed grave reservations about the nurses' ability to defend patients' rights (*Report of the Cervical Cancer Inquiry* 1988). She is reported to have stated:

> Nurses who most appropriately should be the advocates for the patient, feel sufficiently intimidated by the medical staff (who do not hire and fire them) that even today they fail or refuse to confront openly the issues arising from the 1988 trial.
>
> (cited by Bickley 1988, p. 15)

The 'improved' legal status of the nurse — some further considerations

It should be noted that the vulnerability of nurses in the area of medical malpractice is not the only indication that their legal status as authoritative and autonomous professionals has not improved significantly. Indeed, there are other notable indications that the legal status of nurses remains less than optimal; these will be considered briefly below.

The nurse's lack of sovereignty in her own realm of practice

An important indicator of the legal status of the nurse is the degree to which nurses have sovereignty (or rather, a lack of sovereignty) in their own realm of practice. Over the past few decades, the social and economic position of nurses has improved significantly, and the nursing profession as a whole has gained more status as a legitimated profession. Nevertheless, nurses do not have sovereignty in their own realm of practice. As a general rule, nurses do not have the legitimated authority to prescribe patient care (officially, only doctors may do this), and are still not permitted to exercise independent professional nursing judgment in matters of life and death (Gunning 1983, p. 121; Kiefer 1983, p. 562; King and Sagan 1989, p. 59). As already argued, nurses who attempt to prescribe patient care without a doctor's authorisation or who attempt to exercise independent (medically unauthorised) professional nursing judgment, risk being censured for having 'exceeded their scope of authority' — that is, engaged in the illegal practice of medicine (Kiefer 1983, pp. 562, 564). This is so, even in cases where the role of the nurse has been legitimately 'expanded'.

The very essence of professional nursing rests on 'the decision-making on the part of the nurse' (Creighton 1984a, p. 60). Creighton (ibid.) explains: 'The well being, and in some instances, the life of the patient depends on nursing judgment and necessary action based thereon'. Despite this, nurses remain intolerably constrained when making and acting on their own 'best' judgment. Although, as a general rule, nurses are expected to make 'good nursing judgments', these judgments are not meant to stand on 'their own merit' or have overriding authority. At best, they are only meant to 'complement good medical judgment' and be only a 'component of quality [read 'medical'] care' (*Regan Report on Nursing Law* 1980b).

Despite changing legal attitudes towards the nurse's ability to exercise independent professional judgments vis-à-vis the duty to report negligent medical actions, a nurse's judgment is still not recognised as having overriding authority and, in the main, is still regarded as being 'by nature' dependent on and inferior to a doctor's judgment. One doctor (a surgeon and Federal Councillor of the Australian Medical Association) has also suggested that independent professional nursing judgments and actions are not only 'inferior', but 'unconscionable', 'unhealthy' and 'potentially dangerous' (Wertheimer 1990, p. 11). Further to this, rightly or wrongly, the doctor remains 'imbued with a sense of ultimate moral-legal responsibility for the patient', and thus as being 'justified' in assuming total control over patient care matters — including a nurse's professional nursing judgments and actions (Dachelet 1978, p. 40; Lee 1979; *British Medical Journal* 1982). One important consequence of this is that in instances where a nurse's professional judgment does not 'square' with a doctor's professional judgment, the doctor's judgment will, almost without exception, be regarded as having the most weight or authority (*Regan Report on Nursing Law* 1980b). This situation makes it extremely difficult for nurses to practise their profession responsibly, since, in the ultimate analysis, it is the doctor's, not the nurse's judgment which reigns supreme, and the doctor retains the ultimate authority to order a nurse to carry out his or her instructions.

Another problem for nurses is that although they need to — and are expected to — exercise 'good' nursing judgment, and to make recommendations on the basis of their professional judgment, there are strict normative rules governing the way in which they are to make their professional judgment and related recommendations known. For instance, in his influential article entitled 'The doctor-nurse game', Stein (1968, p. 102) explains:

> The nurse is to be bold, have initiative, and be responsible for making significant recommendations, while at the same time she must appear passive. This must be done in such a manner so as to make her recommendations appear to be initiated by the physician . . . the nurse must communicate her recommendations without appearing to be making a recommendation statement. The physician, in requesting a recommendation from a nurse, must do so without appearing to be asking it.

The ultimate aim of this 'doctor–nurse game' is to avoid conflict (read 'maintain the patriarchal political order'), and to ensure that the sovereignty of the doctor in patient care contexts is maintained and reinforced.

There are many examples (too numerous to give in full here) which can be used to demonstrate that nurses do not have sovereignty in their own realm of practice. One common and universal example is that nurses still do not have the independent authority to determine when and if a patient should be on 'bed rest' (that is, kept in bed) or ambulated (that is, got out of bed and mobilised). It has always been and remains the doctor's prerogative to decide and prescribe these things — even though the doctor's decision is invariably dependent on nursing observations and judgment, and even though the care involved (in relation to either bed rest or ambulation) is primarily performed by nurses. Similarly, nurses do not have the legitimated authority to directly admit patients to or discharge patients from hospital on the basis of the patient's nursing care needs — this too is a doctor's prerogative (see, for example, Dunn 1982; Brewer 1988; Fielding 1988; Wertheimer 1990). Doctors can discharge patients from hospital care — even though nurses might not agree with the decision to do so. For instance, a nurse might correctly judge that a patient is not ready to be sent home and could suffer otherwise avoidable harms if discharged from hospital too soon (this is particularly so in instances where a patient has nobody at home to care for her or him upon being discharged from hospital, or where her or his primary lay carer is also an invalid, or where the lay carer simply does not know how to provide certain specialised cares that are required). Conversely, a nurse might correctly judge that the patient would benefit from further nursing care, and that discharge should be delayed accordingly in order to maximise the therapeutic success of the nursing care which has already been given.

Another example of nurses' lack of sovereignty in their own realm of practice can be found in the case of restraining disturbed patients. As a general rule, nurses are not permitted to prescribe the use of 'standard' restraints (for example, 'posey' belts or vests) to restrain disturbed patients who, because of their mental state, are at risk of injuring either themselves or others. Restraints may be used only if authorised by a doctor, although it is generally left to the nurses to decide whether or not to use the restraint once the authorisation has been given (*Regan Report on Nursing Law* 1982b; Staunton and Whyburn 1993, p. 130).

Still another common example demonstrating nurses' lack of sovereignty in their own realm of practice can be found in the case of drug prescribing. As a general rule, nurses have no legal authority to prescribe and supply drugs, or to adjust the time and dosage of an existing medically prescribed drug order to accord with 'patient-specific protocols' (that is, to meet a patient's specific and individual needs). Restrictions on nurses prescribing drugs sometimes include 'over the counter' (OTC) remedies such as paracetamol, aspirin, vitamin C, lotions for dry skin, or glycerine suppositories for constipation. In some hospitals, even these basic items must be ordered by a doctor before a nurse can administer them to a patient (Gunning 1983, p. 121; Hackett 1983, p. 4). Although many hospitals have standard drug protocols or 'standing orders' allowing nurses to use their own discretion and to administer certain drugs or other therapeutic substances, these protocols or standing orders must first be authorised either by the appropriate consultant doctor(s) or health administrators before a nurse can 'safely' use her own discretion and can 'safely' administer the approved drugs named in a given protocol or standing order regime (Staunton and Whyburn 1993, pp. 198–199; see also Greenfield 1975, p. 62; Carlisle 1990b; Smith 1990a).

Legal prohibitions against nurses prescribing drugs have, at times, had a profound and negative impact on the nurse's ability to deliver effective nursing care. In district nursing situations in the United Kingdom, for example, the nurse's inability to prescribe and supply drugs has sometimes meant that

> patients have [had] to wait hours, or even days, for adequate pain relief because the nurse is unable to provide an analgesia ... and yet this suffering could be alleviated by making small amounts of drugs available until a prescription can be obtained.
> (*Nursing Times* 1985c)

Likewise, patients in hospital settings have had sometimes to wait hours for adequate pain relief, night sedation or other needed remedies, because the doctor has been delayed (for example, by an emergency or some other demand) and the nurse has been unable to administer the required drugs without a doctor's prescription (McIntosh 1990, p. 3).

The appropriateness of legal restrictions on nurses prescribing and supplying drugs, and altering the time and dosage of medically prescribed drugs, is questionable — particularly when it is considered that nurses are the ones who are primarily responsible for:

- checking that a doctor has correctly prescribed a patient's drugs, and — in given situations — has administered the correct drug;
- administering prescribed medications to patients;
- monitoring the effects and adverse side effects of medications given to patients (see Carr 1983; Gould 1988).

Furthermore, nurses are the ones who can be (and are) held independently responsible for medication errors — including those made by doctors, as happened in the Somera case cited earlier (see also *Yorston v Pennel* (1959); *Killeen v Reinhardt* (1979); *Dessauer v Memorial General Hospital and Glorious Borque* (1981); Carr 1983; Jones, I.H. 1988).

Legal restrictions on drug prescribing and administration by nurses are also questionable on grounds that they do not reflect the realities of either nursing or medical practice. For instance, although it has not generally been acknowledged, nurses have always made an enormous contribution to prescribing drugs in both hospital and community settings (Carlisle 1990b, p. 17). In Australia, for example, in the private hospital sector where there are often no resident medical officers, it is left to nurses to ascertain, upon admission, what a patient's regular medications are, to note these on a drug prescription form, and to contact the 'attending' (absent) private physician or surgeon to obtain a verbal order for the drugs in question so that they can be administered to the patient (note, verbal drug orders are supposed to be given only in an emergency situation and should be signed by the prescribing doctor within 24 hours). The drug order is eventually signed when the doctor next visits the ward or hospital, which sometimes can be more than 24 hours after the patient's admission. The legalities (or more to the point, the illegalities) of this commonly accepted practice appear not to have been seriously questioned either by nurses or by government authorities (see also Langslow 1985, pp. 54–55).

Nurses working in remote areas of Australia have also long been involved (sometimes illegally) in the storage, prescribing, dispensing and administration of legally restricted drugs. In one of the most comprehensive reports to date on remote area nursing (RAN) practice, Ann Kreger (1991, p. 36) notes that:

> In the absence of pharmacists, RANs accept reponsibility for the ordering, storage and control of substances covered by the Poisons Acts and Regulations in their locations. Some nurses are clearly disturbed by the illegality of their practice in this area. Others are unclear about their responsibilities, terminology and legislation pertinent to the prescription, dispensation, possession, supply and administration of drugs.

Kreger (1991, p. 37) goes on to point out that with the exception of nurses working in the Northern Territory,

> employers, Nurse Registering Authorities and governments have provided little realistic support and guidance to nurses constantly faced with this burden. Generally, the authorities' response has been to deny their responsibility in this matter by hiding behind existing inappropriate legislation and policy, thereby leaving remote area consumers and nurses inadequately protected.

On a more general level, it is evident that nurses have been unofficially prescribing drugs for years, with doctors merely 'rubber-stamping' nurses' decisions (*Nursing Times* 1989g; Andrews 1990, p. 32; Carlisle 1990a, p. 16; Stilwell 1988). A typical example of how a nurse unofficially prescribes a drug is given by Stilwell (1988, p. 33) as follows:

The scene is a nurse's treatment room. Mrs J has come to have her leg redressed and complains that it is painful.

Nurse: 'Have you ever taken pain-killers for this ulcer, Mrs J?'

Mrs J: 'Yes. I did take paracetamol some time ago, but I stopped taking them and didn't know if I should start again.'

Nurse: 'I think that would help, especially if you took them regularly. I'll get Dr S to come and look at your leg.'

Ten minutes later.

Nurse: 'Mrs J is having trouble with her leg, doctor. It's painful. She had paracetamol before, and it helped her.'

Doctor: 'O.K., then Mrs J, *I think* we'll give you some more' [emphasis added].

Although the nurse in this example is perfectly capable of prescribing the paracetamol, she lacks the legitimated authority to do so. Instead, she has to play an 'elaborate game of words with her medical colleague to get the prescription' (ibid.). The absurdity of this situation is highlighted further by the fact that nurses the world over have for years played a major (although an unacknowledged) role in teaching junior doctors how to prescribe medications properly (see also Wolf 1988, p. 169).

Over the past few years there has been increasing recognition by governments, the medical profession and the lay community that the quality of patient care could be greatly enhanced if nurses had the authority to prescribe and supply drugs — particularly in community care settings (for example, involving the palliative care of patients with cancer or full-blown AIDS) (LaBar 1984; Stilwell 1988; Carlisle 1990e, p. 29; Andrews 1990, p. 3; Smith 1990b; Snell et al. 1988). In the United States of America, for example, over 18 states have 'adopted legislation or rules which authorises nurses to write prescriptions' (LaBar 1984, p. 2). And in the United Kingdom, nurses working in community-based health care settings (for example, district nursing, school nursing, community psychiatric nursing, palliative care, diabetic care and stomal therapy) were initially expected to be granted limited prescribing 'privileges' by 1992 (Carlisle 1990e, p. 29; Andrews 1990, p. 3; Smith 1990b). The proposal to give select nurses legitimated prescribing authority did not receive royal assent until early 1992, however, and even then the proposal pertained only to 'district nurses and health visitors working in a particular post' (Sadler 1992, p. 21). Pending legislation has received full government support meanwhile, and is expected to be implemented in October 1993 — exactly seven years after it was first mooted (Moreton 1992). It is unlikely that hospital nurses will be given authority to prescribe drugs — primarily because of medical opposition to the idea.

Despite changing attitudes towards nurses prescribing drugs, there exists a strong body of opinion that prescribing drugs is absolutely and unconditionally a doctor's duty, and even law reforms allowing nurses to prescribe drugs continue to reflect this belief (LaBar 1984, pp. 3–5; Carlisle 1990b, p. 16). Nevertheless, there is an increasing acceptance of the view that prescribing and supplying drugs is 'justifiable nursing care', and not merely a question of nurses once again taking on a 'discarded medical function' (Stilwell 1988, p. 31). However, even when nurses have been granted drug prescribing 'privileges' (note, doctors are generally seen as having drug prescribing 'rights'), their activities have been closely scrutinised and controlled by doctors. Nurses with prescribing 'privileges' may, for instance, be required to follow a pre-existing medical protocol or to enter into an 'honorary contract' with a medical practitioner (Greenfield 1975; Carlisle 1990e, p. 28). In the United Kingdom, for example, doctors have given in principle support to nurses being allowed to prescribe drugs, but have insisted that doctors should retain the 'overall responsibility' for prescribing drugs, and, in the case of community-based nursing, have insisted that ultimately it should be left to the general medical practitioner (GP) 'to judge whether the nurse was competent for the task [of prescribing and supplying drugs]' (*Nursing Times* 1988p). Thus, in the ultimate analysis, it can be seen that drug prescribing by nurses — rather than being an emancipatory professional reform, stands as a medically controlled, if not a medically dependent, act.

It should perhaps be clarified here that the entire system of medical prescribing (whether of drugs or of more specific patient cares) is particularly problematic for nurses since, among other things, it perpetuates the myths that 'the only role of the nurse is to follow the physician's orders' (Gunning 1983, p. 121), and that doctors (men) should 'supervise' nurses (women) whether they are in the presence of these nurses or not (Ashley 1975c, p. 1466). It also perpetuates the myths of medical independence and nurse dependency (even in the absence of a 'supervising' doctor) (Ashley 1976a, p. 117). Furthermore, it works to disguise the fact that, contrary to popular impressions, it is 'the nursing role [that] is paramount and is supported by the medical function', and not vice versa (Fielding 1988, p. 43).

Another indication of the nurse's lack of sovereignty in her or his own realm of practice is that it remains very difficult for a nurse to refuse a directive to work in areas for which she or he lacks the competency or necessary nursing expertise. When, for instance, there is a shortage of nursing staff (as frequently occurs in the specialised areas of intensive care units (ICUs), coronary care units (CCUs), neonatal intensive care units (NICUs), and accident and emergency departments (A&Es)), it is common practice to direct or 'float' nursing staff from one (for example, generalist) area to work in another (for example, specialist) area, or vice versa. For example, if an ICU is short of staff, nurses working in a general medical or surgical ward might be directed by a nursing supervisor to go and work their shift in the ICU. Or, if a general ward is short staffed, specialised ICU nurses might be asked to go and work their shift in that ward. Although commonly accepted, the practice of directing nursing staff to work in areas for which they are neither educationally prepared nor practically experienced to work in, is problematic on a number of grounds. First, it sometimes places nurses in the intolerable position of having to function above their level of competence (interestingly, this is not regarded by the courts as being either illegal or 'contrary to public policy' (see *Regan Report on Nursing Law* 1986; *Francis v Memorial General Hospital* (1986); Langslow 1983b, 1989a, p. 38)). Second, by so doing, it increases the margin for error, and the risk of nursing negligence (Creighton 1982; Cushing 1983). Related to this is a third problem, namely, that it increases the risk of otherwise avoidable harm being caused to patients (see, for example, *Norton v Argonaut Insurance Company* (1962); *Dessaur v Memorial General Hospital and Glorious Borque* (1981)). Finally, on a philosophical level, it demonstrates that in the final analysis there is little (if any) recognition of — or respect for — the fact that competent and responsible nursing requires specialised knowledge and experience, and that it is not the case that 'just anyone' (or indeed any nurse) can work in any area of nursing without the prerequisite (specialist or generalist) knowledge and experience. Significantly this is not a problem that doctors face. As Gunning (1983, p. 115) points out, for example:

> It is difficult to imagine a cardiologist being asked to deliver a baby. Yet, if staffing is inadequate, a nurse who is a specialist may be pulled from a medical floor to work in the obstetrics unit.

The problems for nurses in the case of nursing staff shortages are exacerbated by the facts that:

- the courts do not accept short staffing as an excuse for failing to uphold standards of care (see *Horton v Niagara Falls Memorial Medical Centre* (1976); *HCA Health Services of Midwest Inc v National Bank of Commerce* (1988); Murphy 1988b, p. 116);
- 'inexperience' is no defence in the case of negligence (Tingle 1990a, p. 43);
- a nurse who refuses to follow a directive to work in an unfamiliar area can risk disciplinary action for insubordination (Cushing 1983, p. 297; Creighton 1986, pp. 68–69; *Francis v Memorial General Hospital* (1986;) *Regan Report on Nursing Law* 1986; *Nursing Life* 1987, p. 72).

The dilemma for nurse administrators in the third instance is that they are obliged to direct staff to work in a short staffed area, despite knowing that the staff being sent might not have the required expertise to function in the area concerned (their response to this dilemma is usually to advise the reliever(s): 'just do the best you can'). The dilemma for the 'float' nurses (or 'relief' or 'pool' nurses as they are called in Australia and New Zealand), on the other hand, is that either they work where or as directed (even though this may mean functioning above their level of competence), or they refuse to work where or as directed and risk dismissal or being censured in some other way for insubordination. The float/relief nurse's position is made more intolerable by the fact that

> although education and experience in a particular area will be considered in deciding liability, a nurse cannot use her or his lack of familiarity with a particular specialty as an excuse for not applying the knowledge he or she does possess.
> (Murphy 1988c, p. 378)

What this position fails to recognise, however, is that 'familiarity' with a given area is itself often a necessary prerequisite to the possession and application of specialist or generalist nursing knowledge. For example, a nurse specialising in renal nursing will know, on the basis of her specialised education and experience, that a chronic renal failure patient with hypertension and who is bleeding at a peritoneal dialysis site, can be in clinical shock even though showing a blood pressure recording of 140/90 (a typical blood pressure recording for a person in shock would be around 90/60 or below). A nurse not familiar with renal nursing might, however, fail to recognise that the same patient is in clinical shock — mistakenly judging the 140/90 blood pressure recording to be a 'text-book' example of hypertension (high blood pressure).

A relief or a 'float' nurse's fears that 'if a patient's condition deteriorates, he or she will lack the necessary skill or knowledge to recognise and respond to it' are not only realistic, but are compounded by the fact 'that specialized units often have policies and protocols not known to the generalist nurse' (Cushing 1983 p. 297). The courts, however, appear to have little appreciation of these realities in nursing practice.

There is room to suggest that if nursing was truly recognised as being a knowledge based practice, and if it was recognised that nurses need to have either generalist and/or specialist knowledge and experience to practise competently and safely in given areas, then nurses could not be reasonably expected to work or relieve in areas that they are not familiar with. It is evident, however, that in the final analysis nursing is perceived (by hospital administrators and by the courts) as requiring little more than plain 'common sense'. The assumption that nursing work is carried out 'under the supervision of doctors' also makes it difficult for nurses to justify their refusal to follow a superior's directive to work in a short-staffed area for which they are neither educationally prepared nor practically experienced to work. If the legal status of the nurse as an autonomous and authoritative professional had really improved, nurses having to relieve in or cover unfamiliar areas would possibly be a non-issue altogether.

Law reform and the 'expanding the role' of the nurse

Over the past two to three decades there has been an increasing trend towards changing laws governing nursing practice to 'accommodate an expanded nursing role' (Waters and Arbeiter 1985, p. 38; Young 1985). The need to 'expand the role' of the nurse (which in essence has primarily involved expanding or extending the legal boundaries of nursing practice to allow nurses to perform 'new' (translate as 'medical') tasks without risk of being charged with the illegal practice of medicine) dates back to the 1960s. At this time, a shortage of doctors (or rather, as some have suggested, a 'maldistribution' of doctors) — particularly in the area of maternal and child health care — prompted health organisations around the world (including the World Health Organisation) to consider ways in which the shortage could be accommodated (Carlson and Athelstan 1970; Kadish and Long 1970; Lambertsen 1972; Slater 1974; Parsons 1975; Blower 1977; Trainer et al. 1981). The 'solution' was eventually found in the proposals to:

- train and use medical assistants, or 'physician assistants' as they are now called in the United States of America (note, it was envisaged that this option would 'open up careers' for 'corpsmen' leaving the army (Lambertsen 1972, p. 35));
- 'expand' (translate as 'extend') the role of the nurse[7] (Bullough 1975, p. 57; Blower 1977, p. 28; Mundinger 1980, p. 143; Mechanic 1988, p. 280).

The American Medical Association (AMA) went a step further and announced its 'new plan to turn nurses into physician assistants' (American Nurses' Association et al. 1970, p. 691). The announcement was met with shock and outrage by the American nursing profession which had been neither consulted nor informed about the AMA's plan prior to its announcement. Whereas the AMA confidently speculated that '100 000 nurses could quickly be trained and could markedly expand physicians' ability to serve their patients', and that this new 'role expansion' would 'increase' the nurse's professional status; nurses saw the plan as compounding already existing shortages of nurses and as standing to erode rather than expand the role of the nurse (ibid.; see also Carlson and Athelstan 1970, p. 1858; Kadish and Long 1970, p. 1051; *American Journal of*

Nursing 1972; Parsons 1975, p. 17; Trainer et al. 1981, p. 238). As the distinguished nurse theorist, Dr Martha Rogers, succinctly put it:

> To deliberately seek to make [the nursing] shortage even more critical — to con and coerce these nurses away from nursing — is morally reprehensible and socially irresponsible.
> (Rogers 1972, p. 43)

As at the turn of the century (when nurses were needed to establish the hospital system, and debates raged about the role and legal status of the nurse) it was politics and economic need — not bona fide public interest — that determined the outcome of the 'expanded role' debate (see Young 1985). The first paediatric nurse practitioner's course began at the University of Colorado in 1965 (Parsons 1975, p. 22; Trainer et al. 1981, p. 232). By 1970, the United States of America had 26 paediatric (postgraduate) nurse practitioner (NP) programs running. The graduates of these programs were educationally prepared and able to give total care to more than 75 per cent of all children attending outlets where NPs were practising (Blower 1977, p. 28). In 1971, an article in the *American Journal of Nursing* concluded: 'the pediatric nurse practitioner appears to offer an acceptable, practical and workable contribution toward alleviating the manpower shortage' (Andrews and Yankaver 1971 — cited in Dolan et al. 1983, p. 382; see also Secretary's Committee to Study Extended Roles for Nurses 1972). Other categories of NPs also emerged in the United States of America, namely: family nurse practitioner (FNP), adult nurse practitioner (ANP), obstetrics and gynaecologic nurse practitioner (OB-GynNP) (which, incidentally, effectively replaced midwifery which had been dispensed with earlier in the century (Carlson and Athelstan 1970, p. 1856)), and the psychiatric–mental health nurse practitioner (Kelly 1985, pp. 340–342; Walker 1972).

The NP came to epitomise — or so it was thought — the 'ultimate' of what nurses could achieve; namely, a truly *expanded* as opposed to a merely *extended*[8] role (that is, as a doctor's 'handmaiden') (Murphy 1970; Paxton and Scoblic 1978). Among other things, the NP was seen to gain direct access to patients; to be responsible for all nursing care including health assessments, identification of health needs, decision making, care giving and evaluation, and most important of all, was able to work independently (Kinlein 1972; Walker 1972; Lewis 1974; Parsons 1975; Carr 1982, p. 414; Trainer et al. 1981; Mechanic 1988, p. 280). These developments were generally interpreted as indicating a definite improvement in the professional status of the nurse.

Today, the realities of the NP's position offer quite a different picture of the NP's status. Waters and Arbeiter (1985, pp. 38–39) point out, for example, that in the United States of America few NPs practise independently, and many find it difficult to provide total health care because of:

- not having the authority to prescribe medications;
- the reluctance of and refusal by insurance companies to reimburse patients for a nurse practitioner's services.

Kelly (1985, p. 343) explains that while many NPs are in *private* practice, this should not be confused with their being in *independent* practice. Indeed, most NPs, she claims, are either working in a situation where they are 'backed up' by a physician or where they are in full partnership with a group of doctors in an established medical practice (ibid.). Kelly (1985, pp. 343–344) further notes that a major problem for NPs is 'getting enough patients and reimbursement to earn a living' (see also Styles 1989, p. 42). Another major problem faced by NPs is obtaining hospital privileges, that is, the right

> of a nurse not employed by that institution to admit patients and/or write orders for their care or participate in any part of his or her patient's care. (Kelly 1985, p. 344)

St Amand (1982, p. 407) explains that a hospital's medical by-laws often make 'no provision for nonphysician staff privileges'. She further explains (ibid.) that another obstacle is

> the lack of knowledge on the part of hospital health personnel about the independent nurse practitioner's role within the institution. Physicians [fear] the competition, nurses [worry] about the lack of control, and the hospital community overall [does] not understand the role of an independent nurse practitioner in an acute care setting.

The outcome of the NP movement has been both controversial and disappointing. Waters and Arbeiter (1985, p. 38) note that 'most NPs agree that the speciality hasn't yet attained the status that its creators envisioned'. Gorham (1985, p. 42) argues along similar lines, stating that many NPs have 'hassles with local physicians and difficulty in collecting payment from insurance companies'. As well as this, although many doctors employ NPs, 'the medical establishment still regards them as undertrained but threatening competitors' (ibid.), and many have actively opposed their 'expanded role'. For example, in the early 1970s, the Medical Society of the State of New York vehemently opposed a proposal to change the definition of nursing practice in the state's nurse practice Act. The proposed new definition had been formulated by the board of directors of the New York Nurses Association which had been established in 1969 to study the Act. After wide consultation with nursing groups, the board of directors recommended sweeping changes in the Act, including the definition of the practice of nursing (Driscoll 1972, p. 26). The definition proposed is quoted in full below:

The practice of the profession of nursing as a registered professional nurse is defined as diagnosing and treating human responses to actual or potential health problems through such services as casefinding, health teaching, health counselling, and provision of care supportive to or restorative of life and well-being, and executing medical regimes prescribed by a licensed or otherwise legally authorized physician or dentist.
(quoted in Driscoll 1972, p. 26)

The Medical Society of the State of New York quickly opposed the definition, arguing that it would permit the 'unauthorized practice of medicine' (ibid., p. 27) — in other words, it would permit nurses to function independently of doctors. Fearing that doctors would lose their statutory supervisory control over nursing practice, the Medical Society responded to supporters of the new nursing Bill by arguing:

You can use any words you want to in that definition as long as you make it clear that what nurses do is under the supervision and direction of the physician.
(cited in Driscoll 1972, p. 27)

The new nurses' Bill was approved by both houses of the New York State legislature. However, in a statement described as being 'rife with misinformation', and 'without discussion with those who would have clarified the facts', the New York State Governor vetoed the Bill, thus preserving medicine's statutory supervisory control over nursing practice (Rogers 1972, p. 45; see also Young 1972b, p. 39).

A more recent example of the degree to which some medical groups are threatened by and have opposed the NP can be found in a Missouri case involving two nurses in a family planning clinic who were accused of 'practising medicine without a licence' by the Missouri State Board of Registration for the Healing Arts (to be referred to hereafter as the board) (*Sermchief v Gonzales* (1983); see also Gorham 1985, p. 42; Creighton 1986, p. 18). The services routinely provided by the nurses and the subject of the complaint by the board, included:

taking [health histories]; breast and pelvic examinations; laboratory testing of Papanicolaou (Pap) smears, gonorrhea cultures, and blood serology; the providing and giving of information about oral contraceptives, condoms, and intrauterine devices (IUDs); the dispensing of certain designated medications; and counseling services and community education.
(*Sermchief v Gonzales* (1983), p. 684)

The board is reported to have

threatened to order the ... nurses and [employing] physicians to show cause why the nurses should not be found guilty of the unauthorized

practice of medicine and the physicians guilty of aiding and abetting such unauthorized practice.
(*Sermchief v Gonzales* (1983), p. 685)

As a result of this threat, the nurses and physicians sought relief through the court. Initially, a trial court ordered the nurses to stop doing breast and pelvic examinations, taking pap smears, and dispensing contraceptives (Gorham 1985, p. 42). The trial court's decision was, however, overturned by the Missouri Supreme Court, which found that the nurses' acts were 'authorised' ('all acts were performed pursuant to standing orders and protocols approved by physicians' (*Sermchief v Gonzales* (1983), p. 689)), and hence '[did] not constitute the unlawful practice of medicine' (ibid., p. 690). As well as this, the Supreme Court accepted that the nurses were acting within the scope of the 'specialized education, judgment and skill based on knowledge and application of principles derived from the biological, physical, social and nursing sciences' (ibid., p. 689). Despite this landmark decision, doctors in the United States of America continue to successfully oppose law reforms favouring the expanded role of the nurse — particularly in relation to prescribing and dispensing drugs (especially contraceptives, narcotics and antibiotics).

A similar situation has occurred in the United Kingdom. During the 1980s, for example, moves to 'expand the role' of the nurse in family planning were bitterly opposed by doctors. Although nurses were trained to carry out cervical smears and breast examinations, and to advise on contraception, many doctors considered this an 'encroachment on their territory' (*Nursing Times* 1982b; see also Mitchell 1985). The situation in the United Kingdom will be examined further shortly.

Another major problem faced by NPs is that many have ended up being little more than the 'appendages' or the assistants of doctors (Orr 1988, p. 34; see also Turner 1990a; Smith 1990a; Stilwell 1990). Gorham (1985) notes, for example, that overburdened doctors have discovered the advantages of employing NPs. In one case, a small medical practice of two doctors was able to increase its patient turnover by 40 to 50 patients per day by employing NPs. The doctors in this instance were able to increase their patient turnover and hence their net incomes, while at the same time reducing their own workloads (ibid., pp. 42–43; Turner 1990a). Others have suggested that by employing NPs, an average medical practice could increase its turnover (and hence profit) by 30 to 50 per cent without increasing the workload, time and stress of the medical practitioners themselves (Slater 1975, p. 31).

Another concern — and a further indication that expanded role law reforms have not improved the professional status of nurses — is that even in the case of NPs, it is usually the doctor (for example, a general practitioner or a private medical consultant) who employs the nurse, and not vice versa (Stilwell 1990, p. 34). When 'independent' NPs are in a position to be the employers of doctors — and actually employ doctors in a nursing practice — then the nursing profession might well have some grounds for optimism that its professional status has indeed improved.

It should perhaps be clarified here that the notion of 'role expansion' (taken literally to mean 'multi-directional change') was not restricted to apply only to NPs. Nurses[9] practising in hospitals and other health care agency settings have also experienced 'role expansion' — particularly in the speciality areas such as ICUs, CCUs, NICUs, A&Es. Role expansion (which in reality has been only role extension, namely, as a doctor's assistant (Paxton and Scoblic 1978, p. 271)) remains controversial. Even the concept of 'role expansion' is problematic. For example, Driscoll (1972) — an early critic of the role expansion movement — argues persuasively that the concept of role expansion presupposes that nursing practice 'is merely an extension of medical practice', and that its development essentially involves 'extending' or 'expanding' out from (and transforming itself into) medical practice — which is seen to be central not just to nursing, but to the whole health care domain (see also Keller 1973, p. 236). To describe nursing as merely 'expanding' or 'extending' also denies and undermines its bona fide evolution as a socially relevant profession and its 'keeping pace' with sociological, scientific and technological change — something which, historically, nursing has always done. Comparing the position of nursing with medicine, Driscoll (1972, p. 25) explains:

> Although today's [medical] experts in cardiac and renal surgery bear little resemblance to their historical antecedents — barbers and blood-letters — no one refers to our eminent medical colleagues as 'extended' physicians, nor to their role as the 'expanded' role of the surgeon. The medical profession has *simply kept pace with* and utilized advances in science and technology [emphasis added].

Martha Rogers (1972), another early critic of the role expansion movement, is even more critical of the concept of 'role expansion' and derivatives thereof. In a short but celebrated article entitled 'Nursing: to be or not to be?', Rogers (1972, p. 42) argues:

> Clichés such as 'expanded role,' 'physician's assistants,' 'pediatric associates,' and multiple other meaningless verbosities provide subtle and not so subtle come-ons for the naive — nonsensical nomenclature designed to gull registered nurses into leaving nursing in order to play handmaiden to medical mythology and machines.

She goes on to remind nurses that 'medical knowledge, no matter how relevant to medical practice, is not a substitute for the nursing knowledge that is essential to nursing practice', and concludes:

Persons who choose to leave nursing to become physician's assistants, pediatric associates, and the like must find their identity in the new field they have chosen. They are no longer entitled to identify as nurses. (Rogers 1972, p. 45)

Paradoxically, 'role expansion' has forced nurses to participate in the erosion of their own traditional role. Equally disturbing, it has paved the way for others outside nursing (in particular, physician assistants and even doctors themselves) to encroach on and erode the role of the nurse and nursing practice (Young 1972b, p. 38; see also Lambertsen 1972; *Regan Report on Nursing Law* 1985). A good example of the role erosion that has occurred as a result of 'role expansion' can be found in the following personal commentary by a nurse published in the American nursing periodical *Nursing*. She writes:

Last night in the emergency room, three children cried, three people were nervous, two people said they wanted to talk to me, thirty anxious people passed through the waiting room, three people were cold, and two were hungry. I was too busy to help any of them. What they needed was a nurse.

(Anderson 1977)

Reflecting on why she could not help these people — why she could not help the thirty anxious people, feed the hungry or give blankets to the cold — the nurse concluded that her 'expanded role' had committed her to performing other 'more important' tasks such as inserting two intravenous therapy lines, drawing eight tubes of blood for testing, taking ten blood pressure recordings, auditing an electrocardiogram, and so the list went on. The nurse finished her commentary by warning (ibid.):

We'd better start thinking about our one great contribution to the health field — nursing — and figuring out ways to get back to our job. We've only to compare our 'notes on not-nursing' with Ms Nightingale's *Notes on Nursing* to see how far we've expanded our role. And to see that, if we're not careful, we'll expand ourselves right out of a job.

Dr Hedy Mechanic (1988), an American associate professor of nursing, has similar concerns. She argues that the expanded role movement is at the 'crossroads', and contends:

We can continue to emphasize the medical elements of the extended role or we can choose to redefine the expanded role to reflect the depth and breadth of nursing skills today. (Mechanic 1988, p. 284)

Like Anderson, Mechanic also believes that the expanded role of the nurse in its present form, could 'spell its own demise' — unless it is more reflective of nursing and not merely reflective of the discarded functions of medicine as has tended to be the case (see also Rogers 1972, p. 44; Bellersen 1979; Young 1985; Rowden 1987b).

The legitimated expansion of the nurse's role has done little to improve either the autonomy or authority of professional nurses. Even when in 'independent' practice, nurses are still required to follow medical protocols or guidelines for certain tasks, or to enter into an 'honorary contract' with or work under the 'supervision' of a doctor before being 'allowed' to perform 'new' tasks — for example, perform health assessments, advise on contraception, initiate wound care, treat constipation and prescribe and supply drugs (see, for example, Carlson and Athelstan 1970; Mitchell 1985; Young 1985; Head 1988; Cameron, J. 1990; Stilwell 1990; Turner 1990a). Nurses are still regarded as being intellectually and occupationally inferior to doctors, and for the most part are still viewed by the courts as being dependent on doctors (Murphy 1987a, p. 15).

Perhaps one of the most disturbing outcomes of the expanded role reforms, however, is that nurses are increasingly being held to medical standards of care rather than nursing standards of care in negligence cases in which they are involved (see, for example, *Gugino v Harvard Community Health Plan* (1980); *Planned Parenthood of Northwest Indiana v Vines* (1989); *Regan Report on Nursing Law* 1989; Northrop 1987). The application of medical rather than nursing standards in nursing negligence cases (which is discussed more fully in chapter 8 of this text) has, among other things, served to reinforce the cultural hegemony of medicine, and the medical control of nurses and of defining the 'acceptable' legal boundaries of nursing practice. Thus, in the final analysis, it appears that the so-called *expanded role* reforms in nursing amount to little more than *expanded control* reforms, which in turn have further denied nurses their 'freedom to nurse'. In other words, to borrow from Driscoll (1972, p. 24), 'nursing [continues to be] nursing practiced *under the supervision of doctors* [emphasis added]'.

Equally if not more disturbing, however, is that so-called 'expanded role' reforms are providing an important means by which doctors are increasingly taking over practices and roles traditionally performed and fulfilled by nurses. In the United Kingdom, for example, government reforms mandating a new 'GP contract' are forcing GPs to take a more proactive role in health promotion and preventative medicine. As a result, GPs are taking over the health surveillance of children and the elderly (notably those over the age of 75 years) — a role and practice traditionally performed by nurses (for example, district nurses, community psychiatric nurses, and another category of health worker called 'health visitors') (Smith 1990a; Stilwell 1990; Turner 1990a). GPs are responding to their new contract by increasing their employment of practice nurses to whom they delegate home visiting duties. One commentator has recently pointed out, for example, that:

74% of district nurse contact is made with those over 65, so district nurses could contribute to the regular annual assessment of patients over-75 *on behalf* of the GP.
(Smith 1990a, p. 31)

The outcome of the United Kingdom 'reforms' will probably be akin to the outcome of similar reforms in the United States of America which saw doctors declaring that 'home care services and health maintenance and promotion, initiated more than a century ago by nursing, are a new creation of *their* making' (Rogers 1972, p. 44). This outcome threatens not only to deny the nursing profession's historical front line role in health promotion and primary health care, but to deny nursing's role altogether.

For all the expanded role 'reforms' which have occurred over the past 20 to 30 years, a number of serious questions remain; notably, as Edith Lewis, editor of the American nursing periodical *Nursing Outlook* asks:

Whatever the nurse does, will she do so *in her own right* [emphasis added], as part of the legitimate practice of nursing? or will she continue in a dependent status, under the continuing myth of medical supervision — supervision that is all too often remote, token, and not even related to the patient's *health* care (as opposed to his medical care) needs? supervision that often delays and frustrates the nurse in taking the action that she, out of her nursing knowledge, knows is needed?
(Lewis 1974, p. 21)

At present, the possible answers to these questions give little hope for optimism. Although in practice nurses may exercise independent judgment, their judgments are nevertheless 'legally dependent' in so far as they are still legally subject to 'medical review and direction' — and, it should be added, medical sanction (Slater 1974, p. 32). Furthermore, it is the medical practitioners — not nurses — who, in the final analysis, have the legitimated authority to 'decide what, if any, of [their] present responsibilities [they] will delegate, and under what type of supervision' (ibid., p. 33). Until nurses are really in a legitimated position of power and authority to decide what responsibilities they will accept and when, then the status quo will remain very much intact. Meanwhile, expanded role reforms stand in nursing jurisprudential history as yet another example of 'law reforms going *for* nurses also going *against* them'. To borrow from the early 'crisis school' of thought in the early 1970s[10],

the nurse's step forward into an expanded medical assistant role [is] a step backward into the handmaiden role the nurse has been required to play for the medical profession in the post-Nightingale era.
(Parsons 1975, p. 20)

The powerlessness of the nurse's signature

Historically, nurses (like women generally) have lacked legitimated signing authority. The nurse's signature has always been regarded as having less value and less authority than a doctor's signature (a situation which has its parallel in women's signatures traditionally having less power and authority than men's signatures[11]). Unlike the doctor's signature, which has traditionally been a symbol of authority and approval, the nurse's signature has traditionally been a symbol of compliance and obedience.

The legal status of the nurse's signature has not improved over the years. Today, it is still primarily a symbol or mark of obedience (that is, of having carried out a command) and an admission of responsibility. This contrasts strongly with the doctor's signature which stands as a symbol or mark of authority — of having authorised a command which demands compliance.

As a general rule, nurses have no legal authority to sign important documents relating to matters of life and death. In the past, some hospitals even discouraged nurses from witnessing wills, even though there was no legal reason why nurses should not have undertaken this role (it was thought that nurses might 'unduly' influence a patient and/or be made a beneficiary of a grateful patient's will). Nurses have no legal authority to sign a death certificate — even though they are often the only ones who have attended and witnessed the death and may make the initial judgment that a patient is in fact dead. Nor do nurses have the legitimated authority to specify a patient's cause of death — even though their knowledge of possible causes may be equal to that of a doctor's. Typically, when a patient dies in the absence of an 'attending' doctor, a nurse will notify the 'attending' doctor of the death and will prepare the relevant forms for him or her to sign (CCH et al. 1990, pp. 308–310). Nurses also have no authority to issue and sign a 'sick' certificate authorising a worker to take time off work to recover from an illness or injury. Usually only a doctor has the legitimated authority to sign a 'medical' certificate.

Another example of the nurse's lack of signing authority can be found in the case of legally restricted drugs — which, as discussed earlier in this chapter, nurses have no authority either to prescribe or dispense. Typically, when nurses sign for a drug, their signature means nothing more than that the drug in question has been either examined, verified, checked and/or administered. When doctors sign for a drug, however, this tends to mean that they have commanded or given a direction that the drug in question must be or may be administered.

Perhaps one of the best examples of a nurse's lack of signing authority can be found in the case of passport applications. On the standard Australian passport application form, 25 categories of people are listed who are able to verify an applicant's proof of identity. The categories of people named include: dentists, doctors of medicine, pharmacists and veterinary surgeons. Teachers, policemen, and public servants are also named, as are those of the 'traditional' professions such as judges, barristers, solicitors, bank managers, accountants, and politicians. The category 'nurses', however, is conspicuous by its absence. Just why nurses have not been included on the list is not immediately clear. One possible reason is that since the majority of nurses are women, and since women still tend to be regarded by the state as being by nature 'fickle' and 'rationally incompetent', it may have been deemed 'safer' not to include nurses on the list.

There is a paucity of literature on the question of the legal authority of the nurse's signature, and unfortunately it is beyond the scope of this present inquiry to investigate the issue further. Nevertheless, on the basis of everyday experience, it is evident that the nurse's signature lacks authority, and that this is a reflection of the nurse's lack of authority generally. The essential powerlessness of the nurse's signature, and the essential powerfulness of the doctor's signature is perhaps also a reflection of the continued legitimated cultural hegemony of medicine and the subordination of nursing in the world of everyday affairs. More significantly, the powerlessness of the nurse's signature is possibly also a reflection of the fact that despite demonstrable improvements in the social and legal status of women, the social and legal status of the nurse has not only *not* improved, but has not kept pace with the improved status of women. For instance, whereas the legal status of a woman's signature has greatly improved (women in common law countries no longer need their husbands' signatures to obtain a driver's licence or to open a bank account, for example), the legal status of a nurse's signature has not (nurses, for example, still require the 'authorising' signature of a doctor before being able to initiate certain nursing actions and cares). Had the social and legal position of nurses improved, there is room to speculate that the legal (and professional) authority of their signatures would have likewise improved.

The marginalisation of nurses in legal texts

Another informative example of the nurse's lack of improved legal status can be found in the case of legal texts, and the extent to which nurses have been — and continue to be — marginalised and rendered invisible in law reports, the tables of contents and subject indexes of legal texts, legal dictionaries, legal digests, and so on. As stated earlier in this book, a lack of reported cases involving nurses and nursing practice in Australia and other common law countries has made it extremely difficult, and at times impossible, to construct an account of nursing's historical relationship to and experience of the law in given areas. This has forced a disproportionate reliance on the American experience.

To clarify what is at issue here, law reports are 'reports of cases decided by the courts' (*A concise dictionary of law* (Oxford Reference) 1990, p. 230). It should be noted, however, that not all cases decided by the courts are reported (indeed, there may not even be written judgments for lower court decisions (for example, trial and industrial commission hearings)). Usually, it is only the 'important' (superior court) cases — selected by lawyers, and approved by the judges involved — that are reported (ibid.). Furthermore, the mere reporting of a case does not assure its reliability. Derham et al. (1986, p. 107) point out, for example, that while a court may in principle 'hear citation of a precedent case from *any source which the court decides is reliable* [emphasis added]', normally the courts 'will require the report to be the best available'. A court decision published in the *Australian Nursing Journal* or *The Times* newspaper, for example, would be considered less reliable than a decision published in the prestigious (and authorised) Reports of the Incorporated Council of Law Reporting for England and Wales (ibid.).

The traditional (and patriarchally biased) processes used for reporting 'important' legal cases have historically militated against the development of a substantial and reliable body of law on nursing jurisprudence. It is probable that cases involving nurses have not been reported because the lawyers and jurists involved in selecting and reporting cases have considered nursing cases 'unimportant' and therefore not 'worthy' of reporting (it should be noted here that while a case might be considered 'unimportant' in law, it certainly is not 'unimportant' for the unfortunate nurse having to appear in court and who may have been at the receiving end of an unfavourable decision). A notable example of the failure to report a nursing case can be found in the Australian case *In re Nurses Registration Act 1953 and In re Heathcote and Nurses Registration Board and Walton* (District Court of New South Wales, dated 12 April 1991) cited earlier in this chapter, in the section entitled 'Increased nurse liability for failing to question a doctor's negligent orders'. Despite the profound significance of this case for the nursing profession (it is the first *recorded* case (to be distinguished here from a *reported* case) of its kind in NSW), it has not as yet been formally reported in the 'mainstream' Australian law reports. Indeed, because it was a lower court decision, it probably will not be formally reported. As previously mentioned, the recorded decision of this case has been published in full in the *Australian Nurses Journal*. This journal would probably not be regarded by the courts as a 'reliable' source, however.

A major effect of not reporting decisions involving nurses and nursing practice has been the marginalisation of nurses' experiences in the courts, and the rendering invisible of nursing's relationship to and experience of the law generally. As a result, it has been and remains very difficult for the nursing profession to identify — let alone critically examine — nursing's historical and contemporary relationship to the law and, in particular, to identify and expose the injustices that nurses — both as professionals and as women — have experienced at the hands of the entire legal system. This, in turn, has had the effect of silencing nurses. In particular, it has silenced any dissenting voice that nurses might otherwise have been able to raise had they had access to and full knowledge of the ways in which the courts have historically treated them, and knowledge of the extent to which the courts have been instrumental in structuring, reinforcing and maintaining generally the nursing profession's legitimated subordination to medicine.

Nurses' and the nursing profession's experience of law have been marginalised and silenced in other legal texts besides law reports, however. For instance, the categories 'nurse', 'nursing practice', 'nursing profession', and the like, are either conspicuously absent or are subsumed under 'medicine' in the tables of contents and subject indexes of legal reference texts — including legal digests, legal dictionaries and legal history texts. For example, in the table of contents of *Halsbury's laws of England* 4th edn (1980), the subject 'Nurses, midwives and nurses agencies' is subsumed under the primary subject heading 'Medicine, pharmacy, drugs and medicinal products'. Similarly, in the table of contents of *Halsbury's laws of England: annual abridgement 1990* (1991), the subject of 'Nurses, midwives and health visitors' is likewise subsumed under the subject heading 'Medicine, pharmacy, drugs and medicinal products'. In the *Australian Legal Monthly Digest* (1990), again the subject of nurses or nursing has no discrete listing. And in the 'Key to the Australian digest', the subject 'Nurses and midwives' is subsumed under the subject heading 'Medicine'. Nurses and nursing suffer a similar fate in *The digest: annotated British, Commonwealth and European cases* (1982). In this major reference text, the subject 'Nurses, midwives and nurses agencies' is subsumed under the primary subject listing of 'Medicine, pharmacy, drugs and medicinal products.'

The *Index to the Canadian legal literature* (1989), stands as a particularly good example of the marginalisation and constructed invisibility of the profession and practice of nursing. The subject index of this publication has almost two pages of fine print devoted to identifying an extensive range of subjects relating to the practice and profession of medicine, including, for example: medical care, the cost of medical care, medical corporations, medical disclosure, medical ethics, medical law and ethics, medical examiners, medical experimentation, medical facilities, medical jurisprudence, medical laws and legislation, medical personnel, malpractice, medical profession, medical records, medication errors, and forensic medicine. There is, however, no reference to 'nurses' or 'nursing'.

Nurses and the nursing profession fare no better in the *American digest system*, despite the fact that there is an abundance of reported cases involving nurses in the American law reports. In the 'descriptive word index' of the *Ninth decennial digest, American digest system 1981–1986*, for example, the word 'nurses' is not listed under the index topic 'particular occupations'; nor is the word 'nurses' listed in the general list of 'digest topics'. In the case of the American law reports, all cases involving nurses are firmly subsumed under the topic 'physicians and surgeons'.

The failure to list nurses under their own discrete subject or topic heading not only renders nursing invisible, but, as already stated, makes it difficult to inquire into the whole issue of nursing jurisprudence. Fortunately, inquiry into American nursing jurisprudence, at least, is assisted greatly by the publication of the *Regan Report on Nursing Law*, which is produced monthly and which provides an up-to-date record of recent court cases involving nurses. The proliferation of nursing and the law texts in the United States of America has also greatly assisted the development of nursing jurisprudence research. Nevertheless, as in the case with most law reports outside of the United States, it is still necessary to do a piecemeal search of cases subsumed under the primary topic or subject heading of 'physicians and surgeons' or 'medicine' in order to locate cases which might be of importance to nurses. The task is further complicated by the fact that although nurses may be involved as defendants in a given case, they are not always independently named as defendants (for example, the hospital or a physician/surgeon may be named as the defendant).

Nurses have also been marginalised and rendered invisible in other more general legal texts. In the 'general index' of Holdsworth's (1972) *A history of English law* series, for example, nurses do not rate a mention at all. There is, however, a listing for the subjects 'medical profession', and 'medical jurisprudence'. And in John Saunders' (1989) *Words and phrases legally defined*, although the word 'nurse' is listed, it is inadequately defined. The definition (which, incidentally, could apply to almost anybody) simply reads: '"Nurse" means a nurse for the sick' (*Nurses Agencies Act 1957*, s 8, as amended (Saunders 1989, p. 243)). This definition compares very poorly with the two pages of extremely fine print devoted to defining the term 'medical practitioner'. And whereas no other terms related to the profession and practice of nursing are listed, terms such as 'medical examination', 'medical officer', 'medical treatment', 'medicinal purpose', and 'medicine' are all listed and adequately defined. Overall, Saunders pays inadequate attention to the subject of nurses and nursing practice, compared to other mainstream health professional reference texts which have given very comprehensive definitions of terms relevant to the profession and practice of nursing (see, for example, Miller and Keane's (1987) *Encyclopedia and dictionary of medicine, nursing, and allied health*, 4th edn, pp. 870–873).

Saunders' (1989) text is not alone in its deficient treatment of nurse related terms, however. Hardy Ivamy's (1988) *Mozley and Whiteley's law dictionary* omits the term 'nurse' altogether. The term 'medical practitioner' is included but with a cross-reference to the term 'practitioner'. The term 'practitioner' is defined as 'a doctor, dentist or veterinary surgeon'. The term 'practitioner', in this instance, clearly does not include nurses.

The exclusion of the category 'nurse' or its subsumption under the category 'medicine' in legal texts is another indication that nursing has not yet received full legitimated recognition as an autonomous and authoritative profession in its own right. If and when terms such as 'nurse', 'nurse practitioner', 'nursing profession', 'nursing practice', 'nursing ethics', 'nursing jurisprudence', 'nursing examinations', 'nursing law and ethics', 'nursing research', 'nurse medication errors', 'nursing care facilities', 'nursing personnel', 'nursing malpractice/negligence', 'nursing records', and the like, are given discrete listings in their own right in legal texts, then, and only then, can the nursing profession have some grounds for optimism that it has moved closer to achieving the social and legal recognition for which it has historically fought.

CONCLUSION

In this chapter, an attempt has been made to show that despite so-called 'progressive' law reforms in nursing, and despite legal trends over the past few decades which are seeing nurses being increasingly held independently responsible for their own negligent actions, the legal status of the nurse as an autonomous and authoritative professional has not significantly improved and the nursing profession as a whole remains subject to the dominance and control of doctors. Chapter 8 will provide additional compelling evidence illustrating the fact that the legal status of the nurse as an autonomous professional remains less than optimal.

ENDNOTES

1   See, for example: *Hall v Lees* (1904); *Evans v Liverpool Corporation* (1906); *Hillyer v Governors of St Bartholomew's Hospital* (1909); *Lavere v Smith's Falls Public Hospital* (1915); *Nyberg v Provost Municipal Hospital Board* [1927]; *Byrd v Marion General Hospital* (1932); *Lavelle v Glasgow Royal Infirmary* [1932]; *Logan v Waitaki Hospital Board* [1935]; *Strangeways-Lesmere v Clayton* [1936]; *Vuchar et al. v The Trustees of the Toronto General Hospital* [1936]; *Wardell v Kent County Council* (1938); *Gold v Essex County Council* (1942); *Richardson v Doe* (1964); *Darling v Charleston Community Memorial Hospital* (1965); *Toth v Community Hospital at Glen Cove* (1968); *Re Mount Sinai and Ontario Nurses' Association* (1978); *Flinders Medical Centre Incorporated v Tingay (Appeal) Case* (1984); *Koeniguer v Eckrich* (1988)).

2   A similar position was accepted in the famous unreported Dr Leonard Arthur case in England (see Kuhse 1984; Gunn and Smith 1985; Johnstone 1989, pp. 267–269).

3   Although the court decision in this matter has not been formally reported in the Australian law reports, it has been reprinted in full in the *Australian Nurses' Journal* (1991) (see also Hills 1989–1990, 1991; Harbutt 1991).

4 On 12 April 1991, almost four years after the events of 24 June 1987, the District Court of New South Wales ordered that the action of the NSW Registration Board be 'quashed' and that Sophia Heathcote 'be restored to the position that she was in before that action was taken in relation to her' (*Australian Nurses Journal* 1991, p. 15).

5 Note: selective prosecution is a classic mechanism for controlling subordinates (Thornton, personal communication). A famous military example of this can be found in the case of the My Lai massacre during the Vietnam war, and the selective prosecution of Lieutenant William Calley for his role in the incident (see in particular: Peers 1979; Kelman and Hamilton 1989). Although others (including his superiors) were brought to trial, Calley was the only one convicted for the My Lai crimes (Kelman and Hamilton 1989, pp. 5–6).

6 Note that this reference does not include *nurses*. This is not merely coincidental. Nor is it, I believe, intended to be 'inclusive' of nurses, since an examination of early court cases reveals that as a general rule nurses were not independently named as defendants in negligence torts. Usually it was either the hospital board/trustees or the doctor who was sued.

7 Note: concerns about maternal and child health also prompted governments at the turn of the century to support the state registration of nurses. Swendson (unpub.) notes, for example, that the Queensland government's relatively early state registration of nurses in 1911 was seen as a means of 'preventing maternal and child deaths'.

8 The whole notion of the *expanded* versus the *extended* role of the nurse was and remains a matter of controversy within nursing (see, for example, Murphy 1970; Driscoll 1972; Kinlein 1972; Lambertsen 1972; Lewis 1972, 1974; Rogers 1972; Secretary's Committee to Study Extended Roles for Nurses 1972; Jacobi 1973; Keller 1973; McGivern 1974; Bates 1975; Parsons 1975; Slater 1974; Paxton and Scoblic 1978; Kelly 1985; Young 1985; Rowden 1987b; Head 1988; Mechanic 1988; Smith 1990a; Styles 1989).

9 Note: there is an acknowledged semantic problem with the title 'nurse practitioner'. As Kelly (1985, p. 337) correctly points out, technically speaking all nurses who practise nursing are 'nurse practitioners'.

10 Parsons (1975, p. 20) refers to Dr Martha Rogers as the 'spiritual leader of the crisis school', and thereafter refers to those opposing the expanded role reforms as the 'crisis school'.

11 Signing has always been a male prerogative. In the past, even literate women could not sign on their own behalf, and were required to have the signature of their husbands or a close male relative to authorise or authenticate documents. Frye (1983, p. 63) gives the example that as late as the 1970s, in one liberal college town in the United States of America, a woman could not even get a library card without her husband's signature.

CHAPTER **EIGHT**

Nursing Negligence and the Problem of 'Expert' Witnesses

INTRODUCTION

ON 16 JULY 1974, the jury of an Illinois circuit court rendered a verdict in favour of the plaintiffs and against the hospital and a nurse to the amount of $1 million for their negligence which resulted in a 14-month-old child being left a quadriplegic and mentally retarded (Fiesta 1988, pp. 280–281). The family paediatrician involved in the case was held not negligent. The jury reached its decision 'after a 17-day trial with 29 witnesses, *of whom 24 were physicians* [emphasis added]' (ibid., p. 281). The case, *Hollinger v Children's Memorial Hospital* (No. 70L–10627, Ill Cir Ct, Cook County, 16 July 1974 — cited by Fiesta 1988, p. 281), has not been reported.

As already discussed, many nurse and legal commentators believe that the increase in successful litigation against nurses is a sign that nursing has 'come of age' as an autonomous and socially accountable profession, and that the courts are 'at last' recognising nurses as autonomous and independently accountable health care practitioners. In chapter 7, arguments were advanced to refute this view, and to show that, contrary to superficial appearances, the legal status of the nurse has not improved significantly and, further, that the profession and practice of nursing remains very much subject to the control and dominance of the medical profession. In this chapter, additional arguments are advanced to support further the view that the legal status of nursing as an autonomous profession has not improved significantly. In particular, attention is given to showing that the courts still do not recognise that the nursing profession has its own discrete body of professional *nursing* (as opposed to *medical*) knowledge and has its own discrete nursing (as opposed to medical) standards of care. In demonstrating these points, appeal is made to the distinct body of American law[1] that has emerged over the past 30 or more years on the subject of expert witnesses in cases involving professional nursing negligence.

Owing to a lack of reported cases in Australia, and the apparent lack of an equivalent 'body of law' on the subject of expert nurse witnesses in other common law countries, it has not been possible to undertake a more comprehensive and comparative analysis here. Nevertheless, the American cases reported on and used in this chapter involve situations with which nurses in other common law countries would be familiar. Furthermore, the cases used offer important insights into court attitudes toward nurses and nursing practice that might otherwise not be gained because of the paucity of similar reported cases in those countries. For these reasons, among others, the American focus need not be regarded as problematic or as limiting or undermining the present inquiry.

Before proceeding, the point should perhaps be clarified that there is a significant difference between an expert witness and a non-expert or 'ordinary' witness. Generally speaking, an 'ordinary' witness is someone who gives evidence on what she or he has seen 'as an ordinary member of the public [or profession as the case may be]' (Gee and Mason 1990, p. 26). An expert witness, by contrast, does not have to have 'direct experience of the facts'; he or she is an expert, that is, has 'superior knowledge' of a subject (ibid.; *A concise dictionary of law* 1990; see also *Wood v Rowland* (1978), p. 1335; Cushing 1988, pp. 44–51). It should be clarified further here that not just anybody or any nurse can be an expert witness. Before an expert opinion can be given, two key matters must first be established, namely, that

- the field of knowledge in which the witness professes expertise is outside the ordinary experience of the court;
- the witness has sufficient expertise in that field.

(Langslow 1989b, p. 30)

Thus, in order for a nurse to 'qualify' as an expert witness, the court must firstly be satisfied that the knowledge (in this instance, of nursing practice) in which the nurse professes expertise 'is outside the ordinary experience of the court', and, secondly, that she or he has sufficient expertise in that field (nursing practice) in order to give a 'credible' expert opinion. Whether the courts adhere to their own rhetoric with regards to the need for the above criteria to be met before qualifying expert witnesses — particularly in the case of nursing — is another matter entirely. The discussion below will, I believe, cast considerable doubt on the integrity of the courts in relation to the expert nurse question, and will show that the courts have either not applied or have not correctly applied the above criteria when qualifying expert witnesses to give an opinion on 'acceptable' nursing standards of care.

Determining professional nursing negligence

Every nursing action 'carries the potential for a charge of negligence' (Tingle 1990b, p. 60). In order for a nurse's conduct to be negligent, however, it 'must have fallen below the standard expected of that nurse *given his or her level of training and experience* [emphasis added]' (CCH et al. 1990, p. 14; see also Murchison et al. 1982; O'Sullivan 1983; Creighton 1986; Bernzweig 1987; Northrop and Kelly 1987; Cushing 1988; Fiesta 1988; Guido 1988; Staunton and Whyburn 19). In determining the 'standard expected', it is generally believed (and indeed taught in courses/in-service nursing education programs on nursing and the law) that the matter of a nurse's negligence would be approached by asking the question:

> What would we have expected the ordinary reasonable nurse to do in this situation, given that she has a particular level of skill, knowledge and expertise?
>
> (Staunton and Whyburn 1993, pp. 23–24)

It is further believed (and taught) that a nurse against whom negligence is alleged would be judged by the 'ordinary' or 'normal' standards of nursing care (see also the 'Bolam test' as established by *Bolam v Friern Hospital Management Committee* [1957]; Gee and Mason 1990, p. 169). Or, to be more specific, a nurse against whom negligence is alleged, would

> not be judged by the standards of the least qualified members of his [or her] class, nor by those of the most highly qualified, but by the standard of the ordinary careful and competent practitioner of that class.
>
> (Nathan 1957 — cited in Staunton and Whyburn 1993, p. 24)

In other words, if it is alleged that a nurse has been negligent, her or his conduct will be judged from the standpoint of an 'ordinary, careful and competent' nurse of 'similar education and experience' — or so it is believed (O'Sullivan 1983; Creighton 1986; Bernzweig 1987; Northrop and Kelly 1987; Cushing 1988; Fiesta 1988; Guido 1988; Staunton and Whyburn 1993; CCH et al. 1990; Tingle 1990a, 1990b).

At face value, the legalistic processes and procedures described above seem fair and reasonable, and perhaps offer nurses some degree of reassurance that if it is alleged they have been negligent, they will, at the very least, be judged by professional nursing peers who have the relevant nursing knowledge necessary to make an appropriate and just evaluation of the allegedly negligent conduct in question. The problem is, however, that for all the 'nicety' of legal rhetoric about what ought to happen in a nursing negligence case, the reality is that nurses are rarely judged from the point of view of their own professional nursing peers or on the basis of acceptable professional nursing standards of conduct. To the contrary. If it is alleged that a nurse has been professionally negligent (to be distinguished here from 'ordinary' or 'common' negligence), she or he tends to be judged from the point of view of 'experts' (that is, those most highly qualified and who have special knowledge on the subject at hand), rather than from the point of view of 'ordinary careful and competent' nursing peers; and, more specifically, from the standpoint of medical experts (usually male doctors), rather than nurse experts.

Conversely, if it is alleged that a nurse has been negligent in an 'ordinary' or 'common' sense, he or she tends to be judged from the standpoint of a lay person (or people), rather than from the standpoint of nursing peers; and, more specifically, from the standpoint of male judges and/or lay members of a jury. Either way, the situation is profoundly problematic, not just for individual nurses, but for the nursing profession as a whole — not least because it has totally undermined the nursing profession's ability to control and define the legitimated boundaries and standards of its own professional practice. More specifically, it has ensured that doctors, not nurses, have ultimate control of what the 'acceptable' boundaries of nursing practice should be, what the 'acceptable' standards of nursing care should be, and when and if nursing standards (as opposed to medical or lay standards) should be applied in judging whether a nurse's conduct has been negligent (see Fiesta 1988, p. 47). It is to examining these claims more fully that this discussion will now turn.

The dominance of expert medical witnesses in nursing negligence/malpractice cases

Historically, doctors have played a prominent and dominant role as expert witnesses in cases involving professional nursing negligence. There have been a number of reasons for this. First, as Langslow (1989b, p. 30) points out:

> Traditionally nurses have not been seen as competent to give opinion evidence on matters of diagnosis and the cause of injury.

Indeed, the courts have tended to hold that only doctors are competent and able to testify on 'conditions and causation', and that to allow nurses to testify on such matters would be tantamount to allowing them to 'go beyond the field of nursing and invade that of the physician' (*Belmon v St Frances Cabrini Hospital* (1983), p. 545; see also *McCormick v Avret* (1980); *Mellies v National Heritage, Inc* (1981); *Kuna v Lifemark Hospitals of Texas, Inc* (1987)). Where nurses have been permitted to testify on such matters, they have not always done so in their own right as nurses. Instead, nurses appearing as expert witnesses have often been accepted as qualified by the courts as expert medical witnesses (used here in a generic sense), rather than as expert nurse witnesses (see, for example, *Avret v McCormick* (1980); *McCormick v Avret* (1980); *Maloney v Wake Hospital Systems, Inc* (1980) — see in particular p. 684; *Mellies v National Heritage, Inc* (1981); *Johnson v Hermann Hospital* (1983)). Or, where a nurse's expert testimony has been permitted 'in its own right', its admission by the court has tended to be 'token', rather than necessary. For example, in the Louisiana Court of Appeals case *Belmon v St Frances Cabrini Hospital* (1983), in which the admission of an expert nursing opinion was cited among the grounds for appealing a trial court's judgment for the plaintiff in a negligence case, the court ruled that admitting the testimony of the expert nurse (an assistant professor of nursing) was 'entirely proper'. While acknowledging that the nurse's expert testimony 'addressed a precise issue before the court' (notably, the issue of acceptable nursing standards of care in the management of Heparinised patients) — and had been helpful in that respect — the court nevertheless added that even if the nurse's testimony had been 'disregarded entirely', there was still

> *sufficient medical support in the record* for us [the Court of Appeals] to say that the trial court was not clearly wrong in finding that the conduct of the hospital's employees was below the standard of care required under the circumstances of this case [emphasis added].
> (*Belmon v St Frances Cabrini Hospital* (1983), p. 546)

In other words, the nurse's expert testimony was, in the ultimate analysis, insignificant. And whether the court had admitted it or not, the final outcome of the case in question would have been the same since it was fully supported by the expert medical testimony which had also been given and accepted by the court.

Another and perhaps more compelling example of the trivialisation of an expert nurse's testimony can be found in the North Carolina Court of Appeals case *Page v Wilson Memorial Hospital, Inc* (1980), involving a medical malpractice action brought against a hospital and a nurses' aide as a result of a patient fracturing her hip after falling off a bedpan when the nurses' aide had left the patient's room. The trial judge first hearing the case refused to admit the testimony of an expert nurse witness on grounds that the nurse was not familiar with the standards of nursing care at the hospital in question. The North Carolina Court of Appeals found that the trial court's refusal to admit the nurse's testimony was 'an error', however, and held that the expert nurse was

> eminently qualified to testify as an expert witness concerning the practices and standards of care appropriate when administering a bedpan.
> (*Page v Wilson Memorial Hospital, Inc* (1980), p. 11)

Superficially, this finding seems to be supportive of the authority and expertise of nurses to function as expert nursing witnesses. At a deeper level, however, there is a sense in which the admission of the nurse's testimony in this instance was, in reality, a mockery of expert nursing opinion. For example, in reaching its decision, the court characterised the procedure of giving a bedpan as being 'so routine and uncomplicated' and so 'simple' that there was room to question why the court should have accepted the need to have an expert witness at all (in light of the court's characterisation of the procedure, even an idiot would have been 'eminently qualified' to testify as an expert witness). The seriousness with which the court took this matter is open to further question on account of its citing an appeal case involving the alleged negligence by a veterinarian (*Williams v Reynolds* (1980)), and in which a judge observed

> we are not dealing in this case with a complicated, novel or rare medical procedure, but rather with an operation commonly and routinely performed on certain male animals.
> (cited in *Page v Wilson Memorial Hospital* (1980), p. 11)

While citing *Williams v Reynolds* (1980) may well have assisted the court's reasoning in determining whether expert testimony was required in the case at hand, it is difficult to see how a case involving 'an operation commonly and routinely performed on certain male animals' (in this particular case, the castration of a horse!) could be accepted as seriously supporting the far from trivial issue of whether and on what grounds a nurse can and should be qualified as an expert witness in a case involving negligent injury to a patient. The court was attempting to show that if a procedure like the surgical castration of a male animal was deemed to be 'routine' and 'simple', then, at the very least, the procedures dealing with a patient's use of a bedpan (in this case a frail elderly female patient's use of a bedpan) should not be considered 'complicated', and certainly not more complicated than a simple and uncomplicated 'cutting [surgical] operation' commonly and routinely performed on certain male animals (ibid.). Had the court used an example more relevant to and supportive of the authority and ability of nurses to function as expert witnesses, the nursing profession might well have had firmer grounds for optimism that the question of expert nursing testimony was taken seriously by the court in this case.

The court's reasoning in *Page v Wilson Memorial Hospital, Inc* (1980) not only trivialised the expert nurse witness. It also trivialised the nursing procedure itself. While it is true that administering a bedpan to patients is a 'commonly performed' (that is, 'routine') nursing duty, this should not be taken to mean that it does not require skill to perform (surgeons, for example, 'routinely' perform heart transplants and bowel surgery; however, although these procedures are 'commonly performed', we would, I think, stop short of saying that they do not require skill).

When administering a bedpan, the nurse has to exercise skilled and informed judgment on how best to balance a patient's competing safety and privacy needs. Cultural taboos and norms governing the acts of human defecation and micturition further complicate the nurse's task (see, for example, Wolf 1988; Lawler 1991). It is certainly an 'art' to be able to assist patients to use a bedpan in a way that minimises their embarrassment and loss of dignity, maximises their comfort (in so far as this is possible), ensures their safety, and promotes their ability to eliminate. Furthermore, it should be noted that the risks of injury associated with this procedure are far from trivial.[2] Injuries can include trauma to the skin (including tears, lacerations, decubitus ulcers, and — if over-heated metal bedpans are used — burns), the fracturing of bones as a result of falling (as occurred in the *Page v Wilson Memorial Hospital, Inc* (1980) case given above), and, equally problematic, inhibition to pass urine or faeces resulting in either urinary retention or constipation — both of which are potentially injurious to health. Contrary to the court's perceptions, then, it can be seen that although the administration of a bedpan is a 'commonly performed' nursing duty, it is nevertheless a skilled procedure. It is evident that the courts have a lot to learn about the complexity of so-called 'simple' nursing tasks — as indeed they do about the complexity of so-called 'simple and uncomplicated' veterinarian tasks, such as the gelding of a horse.

A second reason why expert medical witnesses (and in particular male medical witnesses) have played a prominent and dominant role in cases involving nursing negligence is because medical witnesses have been preferred by the courts. There are a number of reasons for this. Firstly, medical practitioners are generally regarded as being the ones 'principally concerned with patient treatment' and therefore as the ones who are most eminently qualified to testify on patient care and treatment matters (see, for example, *Harris v State, through Huey P. Long Hospital* (1979)). Even in instances where a nurse has 'first hand' knowledge of the facts of the matter under investigation, the court will tend to favour a doctor's evidence. In the relatively recent case of *Perez v Hartman* (1989) for example, the Appellate Court of Illinois held that because of the revealed 'difference in medical training, education, knowledge and expertise' between the doctors and the registered nurses involved in the case, an earlier lower (trial) court decision to bar the nurses' evidence had not been in error. In this instance the nurses had been barred from testifying to their opinion on whether a patient had experienced an 'episode of sudden death'. Although the nurses in question — who had been monitoring the patient's heartbeat for any abnormalities, had been the first to detect a condition known as asystole (commonly referred to as 'cardiac arrest' — had initiated and performed cardiopulmonary resuscitation (CPR), had sent out an emergency code, and were fully involved in resuscitating the patient when the defendant doctor arrived, the court still refused to allow the nurses to testify.

In the unreported Australian case *In re Nurses Registration Act 1953 and In re Heathcote and Nurses Registration Board and Walton* (District Court, NSW 1991), discussed in chapter 7 in the section entitled 'Increased nurse liability for failing to question a doctor's negligent orders', a preference for medical testimony is again evident. Although several expert nurse witnesses appeared in this case, only two were named in the final decision and none of the nurse witnesses were quoted in the final report. By contrast, the only expert medical witness appearing in the case, an eminent physician, was both named and extensively quoted in the final decision. While there is no doubt that the expert medical witness' testimony was important to the successful outcome of this case, a good part of his testimony could have been competently given by the nurse witnesses — particularly with regard to the taking of a blood pressure, a task which is formally taught by nurses (not doctors) in schools of nursing, and which is routinely performed by nurses all over Australia.

A second reason why medical practitioners are preferred as expert witnesses in cases involving nursing negligence is that the courts have tended to assume that medical practitioners not only have nursing knowledge, but have it to a 'superior degree' (Murphy 1987a, p. 15). Related to this, it is also evident that the courts have little sympathy for the view that 'only nurses can qualify as experts to testify as to nursing standards of care' (see, for example, *Haney v Alexander* (1984), p. 434). This, of course, contrasts strongly with the view that doctors alone can testify on standards of medical care (see, for example, *Adkins v Ropp* (1938); *Davis v Schneider* (1979); *Emig v Physicians' Physical Therapy Service, Inc* (1982)). Furthermore, although doctors have not studied nursing, are not legally qualified as nurses, and do not practice nursing, the courts have nevertheless been satisfied that they meet the 'similar training and experience' requirement for qualification as expert witnesses on nursing practice and standards of care. In *Goff v Doctors General Hospital of San Jose* (1958), for example, the District Court of Appeals (Third District, California) accepted that a doctor need only be a 'doctor' in order to qualify as an expert witness on nursing. In handing down its decision, the court argued (ibid., p. 33):

> We are convinced also that Dr. Blinn [an expert medical witness appearing for the plaintiff] would be competent to testify as to negligence of the nurses. *Surely, a qualified doctor would know what was standard procedure for nurses to follow* ... We are satisfied that Dr. Blinn ... was fully competent to testify as to the negligence of the appellant nurses [emphasis added].

In *Gugino v Harvard Community Health Plan* (1980), p. 1167, the Supreme Judicial Court of Massachusetts accepted that the plaintiff's expert medical witness was qualified to give an expert opinion on nursing standards of care because he had had 'considerable experience in working with and supervising nurse practitioners'. Meanwhile, in *Haney v Alexander* (1984), pp. 433–434, the North Carolina Court of Appeals likewise held that the plaintiff's medical witnesses were qualified to give an expert opinion on nursing standards of care since they had each, respectively, had 'day-to-day dealings' with nurses, had 'taught nursing students', and had 'taught and worked with [registered] nurses'. In *Avey v St Francis Hospital and School of Nursing, Inc* (1968), p. 1017, the Supreme Court of Kansas even accepted that a medical witness was qualified to give an expert opinion on nursing standards of care when it was revealed that the doctor had read *a* nursing manual and *a* nursing textbook relevant to the evaluation of the nursing conduct under examination by the court.

It is important to note here that doctors themselves also 'prefer themselves' as expert witnesses in cases involving nursing negligence. A good example of this can be found in the cross-examination of a medical witness cited in the Superior Court of Pennsylvania case *Taylor v Spencer Hospital* (1972). In this case, the expert medical witness is quoted to have argued, controversially, that

> the practice of medicine and nursing were two professions which were so interwoven that they would have to be considered *part of a unitary medical profession*[3] [emphasis added].
> (*Taylor v Spencer Hospital* (1972), p. 452)

On cross-examination, this same medical witness was asked: 'And do you believe that every doctor is an expert in nursing service? Every qualified doctor, let's say?'. To which he is reported to have replied (ibid.):

> I would say a doctor knows enough about nursing service to be an expert, yes, because he's in contact with them all the time. He depends upon the nurses to carry out the treatment of his patients and to watch and care for his patients.

Citing a leading Supreme Court of Pennsylvania case *Baur v Mesta Machine Company* (1962), the court accepted that a medical doctor had sufficient knowledge and expertise to give an expert opinion on acceptable standards of nursing care (*Taylor v Spencer Hospital* (1972), p. 453).

A third reason why medical doctors (and in particular, male medical doctors) are preferred as expert witnesses in cases involving nursing negligence is that they are regarded by the courts as having more credibility than 'mere' female nurse witnesses. A paradigmatic example of this patriarchal bias can be found in a recent Australian case involving a barrister who advised two of 'his' female expert nurse witnesses:

> You are not going to like this girls, but we are going to have to put [Dr X] on the stand first thing in the morning . . . If we don't do this, we won't get a 'foot in the door.' The judge doesn't like female witnesses. If we put [Dr X] on the stand, we've got a good chance of impressing his Honour and keeping him 'on side'.
> (Confidential source/personal communication)

Another recent Australian example can be found in the case of a coroner who would not permit the nurse witnesses attending the coroner's court to read their own statements — despite the fact that they had been formally asked to be present at the inquest in question. Instead, the coroner instructed that the nurses' statements be read by a medical witness who had also been asked to be present at the inquest. The nurses' objection to this instruction was rejected. A request to allow a senior nurse administrator to give evidence on the nursing procedures under examination was also rejected. When pressed further to allow the nurses to 'speak for themselves', the coroner is alleged to have responded: 'I've had my expert [medical] witness. I've already made up my mind'. (Confidential source/personal communication).

Judicial antipathy towards nurses as expert witnesses has its origins in judicial antipathy towards women generally as entities who are capable of (or rather incapable of) assuming and performing 'the civil and political duties and obligations of citizenship' (Sachs and Wilson 1978, p. 122). An essential criterion for qualifying as a witness has traditionally been competence to give evidence and/or to testify on oath. Historically only men have 'truly' met this criterion since only men were considered 'competent' and able to 'testify'[4] on oath. It will be recalled that it was only at the turn of this century that women were recognised as 'persons' in law (see *Edwards v Attorney-General for Canada* (1929)), and thus as being competent to, among other things, practise as barristers, serve on juries and be (ordinary and/or expert) witnesses in a court of law. Despite these law reforms, and improvements in the status of women generally, it is apparent that, in the ultimate analysis, women still lack credibility. As Catharine MacKinnon (1987, pp. 132–133) points out in her influential text *Feminism unmodified: discourses on life and law*:

> I notice that law gives me some credibility, but that being woman-identified takes it away. The law gives male credibility; female identification erases it.

The case of expert nurse witnesses stands as a paradigmatic example of 'credibility being taken away' — erased — on account of the witnesses in question (most of whom have been female) being woman-identified. As a point of interest, of all the reported cases cited in this book, not one of the expert medical witnesses testifying on nursing standards of care or nursing practice was female. This should not be interpreted as meaning that female doctors are never involved as expert medical witnesses in cases involving nursing negligence. Such a claim would need to be established by further research, which unfortunately is beyond the scope of this present project to undertake. Nevertheless, I am prepared to speculate that given that female doctors are used as expert medical witnesses in cases involving nursing negligence, their numbers would probably be significantly less and statistically disproportionate to the numbers of male doctors acting in this capacity. I am prepared to speculate further that an under-representation of female medical doctors as expert witnesses could probably be explained by MacKinnon's thesis that being 'woman-identified' erases credibility. This may also help to explain why it is that barristers select those 'experts' considered likely to be most persuasive and 'credible' — that is, male doctors.

Judicial prejudice against qualifying nurses as expert witnesses

It has been and remains extremely difficult for nurses to qualify as credible expert witnesses — in nursing as well as medical negligence/malpractice cases. While it is true that nurses have testified — and do testify — as expert witnesses, their qualifications have had to be exemplary — rather than 'ordinary', and formal — not 'incidental' as has often been the case with expert medical witnesses. Certainly, it is highly unlikely that a court would qualify a nurse as an expert witness on medical or nursing standards of care by virtue of the fact that she or he was 'a nurse' (at least not in the way that being 'a doctor' is accepted for qualifying a witness to give an expert opinion on nursing standards of care). As stated in *Wood v Rowland* (1978), p. 1336, 'merely because the witness was a registered nurse does not automatically qualify her as an expert'. And it is most unlikely that a court would qualify a nurse as an expert witness on medical standards of care simply because he or she has had considerable experience working with and 'supervising' doctors (as happens, particularly in the case of junior or inexperienced doctors), has been in contact with doctors 'all the time', relies on doctors to respond to her or his requests in relation to patient care matters, has taught medical students, or has read a medical manual or a medical textbook on a relevant medical procedure or practice. If a nurse was qualified by a court on these or similar grounds to act as an expert witness on medical standards of care (as doctors in the past have been qualified on these grounds to give an expert opinion on nursing standards of care), no doubt the 'qualification' would be condemned by doctors and jurists alike as being 'outrageous', 'scandalous' and possibly even an 'error of law'.

Significantly, even when nurses have been eminently qualified to offer an expert opinion on medical or nursing standards of care, courts have still refused to qualify them and have deemed their testimonies inadmissible. For example, in an American trial court case involving a medical malpractice action against a doctor who allegedly 'failed to follow standard procedures in keeping sterile a needle used to draw a blood sample' (*McCormick v Avret* (1980), p. 759) and which resulted in the patient developing a severe infection of the radial nerve, the judge refused to permit a nurse witness to provide an expert opinion on the matter, even though the nurse had drawn blood and given injections well over 2000 times. In the appeal and supreme court cases that followed (see *McCormick v Avret* (1980); *and Avret v McCormick* (1980)), it was found that the trial court had

> erred in refusing to qualify as an expert witness a licensed nurse who '[had] drawn blood and given injections in numbers exceeding two thousand, and perhaps double that amount'.
> (*McCormick v Avret* (1980), p. 759)

In short, the court accepted that the nurse in question was an 'expert'. Significantly, although the dissenting judge, Birdsong J, agreed with this finding, he did not agree that the nurse's testimony satisfied the need for

> 'medical' testimony to show the standards of procedure established and accepted generally in the *medical profession* [emphasis added].
> (*McCormick v Avret* (1980), p. 762)

He further contended (ibid.):

> Permitting that nurses normally are best qualified by experience and training to withdraw blood and that medical doctors rarely perform that rather mechanical procedure, this does not qualify a nurse as a member of the medical profession so as to make her opinion as to the proper performance of a technical procedure admissible as a 'medical' opinion by a member of the medical profession. *While a rose may be a rose, a nurse is not a doctor.* As I understand the law, only a doctor can give a medical opinion that a particular procedure meets the standard generally accepted in the medical profession [emphasis added].

Then to emphasise his contention, Birdsong J warned (ibid.):

> I do not consider it *wise* to establish a rule that will allow an 'expert' other than a medical doctor to tell a jury what is an established medical procedure [emphasis added].

In another trial court case, once again the judge refused to allow an eminently qualified nurse to give an expert opinion on the matter under consideration by the court. The case involved a nurse who was alleged to have administered improperly a potassium solution intravenously, causing disfigurement of the skin on the plaintiff's hand. The expert nurse witness in this case had worked as an intravenous therapy specialist, had been responsible for assisting in the organisation and implementation of an intravenous (IV) therapy team at an employing hospital, had served as the president of the American Society of Intravenous Therapy, and had served on a number of important IV committees including an ad hoc committee of the powerful United States Food and Drug Administration Center for Disease Control and the Pharmacy Appeal Convention, for setting standards for the preparation and administration of IV drugs. At the time of the trial court hearing, this nurse witness 'was completing the equivalent of her fifth year of pharmacy school' (*Maloney v Wake Hospital Systems, Inc* (1980), p. 682). The court, however, refused to qualify her as an expert medical witness, primarily on the grounds that she was a nurse — not a medical doctor — and therefore was not qualified to testify on medical standards of care. When counsel for the plaintiff–appellant asked the court if he could ask the nurse witness 'a few further qualifying questions to see if [he could] qualify her', the judge is reported to have replied: 'Yes, you can try that. But it is going to be a long slow road I tell you' — meaning that he was not about to change his mind on the matter (ibid.). However, a subsequent court of appeals case found that the trial court's exclusion of the nurse's testimony was a 'reversible error' and that the nurse should have been permitted to testify (ibid. p. 680).

Another example of patriarchal judicial attitudes toward expert nurse witnesses can be found in the Supreme Court of Nevada case *Wickliffe v Sunrise Hospital, Inc* (1988). The case is particularly interesting from a nursing point of view, since its success hinged on the supreme court finding that a trial court judge in an earlier case had 'violated law of the case' by demeaning the credibility and expertise of the plaintiff's expert nurse witness. The trial court judge's demeaning comments (which were made in his instructions to the jury at the time) are quoted in full below:

> I'm going to instruct you as to these 'so-called experts' that you'll be listening to . . . you're gonna be comparing so-called expert testimony, so that's why I asked you to pay specific attention to the witnesses when they come forward, cause you're gonna have to make that determination . . . I'll give you the appropriate . . . statutory charge on how to view 'expert testimony', you may not think that they're experts but that's up to you, its your determination.
> (*Wickliffe v Sunrise Hospital, Inc* (1988), p. 1324)

The supreme court found that the trial court judge's comments (notably, his reference to the witnesses as 'so-called experts') had demeaned the credibility and expertise of the plaintiff's expert nurse witness. There is, however, room to suggest that the case succeeded not so much because of judicial sympathy for the position of an expert nurse witness specifically, but for the position of expert witnesses generally.

Admittedly, there have been some cases in which a court has explicitly stated that a doctor should not be 'permitted to testify as [a] conclusion that a nurse would be negligent in the practice of her profession under certain circumstances' (see, for example, *Crowe v Provost* (1963), p. 646). There have also been some reported cases in which a doctor's expert opinion on nursing standards was rejected by the court, and some instances of court cases failing 'because the plaintiff relied on a physician to establish the applicable nursing standard' (Cushing 1988, p. 49). These are, however, significantly few in number (see, for example: *Baur v Mesta Machine Company* (1961); *Crowe v Provost* (1963); *Avey v St Francis Hospital and School of Nursing, Inc* (1968); *Taylor v Spencer Hospital* (1972); *Mellies v National Heritage, Inc* (1981); *Sanchez v Bay General Hospital* (1981); *Haney v Alexander* (1984)). Furthermore, it is interesting to note, that if and when an expert medical witness or an expert medical testimony has been rejected by the courts, the rejection has tended to be based on a technical point of law (for example, the violation of a 'locality rule', or the testimony has 'invaded the province of the jury', or the expert witness has relied on 'demonstrably false and unsupportable' assumptions in forming his or her opinion), rather than on grounds that a given expert medical witness was neither competent nor qualified to testify on nursing standards of care per se (see, for example, *Baur v Mesta Machine Company* (1961); *Crowe v Provost* (1963); *Avey v St Francis Hospital and School of Nursing, Inc* (1968)). Indeed, it is generally accepted that doctors are competent to testify in other fields (including and perhaps especially nursing) in which they are not specialised (see, for example, *Hunsaker v Bozeman Deaconess Foundation* (1978)). To borrow from the United States Court of Appeals in *Baerman v Reisinger* (1966), p. 310:

> A physician is not incompetent to testify as an expert merely because he is not a specialist in [the] particular field of which he speaks.

The problem of expert medical witnesses in nursing negligence cases

The use and dominance of medical doctors as expert witnesses in cases involving nursing negligence has had a number of undesirable outcomes for the nursing profession. Among other things, it has served to reinforce the myths that nursing is merely a 'part' of medicine, and that nursing knowledge and practice both comprise and are dependent on medical knowledge and practice. This, in turn, has served to reinforce the myths that nursing does not have its own discrete body of knowledge or its own discrete standards of care. Evidence of this can be found in the fact that when it is alleged that nurses have been professionally negligent, often (although not always) it is medical negligence that is alleged (including the failure to make medical diagnoses and to initiate medical treatments[5]), not nursing negligence (see, for example, *Crowe v Provost* (1963); *Kelly v Hartford Casualty Insurance Company* (1978); *Harris v State, through Huey P. Long*

Hospital (1979); *Page v Wilson Memorial Hospital* (1980); *Johnson v Hermann Hospital* (1983); *Reynolds v Swigert* (1984); *Sheppard v Kimbrough* (1984); *Tripp v Humana* (1985); *Planned Parenthood of Northwest Indiana v Vines* (1989)). This in turn has justified the application of 'higher' medical standards of care rather than nursing standards of care when evaluating a nurse's allegedly negligent actions (see, for example, *Kelly v Hartford Casualty Insurance Company* (1978); *Harris v State, through Huey P. Long Hospital* (1979); *Gugino v Harvard Community Health Plan* (1980); *Belmon v St Frances Cabrini Hospital* (1983); *Planned Parenthood of Northwest Indiana v Vines* (1989)), which in turn has justified the use of medical witnesses as opposed to nurse witnesses to apply those standards (as we have been repeatedly told, only doctors are competent to apply medical standards of care) (see, for example, *Goff v Doctors General Hospital of San Jose* (1958); *Avey v St Francis Hospital and School of Nursing, Inc* (1968); *Laidlaw v Lions Gate Hospital* (1969); *Krujelis v Esdale* (1971); *Gugino v Harvard Community Health Plan* (1980); *Wooten v United States* (1982); *Haney v Alexander* (1984); *Herman v Milwaukee Children's Hospital* (1984); *Reynolds v Swigert* (1984); *Sheppard v Kimbrough* (1984)).

The overall outcome of the prominence and dominance of doctors as expert witnesses in negligence cases involving nurses has been to nursing's serious disadvantage. In particular, it has been instrumental in ensuring that the medical profession rather than the nursing profession has gained ultimate control over defining the 'acceptable' boundaries of nursing practice, and ensuring that these boundaries have not encroached on the established boundaries of medical practice. It has also been instrumental in securing ultimate control over prescribing the 'acceptable' standards of nursing care for the medical profession rather than the nursing profession. This, in turn, has been instrumental in ensuring that nursing has remained legitimately subsumed under medicine, and vicariously dependent on medicine for its professional status (see, in particular, *Green v Berrien General Hospital Auxiliary* (1990); *Roberson v Liu* (1990)). Thus, in the ultimate analysis, it can be seen that rather than providing the nursing profession with an opportunity to express its social and professional accountability, malpractice litigation has merely provided a legitimate means of structuring, reinforcing and maintaining medical dominance and control of the 'expanding' profession and practice of nursing. In short, the patriarchal and pro-medical legalistic processes and procedures commonly used to respond to claims of nursing negligence have, contrary to superficial appearances, served to seriously undermine the legal status of nursing as an authoritative, autonomous and socially accountable profession in its own right.

The legal status of nursing as an autonomous and authoritative profession has not only been undermined by the patriarchal and pro-medical processes and procedures of qualifying and using expert witnesses, however. The use of 'ordinary' (non-medical) witnesses has also seriously undermined the legal status of nursing, as the remainder of this chapter will now attempt to show.

The problem of 'ordinary' negligence

When nurses are held liable for negligence, it is not always professional or medical malpractice/negligence that they are held liable for. Nurses can be and are held liable for 'ordinary' or 'common' negligence.

In the past, it was assumed that nurses could not, strictly speaking, commit or be held liable for professional negligence or malpractice since they were not 'true' professionals (Murchison et al. 1982, p. 49; King and Sagan 1989, p. 58). In the noted American case *Richardson v Doe* (1964), for example, the Supreme Court of Ohio held that the legal definition of the term 'malpractice' (as used in a one-year statute of limitations then under consideration by the court) was limited to the professional misconduct of members of the medical profession and attorneys only and 'was not meant to apply to nurses' (ibid., p. 880). This, the court reasoned, was primarily because only doctors and lawyers exercised independent judgment, whereas the nurse 'by the very nature of her occupation is prohibited from exercising an independent judgment' (note, similar reasoning was recently employed in the dissenting opinion of *Green v Comstock* (1989), and in the Supreme Court of Michigan finding in *Green v Berrien General Hospital Auxiliary* (1990)).

Today, as already argued elsewhere in this text, although nurses are regarded as being sufficiently competent to be held liable for professional negligence — and medical negligence to boot — they are still not regarded by the courts as being 'fully professional'. Indeed, it is apparent that the courts, for the most part, still regard nursing as being an essentially lay practice, not a professional practice — and as primarily involving only 'routine' or 'ministerial' duties, rather than bona fide professional duties or discretionary acts — and thus as being of a nature that lay people are more than competent to evaluate in the case of negligence (see, for example, *Larrimore v Homeopathic Hospital Association of Delaware* (1961); *Jones v Hawkes Hospital of Mt Carmel* (1964); *Fogel v Sinai Hospital of Detroit* (1965); *Gold v Sinai Hospital of Detroit* (1966); *Kelly v Hartford Casualty Insurance Company* (1978); *Royal College of Nursing v DHSS* [1981] (see in particular p. 835); *Green v Comstock* (1989) (note: this is the dissenting opinion); *Green v Berrien General Hospital Auxiliary* (1990)).

In *Larrimore v Homeopathic Hospital Association of Delaware* (1961), p. 367, for example, the Superior Court of Delaware accepted that a nurse's allegedly negligent administration of a drug was 'within the understanding of the ordinary juror', and further that there is evidence[6] in this case from which a jury could conclude, without the aid of experts, that the nurse failed to exercise ordinary care.

And in another American case *Jones v Hawkes Hospital of Mt Carmel* (1964), again the court (in this instance, the Supreme Court of Ohio) accepted that the lay jury was sufficiently competent to judge whether the conduct of the nurses in question was negligent. The case involved a partially sedated obstetrics patient who was injured after falling from her bed when left unattended for between two and five minutes. Although the incident involved discretionary professional nursing acts, the court nevertheless held that expert testimony was not required to establish 'cause and effect under the circumstances presented by the undisputed evidence in this case'. In defending its decision not to include expert testimony, the majority explained:

> The court may take judicial notice that juries of today include women. Many of these woman jurors are mothers, and, in many instances, grandmothers. In the case at bar, there were six women. They know probably as much if not more about child-birth than many experts who might be put on the witness stand.
> (*Jones v Hawkes Hospital of Mt Carmel* (1964), p. 595)

The court quite obviously missed the point in that what was at issue was not childbirth, but the conduct of nurses while acting in their professional capacity and whether their conduct complied with acceptable nursing standards of care. As Duffey J correctly pointed out in his dissenting opinion:

> I fail to see how the majority opinion is strengthened by the fact that some jurors are women (apparently as opposed to men), some of whom the majority assumes to be mothers and whom the majority further assumes to know more about childbirth than 'many experts'. This case involves the conduct of a nurse and not childbirth.
> (*Jones v Hawkes Hospital of Mt Carmel* (1964), p. 598)

Arguably one of the most compelling examples of a court characterising nursing activities as being by nature 'routine' and 'ministerial' as opposed to being 'professional' and 'discretionary' can be found in the Michigan Court of Appeals case of *Green v Comstock* (1989) and the subsequent Supreme Court of Michigan case *Green v Berrien General Hospital Auxiliary* (1990). These two cases involve the same seven-year-old child who died as a result of prolonged oxygen deficiency caused by an upper airway obstruction and cardiac arrest which occurred as a result of gross nursing negligence. The parents of the child sued the treating hospital and nurses, alleging, among other things, that the defendant nurses had breached their duty of care to:

(1) observe and chart the child's breath sounds, (2) suction the endotracheal tube as needed to maintain an airway, (3) discontinue dosages of the drug Demerol when it became apparent the drug should not be given, (4) consider doing blood gases when the decedent [the deceased] continued with distressed breathing, (5) have the proper catheter size available for suctioning, and (6) complete a specific nursing plan to provide for maintaining the decedent's airway.
(*Green v Comstock* (1989), p. 746)

Initially, it was claimed that the nurses' acts were 'discretionary' and therefore 'protected [from liability] under the defence of individual governmental immunity' (a provision which is peculiar to the United States of America and which is probably similar to the old Crown immunity — 'The King can do no wrong' (see *A concise dictionary of law* (1990, p. 110)). The plaintiffs–appellants challenged this immunity, however, on grounds that the nurses' acts were 'ministerial', not 'discretionary' and therefore were not protected under the defence of 'individual governmental immunity'. In the Michigan Court of Appeals case that followed, the majority held that the nurses' actions were 'discretionary', not 'ministerial', and therefore were protected from liability. However, in his dissenting opinion, Murphy J strongly disagreed with the majority finding and argued:

I am hard pressed to imagine how these acts can be anything other than ministerial ones. It surely does not involve significant decision making to observe a patient or record a breath sound.
(*Green v Comstock* (1989), p. 748)

In the ensuing supreme court case, the majority likewise rejected the idea that the nursing actions under consideration were in any way 'discretionary' (professional) (*Green v Berrien General Hospital Auxiliary* (1990)). Rather, the court characterised these highly skilled activities as being merely 'routine' and 'ministerial' and as involving, at best, only 'minor decision making'. In distinguishing between 'discretionary acts' and 'minor decision making', the court explained that unlike discretionary acts which involve 'significant decision making', minor decision making as is sometimes required in the performance of ministerial acts, does not 'require the significant deliberation and judgment characteristic of discretionary acts' (ibid., p. 706). The court went on to illustrate the distinction by explaining that whereas medical decision making is 'inherently discretionary' (although, it should be noted here that it did not make clear upon what basis this judgment was made), the mere execution of a medical decision (the very thing that nurses are supposed to do — and only do) was, at best, only a ministerial act. Citing *Ross v Consumers Power Company* (1984) (of which there is an awesome 61 page report), the court accepted that ministerial acts required no more discretion than did the 'driving of a nail [with a hammer]' (*Green v Berrien General Hospital Auxiliary* (1990), p. 707).

On the basis of its highly dubious and fallacious reasoning, the court made the following judgments on the nursing actions in question. Regarding the specific act of suctioning, the court held that this comprised a ministerial act involving only minor decision making. As for the frequency of suctioning, the court held that this too did not require 'significant decision making', since the question of how frequently to suction the patient was, in effect, already decided by the prior 'discretionary' medical decision to intubate the patient. As to the size of the catheters which should have been used, the court held that

> the choice of either [a number 8 or 10 catheter] would not involve considerable deliberation and judgment from a medical standpoint.
> (*Green v Berrien General Hospital Auxiliary* (1990), p. 708)

As for the nurses' failure properly to observe and chart the patient's breathing sounds (something which, incidentally, requires experience and extremely fine and skillful judgment), again the court held that there were 'no persuasive facts or arguments that these acts necessarily involve[d] significant deliberation or judgment' and, at best, involved only 'routine, minor decision making characteristic of ministerial–operational conduct' (ibid.). Finally, in relation to the nurses' failure to complete a nursing plan as required by 'all applicable standards of [nursing] care', the court held that:

> The completion of a nursing plan in the abstract would appear to involve significant decision making, personal judgment, and deliberation.
>
> We do not deal here in the abstract, however, but in the concrete record before us. It can be inferred from the testimony of Nurse Dennis [a defendant–appellee] that in her view, 'nurses in most institutions find [writing patient care plans] sometimes less significant than doing the nursing care for patients . . .' This statement permits the inference that the completion of nursing care plans is a routine administrative task requiring little deliberation.
> (*Green v Berrien General Hospital Auxiliary* (1990), p. 30)

The court's findings in this instance are incredible and reflect a disturbing lack of knowledge and understanding about the nature and realities of nursing practice. Intensive care nursing is a recognised specialised area of nursing practice. Paediatric nursing (both general and intensive care) is also recognised as a highly specialised area of nursing (Styles 1989). To characterise it as otherwise is to perpetrate a falsehood. On the basis of the realities of intensive care nursing practices, there are substantial grounds for holding that the court in this case seriously erred in holding that the specific acts of suctioning, deciding the frequency of suctioning, choosing the correct catheter size for suctioning, observing and monitoring the patient's breathing, and formulating a nursing care plan involved only 'routine, minor decision making characteristic of ministerial–operational conduct'. As is well known by nurses (and, indeed, doctors), all of these nursing activities require specialist knowledge, skilled judgment and significant discretionary acts (see, for example, Persons 1987; Holloway 1988; Oh 1990).

Green v Berrien General Hospital Auxiliary (1990) is a significant and disturbing case — not least because it demonstrates that judicial views about the professional status of the nurse are still very much conditioned by patriarchal assumptions about the rational incompetence of women (nurses) and the natural inferiority of and subordination of women (nurses) to men (doctors). In this case, it is very clear that the court did not see nursing as a profession — and certainly did not recognise that nursing activities require 'significant deliberation and judgment characteristic of discretionary acts'. In terms reminiscent of those used in *Richardson v Doe* (1964), the court made clear its view that only doctors make significant deliberations and judgments, and that once a doctor makes a judgment, anything that occurs after that (for example, the implementation of nursing care) is elementary, insignificant and unimportant (a similar line of reasoning was also used in the noted English House of Lords case *Royal College of Nursing v DHSS* (1981) (see in particular p. 835)). The bottom line in this instance seems to be not only that nurses are supposedly incapable of engaging in discretionary acts, but that they have no legitimate business to be doing so, since that is entirely the prerogative and province of doctors. Given the catastrophic consequences that can and do occur when nurses fail to exercise 'deliberation and judgment characteristic of discretionary acts', however, it is obvious that nursing actions are considerably more than 'ministerial' and 'routine' in nature.

An important lesson to be gleaned from *Green v Berrien General Hospital Auxiliary* (1990) is that despite so-called 'progressive' law reforms favouring the profession and practice of nursing, it is the courts which retain the ultimate authority to decide how, when, if, and under what circumstances nurses and nursing care can be legitimately described as 'professional'. Nurses should not think that the mere passage of a new law or the reformation of an old one will improve significantly the legal status of nursing. As the Green case has illustrated, old patriarchal attitudes die hard, and the rhetoric of 'law reform' is often little more than that — rhetoric. The case also serves as a timely warning to the nursing profession that its hopes that the nursing process[7] (including the documentation of patient assessment, nursing diagnoses, plans of care, and evaluation of outcomes) would add legal credibility and status to the profession and practice of nursing — and would symbolise the nursing profession's 'new independence, accountability and potential influence on the health care scene' — might be seriously misplaced (Baer 1984, p. 93; see also Feild 1979, p. 497; Fortin and Rabinow 1979, p. 553). Certainly, few nurses would have envisaged or expected that a court would — or could — sweep aside the enormous professional significance that nurses universally have attributed to the nursing process, with the simple and almost barely noticeable statement: 'the completion of nursing care plans is a routine administrative task requiring little deliberation'.

CONCLUSION

The cases used in this chapter are by no means exhaustive, and, as already stated in the introduction, are not binding on other common law countries or indeed on other American states outside of the respective jurisdictions of the courts in question. Nevertheless, I believe the cases are representative, and reflect situations with which nurses in other common law countries would readily identify. In one way or another, the respective experiences of each of the nurses in the cases considered here are potentially every nurse's experience — and will continue to be so for as long as the patriarchal status quo remains. While it is true that the findings of the cases cited here may have since been overturned or may have only limited application in law, taken together, they offer nevertheless an important insight into the pervasiveness of the judiciary's patriarchal and hierarchical attitude towards nurses, and the absolute power of the courts to control the boundaries and professional standards of 'acceptable' nursing practice. Equally important, the collective consideration of these cases demonstrates that despite so-called 'progressive' law reforms in nursing, and the improved social status of nursing generally, the orthodox processes and procedures of law continue to structure and reinforce the traditional principles of nurse (female) incompetence, nurse (female) subordination and medical (male) guardianship and supervision. Given this, it can be seen that much more is required than law reform alone to improve the social and professional status of the nurse and of the nursing profession as a whole. There also needs to be radical reform (or, more to the point, a revolution) of the entire legal system — its procedures, processes and underlying (patriarchal) assumptions about the world and about how people ought to function in it. More than this, there needs to be a radical change in thinking about law itself (its rules, principles, assumptions, doctrines, procedures, and so on) and the role it should or should not play in adjudicating human affairs.

ENDNOTES

1   See, for example: *Goff v Doctors General Hospital of San Jose* (1958); *Baur v Mesta Machine Company* (1962); *Crowe v Provost* (1963); *Jones v Hawkes*

Hospital of Mt Carmel (1964); *Fogel v Sinai Hospital of Detroit* (1965); *Gold v Sinai Hospital of Detroit, Inc* (1966); *Avey v St Francis Hospital and School of Nursing, Inc* (1968); *Laidlaw v Lions Gate Hospital* (1969); *Krujelis v Esdale* (1971); *Taylor v Spencer Hospital* (1972); *Suburban Hospital Association, Inc v Hadary* (1974); *Embrey v Borough of West Mifflin* (1978); *Hunsaker v Boseman Deaconess Foundation* (1978); *Kelly v Hartford Casualty Insurance Company* (1978); *Davis v Schneider* (1979); *Harris v State, through Huey P. Long Hospital* (1979); *Kolakowski v Voris* (1979); *Avret v McCormick* (1980); *Gugino v Harvard Community Health Plan* (1980); *Maloney v Wake Hospital Systems, Inc* (1980); *McCormick v Avret* (1980); *Maslonka v Hermann* (1980); *Page v Wilson Memorial Hospital, Inc* (1980); *Mellies v National Heritage, Inc* (1981); *Sanchez v Bay General Hospital* (1981); *Wooten v United States* (1982); *Belmon v St Francis Cabrini Hospital* (1983); *Johnson v Hermann Hospital* (1983); *Haney v Alexander* (1984); *Herman v Milwaukee Children's Hospital* (1984); *Reynolds v Swigert* (1984); *Sheppard v Kimbrough* (1984); *Tripp v Humana, Inc* (1985); *Breit v St Luke's Memorial Hospital* (1987); *Kuna v Lifemark Hospital of Texas, Inc* (1987); *Wickliffe v Sunrise Hospital, Inc* (1988); *Green v Comstock* (1989); *Perez v Hartmann* (1989); *Phillips v Eastern Maine Medical Center* (1989); *Planned Parenthood of Northwest Indiana v Vines* (1989); *Green v Berrien General Hospital Auxiliary* (1990); see also the Australian case *In re Nurses Registration Act 1953 and In re Heathcote and Nurses Registration Board and Walton* (1991).
2   For example, I can recall the case of an elderly woman who slipped off a bedpan, hitting her head on an adjacent bedside table. She hit the bedside table with such force that she suffered a subarachnoid (brain) haemorrhage and died. Had she been correctly positioned on the bedpan, and had proper attention been given to her safety needs, it is probable that this tragic incident would not have occurred.
3   Note: there is no suggestion here that the practice of medicine might be more appropriately considered part of a unitary nursing profession, despite the fact that such a description would more accurately reflect the relationship between nursing and medicine.
4   As a point of interest the term 'testify' comes from the Latin *testis* meaning witness; testis, however, can also be used to refer to the male gonad, the testicle. Dirckx (1983, p. 48) explains that the term testis goes back at least to Horace's time (the first century BC) and 'is probably derived from the primitive custom of taking an oath with a hand on the testicles'. The ancient Hebrews had a similar practice. In Genesis 24: 2–3, for example, Abraham instructs his oldest servant 'Please, put your hand under my thigh, and I will make you swear by the LORD, the God of heaven and the God of earth'. Since women quite obviously lacked testicles upon which to swear an oath, it is probable that they could not qualify as credible witnesses. Today credibility still rests on male-identified characteristics, such as the wearing of a distinctive pin-striped suit and club tie (as opposed to jeans and a floral tie — and certainly as opposed to wearing a floral dress), and

having the 'right' demeanour (read 'mannerisms culturally specific to the dominant white middle-class Anglo-Saxon male culture') (Gee and Mason 1990, pp. 102–103, 112; see also Rea 1987b, p. 538; Naffine 1990, p. 22; Thornton 1990, p. 1).

5   Alleging that nurses have been negligent in failing to make correct medical diagnoses (to be distinguished here from nursing diagnoses which rely on distinctive nursing diagnostic categories and classifications (see, for example, Carpenito 1987; Gordon 1987; McFarland and McFarlane 1989)) and/or failing to initiate medical treatments (to be distinguished here from planned nursing interventions) has resulted in the absurd situation of nurses being held negligent for failing to engage in the illegal practice of medicine. A paradigmatic example of this can be found in the Australian case *In re Nurses registration Act 1953 and In re Heathcote and Nurses Registration Board and Walton* (1991) discussed in this and the previous chapter, and the noted American case *Baur v Mesta Machine Company* (1962).

It is interesting to note that both the courts and the medical profession consider nurses to have enough medical knowledge to be held liable for medical malpractice, yet not enough medical knowledge to qualify as expert medical witnesses or to provide a competent expert opinion on medical practices and standards of care.

It is also interesting to note that doctors and the courts both expect nurses to exercise discretionary 'medical' judgment — particularly in emergency situations — but are not prepared to recognise formally that nurses do exercise discretionary judgment or that they should have the legitimated authority to exercise it in their clinical practice (see, in particular, *Green v Comstock* (1989); *Green v Berrien General Hospital Auxiliary* (1990)).

6   The 'evidence' being referred to here included an alleged remark by a doctor that the nurse in question 'had made a very bad mistake' (*Larrimore v Homeopathic Hospital Association of Delaware* (1961), p. 368).

7   The nursing process 'is an organized, systematic method of giving individualized nursing care that focuses on the unique human response of a person or group of people to an actual or potential alteration in health' (Alfaro 1986, p. 6). It is, in short, a 'problem-solving process and includes the commonly accepted components of (1) assessment, (2) nursing diagnosis, (3) planning [patient care], (4) implementing [nursing care], and (5) evaluating [the outcomes of nursing care]' (McFarland and McFarlane 1989, p. xi; see also Carpenito 1987; Gordon 1987). It should be noted that the nursing process is widely taught and practised in all common law countries, and in some American states is even specifically mandated by law in the nurse practice Acts (see Feild 1979; Fortin and Rabinow 1979; Fredette and O'Connor 1979; Gordon 1979, 1987; Baer 1984; Gaines and McFarland 1984; Putzier and Padrick 1984; Young and Lucas 1984; Bennett 1986; Carpenito 1987; McFarland and McFarlane 1989).

CHAPTER NINE

The Legal Invalidation of Professional Nursing Ethics

INTRODUCTION

THE NURSE–PATIENT RELATIONSHIP, like any other health professional–patient relationship, is of a profoundly moral nature. A nurse's actions within the nurse–patient relationship never occur in a moral vacuum, and are never free of moral risk. Furthermore, no nursing action or omission is without moral consequence. As the examples given in this book have already shown, a nurse's professional judgment and actions have the substantive capacity either to promote or seriously undermine and/or violate a patient's significant moral interests. It is for these reasons, among others, that nurses are expected to fulfil certain professionally recognised moral obligations and responsibilities to their patients when delivering nursing care. It is generally hoped and expected that by nurses fulfilling their moral obligations and responsibilities to patients, the risk of causing them otherwise avoidable and significant moral harm will at least be minimised, if not prevented.

From the very moment nurses undertake to care for a patient, they are morally (and, it should be added, legally) bound to act in ways which ensure that no undue harm is caused to the patient, and that the patient's 'best interests' are maximised and protected (Creighton 1986; Cushing 1988; Fiesta 1988; Johnstone 1989; CCH et al. 1990; Young 1991; Staunton and Whyburn 1993). There has, however, long been the problem that while the legal dimension of the nurse–patient relationship has been recognised (if only to a limited and qualified degree), the moral dimension has, for the most part, tended to be either trivialised, marginalised, invalidated or completely ignored. This, in turn, has undermined the status of the nurse–patient relationship, and the nurse's moral (and professional) authority and responsibilities within that relationship, as this chapter aims to show.

The moral dimension of the nurse–patient relationship

Nurses have long recognised the moral nature of the nurse–patient relationship, and the many complex moral responsibilities that nurses have within that relationship (see, for example, Curtin 1982; Kohnke 1982; Murphy and Hunter 1983; Watson 1985a, pp. 31–35; Johnstone 1989; Leininger 1990; Neil and Watts 1991). Others outside nursing (for example, medical doctors, hospital administrators, jurists, and the courts) have, however, been less willing to recognise and accept the moral (and related professional) dimension of the nurse–patient relationship or the nurse's moral (and related professional) authority and responsibilities within that relationship (see, for example, *Registered Nurse* 1979; Ashworth 1981; *British Medical Journal* 1982; Dunn 1982; Brewer 1988; Wertheimer 1990). Although doctors and the courts have recognised the existence of the nurse–patient relationship (see, in particular, *Lunsford v Board of Nurse Examiners* (1983), p. 395, s 4), this has been primarily for the purposes of establishing a nurse's responsibility and liability for negligence, not for the purposes of establishing the moral authority or privilege of the nurse–patient relationship per se. It has certainly not been for the purposes of recognising or legitimating the fiduciary or moral nature of the nurse–patient relationship, or the nurse's independent moral authority and moral responsibilities within that relationship. To the contrary. As the cases to be considered briefly in this chapter will demonstrate, the courts have been extremely reluctant to validate nurses' independent moral (and professional) authority and responsibilities to their patients, and indeed have even rejected the citation of codes of ethics or ethical concerns as being 'sufficient to defend a nurse's practice decisions from employer control' (Murphy 1990a, p. 38).

The moral responsibilities of the nurse

Nursing codes of conduct in common law countries around the world have made explicit that the nurse's primary responsibility is to those who require nursing care, and that nurses have a stringent moral responsibility to safeguard the interests and wellbeing of patients in their care. The International Council of Nurses (1973) *Code for nurses* states, for example:

> The nurse's primary responsibility is to those people who require nursing care ... The nurse takes appropriate action to safeguard the individual when his care is endangered by a co-worker or any other person.

The acclaimed United Kingdom Central Council for Nursing, Midwifery and Health Visiting (UKCC) (1984) *Code of professional conduct for the nurse, midwife and health visitor* likewise explicitly states that nurses have a stringent moral responsibility to act 'always in such a way as to promote and safeguard the wellbeing and interests of patients/clients' (Clause One) (reprinted in Jones 1990, pp. 14–15). Similarly, the American Nurses Association (1976) *Code for nurses* states that the nurse has a primary responsibility to act to 'safeguard the client and the public when health care and safety are affected by the incompetent, unethical or illegal practice of any person' (reprinted in Kelly 1985, p. 208). The New Zealand Nurses Association (1988) *Code of ethics* likewise emphasises that nurses have a stringent moral responsibility to act in ways which ensure the welfare and safety of patients (reprinted in Johnstone 1989, pp. 402–410).[1]

The contents of these formally adopted codes of conduct/ethics indicate that the nursing profession believes that nurses are primarily responsible and professionally accountable to the patient, not to other health team workers (for example, doctors), administrators, or even to their employer(s) (see Leddy and Pepper 1989, p. 303). However, employers and the courts take quite a different view. As already argued, the courts tend to view the nurse's primary obligation as being to carry out the doctor's (or a superior's) orders — not to independently respond to and/or uphold a patient's requests or wishes regarding their health care and/or other significant moral interests (see, for example, *Yorston v Pennell* (1959); *Tuma v Board of Nursing of the State of Idaho* (1979); *Warthen v Toms River Community Memorial Hospital* (1985); *Free v Holy Cross Hospital* (1987); *In re the Alleged Unfair Dismissal of Ms K Howden by the City of Whittlesea* (1990)).

Despite the existence and formal adoption of given professional nursing codes of conduct/ethics, it has been — and remains — extremely difficult for nurses to uphold their own professional ethical standards or to fulfil their own very real moral responsibilities to their patients when delivering nursing care. It is apparent that the courts do not recognise the moral nature (to be distinguished here from the contractual or legal nature) of the nurse–patient relationship or the moral authority of the nurse within that relationship. The courts also appear to be reluctant to recognise the moral authority of the nurse to question unscrupulous medical practices, or to make independent moral evaluations about 'commonly accepted' medical practices (see, for example, *Regan Report on Nursing Law* 1993, p. 1). There are a number of reasons for this, which are considered briefly below.

The sacrosanctity of the doctor–patient relationship

Even among men, the doctor–patient relationship has long been recognised and projected as a prototypical professional–client relationship. In health care domains, the doctor–patient relationship tends to enjoy the rather peculiar authority and status of being the only 'true' (or, at least, primary) health professional–patient relationship. The nurse–patient relationship, by contrast, tends to be regarded at best as being only vicarious to or pursuant to the doctor–patient relationship. To borrow from *Roberson v Liu* (1990), p. 1003, just as 'no man is an island . . . no physician acts alone in the discharge of professional, fiduciary duties to a patient'; when nurses perform their 'professional duties' (defined in this case as 'assisting the doctor'), the doctor–patient relationship extends to, and includes, the nurse–patient relationship. This, however, does not apply when nurses are not genuinely 'assisting' physicians in their work, such as when they (nurses) are performing duties which are merely 'ministerial' or 'administrative' in nature, or worse, are independent of the doctor–patient relationship. In such instances, the nurse–patient relationship tends to be viewed as not having any genuine moral authority or independent professional status at all. And any nurse who attempts to act on the assumption that the nurse–patient relationship does have a genuine moral and professional status, risks being legitimately censured for 'overstepping' the boundaries of her or his 'proper sphere' (see, for example, *Tuma v Board of Nursing of the State of Idaho* (1979); *Warthen v Toms River Community Memorial Hospital* (1985); *Free v Holy Cross Hospital* (1987); *In re the Alleged Unfair dismissal of Ms K Howden by the City of Whittlesea* (1990); *Roberson v Liu*, (1990)).

Next to the priest–confessor relationship, the doctor–patient relationship is regarded as one of the most sacrosanct relations in law (*Regan report on nursing law* 1990). One consequence of this has been that doctors have been left almost completely free to determine the ethical standards governing their relationships with patients, and few have dared to challenge this prerogative. The privilege and legitimacy that medical ethics have enjoyed in the past is illustrated in Lord Denning's comments in *Hatcher v Black and others* [1954]. In this case, Lord Denning argued that the court is a court of *law*, not a court of *morals* (he saw morality as the business of moralists and theologians, not of judges[2]), and in the case of medical ethics, 'the law leaves the question of morals to the conscience of the doctor himself' (cited in Denning 1979, p. 243). Although some believe the days of Lord Denning's influence 'are now passed', (Gee and Mason 1990, p. 168), it is evident that medical ethics continues to have considerable authority in the health care arena, and considerably more authority than the professional ethics of other health professional groups (including and perhaps especially nurses). While the courts may indeed stand as being principally concerned with law, not morality, it is apparent that in the case of medical ethics, at least — contrary to their own rhetoric — the courts have played a major role in determining matters 'ethical'. By the mere fact of legitimating the medical profession's prerogative to determine its own ethical standards (a privilege not enjoyed by the nursing profession, as is shown below), the courts take a fundamental role in deciding whose and what ethics will have ultimate authority in the world, and the conditions under which (the when, where and how) those ethics will apply.

Historically, a doctor's ethics and 'conscience' have always had more legitimated authority than those of a non-medical person; and certainly more legitimated authority than a nurse's professional ethics and conscience. In the 1970s, for example, following the legalisation of abortion in the United States of America, many nurses were dismissed from their jobs for refusing conscientiously to participate in abortion procedures (some were expected to participate in as many as ten abortions per day in the absence of the 'supervising' aborting doctor) (Johnstone 1989, pp. 9, 230). Significantly, this was not a problem doctors faced, since, unlike nurses, even junior doctors had the option of refusing to participate in abortion work (ibid., p. 233). The problem of dismissing nurses for conscientious objection became so serious in the United States of America that eventually laws had to be passed to make it an offence to dismiss a nurse for refusing conscientiously to participate in abortion work. Although today conscientious objection to assisting with abortion work is fairly well tolerated (and in some countries, legally supported), nurses are still not legally permitted to refuse conscientiously to participate in other morally controversial medical procedures. For example, in 1988, a Melbourne newspaper reported that nurses 'worried about the ethics of medical procedures such as organ transplants' faced dismissal if they refused to take part (Miller 1988, p. 1). And in the American case *Warthen v Toms River Community Memorial Hospital* (1985), discussed in chapter 6 (in the section entitled 'Detecting medical errors — a matter of professional nursing judgment or mere "ordinary prudence"?'), it will be recalled that the Superior Court of New Jersey totally rejected the nurse-appellant's conscientious objection claim to the medical procedure of dialysing a terminally ill patient — even though her actions were supported by the American Nurses Association (ANA) (1981) *Code for nurses*. It will be recalled further, that the court did not accept that the ANA *Code for nurses* was an 'authoritative statement of public policy', and rejected some of the code's statements on grounds that they served more the interests of the individual nurse and the nursing profession than they did the interests of the public. By taking this position the court effectively invalidated the independent moral authority of both the individual nurse and of the ANA (1981) *Code for nurses* (interestingly, the UKCC (1984) *Code of professional conduct* has suffered a similar fate, and, in at least one case, has apparently been disregarded by a court of law (Rea 1987a, p. 534)). It would be hard to find a comparable example of a medical code of ethics or a doctor's conscientious objection being treated in this dismissive manner.

Nurses have also had difficulty acting in a morally just way even when 'legally required' to do so. For example, in *Free v Holy Cross Hospital* (1987) (also discussed in chapter 6 in the section entitled 'The punishment for insubordination of "questioning" nurses'), involving a nurse who was dismissed for insubordination after she refused to evict a bedridden patient from hospital, the Appellate Court of Illinois did not accept that the *Illinois Nursing Act* — which mandated ethical conduct on the part of a registered nurse — protected the ethical concerns of the nurse in this case (ibid., p. 1190). (It will be recalled that the security officer at the hospital told the nurse that the patient should be removed 'even if removal required forcibly putting the patient in a wheelchair and leaving her in the park' (ibid., p. 1189).) In reaching its decision, the court drew a dubious distinction between 'ethical concerns' and '*sincerely held moral convictions* arising from religious beliefs [emphasis added]'. It then proceeded to characterise the nurse's ethical concerns as being of a *personal* as opposed to a *professional* nature and therefore as falling outside the scope of the *Illinois Nursing Act*. Since the nurse's actions in this case were substantially defensible from a variety of ethical perspectives (including a secular as well as a theological based ethic), it would appear that the court's primary concern in this instance was not 'justice', but maintaining the integrity of employer control. It is apparent that the court certainly was not concerned with upholding the integrity of a nurse's personal or professional morality.

Free v Holy Cross Hospital (1987) stands as a paradigm of the court acting as a court of law, and not as a court of morals. Unlike the case with members of the medical profession, however, it is evident that the court in this case — as in the case of *Warthen v Toms River Community Memorial Hospital* (1985) discussed in chapter 6 (in the section entitled 'Detecting medical errors — a matter of professional nursing judgment or mere "ordinary prudence"?') — was not about to set a precedent of legitimating the moral authority of the nurse's own conscience to determine the moral standards which ought to be applied in the nurse–patient relationship. It certainly was not about to legitimate the 'inferior' moral authority of a nurse (a mere employee) to question the 'superior' moral authority of an employer or doctor, and/or to make profound moral statements concerning what constitutes 'right' and 'wrong' conduct or hospital policy.

The assumed moral incompetence and inferiority of nurses

Another reason nurses have experienced extreme difficulty in having their moral views and standards recognised and legitimated is that they have tended to be regarded (most notably by members of the medical profession) as being morally incompetent. As I have argued elsewhere (Johnstone 1989), even today, in this era of supposed 'enlightened' and 'democratic' bioethical debate, the moral capacity of nurses continues to be undermined and the viewpoints of nurses continue to be marginalised, trivialised and invalidated. In one notable and relatively recent Australian case, for example, a group of registered nurses (many of whom were senior nurse administrators) undertaking a postgraduate course in health administration were told by a lecturer (a medical doctor) that 'nurses were unable to understand the intellectual concept of ethical models'. His reasoning seemed to be that nurses were 'too simplistic and practical', and 'not generally capable of the objective, abstract thought that is required' for ethical reasoning and decision making (*Report of the study of professional issues in nursing* 1988, p. 165).

The attitude of this lecturer is by no means unique. As has been pointed out elsewhere:

> Anecdotal evidence abounds on how nurses are continually told by doctors that nursing practice is devoid of any sort of moral complication and that it is nonsense for nurses to presume they have any independent moral responsibilities when caring for patients.
> (Johnstone 1989, p. 3)

A good example of this can be found in an American case cited by Yarling and McElmurry (1986a), involving a senior physician who objected strongly to the suggestion that nurses have a moral duty to disclose information to terminally ill patients if these patients request it, but an attending physician has expressly ordered that no information be given out. Medical students present at the time were unanimous in suggesting that 'the nurse had a moral duty to disclose and that the physician's order was unjustifiable' (ibid., pp. 65–66). When one of the medical students present asked the physician why he disagreed with their view, the physician replied that 'the nurse's relationship with the patient is different than [read 'inferior to'] the physician's. It does not require independent moral judgment by the nurse' (ibid., p. 66).

A similar attitude exists among some English physicians as well. The *Nursing Times*, for example, has reported recently that a survey of the opinions of 19 doctors at a district general hospital found most believed that nurses ought to evade direct questioning by a patient and should avoid giving patients precise information in response to queries about their medical condition (*Nursing Times* 1990i). Three of the doctors also stated that 'nurses should lie to patients if they were put on the spot by a direct question' (ibid.). As in the American case above, it is apparent that these English physicians likewise do not recognise the moral (or professional) nature of the nurse–patient relationship or that nurses have any independent moral (or professional) responsibilities to their patients.

Interestingly, at an evening seminar in 1991, held at a country hospital in Victoria, I heard some senior physicians and lawyers also assert, incorrectly, that nurses have no independent *legal* responsibilities in their relationships with patients — and, controversially, no moral responsibilities either. These views were stated in the context of a debate on the legal and ethical aspects of 'not-for-resuscitation' (NFR) orders (a common although morally and legally questionable practice involving a medical order not to perform emergency cardiopulmonary resuscitation (CPR) on certain 'medically hopeless' patients in the event of cardiac or respiratory arrest (see Johnstone 1989, pp. 282–302)). Senior physicians and a barrister of criminal law present at the debate argued that since the decision not to resuscitate a patient was, ipso facto, a *medical* decision — not a *moral* decision — and thus 'properly' the prerogative of a doctor to make, the ethical and legal aspects of the matter (if indeed there were any) were not the province of nurses. When the doctors and barrister in question were challenged about the widespread problem of doctors refusing to chart properly their 'clinically sound' NFR orders (that is, put them in writing), it was contended that as an NFR patient would probably be rendered 'brain dead' through non-action, it was unlikely that a nurse could or would be charged with manslaughter or negligence (the assumption being that if a person was already 'dead', then a nurse could not 'kill' that person). This response was, however, unsatisfactory and indeed misleading on a number of accounts. Among other things, it ignored the fact that a nurse is not legally qualified to diagnose 'brain death', which, as legally mandated, can only be diagnosed after a stringent set of tests have been carried out by a qualified medical practitioner of several years (for example, of at least five years) experience. This response also ignored the fact that in the event of a cardiac arrest, ordinary legal standards of care dictate that, unless a patient has explicitly and lawfully refused orthodox medical treatment, resuscitation procedures must be initiated. To do otherwise (that is, to fail to initiate full CPR), would probably be construed by a court as functioning below an acceptable standard of care (Cushing 1981, p. 27). Lastly, the response ignored the reality that, in the event of a court action, an order which is shown not to have been written, would probably be construed as 'an order that was not given' (a problem which is fully understood by nurses). It would be very easy (too easy) for doctors to deny that they gave a verbal order not to resuscitate a patient (as indeed has happened in the past), something which, if it occurred, would undoubtedly leave nurses in an extremely precarious legal position (Adams 1984; Johnstone 1989, pp. 294–298).

Legal aspects of the NFR issue aside, it is evident that nurses are not recognised as having any moral authority to decide the correctness or incorrectness of an NFR order. Nurses who initiate full CPR measures in the face of a medical order not to resuscitate a patient, or who fail to initiate CPR measures when an NFR order has not been given, can face hostility from doctors as well as from other nurses (see also Yarling and McElmurry 1986b). In a noteworthy English case, for example, a nurse was dismissed for failing to call an emergency code and failing to initiate CPR in a cardiac arrest situation when it was revealed that she used her 'own judgment' in letting a 78-year-old man 'die peacefully' (*Nursing Times* 1983f). Although nurses are generally the ones who are left to make the ultimate decision (regardless of a doctor's orders) on whether or not to resuscitate a patient who has suffered a cardiac arrest (largely owing to their immediate presence at the event, and the absence of an 'attending' doctor), in this case it appears that the nurse was disciplined primarily because she used her 'own moral judgment', or, more to the point, had used a judgment which had not been previously 'authorised' by a doctor. The nurse in this case was probably quite capable of making an independent moral decision about whether to resuscitate the patient in question, but nevertheless was without the legitimated authority to do so. In short, to borrow from Yarling and McElmurry (1986b, p. 129), she was 'not free to be moral'. As a consequence, she was 'legitimately' dismissed from her job. This contrasts strongly with the position of doctors who are rarely, if ever, dismissed from their jobs for deciding not to resuscitate a patient — even when they have made their decisions without either the knowledge or consent of the patient concerned, as frequently happens in hospitals around Australia and overseas (Johnstone 1989, pp. 282–302).

Another example of the nurse's lack of legitimated freedom to be moral, can be found in an Australian industrial relations case (*In re the alleged unfair dismissal of Ms K Howden by the City of Whittlesea* (1990), Industrial Relations Commission of Victoria). The case involved a maternal and child health nurse (also a registered nurse (RN)) who was dismissed from her place of employment for 'professional misconduct' after it was alleged she had breached confidentiality while dealing with a case of suspected child (sexual) abuse. The dismissal came after a Ms X, the mother of the child-victim concerned, formally complained to the municipal authority employing the RN, that the RN had acted 'inappropriately' by discussing the case with another (lay) person and had 'maliciously reported [her and her husband] to the Community Services Victoria to be investigated for child abuse' (ibid., p. 5). The 'other person' in this instance was a Ms Y, the mother of another child, who, after observing both her own and Ms X's son playing together in a 'disturbing manner', reported her observations and suspicions of possible child abuse to the RN. Concerned about the information she had received, and after discussing the matter in confidence with her professional colleagues, the RN decided 'that it [the case] was not her area of expertise and that she was going to seek advice from Community Services (a decision that was later vindicated by the Industrial Relations Commission of Victoria) (ibid., p. 3). Concerned about the possible ramifications for the informant mother of the matter being referred to Community Services Victoria, the RN decided (on ethical grounds) to inform Ms Y of what she intended to do with the information she had received from her (Ms Y) about the boy's 'disturbing behaviour'. The municipal authority employing the RN, however, considered this action a breach of confidentiality and thus an instance of professional misconduct, and dismissed her instantly.

There are many other important details of this case worthy of consideration, but unfortunately there is not space to consider these here (see, for example, Kutny 1990; Lamont 1990a, 1990b; *Whittlesea Post* 1990; Czernik 1990). Of particular note, however (and of importance to this discussion), are the grounds upon which the RN was ultimately cleared of the misconduct charges against her, and an order given that she should be reinstated to her former position. Significantly, the commissioner's decision in favour of the RN was based not on the correctness of her professional judgment or moral reasoning in the case, or on her authority as a professional to exercise discretion. Rather, it was based on legal grounds — notably that the RN's 'dismissal was harsh, unjust and unreasonable because she was denied procedural fairness and in particular, was not given a proper opportunity to answer allegations' and 'because she was not guilty of misconduct' (*In re the Alleged Unfair Dismissal of Ms K Howden by the City of Whittlesea* (1990), p. 35). The grounds upon which this decision was supported, included that:

- the RN's action to seek advice from Community Services Victoria was fully in accord with the requirements set down by the *Community Welfare Services Act 1970* (*In re the Alleged Unfair Dismissal of Ms K Howden by the City of Whittlesea* (1990), p. 23);
- the RN 'did not commit a breach of [employer] instructions' because she had 'not been given relevant instructions by her employer' (the commission rested this claim on the basis that the city had 'not developed any protocols, guidelines or instructions for maternal and child health nurses faced with the kind of situation like that [faced by the RN]') (ibid., p. 21);
- the RN did not offend the law relating to breach of confidentiality (which, incidentally, was in essence a medical standard of confidentiality) (ibid., p. 16);
- all of the professional witnesses called by the Australian Nursing Federation (representing the RN) considered the RN's decision to contact Community Services Victoria 'appropriate' (ibid., p. 20).

It is noteworthy, however, that in reaching his decision, the deputy president of the Industrial Relations Commission was particularly critical of the International Council of Nurses (1973) *Code for nurses* which the RN cited in defence of her actions. In response to the RN's defence and referring to the code's statement that 'the Nurse holds in confidence personal information and *uses judgement* [emphasis added] in sharing this information', the deputy president concluded, controversially, that although 'well-meaning', the code's statement was

> so imprecise as to be of limited value in circumstances like those which concerned [the RN] on receiving the information given to her by Ms Y.
> (*In re the alleged unfair dismissal of Ms K Howden by the City of Whittlesea* (1990), p. 13)

Equally disturbing was the deputy president's suggestion that the RN's employer

> would be wise to become involved in the development of [precise and clear-cut] guidelines. Otherwise the City leaves the field to *an imprecise code of Nursing ethics, to standards of a professional peer group with whom the City may disagree* [emphasis added].
> (ibid., p. 29)

The deputy president then advised that if the city wished to dismiss its employees for

> breaches of professional standards where the standards or their application are not clear, the City would have to develop guidelines as to what it expects of employees and make them known to employees.
> (ibid.)

Although the deputy president went on to acknowledge that 'there may always be situations where published guidelines do not specifically cover a particular factual situation', and that in such instances 'as a professional, a Nurse can be expected to use judgment', it is nevertheless apparent that he did not recognise either the ability or the authority of nurses to exercise independent (professional and/or moral) judgments, or, it seems, the competence of nursing peers to testify to the nature and application of otherwise 'unclear' standards of nursing practice. This contrasts strongly with the position of medical practitioners who, as already argued elsewhere in this book, are regarded as having not only the ability and authority to exercise discretion and judgment in relation to professional matters (including otherwise 'unclear' standards of medical practice), but as having these things to a superior and, at times, unqualified (male-qualified?) degree.

Although, as a general rule, nursing standards of conduct and/or ethics have very little legitimated authority, there are some noteworthy exceptions. One such exception can be found in the case of the *Code of professional conduct* (1984) developed and enforced by United Kingdom Central Council for Nursing, Midwifery and Health Visiting (UKCC), a statutory nursing authority established under the 1979 *Nurses, Midwives and Health Visitors Act*. Although the code is *not law*, as Young (1991, p. 6) correctly points out, the UKCC nevertheless has the statutory authority to 'legally prevent a nurse practising if she fails to measure up to the standards' prescribed by the code. Thus, there is a sense in which the UKCC *Code of professional conduct* does have legitimated force even though it is 'not law' (see also Armstrong 1987; Pyne 1987; Rowden 1987a). It should be noted, however, that the code's 'legitimisation' has been at the expense of its 'ethicality'. For instance, nurses can and do face the very real threat of disciplinary action by the UKCC if they fail to uphold the standards specified in the code (see *Nursing Times* 1983d; Carlisle 1990c, p. 26). On account of its legitimated force, adherence to the code is thus not strictly 'voluntary' or morally autonomous, but 'coercive'. An undesirable consequence of this has been that rather than enhance the moral status of the code and the professional nursing ethics it explicates, the statutory authority which it has indirectly been accorded has served more to undermine its normative (ethical) force. Furthermore, contrary to superficial appearances, the legitimisation of the code's professional nursing standards of conduct has not improved the moral status or authority of either individual nurses or of the UK nursing profession as a whole. Instead, it has merely increased state control over defining, interpreting and applying 'acceptable' standards of nursing practice.

Thus, while it appears that the nursing profession has found a 'new' legitimated 'freedom' in determining and enforcing its own standards of conduct, upon closer analysis it is evident that the power to determine and apply professional standards of conduct ultimately rests with the state — not the nursing profession per se. It seems, therefore, that the nursing profession has acquired yet another example of law reform going 'for' nurses also going 'against' them. As a point of interest, this is a situation which the nursing profession in Australia also faces if the newly developed *Code of ethics for nurses in Australia* (1993) is made subject to the legitimated authority of and enforcement by nurse registration boards rather than by nursing peers (something which would most probably receive full support from the health ministry (see Hicks 1985, p. 52)). At the present time, the risk of this happening is very high since it appears that nursing representative organisations are not fully cognisant of the pitfalls of using legal avenues to try to improve the status of nursing as an accountable profession.

The UKCC *Code of professional conduct* has, from the point of view of professional nursing standards of conduct and ethics at least, been an important innovation. Reginald Pyne (1981, p. 102), past Deputy Registrar of the old General Nursing Council for England and Wales (GNC), points out, for example, that codes of practice in the UK have stimulated members of the nursing profession to 'think about their responsibilities in a wider sense than they had before' — a view shared by the General Secretary to the

Royal College of Nursing, Trevor Clay (1987, p. 8). But, as Clay (1987, p. 42) goes on to point out, the full implications of the code 'have not yet been realised by the profession' — and perhaps not even by the UKCC itself. While proponents of the code were cognisant of its ethical implications, it is not clear that they fully appreciated its legal implications (Young 1991, p. vi). The indirect legitimisation of the code has given it draconian force, and is resulting in increasing numbers of nurses being censured for 'professional misconduct' (defined as 'conduct unworthy of a nurse' (read 'good woman')). Young (1991, p. 6) notes, for example, that in the UKCC's *Annual report* (1987–1988),

> the number of nurses appearing before the professional conduct committee and the resulting number where the nurse's name was removed from the Register showed a marked increase over previous years.

What is disturbing about this trend, however, is not just that the number of professional misconduct cases has increased, but the reasons for which nurses are finding themselves being deregistered. Common reasons cited for deregistering a nurse include the practice-related (and it should be added, work-stress related) offences of 'reckless or unskilful practice', 'drug offences' and 'the abuse of patients' (acts which unquestionably deserve the severest professional discipline) (Young 1991, p. 6). There are, however, other common reasons for deregistering a nurse which, while deserving professional discipline, would probably not feature among the kinds of reasons given for disciplining a doctor — for example, 'insensitivity or unkindess to patients' relatives', 'using obscene or indecent language in patient areas', 'misleading vulnerable patients', 'failure to promote a patient's interests' and 'failure to act when knowing that a colleague is improperly treating or abusing patients' — behaviours which, like the more serious practice-related offences identified above, are sometimes stress related and, in some cases, have been directly linked to poor staffing levels and poor working conditions (ibid.; Pyne 1981). While not condoning these immoral and unprofessional acts, there is room to question whether they deserve the punishment of deregistration, as opposed to, say, a punishment of restricted practice under supervision and/or compulsory remedial education, or a fine. The punishment does seem excessive particularly when it is considered that doctors can be found culpable for malpractice in a court of law and yet still not be deregistered — an example of which can be found in the case of the American physician, cited in chapter 7 (at the end of the section entitled 'The symbiosis between medicine and law'), who, it will be recalled, was found guilty of medical malpractice 18 times before the local statutory medical board took disciplinary action and suspended the physician's licence to practice.

The UKCC code (and others like it) stands as an important hallmark of professional accountability. And it is important that professional nursing codes of conduct are formally stated (published) and enforced. What is problematic about the UKCC code, however, and what promises to be problematic about the Australian code, is not the enforcement of the code per se, but the locus from which — and the means by which — it is enforced. A statutory nursing authority is first and foremost an instrument of the state, not of the nursing profession, and is, by its very nature, bound by the state, not the nursing profession. Because of this, a statutory nursing authority cannot be relied upon to fulfil impartially the role of defining, interpreting and enforcing the ethical standards of the nursing profession. And the nursing profession is naive to think otherwise. The ethical standards of the nursing profession should be developed by the profession through its representative and democratically elected nursing organisations, not by the state through its statutorily controlled if not 'hand picked' appointees. The interpretation and application of professional nursing standards of conduct/ethics should, in turn, be determined by nurses (for example, by interpretative position statements, or through voluntary expert testimony in either disciplinary or court hearings), not by the state. The development of new standards should likewise be determined by democratically elected and knowledgeable (sometimes expert) nurses, not by the state.

The state does not have a good 'track record' of protecting the public interest in health care matters, and there is no reason to suggest that by its over-regulation of nursing it will improve its reputation as the guardian of the 'public good' in the health care arena. As shown in the opening chapters of this book, the nursing profession in contrast has developed and upheld exemplary standards of practice long before it became the subject of statutory regulation. Furthermore, it was — and remains — the nursing profession's voluntary ethical standards which ensured the quality of its service, not statutory regulation. As well as this, where the nursing profession has not been able to uphold its ethical standards, it should not be forgotten that this has often been because of legally supported restraints structured against the independent and competent practice of nursing — and not the limitations of nursing's ethical standards of conduct per se. In light of these considerations, there are strong grounds for rejecting even the indirect statutory control and regulation of the nursing profession's codes of professional conduct/ethics.

CONCLUSION

Members of the nursing profession have long recognised the 'special' moral responsibilities they have to people in the community. It is evident, however, that others outside nursing (in particular, doctors, jurists and judges) are not willing to accept the moral (or indeed the professional and therapeutic) dimension and significance of the nurse–patient relationship, or the nurse's moral authority and very real moral responsibilities within that relationship. Rather, the nurse's moral authority (if it is recognised at all) is generally regarded as being inferior and subordinate to the doctor's moral authority. In so far as the nurse's moral responsibilities to patients are concerned, these too are not generally regarded as being genuine. At best, they are regarded as being only vicarious vis-à-vis the doctor–patient relationship, and the doctor's moral responsibilities in that relationship.

As in the case of denying the therapeutic importance of the nurse–patient relationship, denying the moral validity and sanctity of the nurse–patient relationship has, among other things, helped to ensure that independent (medically unauthorised) nursing judgments and actions are constrained, and that nurses have been kept firmly in their 'proper sphere'. It has also been instrumental in structuring, reinforcing and maintaining the primacy of the doctor–patient relationship, and medical control over patient care matters. This, in turn, has made it extremely difficult for nurses to challenge authoritatively unscrupulous medical or general hospital practices. One of the most serious consequences of denying the moral validity and significance of the nurse–patient relationship, however, is that it makes it very difficult for nurses to fulfil their own moral responsibilities to patients. This, in turn, has sometimes resulted in patients being exposed to an unacceptable risk of (or indeed the actuality of) suffering otherwise avoidable moral harms on account of being subject to unscrupulous (and unchecked) health and medical care practices.

Historically, nurses have been well informed of (or, more to the point, indoctrinated about) the moral unacceptability of nurses 'interfering' with the doctor–patient relationship — which, incidentally, has sometimes involved little more than nurses giving patients 'privileged' information about their medical treatment, or advising them to seek a second medical opinion. Nurses have not, however, been so well informed about the moral (and it might be added, clinical) unacceptability of doctors interfering with the nurse–patient relationship — which happens not only regularly, but in ways which seriously threaten the wellbeing and in some instances the life of patients (Johnstone 1989, p. 129). Certainly, we do not see doctors being reported to their state medical boards for the 'professional misconduct' of 'interfering' with the nurse–patient relationship — at least, not in the way that nurses have been reported to their state registration boards for allegedly interfering with the doctor–patient relationship, as occurred in the case of *Tuma v Board of Nursing of the State of Idaho* (1979), discussed in chapter 6 in the section entitled 'The legal reinforcement of nurse incompetency'. As already argued in this book, when a doctor 'interferes' with a nurse–patient relationship (for example, questions and/or overrules a nurse's judgment), this is generally construed as being a 'normal' course of action and even a 'highly professional' or 'ethical' thing to do (see also *Regan Report on Nursing Law* 1982a, p. 1). However, when a nurse attempts to question or overrule a doctor's judgment, this is generally construed as being not only highly 'unprofessional' and 'unethical', but bordering perilously close to illegal and possibly even criminal behaviour (*Regan Report on Nursing Law* 1980d; O'Sullivan 1983, p. 6).

The moral status and authority — or rather, the lack of status and authority — of the nurse–patient relationship stands as another important measure of the extent to which the nursing profession still has not 'come of age' as an autonomous profession. So long as the moral significance, therapeutic importance and sanctity of the nurse–patient relationship is denied, marginalised, trivialised and invalidated there will remain considerable scope to argue that the nurse's status as an autonomous and authoritative professional remains less than optimal, and that nurses are not only 'not free to nurse', as already contended in this book, but, to borrow from Yarling and McElmurry (1986b, p. 129), are 'not free to be moral'.

ENDNOTES

1 An Australian example has not been included here because the newly developed Australian Nursing Council's (1993) *Code of ethics for nurses in Australia* does not contain comparable statements which make explicit that:

- the nurse's primary responsibility is to those people who require nursing care;
- nurses have a stringent moral responsibility to safeguard and if necessary take action in order to protect the interests and wellbeing of people in their care.

The code's primary emphasis is on making explicit six broad values which it is believed the nursing profession in Australia holds. While the code acknowledges that 'nurses provide care and support before and during birth and throughout life, and alleviate pain and suffering during the dying process', and that 'nurses have moral obligations in the provision of nursing care', these statements are not as strong as those expressed in other codes. For example, 'Value statement 1' of the code explicates the value that 'nurses respect persons' individual needs, values and culture in the provision of nursing care'; 'Value statement 3' that 'nurses promote and uphold the provision of quality nursing care for all people'; and 'Value statement 5' that 'nurses respect the accountability and responsibility inherent in their roles'. However, as is self-evident, none of these statements — nor the explanatory statements given with them — make explicit the overriding moral nature of the nurse–patient relationship or the stringent moral responsibilities nurses have in that relationship — at least, not in the way that these things are identified in the other codes quoted.

2   Note: Questions concerning the nature of, and the relationship between, law and morality/ethics have long been the subject of debate among philosophers, jurists and social scientists (see, for example, Hart 1961, 1963, 1968, 1983; Fuller 1969; Mitchell 1970; Wasserstrom 1971; Dworkin 1977, 1985, 1986; Morawetz 1980; Raz 1980; Cohen 1983; Feinberg 1984, 1990; Lyons 1984; Lee 1986; Coleman and Paul 1987; Weinreb 1987; Cotterrell 1989; Bartee and Bartee 1992).

CHAPTER **TEN**

Conclusion: Towards a New Nursing Jurisprudence

The fragility of recent feminist gains must alert us to be ever-watchful, for it is a function of legalism to constrain and hedge in the political gains of women in order to protect and maintain the status quo.
Margaret Thornton (1986, p. 22)

INTRODUCTION

FROM THE VERY MOMENT the early modern nurses first began their quest for legal status as autonomous professionals, they experienced enormous difficulties in establishing their identity and authority as professional women and, more specifically, as qualified professional health care providers. The harder these nurses (and their successors) fought for legal recognition and legitimated authority as autonomous professionals independent of the dominance and control of doctors, the more entwined they became in the inescapable paradoxes of law: law reforms going 'for' nurses, also went 'against' them (adapted from DeCrow 1974, p. 3). Rather than free nurses from medical dominance and control, nursing law reforms served more to legitimate it. And when nurses eventually achieved legal recognition as 'professionals', this proved to be primarily for the purposes of imposing legal responsibility and liability, not authority and autonomous professional agency, and for reinforcing and maintaining the cultural hegemony of medical men in the public health care system.

Despite the apparent improvement in the social position of nurses today (something that is inextricably linked to the improved social position of women), it is evident that the law has failed nurses in their ongoing quest for improved authority and status as autonomous professionals, and that the patriarchal status quo has been preserved. Like their predecessors over a century ago, nurses do not have the authority to match their responsibilities, are subject to the legitimated dominance and control of doctors, and are vulnerable to exploitation and abuse by employers and the state. As the World Health Organisation (WHO) observed in its report entitled *Leadership for health for all: the challenge to nursing: a strategy for action* (1987, p. 5):

> The nursing culture is heavy with subordination without influence. It is burdened with obligation without power — even in directing, heading and controlling its own education, practice, research and management.

In the preceding chapters of this book, a substantial attempt has been made to answer the question of why the nursing profession has not achieved the legal status and authority for which it has historically fought. Given the findings of these chapters, it would not serve the purposes of either this chapter or this book to dwell any further on that question. One pressing question which does remain, however, is what (if anything) can the nursing profession do realistically to improve the status quo? It is the task of this final chapter to try to answer this question.

Challenging the status quo

It is understandable that nurses might feel completely overwhelmed by the patriarchal forces that have been and are pitted against them, and might fall prey to what Sandra Harding (1973–1974) aptly describes in another context as 'cynical indifference to the immediate plight of women' — or, as in this case, the plight of nurses. Nevertheless, for all the odds that continue to militate against the independent profession and practice of nursing, to borrow from Salvage (1988, p. 516): 'the status quo is not an option'. A major reason for this is that too much is at stake — not just for the nursing profession, but more importantly for those who are requiring and/or receiving nursing care. In the case of the nursing profession, if nurses do not challenge the status quo they risk continuing along the path of legitimated powerlessness, exploitation and abuse; and will continue to be subject to a general inability to practise their profession in a safe, clinically competent, therapeutically effective, and ethically responsible manner.

In the case of those requiring and/or receiving nursing care, a failure by nurses to challenge the status quo likewise threatens confinement to an intolerable future. As the examples given throughout this book have shown, the interests of patients have been seriously compromised and violated because nurses have not had the legitimated authority to match their responsibilities, and because nurses have not been 'free to nurse' in the way in which they have been educationally prepared and morally obligated. Furthermore, as has long been recognised in the Western world, nurses are essential to the maximisation of public health and to the success of national health care systems as a whole. Without nurses, the health care system would collapse, and the health interests of the community at large would be put in serious jeopardy. It is for these reasons, among others, that the nursing profession must have the legitimated authority it seeks, and why nurses must continue to challenge the patriarchal political status quo in health care, regardless of the immense political pressures exerted upon them to accept, maintain and reinforce it.

Over a decade ago, the American nurse scholar, Lucy Kelly (1978, p. 468) urged the nursing profession to concentrate its energy on attacking the 'corruption of powerlessness' that had come to envelop and discourage it. Kelly's words remain relevant today. It should be added, however, that the nursing profession must also concentrate its energy on subverting the patriarchal political forces which have historically been stacked against it, on dismantling its legitimated subordination to medicine, and on reasserting itself as an autonomous and authoritative healing profession. Just how this rhetoric can be translated into effective action remains an open question, however. Before addressing this problem, a brief comment is required on the broader issue of legal activism (including law reform), and the extent to which this should or should not be pursued as a means of addressing and remedying the nursing profession's problems.

The paradoxes of engaging in legal activism

It is tempting to assert that the panacea for all of nursing's ills is to engage in a rigorous campaign of legal activism with a focus on law reform. As Thornton (1991) points out in another context, legal activism is 'an important public site of political activity' and has the power to 'challenge private dominance which would otherwise go unchecked'. It should be added that legal activism also has the power to challenge public dominance which would otherwise go unchecked — as in the paradigmatic case of medicine's largely unchecked and very public legitimated dominance of nursing.

While legal activism is obviously an important option in the battle for improving the status of nursing, it should be noted that it is not without its risks — not least that of cooption, complicity and assimilation to the ideologies, processes and procedures of law (Lahey 1991, p. 4). Furthermore, there is an acknowledged danger (and paradox) that 'engaging with the law' (whether for the purposes of critiquing it or reforming it) could have the morally undesirable consequences of increasing nursing's dependency on the law (and the state), of further subverting nursing's demands, of replicating the very injustices that nurses are trying to eradicate, and of further legitimating and reinforcing the centrality of law in nursing discourse (see also Thornton 1986, 1990, 1991; Stubbs 1986; Lacey 1989; Fineman 1990; Lahey 1991). Nevertheless, the alternatives (for example, of falling prey to cynical indifference, and/or a sense of hopelessness and despair) are equally pessimistic, subordinating and imprisoning, and could ultimately have the effect of also supporting the status quo. Neither is nihilism an option: blowing up the supreme court (or nurse registration boards, for that matter) will not pave the way for the establishment of a nursing utopia.

Given the practical realities of their predicament, it is apparent that nurses have little choice but to 'engage in law'. As Smart and Brophy (1985, p. 16) writing in another context concede, the law 'affects our daily lives whether we choose it or not'. And, in the case of nursing, law affects our daily practise whether we choose it or not. Indeed, there is hardly a nursing action which is not legally restricted or controlled in some way. For example, every time nurses sign for a drug they have administered, they are fulfilling a legal (not merely an institutional policy) requirement. Thus, while nurses may choose ultimately to either reject or accept the law as it is, they cannot ignore it — or its prominent and up until now central role as a powerful instrument of social (and, in this case, professional) control and change (see also O'Donovan and Szyszczak 1988, p. 45).

The challenge for the nursing profession at this time is not how to avoid the law (this is impossible, even in death), but — to borrow from Thornton (1991) — how to engage in law without being tantalised by its (false) promises, and how to reform it without being caught in one of its 'many concealed traps' (ibid.). Although it may not be possible to avoid totally the 'many concealed traps' of law, or to achieve genuine law reform,[1] this should not be taken as ground for abandoning altogether the quest for professional nursing justice. The nursing profession can do a great deal to challenge the status quo, to subvert both the law's and the medical profession's patriarchal assumptions about nurses and nursing practice, and to move a firm (albeit slow) step closer towards achieving its ultimate goal of professional emancipation. As a point of encouragement, nurses should not forget their extraordinary history of establishing nursing as a respectable and quality controlled profession at a time when women did not have legal status as persons, and did not have the legal right to enter into a profession of their own choosing. This highlights an additional challenge for the nursing profession: namely, how to reclaim its lost heritage and to emerge once again one step ahead of the law — only this time, in a form not so vulnerable to the influences and assaults of patriarchy.

Strategies for change

While not wishing to end this book by offering a 'shopping list' of remedies which the nursing profession might find useful in its ongoing quest for legitimated status as an autonomous profession, there are a number of strategies which warrant some mention here — and which the nursing profession would, arguably, be well advised to consider seriously.

Exposing the injustices of law

In their influential text *Sexism and the law*, Sachs and Wilson (1978, p. 136) argue:

> There is no such thing as a self-evident injustice — the beneficiaries of inequality will always justify it, while its victims will have to struggle to get its very existence acknowledged ... Injustice only becomes self-evident retrospectively, that is, after it has been removed.

As demonstrated in the previous chapters of this book, nurses have suffered enormous injustices over the years: exploited by unscrupulous employers (including the state), forced to endure intolerable work conditions, used as scapegoats by more powerful others, treated as objects, denied recognition as rationally competent professionals, and so on. What has been problematic about these injustices is not only that they occurred, but that, in many instances, were permitted — and in some instances were supported fully — by the law. Not surprisingly, those who stood to benefit from the unfair treatment of nurses always justified it, and, more to the point, justified it (and sought to legitimate it) in the name of the 'public good' — regardless of the many and demonstrable harmful consequences to nurses (including ill health and even death).

Nurses know intimately the injustices they have been forced to endure. Others outside nursing, however, remain largely ignorant of the injustices that nurses have suffered, and of the extent to which the law not only failed to remedy these injustices but in fact contributed to them. Given this, there is room to suggest that one of the most important — if not *the* most important — political acts that the nursing profession could undertake at this time, is to expose the unjust, deceitful and patriarchally biased way that the law (or, more to the point, those whose dominant interests have been supported in and by the law) has historically treated nurses and nursing practice. By doing this, nurses stand not only to break free of their constructed silence and manipulated passivity, but — equally important — stand to break free of the dominant medical and legal discourse that has historically imprisoned them and denied them status and authority as autonomous health professionals (see Thornton 1986, p. 15).

There is, however, the problem that many nurses may themselves need to be convinced of the extent to which the law has been instrumental in subordinating the nursing profession, and has contributed directly and indirectly to the many hardships and injustices that nurses — both individually and as a group — have experienced. Given this, it is evident that 'legal activism' needs to extend far beyond the parameters of law reform, and to penetrate other areas such as nurse education, nursing research, and nursing academia generally.

Reforming the legal education of nurses

In chapter 2 of this text it was argued that nurses need to develop a radically different way of thinking about the law from the way they have historically done so. For this to happen, however, it is apparent that there needs to be a radical change in *what* and *how* nurses are taught about the law.

Traditionally, legal issues in nursing have tended to be addressed in a descriptive, explanatory and positivistic way, rather than a critical and socially and professionally relevant way. While not wishing to deny the importance of nurses learning about the nature of law in its present form, and the various traditional legal doctrines, principles, and rules of law which apply to nurses and nursing practice, this is clearly not enough. As previously argued, much greater attention needs to be given to examining critically the nature and (in)adequacy of traditionally accepted legal doctrines and concepts, legal rules and principles, legal processes, the way the law has operated — and continues to operate — in the specific field of nursing, and the extent to which the law has been instrumental in structuring, reinforcing and maintaining the subordination of nursing. Sustained attention also needs to be given to examining and 'making visible' nursing's historical relationship to and experience of the law, to identifying and critiquing the law's patriarchal assumptions about nurses and nursing practice, and to examining ways in which nurses can challenge effectively nursing's legitimated subordination to medicine (and the legitimated cultural hegemony of medicine in health care generally). Further to this, much greater attention needs to be given to the decentring of law in nursing discourse — to demystifying the law's so readily accepted power, and to the breaking free of its 'theoretical privilege and sovereignty' (Foucault 1978, pp. 86–102). In short, to borrow from Foucault (1978, p. 89), the nursing profession needs to 'cut off the head of the king'.

No doubt there will be some nurses (for example, those in administrative positions charged with the responsibility of 'keeping the peace') who would regard the suggestions being made here as 'threatening' and possibly even 'unprofessional' (read 'not in accordance with the traditional standards of what constitutes a "good woman"'). The point remains, however, that unless nurses challenge and break free of the 'theoretical privilege and sovereignty' of law, they will never be in a position to challenge, let alone break free of their 'subordination without influence' and their 'burden of obligation without power'. Instead, they will remain imprisoned in the dominant medical and legal discourse which has historically undervalued them as women, and which has denied them full legitimated status and authority as autonomous health professionals in the 'public sphere' (see also Thornton 1986, p. 15).

Reforming nursing jurisprudential scholarship and research

In chapter 2 of this text, it was pointed out that there is a surprising lack of critical scholarship on legal issues in nursing. As in the case of nurse education, nursing jurisprudential scholarship has tended to be descriptive and explanatory in nature rather than critical. Nursing legal texts have, for example, tended to concentrate on outlining the history of Anglo-American/Australian law; and on describing and explaining legal doctrines, rules and principles, the hierarchy of the courts, the key players in law enforcement, the processes and procedures of law, and what nurses can do to avoid litigation. Considerable attention has also been given to examining various legal cases involving nurses, and to 'pointing the finger' at those 'errant' nurses who 'did not know better what to do' because they did not have the rudimentary legal knowledge of their practice otherwise necessary for avoiding the very kind of predicaments in which they have found themselves.

However, little if any attention has been given to examining critically whether the law has been fair in its treatment of nurses, to the politics of law and law reform, to nursing's historical relationship to and experience of the law, or indeed to any of the issues identified above, such as examining critically the nature and (in)adequacy of traditionally accepted legal doctrines and concepts, legal rules and principles, legal processes, the way the law has operated — and continues to operate — in the specific field of nursing, the extent to which the law has been instrumental in structuring, reinforcing and maintaining the subordination of nursing.

It is evident that if the nursing profession is to develop a better position from which to challenge and subvert the legitimated patriarchal status quo, it will need to give much more attention to examining critically the above issues and to developing a more substantial body of nursing jurisprudential literature than is presently available. It is also evident that much more attention needs to be given to nursing jurisprudential research — something which, in the past, has not featured prominently on the nursing research agenda. Furthermore, it is evident that there needs to be a radical change in what is written about the law (including legal briefs and analyses of legal cases involving nurses), with more sustained attention being given to demystifying the law and, as stated above, to breaking free of its 'theoretical privilege and sovereignty' in nursing's affairs (adapted from Foucault 1978, pp. 86–102).

Improving the status of nursing jurisprudence in nursing academia

Another strategy for helping to translate the rhetoric of legal activism into effective action is for nurses to adopt a radical change in attitude towards the importance of, and the priority which should be given to, (feminist) nursing jurisprudence in nursing academia. In the past, nursing jurisprudence has tended to be given a low priority and low profile in departments and schools of nursing — something which has been to nursing's disadvantage.

Significantly, medicine has had chairs and lectureships in medical jurisprudence since the early 1800s[2] (a factor which may account for medicine's legal literacy which, in turn, may have contributed significantly to the development of the medical profession's ability to exploit the law fully to its own advantage). By contrast, and equally significant, there are few, if any, equivalent academic positions in nursing. Although, there are a significant number of nurse–lawyers/nurse–attorneys (nurses who have dual qualifications in nursing and in law) employed in nursing faculties, these entities tend to be employed first as clinical nurse specialists/educationalists, rather than as nurse lawyers per se (a fate also shared by nurse ethicists). Dr Helen Creighton, for example, a distinguished American nurse attorney, noted for her prolific writing on the subject of nurses and the law, was appointed as a professor of nursing, not as a professor of nursing jurisprudence/law. While it is certainly true that by being appointed in general academic nursing positions (either as lecturers or as professors), nurse–lawyers/nurse–attorneys have been able to pursue and develop their nursing jurisprudence scholarship, and have been able to speak with relative authority and freedom on nursing jurisprudence questions (a freedom usually denied nurses working in hospitals or private agencies), their nursing jurisprudence scholarship and related activities have nevertheless been denied the legitimated authority of being a primary (and hence prominent) focus of attention in nursing academia or in academia generally. Arguably, one way to rectify this situation would be to establish academic chairs and lectureships specifically in nursing jurisprudence, and — given its close relationship with questions of social and professional values — ethics (for example, 'Lecturer/Professor of Nursing Law and Ethics' or 'Lecturer/ Professor of Nursing Ethics and Legal Studies'). The political importance of an initiative such as this should not be underestimated, trivialised or scorned. While establishing lectureships and chairs specifically in nursing jurisprudence and ethics might well have the appearance of being an act of 'assimilation' to the mainstream ('malestream') legalistic and patriarchal culture, at a deeper level (depending, of course, on how these positions were structured, filled, and administered) it would nevertheless stand as an important and significant political act of *naming* and *legitimising* nursing jurisprudence (and ethics) as a bona fide discipline in its own right and as an area of serious concern not just to nurse academics, but to the broader nursing profession as well. This in turn would give the nursing profession more authority to 'speak on its own behalf' and to break free of the constructed silence which has historically been imposed upon it by the dominant patriarchal elite.

The use of nurse lawyers/attorneys to challenge the status quo

It might be suggested here that a major solution to nursing's problems would be to encourage nurses to undertake law degrees, and to practise as nurse lawyers/attorneys with a view towards making the law more responsive to nurses' lived experiences, and the realities and complexities of nurses' everyday practice. While this suggestion has some merit, it is nevertheless problematic for the reasons outlined below.

It would be naive to expect that a sudden rush of nurses into law would have the effect of 'nursefying' law (that is, making law more responsive to the needs and lived experiences of nurses), in much the same way that it would be naive to expect that an increase of women in law will necessarily have the effect of feminising law. Nurse lawyers are just as prone as are women lawyers generally to becoming socialised into accepting the traditional structures, processes and procedures of law, and hence into supporting rather than challenging the status quo. Just as blowing up the supreme court is not the solution to nursing's problems, neither is securing an increase of nurse lawyers practising, writing about and/or teaching 'nursing law'. It cannot be assumed that just because nurses are lawyers — or lawyers are nurses — they will be able — or willing — to challenge and change the status quo.

This is not to say, however, that nurses who have studied law and who are qualified to practise law, do not have an important role to play in assisting the broader nursing profession to deal with the law in its present form, and to critique its treatment of nurses and nursing practice with a view towards challenging and changing the status quo. Whether nurse lawyers/attorneys will be able to — or indeed will be willing to — undertake such a role may, however, depend ultimately on whether they themselves are able to escape the hegemony and authority of law (see Greer 1982; Polan 1982), and are able to challenge law's own account of itself as 'rational, fair and objective and hence adequate in its treatment of women' (Naffine 1990, p. 2) — or, more specifically, as in this case, nurses.

The question of nurse-lawyers has not been formally investigated. Thus, it is not known what, if any, impact they have had on changing (or perpetuating) traditional (patriarchal) legal attitudes towards nurses and nursing practice. Before the nursing profession embraces any idea of encouraging some of its members to become lawyers with a view towards improving the legal position of nurses, it should first investigate the extent to which (if at all) nurse lawyers can be effective as agents of professional, social and legal reform.

CONCLUSION

In chapter 2 of this text, it was contended that in developing a new substantive nursing jurisprudence, more is required than mere 'compensatory scholarship' — the 'add-on-and-stir' approach which was characteristic of the first phase of feminist jurisprudence scholarship. It was also contended that more is required than merely focusing on 'recovering that which has been silenced', namely, nursing's experience of the law from the point of view of nurses — as opposed to the point of view of eminent jurists clad in their distinctive pin-striped suits and club ties. And it was contended that it is not sufficient merely to criticise the law, legal scholarship and society for its failure to address nursing concerns and its failure to redress the marginalisation, trivialisation and invalidation of nursing's historical experience of the law — although it is conceded here that all of these approaches are critical to the development of the nursing jurisprudence debate. As stated earlier, what is also crucial, is that nurses and nursing jurisprudential scholars engage in 'a positive project of constructing and developing alternative models, methods, procedures, discourses, etc' (Gross 1986, p. 195), and, as alluded to above, to engage in the positive project of 'decentering law in the hierarchy of discourses' (Smart 1989, pp. 88–89). These and other activites are all essential to the development of a substantive nursing jurisprudence, and, even at the risk of duplicating the evolutionary process and findings of feminist jurisprudential thinking on the law, warrant special and urgent attention by the nursing profession.

The issues raised and examined in this book represent only a very modest beginning to the development of a new substantive nursing jurisprudence. There are a number of other issues warranting investigation, but which, for reasons outlined in the beginning of this book, could not be considered here. As stated earlier, it has not been possible to address such issues as industrial law, disciplinary action by statutory authorities,[3] the patriarchal biases of other Acts and statutes (that is, other than nurse registration Acts) which have a bearing on nursing practice, the practice of other nursing specialities, the general physical and verbal abuse of nurses (for example, by doctors, employers, and patients), private agency nursing, men in nursing, and overseas qualified nurses, to name some. These issues are all worthy of investigation, and hopefully will be investigated by the nursing profession in the not too distant future. Research findings into these and other issues promise to contribute substantially to the development of a new substantive nursing jurisprudence, and to the long overdue decentring of law in nursing discourse.

Although not exhaustive, the arguments presented throughout this book mark an important turning point in the nursing jurisprudence debate, and reflect the 'radical change of thinking' that is required on the part of nurses if they are to challenge successfully the patriarchal status quo which has historically obstructed the professional development of nursing. The arguments presented also reflect the kinds of 'new things' that nurses must and can think about as part of their new found legal activism aimed at subverting law's patriarchal assumptions about nurses and nursing practice, and at exposing the patriarchal biases and injustices of law generally. If successful, the nursing profession will find itself in a better position to shed its 'subordination without influence' and its burden of 'obligation without power'. More importantly, nurses will be in a better position to secure their 'freedom to nurse', to gain sovereignty in their own realm of practice, and, not least, to secure and strengthen once and for all the role, function and status of nursing as a socially relevant, therapeutically effective, ethically responsible and accountable professional service that is committed to promoting the health and wellbeing of the individuals, groups and communities requiring and/or receiving nursing care.

ENDNOTES

1 Note: It is widely acknowledged within feminist jurisprudence that the patriarchal structures of law may, in the end, make it impossible to achieve genuine law reform.

2 The first UK chair of medical jurisprudence was established at Edinburgh as early as 1807, followed by Glasgow (1839), and Aberdeen (1875). Lectureships in medical jurisprudence, meanwhile, were established at Guy's Hospital in 1831, followed by Charing Cross Hospital in 1838. Textbooks on medical jurisprudence and forensic medicine were published as early as 1816 onward (Gee and Mason 1990, p. 24). By contrast, the earliest nursing law texts were not published until around the early 1930s — over one hundred years later. One of the first of these texts was co-authored by Eleanor McGarvah, a registered nurse and a member of the Michigan Bar, who is believed to be the first American nurse attorney (Northrop and Kelly 1987, p. vii). Her co-authored text *Jurisprudence for Nurses* was first published in 1931, with two further editions being published in 1939 and 1945. The text was, at the time, heralded by the legal establishment as being a 'newborn babe in the world of nursing texts' (ibid.).

3 As pointed out in the preface to this text, it is known that nurses can and do suffer a range of health problems before, during and/or after disciplinary hearings. For example, in one unpublished case, a nurse, ultimately vindicated of the

professional misconduct charge against her, had to be admitted to hospital for treatment after becoming severely depressed following the completion of the professional misconduct proceedings initiated against her. In another reported case, a charge nurse facing a disciplinary hearing because of a disagreement with a senior nursing officer, committed suicide (*Nursing Times* 1983c). And in another case, a director of nursing committed suicide after being sacked following a long internal wrangle and a 'confused' use of disciplinary procedures (Slack 1982).

LEGISLATION TABLE

New South Wales Legislation

Nurses' Registration Act 1924

Victorian Legislation

Community Welfare Services Act 1970
Drugs, Poisons and Controlled Substances Act 1981
Drugs, Poisons and Controlled Substances (Amendment) Regulations 1985
Drugs, Poisons and Controlled Substances Regulations 1985
Nurses Registration Act 1923
Nurses Act 1928
Nurses Act 1931
Nurses Act 1958
Nurses (Amendment) Act 1985

Queensland Legislation

Health Act 1911
Health Act Amendment Acts 1911
Nurses and Masseurs Registration Acts 1928
Nurses and Masseurs Registration Act 1928–1933
Nurses and Masseurs Registration Acts Amendment Act 1938
Nurses Act 1964
Nurses Act 1976

South Australian Legislation

Nurses Registration Act 1920
Nurses Registration Act, 1920–1934

Western Australian Legislation

Nurses Registration Act 1922

Tasmanian Legislation

Nurses Registration Act 1927
Nurses Registration Act 1952

Northern Territory Legislation

Nurses and Midwives Registration Ordinance 1928–1957

Australian Capital Territory Legislation

Nurses Registration Ordinance 1933

New Zealand Legislation

Nurses Registration Act 1901

United Kingdom Legislation

Nurses Registration Act 1919
Nursing Profession (Wages and Hours) Bill 1930
Nurses Act 1943
Nurses, Midwives and Health Visitors Act 1979

CASES TABLE

Adkins v Ropp 14 NE 2d 727 (1938)

Avret v McCormick Ga 271 SE 2d 832 (1980)

Avey v St Francis Hospital and School of Nursing, Inc 442 P 2d 1013 (1968)

Baerman v Reisinger 363 F 2d 309 (1966)

Bamert v Central General Hospital App Div 430 NYS 2d 336 (1980)

Baur v Mesta Machine Company 176 A 2d 684 (1962)

Belmon v St Francis Cabrini Hospital 427 So 2d 541 (La App 3 Cir 1983)

Benedict v Bondi 122 A 2d 209 (1956)

Bolam v Friern Hospital Management Committee [1957] 1 WLR 582

Bradwell v State of Illinois 83 US 130 (1873)

Breit v St Luke's Memorial Hospital 743 P 2d 1254 (Wash App 1987)

Brinson v Bethesda Hospital, Inc 504 NE 2d 496 (Ohio Com Pl 1985)

Bugden v Harbour View Hospital (1947) 2 DLR 338

Buzan v Mercy Hospital, Inc Fla 203 So 2d 11 (1967)

Byrd v Marion General Hospital 162 SE 738 (1932)

Cassidy v Ministry of Health (1951) 2 KB 343

Cedars of Lebanon Hospital v Silva 476 So 2d 696 (Fla App 3 Dist 1985)

Cignetti v Camel 692 SW 2d 329 (Mo App 1985)

Crawford v Board of Governors, Charing Cross Hospital [1953] TLR 1

Crowe v Provost 374 SW 2d 645 (1963)

Czubinsky v Doctors Hospital 188 Cal Rptr 685 (App 1983)

Daley v St Agnes Hospital, Inc 490 F Supp 1309 (1980)

Daniel v St Francis Cabrini Hospital of Alexandria, Inc La App 415 So 2d 586 (1982)

Darling v Charleston Community Memorial Hospital 211 NE 2d 253 (1965)

Davis v Schneider 395 NE 2d 283 (1979)

Hillyer v Governors of St Bartholomew's Hospital (1909) 2 KB 820

Horton v Niagara Falls Memorial Medical Centre 380 NYS 2d 116 (NY 1976)

Hucks v Cole and Another [1968] The Times 9 May

Hunsaker v Bozeman Deaconess Foundation 588 P 2d 493 (1978)

In re the Alleged Unfair Dismissal of Ms K Howden by the City of Whittlesea 6/9/90 (Case No 90/3672, Decision D90/1933), IRCV (unreported)

In re French (1905) 37 NBR 359

In re Nurses Registration Act 1953 and In re Heathcote and Nurses Registration Board and Walton 12/4/91 (No 3223 of 1989), District Court of New South Wales (unreported)

In re Parkes District Hospital and the New South Wales Nurses' Association 12/12/79 (No 703 of 1979), NSWIRC (unreported)

In re Standard Hours — Nursing Staff in Hospitals (1934) IARNSW 316

In re Tingay and Flinders Medical Centre Incorporated 2/12/83 (No 108 of 1983, Decision M.58/1983), SAIRC (unreported)

Johnsen v Independent School District No 3 of Tulsa County 891 F 2d 1485 (10th Cir 1989)

Johnson v Hermann Hospital 659 SW 2d 124 (Tex App 14 Dist 1983)

Jones v Hawkes Hospital of Mt Carmel 196 NE 2d 592 (1964)

Jones v Memorial Hospital System 677 SW 2d 221 (Tex App 1 Dist 1984)

Kelly v Hartford Casualty Insurance Company Wis 271 NW 2d 676 (1978)

Killeen v Reinhardt 419 NYS 2d 175 (1979)

Koeniguer v Eckrich 422 NW 2d 600 (SD 1988)

Kolakowski v Voris 395 NE 2d 6 (1979)

Krujelis v Esdale (1971) 25 DLR (3d) 557

Kuna v Lifemark Hospitals of Texas, Inc 743 SW 2d 705 (Tex App — Houston [1st Dist] 1987)

Laidlaw v Lions Gate Hospital (1969) 8 DLR (3d) 730

Lampe v Presbyterian Medical Centre Colo App 590 P 2d 513 (1978)

Larrimore v Homeopathic Hospital Association of Delaware 176 A 2d 363 (1961)

Lavelle v Glasgow Royal Infirmary [1931] SLT 220

Lavelle v Glasgow Royal Infirmary [1931] SC (HL) 34

Lavelle v Glasgow Royal Infirmary [1932] SC 245

Lavere v Smith's Falls Public Hospital (1915) 35 OLR 98

Leonard v Watsonville Community Hospital 305 P 2d 36 (1956)

Lindsey County Council v Marshall [1937] AC 97

Logan v Waitaki Hospital Board [1935] NZLR 385

Lunsford v Board of Nurse Examiners 648 SW 2d 391 (Tex App 3 Dist 1983)

McCormack v Redpath Brown and Co [1961] The Lancet 736

McCormick v Avret Ga App 267 SE 2d 759 (1980)

Maloney v Wake Hospital Systems, Inc NC App 262 SE 2d 680 (1980)

Marshall v Lindsey County Council [1935] 1 KB 516

Maslonka v Hermann NJ Super AD 414 A 2d 1350 (1980)

Massey v Heine Ky 497 SW 2d 564 (1973)

Mellies v National Heritage, Inc Kan App 636 p 2d 215 (1981)

Misericordia Hospital Medical Center v NLRB 623 F 2d 808 (1980)

Montgomery v Department of Registration and Education 496 NE 2d 1100 (Ill App 1 Dist 1986)

Muller v State of Oregon 208 US 412 (1908)

NLRB v Mount Desert Island Hospital 695 F 2d 634 (1982)

Norton v Argonaut Insurance Company 144 So 2d 249 (1962)

Nyberg v Provost Municipal Hospital Board [1927] SCR 226

Page v Wilson Memorial Hospital, Inc NC App 272 SE 2d 8 (1980)

Perez v Hartmann 543 NE 2d 1023 (Ill App 1 Dist 1989)

Perionowsky v Freeman (1866) 4 F & F 976 NS (176 ER 873)

Petrillo v Syntex Laboratories, Inc 499 NE 2d 952 (Ill App 1 Dist 1986)

Phillips v Eastern Maine Medical Center 565 A 2d 306 (Me 1989)

Pillai v Messiter [No 2] (1989) 16 NSWLR 197

Planned Parenthood of Northwest Indiana v Vines 543 NE 2d 654 (Ind App 3 Dist 1989)

Plutshack v University of Minnesota Hospitals Minn 316 NW 2d 1 (1982)

Polischek v United States 535 F Supp 1261 (1982)

Poor Sisters of St Francis v Catron Ind App 435 NE 2d 305 (1982)

Porter v Department of Employment Security Vt 430 A 2d 450 (1981)

Powell and Wife v Streatham Manor Nursing Home [1935] AC 243

Re Mount Sinai Hospital and Ontario Nurses' Association (1978) 17 LAC (2d) 242

Reidford v Magistrates of Aberdeen [1933] SC 276

Reynolds v Swigert 697 P 2d 504 (NM App 1984)

Richardson v Doe 199 NE 2d 878 (1964)

Ritchie v People 40 NE 454 (1895)

Roberson v Liu 555 NE 2d 999 (Ill App 5 Dist 1990)

Roe v Minister of Health [1954] 2 QB 66

Ross v Consumers Power Company 363 NW 2d 641 (Mich 1984)

Royal College of Nursing v DHSS (CA) [1981] AC 800

Sanchez v Bay General Hospital App 172 Cal Rptr 342 (1981)

Scottish Insurance Commissioners v Edinburgh Royal Infirmary [1913] SC 751

Seery v Yale-New Haven Hospital 554 A 2d 757 (Conn App 1989)

Sermchief v Gonzales 600 SW 2d 683 (Mo. banc 1983)

Sheppard v Kimbrough 318 SE 2d 573 (SC App 1984)

Sidaway v Bethlem Royal Hospital [1984] 1 All ER 1018

Sides v Duke Hospital 328 SE 2d 818 (NC App 1985)

Smith v Martin and Kingston-upon-Hull Corporation [1911] 2 KB 775

Somera Case GR 31 693 (Supreme Court, Phillipine Islands 1929) (unreported)

Stone v Sisters of Charity of House of Providence Wash App 469 P 2d 229 (1970)

Strangways-Lesmere v Clayton [1936] 2 KB 11

Su v Perkins 211 SE 2d 421 (1974)

Suburban Hospital Association, Inc v Hadary 322 A 2d 258 (1974)

Swigerd v City of Ortonville 75 NW 2d 217 (1956)

Taylor v Spencer Hospital Pa Super 292 A 2d 449 (1972)

Toth v Community Hospital at Glen Cove 239 NE 2d 368 (1968)

Tripp v Humana, Inc 474 So 2d 88 (Ala 1985)

Truhitte v French Hospital App 180 Cal Rptr 152 (1982)

Tuma v Board of Nursing of the State of Idaho 593 P 2d 711 (1979)

Utter v United Hospital Center, Inc 236 SE 2d 213 (1977)

United States v Anthony 24 Fed Cas 830 (Cir Crt New York 1873)

Vassey v Burch NC App 262 SE 2d 865 (1980)

Vuchar et al. v The Trustees of the Toronto General Hospital [1936] OR 387

Wardell v Kent County Council (1938) 54 TLR 1026 (15 July)

Warthen v Toms River Community Memorial Hospital 488 A 2d 229 (NJ Super AD 1985)

Washington State Nurses Association v Board of Medical Examiners Wash 605 P 2d 1269 (1980)

Whitehouse v Jordon [1980] 1 All ER 650

Wickliffe v Sunrise Hospital, Inc 766 P 2d 1322 (Nev 1988)

Williams v Reynolds NC App 263 SE 2d 863 (1980)

Wood v Miller 76 P 2d 963 (1938)

Wood v Rowland Colo App 592 P 2d 1332 (1978)

Wooten v United States 574 Fed Supp 200 (1982)

Wrighten v Metropolitan Hospitals, Inc 726 F 2d 1346 (1984)

Ybarra v Spangard 154 P 2d 687 (1944)

Yorston v Pennell 153 A 2d 255 (1959)

BIBLIOGRAPHY

'A' (1911), 'Some plain truths about private nurses', *Una*, 9(7), 30 September, pp. 153–154.

A Barrister-at-Law (1911), 'Injuries to patients: who is liable for them?', *Una*, 8(12), 28 February, pp. 212–213.

A former House-Surgeon of Guy's (1880), Letter — 'Guy's Hospital and nursing system', *British Medical Journal*, 14 February, p. 272.

Aaronson, L. S. (1989), 'A challenge for nursing: re-viewing a historic competition', *Nursing Outlook* 37(6), November/December, pp. 274–279.

Abel-Smith. B. (1960), *A history of the nursing profession*, Heinemann, London.

—— (1964), *The hospitals 1800–1948*, Heinemann, London.

Achterberg, J. (1991), *Woman as healer*, Rider, London.

Adams, M. (1984), 'On life . . . and death . . . and dots', *Nursing 84*, 14(6), June, pp. 53–58.

Aikens, C.A. (1943), *Studies in ethics for nurses*, W.B. Saunders, Philadelphia (first published in 1916).

Alfaro, R. (1986), *Application of nursing process: a step-by-step guide*, JB Lippincott Co., Philadelphia.

Altekruse, J.M. and McDermott, S.W. (1988), 'Contemporary concerns of women in medicine', in S.V. Rosser (ed), *Feminism within the science and health care professions: overcoming resistance*, Pergamon Press, Oxford.

American digest system, ninth decennial digest, Part 2, 1981–1986, Descriptive Word Index, West Publishing Co., St Paul, Minn.

American Journal of Nursing (1972), 'AMA endorses expanded role for nurses, seeks study of RN and PA functions', 72(8), August, p. 1365.

—— (1974), 'California's officialdom questions legality of extended RN practice', 74(3), March, pp. 416, 420.

—— (1975), 'Firing of Nursing Director sparks demonstration over who runs nursing', 75(3), August, pp. 383–385, 1376.

—— (1983), 'Hospitals must cost out nursing care under landmark Maine law', 83(9), September, pp. 1251, 1262.

American Nurses Association and other sources (1970), 'AMA unveils surprise plan to convert RN to medic', *American Journal of Nursing*, 70(4), April, pp. 691–693, 724, 727.

American Nurses Association (1976), *Code for nurses*, American Nurses Association, Kansas City, Mo.

American Nurses Association (1981), *Code for nurses*, American Nurses Association, Kansas City, Mo.

Ampthill, Lord (1919), Debate on Nurses Registration Bill, 27 May, *House of Lords Parliamentary Debates, fifth series*, Vol. 34, HMSO, London, pp. 822–834.

Anderson, A.V.M. (1908), 'Nursing', *Una*, 6(8), 30 October, pp. 119–127.

Anderson, B.S. and Zinsser, J.P. (1988), *A history of their own: women in Europe from prehistory to the present*, Vol. 1, Harper and Row, New York.

Anderson, M. (1977), 'Our expanding role: notes on not nursing', *Nursing 77*, 7(1), January, p. 16.

Andrews, S. (1990), 'Nurse prescribing — a very select group', *Nursing Times*, 86(29), 18 July, pp. 31–32.

Ardener, S. (ed) (1975), *Perceiving women*, J.M. Dent & Sons Ltd., London.

Argus, The (1904), 'As others see us', *Una*, 2(5), 20 July, pp. 77–78.

Aristotle (1957), *The politics*, Penguin, Hammondsworth, Middlesex.

Armstrong, G. (1977), 'Females under the law — "protected" but unequal', *Crime and Delinquency*, 23(2), pp. 109–120.

Armstrong, M. (1987), 'Contemporary ethics', *Nursing: The Add-On Journal of Clinical Nursing*, 3(14), February, pp. 518–520.

Aroskar, M.A. (1982), 'Establishing limits to professional autonomy: whose responsibility? A nursing perspective', in N.K. Bell (ed), *Who decides? Conflicts of rights in health care*, Humana Press, Clifton, NJ, pp. 67–82.

Ashe, M. (1987), 'Mind's opportunity: birthing a post-structuralist feminist jurisprudence', *Syracuse Law Review*, 38, pp. 1129–1173.

Ashley, J. (1973), 'About power in nursing', *Nursing Outlook*, 21(10), pp. 637–641.

—— (1975a), 'Power, freedom and professional practice in nursing', *Supervisor Nurse*, 6(1), January, pp. 12–14, 17, 19–20, 22–24, 29.

—— (1975b), 'Reforms in nursing and health care: industrial nurses can lead the way', *Occupational Health Nursing*, 23(6), pp. 1–14.

—— (1975c), 'Nursing and early feminism', *American Journal of Nursing*, 75(9), pp. 1465–1467.

—— (1976a), *Hospitals, paternalism, and the role of the nurse*, Teachers College Press, Columbia University, New York.

—— (1976b), 'Nurses and the meaning of law and order', *Imprint (NSNA)*, 23(4), pp. 24–25.

—— (1976c), 'Nursing power: viable, vital visible', *Texas Nursing*, August, pp. 11–16, 18.

—— (1980), 'Power in structured misogyny: implications for the politics of care', *Advances in Nursing Science*, 2(3), April, pp. 3–22.

Ashworth, H. (1981), 'Where's nurse?', *Nursing Times*, 77(39), 23 September, p. 1654.

Astor, Major (1919), Debate on Nurses' Registration Bill, second reading, 28 March, 114 HC Deb 5 s, HMSO, London, pp. 812–814.

Atkins, S. and Hoggett, B. (1984), *Women and the law*, Basil Blackwell, Oxford.

Austin, R. (1977a), 'Sex and gender in the future of nursing 1', Occasional Papers, *Nursing Times*, 73(34), 25 August, pp. 113–116.

—— (1977b), 'Sex and gender in the future of nursing 2', Occasional Papers, *Nursing Times*, 73(35), 1 September, pp. 117–119.

Australasian Medical Gazette (1898), 'Midwifery Nurses' Bill', 21 November, pp. 480–483.

Australasian Nurses Journal (1904), 'State registration of nurses', 2(3), October, pp. 80–81.

—— (1907), 'The responsibility of nurses', 5(3), 15 March, pp. 67–68.

—— (1907), 'State registration', 5(12), 16 December, pp. 359–362.

—— (1908), 'A code of ethics', 6(2), 15 February, pp. 65–67.

—— (1909), 'The English Bill for the registration of nurses', 7(7), 12 July, pp. 257–259.

—— (1910a), 'Editorial — Shorter hours', 8(1), 15 January, pp. 1–2.

—— (1910b), 'The state registration of trained nurses', 8(4), 15 April, pp. 130–131.

—— (1911a), 'The limitations of a nurse', 9(6), 15 June, p. 181.

—— (1911b), 'The exploiting of the private nurse', 9(8), 15 August, p. 270.

—— (1912a), 'The abuse of the hypodermic syringe', 10(6), 15 June, pp. 181–182.

—— (1912b), 'Editor to J. Bell's letter of 14 June 1912', 10(7), July 15, p. 247.

—— (1917), 'Registration in Great Britain', 15(4), April, pp. 136–137.

—— (1920), 'Nursing as a profession', 18(6), June, pp. 181–182.

Australian Legal Monthly Digest (1990), The Law Book Company, Sydney.

Australian Nurses' Journal (1954), 'Editorial — Surprise move by minister', 52(8), August, p. 175.

—— (1955), 'Editorial — Some reflections for the new year', 53(1), January, p. 1.

—— (1990), 'VNC chairperson', 19(6), December/January, p. 19.

—— (1991), 'Sophia Heathcote vindicated', 21(1), July, pp. 10–15.

Australian Nursing Federation (1946), Meeting of Federal Council, February, *Australasian Nurses Journal*, 44(4&5), April–May, pp. 57–60.

Backhouse, C.B. (1985), '"To open the way for others of my sex": Clara Brett Martin's career as Canada's first woman lawyer', *Canadian Journal of Women and the Law*, 1(1), pp. 1–41.

Baer, C.L. (1984), 'Nursing diagnosis: a futuristic process for nursing practice', *Topics in Clinical Nursing*, January, pp. 89–97.

Balfour, K. (1905), Comments minuted at paragraph 1239 of the *Report from the Select Committee on Registration of Nurses*, HMSO, London, p. 71.

Barclay, H.C. (1912), 'Discipline and etiquette', *Australasian Nurses Journal*, 10(7), 15 July, pp. 227–232.

Barnett, Major (1919), 'Debate on Nurses' Registration Bill, second reading', 28 March 114 HC Deb 5 s, pp. 771–777.

Bart, Sir H.R. (1929), 'The nurse from the physician's point of view', *Una*, 27(4), 1 April, pp. 119–122.

Bartee, W.C. and Bartee, A. F. (1992), *Litigating morality: American legal thought and its English roots*, Praeger, New York.

Bates, B. (1975), 'Physician and Nurse Practitioner: conflict and reward', *Annals of Internal Medicine*, 82, pp. 702–706.

Beard, R.O. (1913), 'The trained nurse of the future', *Journal of the American Medical Association*, 61(24), 13 Decmber, pp. 2149–2152.

Beattie, A.C. (1950), 'Industrial law and the nursing profession', *The Lamp*, 7(10), October, pp. 8–12.

Beaumont, M. (1990), 'An historical perspective on registration', *Australian Nurses Journal*, 19(6), December/January, p. 9.

Beith, J.H. (1935), 'The privileged profession', *The Lancet*, 2, 5 October, pp. 799–800.

Bell, J. (1912), 'Letter to the Editor — State registration of nurses', *The Australasian Nurses' Journal*, 10(7), 15 July, pp. 244, 245.

—— (1937), 'The need for compulsory state registration of nurses', *The Australasian Nurses' Journal*, 35(8), 16 August, pp. 159–161.

Bellersen, R. (1979), 'Has the "expanded role" destroyed nursing', *Registered Nurse*, 42(6), June, pp. 83–85.

Bendall, E.R.D and Raybould, E. (1969), *A history of the General Nursing Council 1919–1969*, H.K. Lewis and Co., London.

Benner, P. (1984), *From novice to expert: excellence and power in clinical nursing*, Addison-Wesley Publishing Company, Nursing Division, Calif.

—— and Wrubel, J. (1989), *The primacy of caring: stress and coping in health and illness*, Addison-Wesley Publishing Company, Health Sciences Division, Calif.

Bennett, M. (1986), 'Nursing diagnosis: in the beginning . . .', *Australian Journal of Advanced Nursing*, 4(1), September/November, pp. 41–46.

Bentzon, A.W. (1986), 'Comments on women's law in Scandinavia', *International Journal of the Sociology of Law*, 14(3/4), pp. 249–254.

Bergman, R. (1973), 'Ethics — concepts and practice', *International Nursing Review*, 20(5), pp. 140–142.

Bernzweig, E. (1987), *The nurse's liability for malpractice: a programmed course*, 4th edn, McGraw-Hill Book Co., New York.

Bevis, E. O. and Watson, J. (1989), *Toward a caring curriculum: a new pedagogy for nursing*, National League for Nursing, New York.

Bickley, J. (1988), 'What the cervical cancer inquiry report means for nurses', *The New Zealand Nursing Journal*, 81(9), pp. 14–15.

Birkholz, G. (1989), 'Supervising unlicensed technicians in critical care', *Dimensions of Critical Care Nursing*, 8(5), September/December, pp. 317–323.

Birnbach, N. (1985), 'The nurse registration movement in Great Britain', *Advances in Nursing Science*, 7(2), January, pp. 13–19.

Bishop, A.H. and Scudder, J.R. (1991), *Nursing: the practice of caring*, National League for Nursing Press, New York.

Blatch, J.C., Adronicos, C. and Rob, M.I. (1979), *Survey of nurses' lifestyles*, (NHMRC Working Paper No. 48 (July)), Research and Planning Unit, Health Commission of New South Wales, Northern Metropolitan Region, Sydney.

Blower, C. (1977), 'Nursing and primary medical care', *The Lamp*, 34(12), December, pp. 23–31.

Bowe, E.J. (1961), 'The story of nursing in Australian since foundation day', *Australian Nurses Journal*, 59(4), pp. 89–95.

Brand, K.L. and Glass, L.K. (1975), 'Perils and parallels of women and nursing', *Nursing Forum*, 14(2), pp. 161–174.

Brann, J. (1980), 'Preparing nurses for an expanded role in primary health care delivery', *Australian Nurses Journal*, 10(4), October, pp. 28–29, 41.

Breay, M. and Fenwick, E.G. (1931), *History of the International Council of Nurses, 1899–1925*, The International Council of Nurses, Geneva.

Brewer, C. (1988), 'Should doctors control discharge? The case for', *Nursing Times*, 84(3), January, p. 42.

Briant, Mr. (1919), 'Debate on Nurses' Registration Bill, second reading', 28 March, 114 HC Deb 5 s, HMSO, London, pp.778–781.

Bridges, D.C. (1967), *A history of the International Council of Nurses, 1899–1964: the first sixty-five years*, Pitman Medical Publishing, London.

—— (1968), '"International Nursing Review": past, present — and progress?', *International Nursing Review*, 15(1), pp. 9–15.

British Journal of Nursing (incorporating the *Nursing Record*) (1919), 'Editorial — Second reading of our Nurses' Registration Bill', 62(1617), 29 March.

—— (1931), 'Editorial — Patients first: is nursing a profession or a trade?', 79(1952), March.

British Medical Journal (1911), 'Nurse or minor medical practitioner?', in *Australasian Nurses Journal*, 9(6), 15 June 1911, pp. 185–187.

—— (1959), 'Medical-legal: the defence of "usual practice" in negligence cases', Vol. II, 28 November, pp. 1190–1191.

—— (1982), 'Changing relations between doctors and nurses', 285(6348), 16 October, pp. 1130–1132.

Brittan, A. (1989), *Masculinity and power*, Basil Blackwell, Oxford.

Broad, W. and Wade, N. (1982), *Betrayers of the truth: fraud and deceit in science*, Oxford University Press, Oxford.

Brockway, F. (1930), Motion moved 10 December re: Nursing Profession (Wages and Hours), 246 HC Deb 5 s (8–19 December, 1930), HMSO, London, pp. 415–418.

Brophy, J. and Smart, C. (eds) (1985), *Women in law: explorations in law, family and sexuality*, Routledge and Kegan Paul, London.

Brown, E. (1943), Debate on Nurses Bill (24 March), 387 HC Deb 5 s 23/2/43–25/3/43, HMSO, London, pp. 1648–1653.

Brown, J., Kitson, A. and McKnight, T. (1992), *Challenges in caring: explorations in nursing and ethics*, Chapman and Hall, London.

Buckmaster, Lord (1919), Debate on Nurses Registration Bill, 27 May, in *House of Lords Parliamentary Debates, fifth series*, Vol. 34, HMSO, London, pp. 848–850

Bullough, B. (ed) (1975), *The law and the expanding role of the nurse*, Appleton-Century-Crofts, New York.

Bullough, V.L. and Bullough, B. (1969), *The emergence of modern nursing*, 2nd edn, The Macmillan Company, Collier-Macmillan Ltd, London.

Burton, C. (1985), *Subordination: feminism and social theory*, George Allen & Unwin, Sydney.

—— (1991), *The promise and the price: the struggle for equal opportunity in women's employment*, Allen and Unwin. Sydney.

—— Hag, R. and Thompson, G. (1987), *Women's worth: pay equity and job excellence in Australia*, Australian Government Publishing Service, Canberra.

Buzzard, A.J., Hughes, E., Hughes, G.L. and Wells, J.D.B. (1986), *Medicine and surgery for lawyers*, The Law Book Company, Sydney.

Caine, B., Grosz, E.A., and de Lepervanche, M. (eds) (1988), *Crossing boundaries: feminisms and the critique of knowledges*, Allen & Unwin, Sydney.

Cameron, D. (ed) (1990), *The feminist critique of language: a reader*, Routledge, London and New York.

Cameron, J. (1990), 'News focus — Unpopular practices', *Nursing Times*, 86(15), 11 April, p. 18.

Cameron, S.L. (unpub.), The ANRAC competencies: fostering autonomy in practice, paper presented at the 13th National Conference, Royal College of Nursing, Australia: 'Controlling Nursing's Destiny', Brisbane, (1991).

Campazzi, B.C. (1980), 'Nurses, nursing and malpractice litigation: 1967–1977', *Nursing Administration Quarterly*, 5(1), pp. 1–18.

Campbell, D. (1988), 'Who will run the homes?', *Nursing Times*, 84(22), 1 June, pp. 16–17.

Canadian abridgment, The, 2nd edn: index to Canadian legal literature 1989 (1990), Carswell, Toronto.

Carlen, P. (1983), *Women's imprisonment: a study in social control*, Routledge and Kegan Paul, London.

—— (1985), 'Criminal women: myths, metaphors and misogyny', in P. Carlen (ed), *Criminal women*, Polity Press, Cambridge, UK, pp. 1–13.

Carlisle, D. (1989), '. . . But who will make the beds?', *Nursing Times*, 85(37), 13 September, p. 18.

—— (1990a), 'News focus — Just what the nurse ordered', *Nursing Times*, 86(2), 10 January, pp. 16–17.

—— (1990b), 'News focus — Who prescribes?', *Nursing Times*, 86(9), 28 February, pp. 16–17.

—— (1990c), 'Are you accountable?', *Nursing Times*, 86(21), 23 May, pp. 26–31.

—— (1990d), 'News focus — Prescribing conflict', *Nursing Times*, 86(22), 30 May, pp. 20–21.

—— (1990e), 'Nurse prescribing — Just what the nurse ordered?', *Nursing Times*, 86(29), 18 July, pp. 26–29.

—— (1990f), 'The road to nowhere?', *Nursing Times*, 86(30), 25 July, pp. 16–17.

Carlson, C.L. and Athelstan, G.T. (1970), 'The physician's assistant: versions and diversions of a promising concept', *Journal of the American Medical Association*, 214(10), 7 December, pp. 1855–1861.

Carlson, R.J. (1975), *The end of medicine*, John Wiley & Sons, New York.

Carpenito, L. (1987), *Nursing diagnosis: application to clinical practice*, JB Lippincott Co., Philadelphia, Pa.

Carr, A. (1983), 'Who keeps the keys?', *Nursing Mirror*, 157(8), 24 August, p. 27.

Carr, E. (1982), 'A model for private practice: requirements for success', in J. Muff (ed), *Socialization, sexism, and stereotyping: women's issues in nursing*, C.V. Mosby, St Louis, Mo, pp. 413–423.

Carson, V.B. (1989), *Spiritual dimensions of nursing practice*, W.B. Saunders Company, Harcourt Brace Jovanovich, Inc, Philadelphia, Pa.

Carter, J. (1990), 'Tell me why', *Nursing Times*, 86(30), 25 July, p. 19.

Cazalas, M.W. (1978), *Nursing and the law*, 3rd edn, Aspen System Corporation, Germantown, Md.

CCH health and medical law editors in conjunction with Laufer, S. (1990), *Law for the nursing profession*, CCH Australia Ltd., North Ryde, NSW.

Chapman, P. (1990), 'Helping hands: "We can do that!"', *Nursing Times*, 86(16), 18 April, p. 34.

Chaska, N.L., Clark, D., Rogers, S.M. and Deets, C.A. (1990), 'Nurses' and physicians' expectations and perceptions of staff nurse role performance as influenced by status consistency', in N.L. Chaska (ed), *The nursing profession: turning point*, The C.V. Mosby Company, St Louis, Mo, pp. 289–303.

Chesler, P. (1972), *Women and Madness*, Avon Books, New York.

—— (1986), *Mothers on trial: the battle for children and custody*, McGraw-Hill Book Company, New York.

Chesney-Lind, M. (1977), 'Judicial paternalism and the female status offender: training women to know their place', *Crime and Delinquency*, 23(2), pp. 121–130.

Chinn, P.L. (ed) (1991), *Anthology on caring*, National League for Nursing Press, New York.

Christy, T. (1972), 'Liberation movement: impact on nursing', *American Operating Room Nurses*, 15(4), pp. 67–72.

—— (1975), 'Portrait of a leader: Sophia F. Palmer', *Nursing Outlook*, 23(12), December, pp. 746–751.

—— (1980), 'Entry into practice: a recurring issue in nursing history', *American Journal of Nursing*, 80(3), March, pp. 485–487.

Chudley, P. (1988a), 'Waiting in the wings', *Nursing Times*, 84(17), 27 April, p. 20.

—— (1988b), 'One step forward . . .', *Nursing Times*, 84(43), 26 October, pp. 16–17.

Clarke, A.R. (1948), 'RN speaks: compromise or conversion?' *Registered Nurse*, 12, November, pp. 30–31, 64, 66, 68, 71–2.

Clay, T. (1987), *Nurses: power and politics*, Heinemann Nursing, London.

Cleary, D.M. (1975), 'A nonstrike for patient care', *Modern Healthcare*, 3(6), pp. 43–44.

Code of ethics for nurses in Australia (1993), Australian Nursing Council, Canberra, July.

Cohen, H. (1981), *The nurse's quest for a professional identity*, Addison-Wesley Publishing Company, Menlo Park, Calif.

Cohen, M. (ed) (1983), *Ronald Dworkin and contemporary jurisprudence*, Duckworth, London.

Coleman, J. and Paul, E.F. (eds) (1987), *Philosophy and law*, Basil Blackwell, Oxford.

Committee of Inquiry into Allegations Concerning the Treatment of Cervical Cancer at National Women's Hospital and into Other Related Matters (1988), *Report of the cervical cancer inquiry*, Government Printing Office, Auckland.

Concise dictionary of law, a (1990), 2nd edn, Oxford University Press, Oxford, UK.

Coney, S. (1988), *The unfortunate experiment*, Penguin Books, Auckland.

—— (1990), *Out of the frying pan: inflammatory writing 1972–89*, Penguin Books, Auckland,.

Conley, J. (1988), 'Outback nurses may get right to supply drugs', *The Age*, (Melbourne), 13 May, p. 10.

Connell, R.W. (1987), *Gender and power*, Allen & Unwin, Sydney.

Cook, E. (1913a), *The life of Florence Nightingale*, Vol. 1, MacMillan and Co., London.

—— (1913b), *The life of Florence Nightingale*, Vol. 2, MacMillan and Co., London.

Cope, Z. (1958), *Florence Nightingale and the doctors*, Museum Press, London.

Corea, G. (1977), *The hidden malpractice: how American medicine treats women as patients and professionals*, William Morrow and Company, New York.

Cott, N.F. (1987), *The grounding of modern feminism*, Yale University Press, New Haven and London.

Cotterrell, R. (1989), *The politics of jurisprudence: a critical introduction to legal philosophy*, Butterworths, London and Edinburgh.

Cowan, D.R.W. (1946), 'Tuberculosis and nurses', *Australian Nurses Journal*, 64(6), June, pp. 93–94.

Crabbe, G. (1989), 'Looking for liberation', *Nursing Times*, 85(1), 4 June, p. 18.

Creighton, H. (1975a), *Law every nurse should know*, 3rd edn, W.B. Saunders, Philadelphia, Pa.

—— (1975b), 'The whistle blower', *Supervisor Nurse*, 6(11), November, pp. 11–12, 57.

—— (1981), 'Refusal to treat patient', *Supervisor Nurse*, 12(4), April, pp. 67, 70.

—— (1982), 'Liability of nurse floated to another unit', *Nursing Management*, 13(3), March, pp. 54–55.

—— (1984a), 'Nursing judgment', *Nursing Management*, 15(5), May, pp. 60–63.

—— (1984b), 'RN advocate and the law', *Nursing Management*, 15(12), December, pp. 14–17.

—— (1986), *Law every nurse should know*, 5th edn, W.B. Saunders, Philadelphia, Pa.

Curtin, L. (1982), 'The nurse–patient relationship: foundation, purposes, responsibilities, and rights', in L. Curtin and J.M. Flaherty, *Nursing ethics: theories and pragmatics*, Brady Communications (Prentice-Hall), Bowie, Md, pp. 79–96.

Cushing, M. (1981), 'No code orders: current developments and the nursing director's role', *Journal of Nursing Administration*, 11(26), April, pp. 22–29.

—— (1982), 'A matter of judgment', *American Journal of Nursing*, 82(6), June, pp. 990–992.

—— (1983), 'Fears of a float nurse', *American Journal of Nursing*, 83(2), February, pp. 297–298.

—— (1988), *Nursing jurisprudence*, Appleton & Lange, Norwalk, Conn./San Mateo.

Cuthbert, M. (1987), 'DRG's: determining the real cost of nursing care', *The Lamp*, 44(5), July, pp. 15–18.

Czernik, K. (1990), 'Officer backed in Howden case', *Whittlesea Post*, (Melbourne), 27 November, p. 3.

Dachelet, C. (1978), 'Nursing's bid for increased status', *Nursing Forum* 1(1), pp. 18–45.

Dahl, R.A. (1984), *Modern political analysis*, 4th edn, Prentice Hall, Englewood Cliffs, NJ.

Dahl, T.S. (1986), 'Taking women as a starting point: building women's law', *International Journal of the Sociology of Law*, 14(3/4), pp. 239–247.

—— (1987), *Women's law: an introduction to feminist jurisprudence*, Norwegian University Press, Oslo.

Dalton, C. (1988), 'Where we stand: observations on the situation of feminist legal thought', *Berkeley Women's Law Journal*, 3, pp. 1–13.

Daly, M. (1978), *Gyn/ecology*, The Women's Press, London.

Darbyshire, P. (1987), 'The burden of history', *Nursing Times*, 83(5), 28 January, pp. 32–34.

Dean, P. G. (1982), 'Go ahead, I'm behind you . . . way behind you', in J. Muff (ed), *Socialization, sexism, and stereotyping: women's issues in nursing*, The C.V. Mosby Company, St Louis, Mo, pp. 321–336.

DeCrow, K. (1974), *Sexist justice*, Vintage Books, Random House, New York.

Delamothe, T. (1988a), 'Nursing grievances, I: Voting with their feet', *British Medical Journal*, 296(6614), 2 January, pp. 25–28.

—— (1988b), 'Nursing grievances, II: Pay', *British Medical Journal*, 296(6615), 9 January, pp. 120–123.

—— (1988c), 'Nursing grievances, III: Conditions', *British Medical Journal*, 296(6616), 16 January, pp. 182–185.

—— (1988d), 'Nursing grievances, IV: Not a profession, not a career', *British Medical Journal*, 296(6617), 23 January, pp. 271–274.

—— (1988e), 'Nursing grievances, V: Women's work', *British Medical Journal*, 296(6618), 30 January, pp. 345–347.

—— (1988f), 'Nursing grievances, VI: Other places, other solutions', *British Medical Journal*, 296(6619), 6 February, pp. 406–408.

Denning, Rt. Hon. Lord (1979), *The discipline of law*, Butterworths, London.

Department of Health, New South Wales (1989), *Health Services of New South Wales Code of Conduct and Ethics*, Department of Health, NSW, Sydney.

Derham, D.P., Maher, F.K.H. and Waller, P.L. (1986), *An introduction to law*, 5th edn, The Law Book Company Limited, Sydney.

Digest, The: annotated British, Commonwealth and European cases (1982), Butterworths, London.

Dimond, B. (1987), 'Your disobedient servant', *Nursing Times*, 83(5), 28 January, pp. 28–31.

Dingwall, R., Rafferty, A.M. and Webster, C. (1988), *An introduction to the social history of nursing*, Routledge, London.

Dirckx, J.H. (1983), *The language of medicine: its evolution, structure, and dynamics*, 2nd edn, Praeger Publishers, New York (first edition published by Harper & Row/Lippincott, 1976).

Dock, L.L. (1904a), 'The duty of this society in public work', in *Proceedings of the 10th Annual Convention of the American Society of Superintendents of Training Schools, held Pittsburgh, October 7–9, 1903*, J.H. Furst Co., Baltimore, Md., pp. 77–84.

—— (1904b), 'The International Council of Nurses', *Una*, 2(9), 21 November, pp. 139–143.

—— (1905), 'Evidence to Select Committee on Registration of Nurses (11 May)', in *Report from the Select Committee on Registration of Nurses*, HMSO, London, pp. 40–45, 61.

—— (1906), 'The progress of registration', *Una*, 4(1), 30 March, pp. 9–10.

—— (1913), 'Status of the nurse in the working world', *Una*, 11(9), 29 November, pp. 227–228.

—— and Stewart, I.M. (1938), *A short history of nursing*, 4th revised edn, G.P. Putnam's Sons, New York.

Dolan, J.A., Fitzpatrick, M.L. and Herrmann, E.K. (1983.), *Nursing in society: a historical perspective*, 15th edn, W.B. Saunders Co., Philadelphia, Pa.

Donnelly, G., Mengel, A. and King, E. (1975), 'The anatomy of a conflict', *Supervisor Nurse*, 6(11), pp. 28–38.

Dopson, L. (1990), 'Nursing without nurses', *Nursing Times*, 86(14), 4 April, pp. 46–48.

Driscoll, V. (1972), 'Liberating nursing practice', *Nursing Outlook*, 20(1), January, pp. 24–28.

DuBois, E.C., Kelly, G.P., Kennedy, E. L., Korsmeyer, C.W. and Robinson, L.S. (1987), *Feminist scholarship kindling in the groves of academe*, University of Illinois Press, Urbana and Chicago.

Dunn, A. (1982), 'A denial of rights?', *Nursing Times*, 78(43), 27 October, p. 1794.

'Duty' (1914), 'An eight-hour day', *Australasian Nurses Journal*, 12(3), 16 March, pp. 75–76.

Dworkin, R. (1977), *Taking rights seriously*, Duckworth, London.

—— (1985), *A matter of principle*, Oxford University Press, Oxford.

—— (1986), *Law's empire*, Fontana Press, London.

Easteal, P.W. (1993), *Killing the beloved: homicide between adult sexual intimates*, Australian Institute of Criminology, Canberra.

Eaton, M. (1986), *Justice for women? Family, court and social control*, Open University Press, Milton Keynes, UK.

Eddy, J.P. (1956), *Professional negligence*, Stevens & Sons, London.

Edwards, J. (1911), 'Private nurses and the special meeting', *Australasian Nurses Journal*, 9(10), 16 October, pp. 352–355.

Edwards, S. (ed) (1985), *Gender, sex and the law*, Croom Helm, London.

Ehrenreich, B. and English, D. (1973a), *Witches, midwives, and nurses: a history of women healers*, The Feminist Press, Old Westbury, New York.

—— (1973b), *Complaints and disorders: the sexual politics of sickness*, Writers and Readers Publishing Cooperative, London.

—— (1979), *For her own good: 150 years of the experts' advice to women*, Pluto Press, London.

Eisenstein, H. (1984), *Contemporary feminist thought*, Unwin Paperbacks, London.

Eisenstein, Z.R. (1988), *The female body and the law*, University of California Press, Berkeley, Los Angeles, Calif.

Eisler, R. (1987), 'Human rights: toward an integrated theory of action', *Feminist Issues*, 7(1), pp. 25–46.

Eisner , M. and Wright, M. (1986), 'A feminist approach to general practice', in C. Webb (ed) and contributors, *Feminist practice in women's health care*, John Wiley & Sons, Chichester, UK, pp. 113–145.

Ellis, J.R. and Hartley, C.L. (1984), *Nursing in today's world: challenges, issues and trends*, J.B. Lippincott, Philadelphia, Pa.

Erickson, N.S. (1982), 'Historical background of "protective" labor legislation: *Muller v Oregon*', in D.K. Weisberg (ed), *Women and the law: a social historical perspective, Vol. 2, Property, family and the legal profession*, Schenkman Publishing, Cambridge, Mass., pp. 155–186.

Erika, S. (1986), 'Patriarchy and the state', *Australian Journal of Law and Society*, 3, pp. 53–62.

E.S. (1912), 'Letter to the editor', *Una*, 10, September, p. 165.

Everington, S. (1985), 'Why do nurses not extend their role more?', *Nursing Times*, 81(50), 11 December, p. 10.

Fagin, C. and Diers, D. (1987), 'Nursing as metaphor', *New England Journal of Medicine*, 309(1), 14 July, pp. 116–117.

Fardell, J. (1989a), 'Short cut or short change?', *Nursing Times*, 85(7), 15 February, pp. 30–31.

—— (1989b), 'Ominous silence?', *Nursing Times*, 85(27), 5 July, p. 20.

Farquharson, Miss (1929), 'Nursing ethics', *Una*, 27(11), pp. 339–340.

Fasser, C.E. (1972), 'Physician's assistant: why, who and how?', *American Operating Room Nurses*, 15(4), April, pp. 51–54.

Feelgood, G.I. (1986), 'Nurses knew their place in the good old days', *Australian Hospital*, May, p. 11.

Feild, L. (1979), 'The implementation of nursing diagnosis in clinical practice', *Nursing Clinics of North America*, 14(3), September, pp. 497–508.

Feinberg, J. (1984), *Harm to others: the moral limits of the criminal law*, Vol. 1, Oxford University Press, New York.

—— (1990), *Harmless wrongdoing: the moral limits of the criminal law*, Vol. 4, Oxford University Press, New York.

Fenwick, B. (1904), 'Evidence to Select Committee on Registration of Nurses (7 July)', in *Report from the Select Committee on Registration of Nurses*, HMSO, London, pp. 1–14.

Fenwick, E.G. (1890), 'Evidence to The Select Committee on Metropolitan Hospitals (31 July)', in *Report from the Select Committee of the House of Lords on Metropolitan Hospitals*, Vol. 16, Facsimile, The Irish University Press series of British Parliamentary Papers (1970), Dublin, pp. 545–557.

—— (1905), 'Evidence to Select Committee on Registration of Nurses (11 May)', in *Report from the Select Committee on Registration of Nurses*, HMSO, London, pp. 30–40.

—— (1919), Editorial — second reading of our nurses' registration bill, *British Journal of Nursing* (incorporating *The Nursing Record*), 1617(62), 29 March.

Feyerherm, W. (1981), 'Measuring gender differences in delinquency: self-reports versus police contact', in M.Q. Warren (ed), *Comparing female and male offenders*, Sage Publications, Beverley Hills, Calif., pp. 46–54.

Fickeissen, J.L. (1986), 'Lobbying for registration laws: letters from the past', *Journal of Nursing History*, 1(2), April, p. 12–19.

Fielding, P. (1988), 'The case against', *Nursing Times*, 84(3), 20 January, p. 43.

Fiesta, J. (1988), *The law and liability: a guide for nurses*, 2nd edn, John Wiley and Sons, New York.

Fineman, M.A. (1990), 'Introduction', in M.A. Fineman and N.S. Thomadsen (eds), *At the boundaries of law: feminism and legal theory*, Routledge, New York and London, pp. xi–xvi.

—— and Thomadsen, N.S. (eds) (1991), *At the boundaries of law: feminism and legal theory*, Routledge, New York and London.

Fineman, S. (1982), 'Nurses on the dole: job loss and job change', *Nursing Times*, 78(47), 24 November, pp. 1978–1980.

Fitzgerald, T.N. (1890), 'Evidence to Royal Commission on Charitable Institutions (27 June)', in *Papers Presented to Parliamentary, Session 1892–3*, Vol. 4, Robt. S. Brain, Government Printer, Melbourne, pp. 227–237.

Fitzpatrick, J. (1990), 'Letter-to-editor', *The Lamp*, 47(2), p. 3.

Flanagan, M.K. (1982), 'An analysis of nursing as a career choice', in J. Muff (ed) *Socialization, sexism, and stereotyping: women's issues in nursing*, The C.V. Mosby Co, St Louis, pp. 169–177.

Flash, A.H. (1915), 'High ideals in nursing', *Transactions of American Hospital Association*, 17(7936), June, pp. 438–447.

Fleming, J. (1981), 'Doctors not deities', *Nursing Times*, 77(36), 2 September, p. 1533.

Florence Nightingale pledge for nurses (1893), in L.Y. Kelly (1985), *Dimensions of professional nursing*, 5th edn, Macmillan Publishing Co., New York, p. 44.

Fondiller, S.H. (1986), 'Licensure and titling in nursing and society: a historical perspective', in National League for Nursing, *Looking beyond the entry issue: implications for education and service*, National League for Nursing, New York, pp. 3–19.

Ford, L. (1972), 'Physician's assistant: why, who and how?' *American Operating Room Nurses*, 15(4), April, pp. 41–46.

Forsyth, P. (1990), 'Councillor's report', *Chapter Chatter*, (Newsletter of the Royal College of Nursing, Australia, Victorian Chapter), 1(1), Winter, p. 2.

Fortin, J.D. and Rabinow, J. (1979), 'Legal implications of nursing diagnosis', *Nursing Clinics of North America*, 14(3), September, pp. 553–561.

Foucault, M. (1972), *The archaelogy of knowledge and the discourse on language*, Pantheon Books, New York.

—— (1973), *The birth of the clinic: an archaeology of medical perception*, Tavistock Publications, London.

—— (1975), *Pierre Rivière, having slaughtered my mother, my sister, and my brother . . . : a case of parricide in the 19th century*, University of Nebraska Press, Lincoln and London.

—— (1977), *Discipline and punish: the birth of the prison*, Penguin Books, London.

—— (1978), *The history of sexuality: an introduction*, Penguin Books, London.

Franzway, S., Court, D. and Connell, R.W. (1989), *Staking a claim: feminism, bureaucracy and the state*, Allen & Unwin, Sydney.

Fraser, N. (1989), *Unruly practices: power, discourse and gender in contemporary social theory*, Polity Press, Cambridge, UK.

Fredette, S. and O'Connor, K. (1979), 'Nursing diagnosis in teaching and curriculum planning', *Nursing Clinics of North America*, 14(3), September, pp. 541–552.

Freedman, A.E. (1983), 'Sex equality, sex difference, and the Supreme Court', *The Yale Law Journal*, 92(6), pp. 913–968.

Freidson, E. (1970), *Professional dominance: the social structure of medical care*, Aldine Publishing Co., New York.

—— (1973), *The professions and their prospects*, Sage Publications, Beverly Hills/London.

—— (1988), *Profession of medicine: a study of the sociology of applied knowledge*, The University of Chicago Press, Chicago and London.

Fremantle, Lieutenant-Colonel (1930), Parliamentary debate on *Nursing Profession (Wages and Hours) Bill* (10 December), in *House of Commons Parliamentary Debates*, 5th series, Vol. 252, HMSO, London, p. 2188.

Friedman, L.M. (1965), 'Freedom of contract and occupational licensing 1890–1910: a legal and social study', *California Law Review*, 53, pp. 487–534.

Friend, B. (1990a), 'Training for the dole', *Nursing Times*, 86(6), 7 February, p. 18.

—— (1990b), 'Counselled out', *Nursing Times*, 86(22), 30 May, p. 18.

Frye, M. (1983), *The politics of reality: essays in feminist theory*, The Crossing Press, Trumansburg, New York.

Fuller, L.L. (1969), *The morality of law*, Yale University Press, New Haven and London.

Gaines, B.C. and McFarland, M.B. (1984), 'Nursing diagnosis: its relationship to and use in nursing education', *Topics in Clinical Nursing*, January, pp. 39–49.

Gamma (1880), 'Letter — Nursing in hospitals', *British Medical Journal*, 6 March, p. 389.

Gardiner, L. (1968), *The eye and ear: the Royal Victorian Eye and Ear Hospital centenary history*, Robertson and Mullens, Melbourne.

Gamarnikow, E. (1991), 'Nurse or woman: gender and professionalism in reformed nursing 1860–1923', in P. Holden and J. Littlewood (eds), *Anthropology and nursing*, Routledge, London, pp. 110–129.

Gaston, C. (unpub.), Product costing activities in South Australia — casemix and nursing acuity, paper presented at the 13th National Conference, Royal College of Nursing, Australia: 'Controlling Nursing's Destiny', 31 May, Brisbane, (1991).

Gaut, D.A. (ed), (1992), *The presence of caring in nursing*, National League for Nursing Press, New York.

—— and Leininger, M. (eds) (1991), *Caring: the compassionate healer*, National League for Nursing Press, New York.

Gavron, H. (1966), *The captive wife: conflicts of household mothers*, Routledge and Kegan Paul, London.

Gaze, H. (1983), 'The cuts that nurses cannot ignore', *Nursing Times*, 79(32), pp. 11–12.

—— (1990a), 'The forgotten fifty thousand', *Nursing Times*, 86(6), 7 February, pp. 28–31.

—— (1990b), 'Dangerous economics', *Nursing Times*, 86(14), 4 April, p. 19.

—— (1990c), 'Helping hands: a glimpse into the future', *Nursing Times*, 86(16), 18 April, pp. 28–31.

Gee, D.J. and Mason, J.K. (1990), *The courts and the doctor*, Oxford University Press, Oxford.

Gelfand, G., Long, P., McGill, D. and Sheerin, C. (1990), 'Prevention of chemically impaired nursing practice', *Nursing Management*, 21(7), July, pp. 76–78.

Gillespie, C.K. (1989), *Justifiable homicide: battered women, self-defence, and the law*, Ohio State University Press, Columbus.

Gladwin, M.E. (1930), *Ethics talks to nurses*, W.B. Saunders, Philadelphia, Pa.

Godden, J. (1989a), 'Jessie Street and the formation of the NSW Nurses' Association', *The Lamp*, 46(7), July, pp. 14–17.

—— (1989b) 'Jessie Street and the formation of the NSW Nurses' Association', *The Lamp*, 46(8), August, pp. 26–29.

Goodhart, A.L. (1938), 'Hospitals and trained nurses', *The Law Quarterly Review*, 54(216), October, pp. 553–575.

Gordon, M. (1979), 'The concept of nursing diagnosis', *Nursing Clinics of North America*, 14(3), September, pp. 487–496.

—— (1987), *Nursing diagnosis: process and application*, 2nd edn, McGraw-Hill Book Co., New York.

Gordon, O. (1920), The National Council of Women of Great Britain and Ireland report of the Special Committee on the Economic Position of Nurses, *Australasian Nurses Journal*, 18(3), March, pp. 89–100.

Gorham, J. (1985), 'This NP covers for a physician', *Registered Nurse*, October, pp. 40–43.

Gould, D. (1988), 'Drug administration — called to account', *Nursing Times*, 84(12), 23 March, pp. 28–31.

Graddol, D. and Swann, J. (1989), *Gendered voices*, Basil Blackwell, Oxford.

Granshaw, L. and Porter, R. (1989), *The hospital in history*, Routledge, London and New York.

Graycar, R. (ed) (1990), *Dissenting opinions: feminist explorations in law and society*, Allen & Unwin, Sydney.

—— and Morgan, J. (1990), *The hidden gender of law*, The Federation Press, Annandale, NSW.

Greenfield, S. (1975), 'Protocols as analogs to standing orders', in B. Bullough (ed), *The law and the expanding nursing role*, Appleton-Century-Crofts, New York, pp. 62–81.

Greenlaw, J. (1982), 'Can you be fired for speaking out?' *Registered Nurse*, 45(8), August, pp. 71–72.

Greer, E. (1982), 'Antonio Gramsci and "Legal Hegemony"', in D. Kairys, *The politics of law: a progressive critique*, Pantheon Books, New York, pp. 304–309.

Gregory, H. (1988), *A tradition of care: a history of nursing at the Royal Brisbane Hospital*, Boolarong Publications, Brisbane.

Gregory, J. (1987), *Sex, race and the law: legislating for equality*, Sage Publications, London.

Greig, M. (1977), 'The case in favour of nurses having legal indemnity', *Australian Nurses Journal*, 7(2), August, pp. 49–51.

Grennan, E. (1930), 'The Somera case', *International Nursing Review*, 5, December/January, pp. 325–333.

Griffin, V. (1990), 'The $100-a-week earning gap' — male and female registered nurses', *Queensland Nurse*, 9(1), January/February, pp. 8–10, 16.

Griffiths Report (1983), *Recommendations on the effective use of manpower and related resources*, HMSO, London.

Grigg, L. (1987), 'Planning the future nursing workforce', *Nurses Action*, (ANF (Victorian Branch) Newsletter), September, p. 1.

Gross, E. (1986), 'Conclusion: What is feminist theory?' in C. Pateman and E. Gross, *Feminist challenges: social and political theory*, Allen & Unwin, Sydney, pp. 190–204.

Guido, G.W. (1988), *Legal issues in nursing: a source book for practice*, Appleton & Lange, Norwalk, Conn./San Mateo.

Gullan, Miss (1925), 'Private nursing ethics', *Una*, 23(10), 1 December, p. 260.

Gunn, M.J. and Smith, J.C. (1985), 'Arthur's case and the right to life of a Down's syndrome child', *The Criminal Law Review*, November, pp. 705–715.

Gunning, C. (1983), 'The profession itself as a source of stress', in S.F. Jacobson and H.M. McGrath (eds), *Nurses under stress*, John Wiley & Sons, New York, pp. 113–126.

Hackett, R. (1983), 'Petty rulings on nursing duties', *Nursing Times*, 79(32), 10 August, p. 4.

Halsbury's laws of England, 4th edn (1980), Butterworths, London.

Halsbury's laws of England: annual abridgement 1990 (1991), Butterworths, London.

Hambridge, R. (1950), 'Tuberculosis', *Australasian Nurses Journal*, 48(11), November, pp. 176–178.

Harbutt, K. (1991), 'Suspended nurse to appeal against ruling', *The Australian*, 10 January.

Harding, S. (1973–1974), 'Feminism: reform or revolution?' *Philosophical Forum*, 5(1–2), Fall/Winter, pp. 271–284.

—— (ed) (1987), *Feminism and methodology*, Indiana University Press, Bloomington and Indianapolis, and Open University Press, Milton Keynes, UK.

Hardy Ivamy, E.R. (ed) (1988), *Mozley and Whiteley's law dictionary*, 10th edn, Butterworths, Sydney.

Harrington, F.E., Myers, J.A. and Levine, I. (1935), 'Tuberculosis among employees of the Minneapolis schools', *Journal of the American Medical Association*, 104(21), 25 May, pp. 1869–1874.

Harris, M. L. (1911), 'What should be the attitude of the state toward the practice of medicine?' *Journal of the American Medical Association*, 56(18), 6 May, pp. 1319–1322.

Hart, H.L.A. (1961), *The concept of law*, Oxford University Press, (Clarendon Law Series), Oxford, UK.

—— (1963), *Law, liberty and morality*, Stanford University Press, Stanford, Calif.

—— (1968), *Punishment and responsibility: essays in the philosophy of law*, Clarendon Press, Oxford, UK.

—— (1983), *Essays in jurisprudence and philosophy*, Clarendon Press, Oxford, UK.

Hase, S. (1977), 'The role of the man in nursing', *Australian Nurses Journal*, 7(1), July, pp. 52–53, 80.

Hawke, R. J. L. (1988), Message from the Prime Minister of Australia to Thirty-nineth Annual Meeting of the College of Nursing, Australia, School of Music, Australian Capital Territory, 25 May. (Reprinted in full in P. Wood (1990), *Nursing: progress through partnership 1921–1991*, Commonwealth of Australia, AGPS, Canberra, Appendix xvii, p. 321.)

Head, S. (1988), 'Nurse practitioners: the new pioneers', *Nursing Times*, 84(26), 29 June, pp. 26–28.

Heath, S. (1991), 'Specialists support "selfish" campaign for doctors' pay rise', *The Age* (Melbourne), 9 August, p. 3.

Health Department Victoria (1987), *General nurse workforce planning: Discussion paper*, Health Department Victoria, Victorian Health Plan, Melbourne.

Hector, W. (1973), *The work of Mrs Bedford Fenwick and the rise of professional nursing*, Royal College of Nursing and National Council of Nurses of the United Kingdom, London.

Hefferon, L. (1972), 'Physician's assistant: why, who and how?', *American Operating Room Nurses*, 15(4), April, pp. 46–51.

Heide, W.S. (1973), 'Nursing and women's liberation: a parallel', *American Journal of Nursing*, 73(5), pp. 824–827.

Heidensohn, F. (1985), *Women and crime: the life of the female offender*, New York University Press, New York.

Helfield, R. (1990), 'Female poisoners of the nineteenth century: a study of gender bias in the application of the law', *Osgoode Hall Law Journal*, 28(1), Spring, pp. 53–101.

Hemmeter, J.C. (1906), 'Science and art in medicine: their influence on the development of medical thinking', *Journal of the American Medical Association*, 46(4), 27 January, pp. 243–248.

Henderson, V. (1969), *Basic principles of nursing care*, International Council of Nurses, Geneva.

Herter, C.A. (1910), 'Imagination and idealism in the medical sciences', *Journal of the American Medical Association*, 54(6), 5 February, pp. 423–430.

Hester, M. (1992), *Lewd women and wicked witches: a study of the dynamics of male domination*, Routledge, London and New York.

Hicks, C. (1982), 'Nurses on the dole', *Nursing Times*, 78(47), 24 November, pp. 1974–1977.

Hicks, N. (1985), 'The history and politics of legislation for nursing status', *Australian Journal of Advanced Nursing*, 2(3), March/May, pp. 46–54.

Hill, A.C. (1979), 'Protection of women workers and the courts: a legal case history', *Feminist Studies*, 5(2), pp. 247–273.

Hills, B. (1989–1990), 'The sacrifice of Sister Sophia', *The Lamp*, 46(11), pp. 24–27.

—— (1991), 'A 90-second telephone call holds key to nurse's future', *Sydney Morning Herald*, 12 February, p. 5.

Hirsh, H.L. (1982), 'TLC plus', *Nursing Homes*, 31(6), November/December, pp. 37–38.

Hobbs, A.J. (1904), Evidence to Select Committee on Registration of Nurses (21 July), in *Report from the Select Committee on Registration of Nurses*, HMSO, London, pp. 67–77.

Hogrefe, P. (1972), 'Legal rights of Tudor women and their circumvention by men and women', *Sixteenth Century Journal*, 3(1), pp. 97–105.

Holden, P. (1991), 'Colonial sisters: nurses in Uganda', in P. Holden and J. Littlewood (eds), *Anthropology and nursing*, Routledge, London and New York, pp. 67–83.

—— and Littlewood, J. (eds) (1991), *Anthropology and nursing*, Routledge, London and New York.

Holdsworth, W. (1972), *A history of English law*, Methuen & Co., London (see J. Burke (1972), *General index to a history of English law*, Vol. 17, Methuen & Co., London).

Holland, S. (1904), Evidence to Select Committee on Registration of Nurses (14 July and 19 July), in *Report from the Select Committee on Registration of Nurses*, HMSO, London, pp. 28–42, 51–58.

Holleran, C. (1986), Foreword in M. Styles, *Report on the regulation of nursing: a report on the present, a position for the future*, International Council of Nurses, Geneva, p. 3.

Holloway, N.M. (1988), *Nursing the critically ill adult*, Addison-Wesley Publishing Company, Health Sciences Division, Menlo Park, Calif.

Holy Bible: New King James version (1982), Thomas Nelson Publishers, Nashville, Tenn.

Homes, P. (1985), 'News focus: who's afraid of Virginia Henderson?', *Nursing Times*, 81(32), 7 August, pp. 16–17.

Horsley, J.E. (1979), 'You can be sued for doing the right thing, too', *Registered Nurse*, 42(6), June, pp. 79–80.

Horsley, V. (1905), Evidence to Select Committee on Registration of Nurses (18 May), in *Report from the Select Committee on Registration of Nurses*, HMSO, London, pp. 61–73.

Howse, C. (1989), 'Registration a minor victory?', *Nursing Times*, 85(49), 6 December, pp. 32–34.

Hunter, G. (1984), 'Nurse gets $8000 in settlement', *The Advertiser* (Adelaide), 24 July.

Hutter, B. and Williams, G. (eds) (1981), *Controlling women: the normal and the deviant*, Croom Helm, London.

Illich, I., Zola, I.K., McKnight, J., Caplan, J. and Shaiken, H. (1977), *Disabling professions*, Marion Boyars, New York.

Index to Canadian legal literature (1989), L.P. Mirando (ed) (1990), Carswell, Toronto, Calgary, Vancouver.

Inlander, C.B., Levin, L.S. and Weiner, E. (1988), *Medicine on trial: the appalling story of ineptitude, malfeasance, neglect, and arrogance*, Prentice Hall Press, New York.

International Council of Nurses (nd), The International Nurses' Pledge, International Council of Nurses, Geneva, in *Australian Nurses Journal* (1965) 63(4), April, p. 79.

—— (1973), *Code for Nurses*, International Council of Nurses, Geneva.

—— (1986a), *Report on the regulation of nursing: a report on the present, a position for the future*, International Council of Nurses, Geneva.

—— (1986b), *Nursing authority* (position statement), International Council of Nurses, Geneva.

—— (1986c), *Nurses' accountability for defining the nursing role* (position statement), International Council of Nurses, Geneva.

—— (1986d), *Educational standards in nursing* (position statement), International Council of Nurses, Geneva.

International Code of Nursing Ethics 1953, adopted by the grand council of the ICN, Sao paulo, Brazil, 10 July 1953, reprinted in ICN 1977, *The nurse's dilemma: ethical considerations in nursing practice*, ICN, Geneva, pp. 73–74.

The international nurses' pledge (1965), Reprinted in *Australian Nurses Journal*, 63(4), April, p. 79.

Jackson, A. (1983), 'Accountability in nursing — 2. The practitioner's view', *Nursing Times*, 79(36), 7 September, pp. 67–68.

Jacobi, E.M. (1973), 'Accountability of the nurse: are there barriers in licensing laws?', in *Proceedings of the American Nurses' Association 48th Convention, Accountability of the Nurse: Are there Legal Barriers to Assuming Full Professional Responsibility?*, American Nurses Association, Kansas City, Mo., pp. 1–3.

Jacobson, S.F. and McGrath, H.M. (eds) (1983), *Nurses under stress*, John Wiley & Sons, New York.

Jaggar, A.M. (1983), *Feminist politics and human nature*, Rowman and Allanheld, Totowa, NJ.

Jamme, A.C. (1915), 'The effects of legislation upon schools of nursing in California', *Transactions of American Hospital Association, 18th Annual Conference*, 17(7936), June, pp. 124–131.

Jarrett, L.E. (1939), 'Professional standards affecting hospital practice', *Hospital*, 13(7), July, pp. 75–77.

Jarrold, K. (1986), 'Cost-effective quality', *Nursing Times*, 82(50), 10 December, pp. 38–39.

Johnson, Cathy (1991), 'We don't need you after all, Govt tells nurses', *Sydney Morning Herald*, 18 September, p. 1.

Johnston, Claire (1989), 'Who is the support worker?', *Nursing Times*, 85(7), 15 February, pp. 26–28.

Johnston, J. D. and Knapp, C. L. (1971), 'Sex discrimination by law: a study in judicial perspective', *New York University Law Review*, 46, pp. 675–747.

Johnston, R. (1976), 'Nurses and job satisfaction: a review of some research findings', *Australian Nurses Journal*, 5(11), May, pp. 23–27.

Johnstone, M. (1989), *Bioethics: a nursing perspective*, W.B. Saunders/Baillière Tindall, Sydney.

—— (1990), Reading 2.1, *Ethics and nursing, Module 601 Distance Education Course for Registered Nurses, Book of readings*, Royal College of Nursing, Australia, Melbourne.

Jones, A.H. (ed) (1988), *Images of nurses: perspectives from history, art, and literature*, University of Pennsylvania Press, Philadelphia, Pa.

Jones, I.H. (1988), 'Code of conduct — the buck stops here', *Nursing Times*, 84(17), 27 April, pp. 50–52.

—— (1990), *The nurse's code: a practical approach to the Code of Professional Conduct for Nurses, Midwives and Health Visitors*, Macmillan Education, Houndmills, Basingstoke, Hampshire and London.

Jones, M.A. (1904), Letter to the Editor, *Una*, 2(4), 20 June, p. 64.

Journal of the American Medical Association (1901), 'The unsentimental nurse', 37, 6 July, p. 33.

—— (1906a), 'Superstitions in medicine', 46(1), 6 January, pp. 40–41.

—— (1906b), 'Another judge defines practice of medicine', 46(6), 10 February, p. 438.

—— (1906c), 'Nurses' schools and illegal practice of medicine', 47(22), 1 December p. 1835.

Kadish, J. and Long, J.W. (1970), 'The training of physician assistants: status and issues', *Journal of the American Medical Association*, 212(6), 11 May, pp. 1047–1051.

Kairys, D. (ed) (1982), *The politics of law: a progressive critique*, Pantheon Books, New York.

Kalisch, B.J. and Kalisch, P.A. (1975), 'Slaves, servants, or saints? (An analysis of the system of nurse training in the United States 1873–1948)', *Nursing Forum*, 14(3), pp. 222–263.

Kalisch, P.A. and Kalisch, B.J. (1978), *The advances of American nursing*, Little, Brown and Company, Boston, Mass.

Kanowitz, L. (1969), *Women and the law: the unfinished revolution*, University of New Mexico Press, Albuquerque, NM.

Kaplan, A. (1933), 'Work sharing at the Beth Moses Hospital', *American Journal of Nursing*, 33(1), January, p. 36.

Karll, A. (1926), 'Sidelights upon professional ethics: loyalty', *Una*, 24(10),1 December, pp. 272–275.

Keddy, B., Gillis, M., Jacobs, P., Burton, H. and Rogers, M. (1986), 'The doctor–nurse relationship: an historical perspective', *Journal of Advanced Nursing*, 11(6), pp. 745–753.

Keller, N.S. (1973), 'The nurse's role: is it expanding or shrinking', *Nursing Outlook*, 21(4), April, pp. 236–240.

Kelly, D. N. (1975), 'Editorial — Power and its abuse', *Supervisor Nurse*, 6(11), November, pp. 7–8.

Kelly, L.Y. (1978), 'The power of powerlessness', *Nursing Outlook*, 26(7), July, p. 468.

—— (1985.), *Dimensions of professional nursing*, 5th edn, Macmillan Publishing Co., New York.

—— (1990), 'Nursing's velvet revolution', *Nursing Outlook*, 38(1), January/February, p. 15.

Kelman, H.C. and Hamilton, V.L. (1989), *Crimes of obedience*, Yale University Press, New Haven and London.

Kennedy, H. (1992), *Eve was framed: women and British justice*, Chatto and Windus, London.

Kennedy, I. (1988), *Treat me right: essays in medical law and ethics*, Clarendon Press, Oxford.

Kent, B. (1905), Evidence to Select Committee on Registration of Nurses (23 May), in *Report from the Select Committee on Registration of Nurses*, HMSO, London, pp. 92–95.

—— (1918), 'The trained nurses' protection committee', *Una*, 16(5), 30 July, pp. 143–144.

Keys, T.E. (1978), *The history of surgical anesthesia*, Robert E. Krieger Publishing Company, Huntington, New York.

Kiefer, M.J. (1983), 'The law and speciality health care practitioners', *Journal of the American Association of Nurse Anesthetists*, 51(6), December, pp. 562–564.

King, E.W. and Sagan, P.R. (1989), 'Nurse practitioner liability and authority', *Nursing Administration Quarterly*, 13(4), Summer, pp. 57–60.

King, H. (1991), 'Using the past: nursing and the medical profession in ancient Greece', in P. Holden and J. Littlewood (eds), *Anthropology and nursing*, Routledge, London and New York, pp. 7–24.

King, P.A. (1985), 'Unprofessional conduct and the nursing profession: the Tuma case', *Bioethics Reporter*, n.6/7, pp. 159–162.

Kinlein, L. (1972), 'Independent nurse practitioner', *Nursing Outlook*, 21(1), January, pp. 22–24.

Kirov, S.M. (1991), 'Women in medical research and academia: what future?', *Australian Universities' Review*, 34(1), pp. 38–43.

Kitzinger, S. (ed) (1988), *The midwife challenge*, Pandora, London.

Kohnke, M.F. (1982), *Advocacy: risk and reality*, The C.V. Mosby Company, St Louis, Miss.

Kreger, A. (1991), *Remote area nursing practice: a question of education*, Council of Remote Area Nurses of Australia (CRANA), Broome, WA.

Kuhse, H. (1984), 'A modern myth. That letting die is not the intentional causation of death: some reflections on the trial and acquittal of Dr Leonard Arthur', *Journal of Applied Philosophy*, 1(1), pp. 21–38.

Kutny, T. (1990), 'Sacking "unfair"', *Whittlesea Post* (Melbourne), 25 September, pp. 1–2.

Kyogle, G.M.B. (1908), 'The power of judgment', *Australasian Nurses Journal*, 6(12), 15 December, p. 417.

LaBar, C. (1984), *Prescribing privileges for nurses: a review of current law*, Center for Research, American Nurses' Association, Kansas City, Mo.

Lacey, N. (1989), 'Feminist legal theory', *Oxford Journal of Legal Studies*, 9(3), pp. 383–394.

Lahey, K.A. (1985), '. . . Until women themselves have told all that they have to tell . . .', *Osgoode Hall Law Journal*, 23(3), pp. 519–541.

—— (1991), 'Reasonable women and the law', in M.A. Fineman and N.S. Thomadsen (eds), *At the boundaries of law: feminism and legal theory*, Routledge, New York, pp. 3–21.

Lambertsen, E.C. (1972), 'Perspective on the physician's assistant', *Nursing Outlook*, 20(1), January, pp. 32–36.

Lamont, L. (1990a), 'Socialist Left council hires an arch foe Liberal to fight union', *The Age* (Melbourne), 22 October, p. 3.

—— (1990b), 'Council red-faced over legal choice', *The Age* (Melbourne), 24 October, p. 17.

The Lamp (1975), 'The medication void and the need for nursing and pharmacy staff co-operation', 32(8), August, pp. 28–30.

—— (1976), 'ILO advocates international standards', 33(5), May, pp. 15–17.

—— (1990), 'Media watch — Dr. Yeo and the nursing shortage', 47(4), May, p. 26.

Langslow, A. (1983a), 'The nurse and the law — drug "reactions"', *Australian Nurses Journal*, 12(6), December/January, pp. 32–34.

—— (1983b), 'The nurse and the law. The dangers of inexperience, traps for young players (pt. 2)', *Australian Nurses Journal*, 12(8), March, pp. 28–29.

—— (1983c) 'The nurse and the law. Finding homes for problems', *Australian Nurses Journal*, 13(4), October, pp. 31–33.

—— (1985), 'Nurse & the law — drug orders must be written up', *Australian Nurses Journal*, 15(3), September, pp. 54–55, 61.

—— (1989a), 'Nurse and the law', *Australian Nurses Journal*, 18(10), May, pp. 37–38.

—— (1989b), 'Nurse and the law. Expert evidence', *Australian Nurses Journal*, 19(5), November, pp. 30–31.

The Lancet (1904), 'The state registration of nurses', 2 April, p. 946.

LaSor, B. and Elliott, M.R. (1977), *Issues in Canadian nursing*, Prentice-Hall of Canada, Scarborough, Ontario.

Laufer, S. (1990), Preface in CCH Health and Medical Law Editors, *Law for the nursing profession*, CCH Australia, North Ryde, NSW, pp. v–vi.

Laurent, C. (1989), 'More questions than answers', *Nursing Times*, 85(7), 15 February, pp. 28–29.

Lawler, J. (1991), *Behind the screens: nursing, somology, and the problem of the body*, Churchill Livingstone, Melbourne.

Leddy, S. and Pepper, J.M. (1989), *Conceptual bases of professional nursing*, J.B. Lippincott Company, Philadelphia, Pa.

Lee, A.A. (1979), 'How nurses rate with MDs: still the handmaiden', *Registered Nurse*, 42(7), July, pp. 21–30.

Lee, S. (1986), *Law and morals: Warnock, Gillick and beyond*, Oxford University Press, Oxford.

Leeson, J. and Gray, J. (1978), *Women and medicine*, Tavistock Publications, London.

Leininger, M.M. (ed) (1988a), *Caring: an essential human need*, Wayne State University Press, Detroit, Mich.

—— (1988b), *Care: the essence of nursing and health*, Wayne State University Press, Detroit, Mich.

—— (1988c), *Care: discovery and uses in clinical and community nursing*, Wayne State University Press, Detroit, Mich.

—— (1990), 'Culture: the conspicuous missing link to understand ethical and moral dimensions of human care, in M.M. Leininger (ed), *Ethical and moral dimensions of care*, Wayne State University Press, Detroit, pp. 49–66.

—— and Watson, J. (eds) (1990), *The caring imperative in education*, National League for Nursing, New York.

Lena, Sister (1903), 'Difficulties and dangers in private house nursing', *Una*, 1(3), October, pp. 46–50.

Leonard, E.B. (1982), *Women, crime and society: a critique of theoretical criminology*, Longman, New York.

Lerner, G. (1986), *The creation of patriarchy*, Oxford University Press, New York.

Lesnik, M.J. (1953), 'Nursing functions and legal control', in M.V. Dryden (ed) (1968), *Nursing trends*, Wm. C. Brown, Dubuque, Ia., pp. 148–156.

Levine, I. (1983), 'Machismo and the male nurse', *Nursing Times*, 79(21), 25 May, pp. 50–51.

Lewis, E.P (1972), 'Editorial — A nurse is a nurse — or is she?', *Nursing Outlook*, 20(1), January, p. 21.

—— (1974), 'Editorial — A role by any name', *Nursing Outlook*, 22(2), February, p. 21.

Lloyd, G. (1984), *The man of reason: 'male' and 'female' in Western philosophy*, Methuen, London.

London, F. (1987), 'Should men be actively recruited into nursing?', *Nursing Administration Quarterly*, 12(1), Fall, pp. 75–80.

Loseby, Captain (1919), Debate on Nurses' Registration Bill, 2nd reading, 28 March, 114 HC Deb 5 s, pp. 806–807.

Lovell, M. (1982), 'Daddy's little girl: the lethal effects of paternalism in nursing', in J. Muff (ed), *Socialization, sexism, and stereotyping: women's issues in nursing*, The C.V. Mosby Company, St. Louis, Mo., pp. 210–220.

—— (1986), 'The politics of medical deception: challenging the trajectory of history' in P. Chinn (ed), *Ethical issues in nursing*, Aspen Systems, Rockville, Maryland, pp. 55–68.

Lowery-Palmer, A. (1982), 'The cultural basis of political behaviour in two groups: nurses and political activitists', in J. Muff. (ed), *Socialization, sexism, and stereotyping: women's issues in nursing*, The C.V. Mosby Company, St. Louis, Mo., pp. 189–202.

L.R.C.P.L. (1880), Letter — Nurses and doctors, *British Medical Journal*, 13 March, p. 425.

Lyle, Mr (1919), Debate on Nurses' Registration Bill, 2nd reading, 28 March, 114 HC Deb 5 s, pp. 788–793.

Lyon, B. (1990), 'Getting back on track: nursing's autonomous scope of practice', in N.L. Chaska (ed), *The nursing profession: turning point*, The C.V. Mosby Company, St Louis, Mo., pp. 267–274.

Lyons, D. (1984), *Ethics and the rule of law*, Cambridge University Press, Cambridge, UK.

Lyons, G. (1912), 'The conditions of nursing in London', *Una*, 10(10), 30 December, p. 241.

M.A.B. (1979), 'Sinners or saints?', *The Canadian Nurse*, 75(6), p. 4.

Maas, M.L. (1973), 'Nurse autonomy and accountability in organized nursing services', *Nursing Forum*, 12(3), pp. 237–259.

McCawley, T.W. (1921), 'Nurses' Award — State', *Australasian Nurses Journal*, 19(7), 15 July, pp. 218–219.

MacDonald, I. (1931), 'Nursing Profession (Wages and Hours) Bill', *British Journal of Nursing*, March, p. 72.

McFarland, G.K. and McFarlane, E.A. (1989), *Nursing diagnosis and intervention: planning for patient care*, The C.V. Mosby Company, St Louis, Mo.

McGivern, D. (1974), 'Baccalaureate preparation of the nurse practitioner', *Nursing Outlook*, 22(2), February, pp. 94–98.

McIntosh, P. (1990), 'Inadequate treatment leaves patients in pay, says report', *The Age* (Melbourne), 8 January, p. 3.

McKeown, T. (1979), *The role of medicine: dream, mirage or nemesis?*, Princeton University Press, Princeton, NJ.

MacKinnon, C.A. (1983), 'Feminism, marxism, method and the state: toward feminist jurisprudence', *Signs: Journal of Women in Culture and Society*, 8(4), pp. 635–658.

—— (1987), *Feminism unmodified: discourses on life and law*, Harvard University Press, Cambridge, Mass.

—— (1989), *Toward a feminist theory of the state*, Harvard University Press, Cambridge, Mass.

Mackinolty, J. and Radi, H. (eds) (1979), *In pursuit of justice: Australian women and the law 1788–1979*, Hale and Iremonger, Sydney.

McLean, I. (1980), *The Renaissance notion of woman: a study in the fortunes of scholasticism and medical science in European intellectual life*, Cambridge University Press, Cambridge, Mass.

MacLean, Miss (1903), 'Lecture by Miss MacLean to the Nurses of the Victorian Trained Nurses' Association, 24 June, 1903', *Una*, 1(2) July, pp. 34–35.

McLean, S. (1981), 'Negligence — a dagger at the doctor's back?', in P. Robson, and P. Watchman (eds), *Justice, Lord Denning and the Constitution*, Gower, Westmead, UK, pp. 99–112.

McMillan, C. (1982), *Women, reason and nature: some philosophical problems with feminism*, Princeton University Press, Princeton, NJ.

McNeill, R.H. (1910), 'The ideal nurse', *Australasian Nurses Journal*, 8(6), 15 June, p. 194–195.

Maggs, C.J. (1981a), 'Control mechanisms and the "new nurse" 1881–1914', *Nursing Times*, 77(25), 2 September, occasional papers (supplement), pp. 97–100.

—— (1981b), 'The register of nurses in the Scottish Poor Law service 1885–1919', *Nursing Times*, 77(33), 25 November, occasional papers (supplement), pp. 129–32.

—— (1983), *The origins of general nursing*, Croom Helm, London.

—— (1987), 'Profit and loss and the hospital nurse', in C.J. Maggs (ed), *Nursing history: the state of the art*, Croom Helm, London.

Malby, R. (1990), 'Helping hands: vocational support', *Nursing Times*, 86(16), 18 April, pp. 31–33.

Marquess of Dufferin and Ava (1919), Debate on Nurses Registration Bill, 27 May, *House of Lords Parliamentary Debates*, 5th series, Vol. 34, HMSO, London, p. 843.

Marriner-Tomey, A. (ed) (1989), *Nursing theorists and their work*, 2nd edn, The C.V. Mosby Company, St Louis, Mo.

Masson, V. (1985), 'Nurses and doctors as healers: personal observations on the relationship — and the distinctions — between nursing and medicine', *Nursing Outlook*, 33(2), March/April, pp. 70–73.

Matthews, J.J. (1984), *Good and bad women: the historical construction of femininity in twentieth-century Australia*, George Allen & Unwin, Sydney.

Mavor, O.H. (1943), 'Nurses' pay and hours', *British Medical Journal*, 21 August, p. 248.

Mechanic, H.F. (1988), 'Redefining the expanded role', *Nursing Outlook*, 36(6), November/December, pp. 280–284.

Medical Journal of Australia (1916), 'Nurses and dispensing', 1(15), 8 April, p. 309.

—— (1921), 'A trade union award for nurses', 1(15), 9 April, pp. 301–302.

—— (1921), 'Nurses and hospitals', 2(3), 16 July, pp. 47–48.

Medical Times and Hospital Gazette (1904), 'The nursing question in England', *Una*, 2(5), 20 July, pp. 75–76.

Melosh, B. (1982), *'The physician's hand': work culture and conflict in American nursing*, Temple University Press, Philadelphia, Pa.

Menkel-Meadow, C. (1987), 'Excluded voices: new voices in the legal profession making new voices in the law', *University of Maimi Law Review*, 42(29), pp. 29–53.

—— (1988), 'Feminist legal theory, critical legal studies, and legal education or "The fem-crits go to law school"', *Journal of Legal Education*, 38, pp. 61–85.

Meredith, S. (1987), 'Lavinia L. Dock: calling nurses to support women's rights, 1907–1923', *Journal of Nursing History*, 3(1), pp. 70–78.

Midgley, M. (1980), *Beast and man: the roots of human nature*, Methuen, London.

—— and Hughes, J. (1983), *Women's choices: philosophical problems facing feminism*, Weidenfeld and Nicolson, London.

Milburn, C. (1989), 'Doctors launch $10 million lobbying group', *The Age* (Melbourne), 7 July, p. 17.

Miller, B.F. and Keane, C.B. (1987), *Encyclopedia and dictionary of medicine, nursing, and allied health*, 4th edn, W.B. Saunders Company, Philadelphia, Pa.

Miller, C. (1988), 'Transplant row: nurses fear sack', *The Herald* (Melbourne), 18 July, p. 1.

Minchin, M.K. (1977), *Revolutions and rosewater: the evolution of nurse registration in Victoria 1923–1973*, Victorian Nursing Council, Melbourne.

Minow, M. (1987), 'The Supreme Court 1986 term — Forward: justice engendered', *Harvard Law Review*, 101(10), pp. 10–95.

—— (1988), 'Feminist reason: getting it and losing it', *Journal of Legal Education*, 38, pp. 47–60.

Mitchell, B. (1970), *Law, morality, and religion in a secular society*, Oxford University Press, London.

Mitchell, D. (1985), 'Partners in practice', *Nursing Mirror*, 161(7), 14 August, p. 3.

Mitchell, J. and Oakley, A. (ed) (1986), *What is feminism?*, Basil Blackwell, Oxford, UK.

Molson, Major (1919), Debate on Nurses' Registration Bill, 2nd reading, 28 March, 114 HC Deb 5 s, HMSO, London, pp. 786–787.

Montgomery, J. (1989), 'Medicine, accountability, and professionalism', *Journal of Law and Society*, 16(2), Autumn, pp. 319–339.

Morawetz, T. (1980), *The philosophy of law: an introduction*, Macmillan Publishing Co., New York.

Moreton, J. (1992), 'Nurse prescribing: how and when', *Health Visitor*, 65(3), March, p. 90.

Morgan, A.F. (1918), 'A new ideal of public service in the nursing profession', *Australasian Nurses Journal*, 16(3), 15 March, pp. 100–107.

Morgan, J. (1987–1988), 'Feminist theory as legal theory', *Melbourne University Law Review*, 16, pp. 743–759.

—— (1989), 'New directions in legal theory: law and feminism', *Law Institute Journal*, 63(7), pp. 620–621.

Morieson, B. (1987), 'Maintaining nursing for nurses', *Nurses Action*, (ANF (Victorian Branch) Newsletter), August.

—— (1988), 'Nursing — change by degrees', *Nurses' Action* (ANF (Victorian Branch) Newsletter), March.

Morris, A. (1987), *Women, crime and criminal justice*, Basil Blackwell, Oxford, UK.

Morris, E. (1892), Evidence to Royal Commission on Charitable Institutions, in *Papers Presented to Parliamentary Session 1892–3*, Vol. 4, Robt. S. Brain, Government Printer, Melbourne, pp. 469–474.

Morrow, H. (1986), 'Nurses, nursing and women', *World Health Organisation Chronicle*, 40(6), pp. 216–221.

Mossman, M.J. (1986), 'Feminism and legal method: the difference it makes', *Australian Journal of Law and Society*, 3, pp. 30–52.

—— (1988), '"Invisible" constraints on lawyering and leadership: the case of women lawyers', *Ottowa Law Review*, 20(3), pp. 567–600.

—— (1990) 'Women lawyers in twentieth century Canada: rethinking the image of "Portia"', in R. Graycar (ed), *Dissenting opinions: feminist explorations in law and society*, Allen & Unwin, Sydney, pp. 80–95.

Muff, J. (ed) (1982), *Socialization, sexism, and stereotyping: women's issues in nursing*, The C.V. Mosby Company, St Louis, Mo.

Mukherjee, S.K. and Scutt, J.A. (eds) (1981), *Women and crime*, Allen & Unwin, Sydney.

Mundinger, M. O'Neil (1980), *Autonomy in nursing*, Aspen Systems Corporation, Germantown, Md.

Murchison, I., Nichols, T.S. and Hanson, R. (1982), *Legal accountability in the nursing process*, 2nd edn, The C.V. Mosby Company, St Louis, Mo.

Murphy, C.P. and Hunter, H. (eds) (1983), *Ethical problems in the nurse–patient relationship*, Allyn and Bacon Inc., Boston, Mass.

Murphy, E. (1987a), 'The professional status of nursing: a view from the courts', *Nursing Outlook*, 35(1), January/February, pp. 12–15.

—— (1987b), 'OR nursing law — Preventing a successful malpractice claim', *American Operating Room Nurses*, 46(1), July, pp. 106–110.

—— (1987c), 'OR nursing law — establishing the legal standard of care', *American Operating Room Nurses*, 46(2), August, pp. 188–192.

—— (1988a), 'OR nursing law — Working in a stressful environment does not supersede the right to be free from verbal or physical abuse', *American Operating Room Nurses*, 47(2), February, pp. 579–584.

—— (1988b), 'OR nursing law — Assessing the nurses' liability exposure when short staffed', *American Operating Room Nurses*, 48(1), July, pp. 116–119.

—— (1988c), 'OR nursing law — Liability exposure when a nurse "floats" to an unfamiliar area'. *American Operating Room Nurses*, 48(2), August, pp. 376–380.

—— (1990a), The legal perspective of nurse autonomy, in N.L. Chaska (ed), (1990), *The nursing profession: turning point*, The C.V. Mosby Company, St Louis, pp. 32–39.

—— (1990b), 'OR nursing law — Legal concerns of the next decade', *American Operating Room Nurses*, 51(1), January, pp. 258–261.

—— (1990c), 'OR nursing law — Intraoperative injury does not always mean liability', *American Operating Room Nurses*, 52(1), January, pp. 19–22.

Murphy, J.F. (1970), 'Role expansion or role extension: some conceptual differences', *Nursing Forum*, 9(4), pp. 381–389.

Naffine, N. (1987), *Female crime: the construction of women in criminology*, Allen & Unwin, Sydney.

—— (1990), *Law and the sexes: explorations in feminist jurisprudence*, Allen & Unwin, Sydney.

National Health and Medical Research Council (1991), *The role of the nurse in Australia*, Commonwealth of Australia, AGPS, Canberra.

National Hospital Record (1908), 'The eight-hour day', 11(15), January, p. 3.

Neil, R.M. and Watts, R. (eds) (1991), *Caring and nursing: explorations in feminist perspectives*, National League for Nursing, New York.

Newberry, S. (1985), 'For better or for worse', *Nursing Mirror*, 160(6), 6 February, p. 27.

New Zealand Herald (1987), 'Cancer cases quoted', 12 August, p. 13.

New Zealand Nurses Association (1988), *Code of Ethics*, New Zealand Nurses Association, Wellington.

Nightingale, F. (1968), *Notes on hospitals*, facsimile copy of the 3rd edn of 1863, Longman, Green, Longman, Roberts, and Green, London (first published 1858).

—— (1970), *Notes on nursing*, Duckworth, London (first published in 1859).

—— (1979), *Cassandra: an essay by Florence Nightingale*, The Feminist Press, New York (first published 1852).

Norman, R.C. (1890), Evidence to Royal Commission on Charitable Institutions (6 June), in *Papers Presented to Parliamentary, Session 1892–3*, Vol. 4, Robt. S. Brain, Government Printer, Melbourne, pp. 138–156.

Northrop, C.E. (1987), 'Judicial perspectives on nursing', *Nursing Outlook*, 35(3), May/June, p. 150.

—— (1989a), 'Legal outlook — Legal content in the nursing curriculum: what students need and how to provide it', *Nursing Outlook*, 37(4), July/August, p. 200.

—— (1989b), 'Legal outlook — Current case law involving nurses: lessons for practitioners, managers, and educators', *Nursing Outlook*, 37(6), November/December, p. 296.

—— and Kelly, M.E. (1987), *Legal issues in nursing*, The C.V. Mosby Company, St Louis, Mo.

Nursing 88 (1988), 'Choosing hospitals', 18(10), October, p. 12.

Nursing Life (1987), 'Fear of floating', 7(5), September/October, p. 72.

Nursing Mirror (1909), 'The relationship between nurse and medical officer', *Una*, 7(9), 30 November, pp. 142–143.

—— (1984), 'Nursing officer struck off register for giving unauthorised drugs', 158(24), 20 June, p. 3.

—— (1985), 'NM's stress survey cited at dismissal hearing', 161(6), 7 August, p. 6.

Nursing Outlook (1974), 'Theme: the nurse practitioner: preparation and practice', 22(2), February, (entire issue).

Nursing Record (1892), 'A slave-drivers union', 5 May, pp. 350–351.

Nursing Times (1907) 'A code of ethics', 12 October.

—— (1913), 'The relation between sister and nurses', *Una*, 11(1), 31 March, p. 9.

—— (1931), 'Not a nurses' Bill', 27(1348), 28 February, pp. 219–220.

—— (1981a), 'Nurse suspended in transfer row', 77(45), 4 November, p. 1908.

—— (1981b), 'Sister sacked in "malicious behaviour" case', 77(48), 25 November, p. 2034.

—— (1982a), 'Baby dies after drug mishap', 78(43), 27 October, p. 1790.

—— (1982b), 'FP nurses' bitter pill for doctors', 78(48), 1 December, p. 2011.

—— (1983a), 'Redundant nurses not re-instated', 79(14), 6 April, p. 18.

—— (1983b), 'New legislation "a political weapon"', 79(17), 27 April, p. 18.

—— (1983c), 'Suicide case leads to DHA inquiry', 79(18), 4 May, p. 18.

—— (1983d), 'New code, old problems', 79(22), 1 June, p. 14.

—— (1983e), 'Lack of staff leads to patient injuries', 79(24), 15 June, p. 19.

—— (1983f), 'Claim of "unfair dismissal" rejected', 79(26), 29 June, p. 19.

—— (1983g), 'Patient's death due to heavy workload', 79(27), 6 July, p. 17.

—— (1983h), 'More nurses need help with drink problems', 79(28), 13 July, p. 18.

—— (1983i), 'Nurses may face the sack', 79(30), 27 July, p. 17.

—— (1983j), 'Sacked ECT student presses for new hearing', 79(32), 10 August, p. 18.

—— (1984), 'DNs must back-up registration plea', 80(31), 1 August, p. 8.

—— (1985a), 'Editorial — As yet it is only the "indians" who have found themselves impaled on the railings of misconduct', 81(30), 24 July, p. 3.

—— (1985b), 'Bury nurses' fight plans to abolish DNO post', 81(35), 28 August, p. 7.

—— (1985c), 'Forum advises on updating controlled drugs law', 81(36), 4 September, p. 7.

—— (1986), 'Editorial — Community nurses manage in the way nurses have traditionally done: they "cope"', 82(43), 22 October, p. 3.

—— (1987a), 'Leading hospital rapped for swapping ENs and RGNs', 83(1), 7 January, p. 7.

—— (1987b), 'Shortages blamed for patient's death', 83(5), 4 February, p. 6.

—— (1987c), 'Inquiry into woman's death angers nurses', 83(5), 11 February, p. 6.

—— (1988a), 'Elderly woman died after moving to freezing ward', 84(3), 20 January, p. 6.

—— (1988b), 'Nurse shortage blamed for cuts', 84(3), 20 January, p. 9.

—— (1988c), 'Rise in infant deaths linked to nurse shortage', 84(12), 23 March, p. 8.

—— (1988d), 'New budget blow costs nurses dear', 84(14), 6 April, pp. 22–23.

—— (1988e), 'Charge nurse disappeared', 84(17), 27 April, p. 10.

—— (1988f), 'Editorial — The alternative to tackling retention is an aimless drift towards a smaller profession supported by a larger number of helpers', 84(18), 4 May, p. 3.

—— (1988g), 'RCN consults on use of YTS trainees', 84(18), 4 May, p. 6.

—— (1988h), 'Editorial — Would it not be better to face up to the inevitability of a smaller profession than swell the ranks of unsuitable recruits', 84(22),1 June, p. 3.

—— (1988i), 'Fewer trained nurses in future, warns UKCC', 84(22), 1 June, p. 5.

—— (1988j), 'Editorial — We must not watch nursing retreat into high-tech areas leaving the elderly, the mentally ill and handicapped and the chronically sick in untrained hands', 84(23), 8 June, p. 3.

—— (1988k), 'Tribunal clears nurse', 84(31), 3 August, p. 6.

—— (1988l), 'Nurses urged to become active in management', 84(31), 3 August, p. 7.

—— (1988m), 'Editorial — The nurse-auxiliary relationship has all too often provided a mirror image of the doctor-nurse relationship', 84(32), 10 August, p. 3.

—— (1988n), 'Doctors' plans cause uproar among nurses', 84(32), 10 August, p. 9.

—— (1988o), 'Editorial — Concern about support workers delivering care should not lead to the profession rejecting evidence that others can contribute to patients' welfare', 84(34), 24 August, p. 3.

—— (1988p), 'Doctors agree to nurses prescribing', 84(50), 14 December, p. 9.

—— (1989a), 'Editorial — At the heart of the debate on support worker training lies the question of the extent to which vocational training and professional education can coalesce', 85(5), 1 February, p. 3.

—— (1989b), 'Junior doctors may delegate to nurses' 85(5), 1 February, p. 5.

—— (1989c), 'View from the frontline', 85(7), 15 February, pp. 32–33.

—— (1989d), 'Support workers "no substitute for students"', 85(39), 27 September, p. 6.

—— (1989e), 'Report urges some prescribing power for nurses', 85(41), 11 October, p. 8.

—— (1989f), 'Whistleblowing students subject to intimidation', 85(20), 20 November, p. 7.

—— (1989g), 'Editorial — It is to be hoped that the reality of nurse prescribing to which Mrs Bottomley referred will dawn very early in 1990 and no later', 85(48), 29 November, p. 3.

—— (1990a), 'Newly qualified nurses forced to join dole queue', 86(4), 24 January, p. 9.

—— (1990b), 'Comment', 86(16), 18 April, p. 3.

—— (1990c), 'ENB demands prescribing training', 86(16), 18 April, p. 6.

—— (1990d), 'Comment', 86(21), 23 May, p. 3.

—— (1990e), 'Government denies survey claim of nurse shortages', 86(21), 23 May, p. 6.

—— (1990f), 'Comment', 86(26), 27 June, p. 3.

—— (1990g), 'Campaigner Graham Pink proved right by expert', 86(26), 27 June, p. 5.

—— (1990h), 'Call to stop scandal of nurses on dole', 86(27), 4 July, p. 6.

—— (1990i), 'Nurses obliged to lie to cancer patients', 86(28), 11 July, p. 9.

—— (1990j), 'Comment', 86(30), 25 July, p. 3.

—— (1990k), 'Challenge doctors or face charges', 86(31), 1 August, p. 8.

Nutting, M.A. (1924), 'How can we care for our patients and educate the nurse?', *Australasian Nurses Journal*, 22(8), 15 August, pp. 376–389.

Oakley, A. (1981), *Subject women*, Fontana Press, London.

—— (1986), *Telling the truth about Jerusalem*, Basil Blackwell, Oxford.

O'Brien, M. (1981), *The politics of reproduction*, Routledge & Kegan Paul, London and New York.

—— (1989), *Reproducing the world: essays in feminist theory*, Westview Press, Boulder, San Francisco & London.

O'Donovan, K. and Szyszczak, E. (1988), *Equality and sex discrimination law*, Basil Blackwell, Oxford.

Ogilvie, S. (1988), 'ODAs are not interchangeable with nurses', *Nursing Times*, 84(21), 25 May, p. 13.

Oh, T.E. (1990), *Intensive care manual*, 3rd edn, Butterworths, Sydney.

Olsen, F. (1990), 'Feminism and critical legal theory: an American perspective', *International Journal of the Sociology of Law*, 18, pp. 199–215.

"On the record" (1990a), 'Nurses impose bans to ensure patient care', June, p. 3 (published by the ANF (Victorian Branch)).

—— (1990b), 'Deregistration of nursing homes', April, p. 3.

—— (1990c), 'Back injuries — a new approach', September, p. 3.

Ooi, C. (unpub.), Paediatrics: a new version by a medical defence union, (1988).

Orr, J. (1988), 'Vested interests', *Nursing Times*, 84(14), 6 April, p. 34.

O'Sullivan, J. (1983), *Law for nurses and allied health professionals in Australia*, 3rd edn, The Law Book Company, Sydney.

Owens, P. and Glennerster, H. (1990), *Nursing in conflict*, MacMillan, London.

Pacific Coast Journal (1920), 'Nursing procedures', *Una*, 17(12), 28 February, pp. 384–385.

Palmer, P. Niessner (1989), 'The AMA proposal for registered care technologists is ludicrous and insulting', *The Lamp*, 46(5), June, pp. 28–29.

Parkes, R. (1991), 'Editorial — Nurses to be invaded?' *Australian Nurses Journal*, 20(8), April, pp. 7–9.

Parsons, R. (1975), 'Nurse practitioner as medical assistant', *The Lamp*, 32(11), November, pp. 15–24.

Parsons, S.A. (1916), *Nursing problems and obligations*, Whitcomb and Barrows, Boston, Mass.

Pascall, G. (1986), *Social policy: a feminist analysis*, Tavistock Publications, London and New York.

Passau-Buck, S. (1982), 'Caring vs. curing: the politics of health care', in J. Muff (ed), *Socialization, sexism, and stereotyping: women's issues in nursing*, The C.V. Mosby Company, St Louis, Mo., pp. 203–209.

Pateman, C. (1988), *The sexual contract*, Polity Press, Cambridge, UK.

—— (1989), *The disorder of women*, Polity Press, Cambridge, UK.

—— and Gross, E. (1986), *Feminist challenges: social and political theory*, Allen & Unwin, Sydney.

Patrick, C. (1988), 'Unskilled agency staff', *Nursing Times*, 84(43), 26 October, p. 12.

Pavitt, L. (1985), 'Don't sweep it under the carpet, Ken', *Nursing Mirror*, 161(6), 7 August, p. 8.

Paxton, C.S. and Scoblic, M.A. (1978), 'Defining and developing protocols for the nurse practitioner', *Nursing Forum*, 17(3), pp. 268–281.

Peers, Lt. Gen. W.R. (1979), *The My Lai Inquiry*, W.B. Norton & Company, New York.

Pelling, H. (1963), *A history of British trade unionism*, Penguin Books, Harmondsworth, Middlesex, UK.

Pensabene, T.S. (1980), *Health research project: the rise of the medical practitioner in Victoria*, research monograph 2, The Australian National University, Canberra.

Pence, T. and Cantrall, J. (eds) (1990), *Ethics in nursing: an anthology*, National League for Nursing, New York.

Persons, C.B. (1987), *Critical care procedures and protocols: a nursing process approach*, J. B. Lippincott Co., Philadelphia, Pa.

Peterson, R.L. (1972), 'Physician's assistant: why, who and how?', *American Operating Room Nurses*, 15(4), April, pp. 54–56.

Peterson, T. (unpub.), 'Nurses Act review: industrial implications', paper presented at Australian Nursing Federation (Victorian Branch) seminar entitled 'Review of the Nurses Act', 2 February, Prince Henry Hospital, Melbourne, (1990).

Pinkerton, S.E. (1981), 'Legislative issues in licensure of registered nurses', in J C. McCloskey and H.K. Grace (eds), *Current issues in nursing*, Blackwell Scientific Publishing, Oxford, UK, pp. 327–336.

Pirquet, C. (1927), 'Should the nurse take part in the scientific work of the medical profession', *Australasian Nurses Journal*, 25(11), 15 November, pp. 343–344.

Polan, D. (1982), 'Toward a theory of law and patriarchy', in D. Kairys (ed), *The politics of law: a progressive critique*, Pantheon Books, New York, pp. 294–303.

Post-registration student nurse (1983), 'Letter to the editor — Unqualified staff in responsible positions', *Nursing Times*, 79(14), 6 April, p. 6.

Pound, R. (1909), 'Liberty of contract', *Yale Law Journal*, 18(7), pp. 454–487.

Price, M. (1987), 'Industrial democracy', *Nurses Action*, (ANF (Victorian Branch) Newsletter), March.

Putzier, D. and Padrick, K.P. (1984), 'Nursing diagnosis: a component of nursing process and decision making', *Topics in Clinical Nursing*, January, pp. 21–29.

Pyne, R.H. (1981), *Professional discipline in nursing: theory and practice*, Blackwell Scientific Publications, Oxford, UK.

—— (1987), 'The UKCC Code of Conduct', *Nursing: The Add-On Journal of Clinical Nursing*, 3(14), February, pp. 510–511.

Raymond, M. (1890), Evidence to the Select Committee on Metropolitan Hospitals (30 June), in *Report from the Select Committee of the House of Lords on Metropolitan Hospitals*, (1890), Vol. 16, facsimile, The Irish University Press series of British Parliamentary Papers (1970), Dublin. pp. 307–313.

Raz, J. (1980), *The concept of a legal system: an introduction to the legal theory of legal system*, 2nd edn, Clarendon Press, Oxford, UK.

R.D.K.L. (1904), 'Letter to the Editor', *Una*, 2(5), 20 July, p. 79.

Rea, K. (1987a), 'Negligence', *Nursing: The Add-On Journal of Clinical Nursing*, 3(14), February, pp. 533–536.

—— (1987b), 'The UK legal system', *Nursing: The Add-On Journal of Clinical Nursing*, 3(14), February, pp. 537–539.

Regan, W.A. (1983a), 'Legally speaking — when in doubt, check it out', *Registered Nurse*, 46(5), May, pp. 87–88.

—— (1983b), 'Legally speaking — when a problem of personality compromises care', *Registered Nurse*,, October, pp. 21–22.

Regan Report on Nursing Law (1980a), 'Emergency codes: nurse's role in crisis', 20(8), January.

—— (1980b), 'Doctors' orders and nursing judgment', 20(10), March, p. 1.

—— (1980c), 'Charting: importance of nurses notes', 20(12), May, p. 1.

—— (1980d), 'Doctor's orders and nurse's judgment', 21(4), September, p. 1.

—— (1980e), 'RN Legal rights: right to complain', 21(5), October, p. 1.

—— (1980f), 'Breast cancer — MD/RN malpractice: $185,000.00!', 21(7), December, p. 2.

—— (1981a), 'Liberated nurses: assessment/judgment', 22(1), June, p. 1.

—— (1981b), 'Blockbuster lawsuits: nurse defendants', 22(3), August, p. 1.

—— (1982a), 'Nurses complaints about doctors: legal aspects', 23(2), July, p. 1.

—— (1982b), 'Physician assistants and quality patient care', 23(3), August, p. 1.

—— (1982c), 'Education and professional nursing: priority', 23(7), December, p. 1.

—— (1983), 'Executing doctors' orders: nursing judgment', 23(11), April, p. 4.

—— (1985), 'Nurses Assn. challenges regulation: nurse practitioners', 25(8), January, p. 2.

—— (1986), 'Nurse refuses to "float": sunk', 27(7), December, p. 1.

—— (1989), 'Nurse practitioners held to higher standards', 30(6), November.

—— (1990), 'Is there a nurse–patient privilege?', 31(4), September, p. 2.

—— (1993), 'Nurses' opinions on Dr.'s malpractice prohibited', 33(12), May, p. 1.

Registered Nurse (1979), 'How nurses rate with the public: how — and where — the handmaiden image is changing', 42(6), June, pp. 36–39.

Reinhard, S.C. (1988), 'Jurisdictional control: the regulation of nurses' aides', *Nursing and Health Care*, 9(7), September, pp. 373–375.

Report from the Select Committee of the House of Lords on Metropolitan Hospitals (1890), Vol. 16, facsimile, The Irish University Press series of British Parliamentary Papers (1970), Dublin.

Report from the Select Committee on the Registration of Nurses (1904), HMSO, London.

—— (1905), HMSO, London.

Report of the cervical cancer inquiry (1988), prepared by the Committee of Inquiry into Allegations Concerning the Treatment of Cervical Cancer at National Women's Hospital and into Other Related Matters, Government Printing Office, Auckland, New Zealand.

Report of the Study of Professional Issues in Nursing (1988), Health Department (Victoria), Melbourne.

Reverby, S.M. (1987), *Ordered to care: the dilemma of American nursing 1850–1945*, Cambridge University Press, Cambridge, UK.

Rhode, D.L. (1986), 'Feminist perspectives on legal ideology', in J. Mitchell and A. Oakley (eds), *What is feminism?*, Basil Blackwell, Oxford, UK, pp. 151–160.

—— (1988), 'The "woman's point of view"', *Journal of Legal Education*, 38, pp. 39–46.

—— (1989), *Justice and gender: sex discrimination and the law*, Harvard University Press, Cambridge, Mass.

Rhodes, B. (1983), 'Accountability in nursing — 1 Alternative perspectives', *Nursing Times*, 79(36), 7 September, pp. 65–66.

Rice, S. (1988), *Some doctors make you sick: the scandal of medical incompetence*, Angus & Robertson Publishers, Sydney.

Rich, A. (1979), *On lies, secrets and silence: selected prose 1966–1978*, Virago Press, London.

Richards, J.R. (1980), *The sceptical feminist: a philosophical enquiry*, Penguin Books, Harmondsworth, Middlesex, UK.

Rimmer, C. (1989), 'The medical report — legal requirements', in R. Winfield (ed), *The expert medical witness*, The Federation Press, Sydney, pp. 1–27.

Roach, M.S. (1987), *The human act of caring: a blueprint for the health professions*, Canadian Hospital Association, Ottawa, Ontario.

Roberts, F. (1919), Debate on Nurses' Registration Bill, 2nd reading, 28 March, 114 HC Deb 5 s, HMSO, London, pp.794–797.

Roberts, S. (1989), 'Going, going, gone?', *Nursing Times*, 85(40), 4 October, pp. 61–65.

Robson, R. (1992), *Lesbian (out)law: survival under the rule of law*, Firebrand Books, Ithaca, New York.

Roche, H. (1953), 'Tuberculosis', *Australian Nurses Journal*, 51(3), March, pp. 48–50.

Rogers, M.E. (1972), 'Nursing: to be or not to be?', *Nursing Outlook*, 20(1), January, pp. 42–46.

Rosen, G. (1963), 'The hospital: historical sociology of a community institution', in E. Freidson (ed), *The hospital in modern society*, The Free Press of Glencoe, Collier-MacMillan, London, pp. 1–36.

Rothman, D.A. and Rothman, N.L. (1977), *The professional nurse and the law*, Little, Brown and Company, Boston, Mass.

Roundell, Lieutenant-Colonel (1919) Debate on Nurses' Registration Bill, 2nd reading, 28 March, 114 HC Deb 5 s, pp. 787–788.

Rowden, R. (1987a), 'The UKCC Code of Conduct: accountability and implications', *Nursing: The Add-On Journal of Clinical Nursing*, 3(14), February, pp. 512–514.

—— (1987b), 'The extended role of the nurse', *Nursing: The Add-On Journal of Clinical Nursing*, 3(14), February, pp. 516–517.

Rowland, R. (1988), *Woman herself: a transdisciplinary perspective on women's identity*, Oxford University Press, Melbourne.

Royal College of Nursing, Australia, Australian Nursing Federation, Florence Nightingale Committee, Australia, and the New South Wales College of Nursing (1991), *Nursing research targets into the twenty first century: discussion paper and first draft policy statement June 1991*, Royal College of Nursing, Australia, Melbourne.

Royal College of Nursing, Australia (Victorian Chapter) (unpub.), Personal care attendants (position paper), 6 August (1991).

Royal Commission on Charitable institutions (1890), in *Papers Presented to Parliamentary Session 1892–3*, Vol. 4, Robt. S. Brain, Government Printer, Melbourne.

Royal Victorian Trained Nurses Association (1923), 'Nurses Registration Bill', *Una*, 21(9), 1 November, pp. 167–168.

Russell, Earl (1919), Debate on Nurses Registration Bill, 27 May, *House of Lords Parliamentary Debates*, 5th series, Vol. 34, HMSO, London, pp. 846–850.

Russell, R.L. (1990), *From Nightingale to now: nurse education in Australia*, W.B. Saunders/Baillière Tindall, Sydney.

Ryan, E. and Conlon, A. (1975), *Gentle invaders*, Penguin, Ringwood, Victoria.

Rye, D. (1983), 'Accountability in nursing — 3. The story so far', *Nursing Times*, 79(37), 14 September, pp. 64–65.

Sachs, A. and Wilson, J.H. (1978), *Sexism and the law*, Martin Robertson, Oxford, UK.

Sadler, C. (1988), '1000 fatal errors', *Nursing Times*, 84(3), 20 January, p. 18.

—— (1992), 'Prescribing timetable', *Nursing Times*, 88(15), April, pp. 20–21.

Sadler, M. (1920), 'Brains in nursing', *Una*, 20(3), 1 May, pp. 56–57.

St Amand, S. (1982), 'Getting a foot in the door: one nurse's experience in obtaining hospital privileges', in J. Muff (ed), *Socialization, sexism, and stereotyping: women's issues in nursing*, The C.V. Mosby Company, St Louis, Mo., pp. 406–408.

Salvage, J. (1985), *The politics of nursing*, Heinemann Nursing, London.

—— (1988), 'Professionalization — or struggle for survival? A consideration of current proposals for the reform of nursing in the United Kingdom', *Journal of Advanced Nursing*, 13(4), July, pp. 515–519.

Sandroff, R. (1981), 'Is it right? Protect the MD . . . or the patient?', *Registered Nurse*, 44(2), February, pp. 28–33.

Sarner, H. (1968), *The nurse and the law*, W.B. Saunders, Philadelphia, Pa.

Satterthwaite, T.E. (1910), 'Private nurses and nursing; with recommendations for their betterment', *New York Medical Journal*, 15 January, pp. 108–110.

Saunders, J.B. (ed) (1989), *Words and phrases legally defined*, 3rd edn, Butterworths, London.

Savage, E. (1952), 'Fifty years' nursing progress in Australia', *Australian Nurses Journal*, 50(1), January, pp. 2–6.

Savage, J. (1987), *Nurses, gender and sexuality*, Heinemann Nursing, London.

Scales, A.C. (1986), 'The emergence of feminist jurisprudence: an essay', *The Yale Law Journal*, 95(7), pp. 1373–1403.

Scheffel, C. (1931), *Jurisprudence for nurses: legal knowledge bearing upon acts and relationships involved in the practice of nursing*, Lakeside Publishing Co., New York.

Schwartz, L. (1991), 'Nurses with attitude', *Sunday Age* (Melbourne), 18 August, Agenda pp. 1–2.

Scutt, J.A. (1976), 'Role conditioning theory: an explanation for disparity in male and female criminality', *Australian and New Zealand Journal of Criminology*, 9, pp. 25–35.

—— (1981), 'Sexism in criminal law', in S.K. Mukherjee and J.A. Scutt (eds), *Women and crime*, Allen & Unwin, Sydney, pp. 1–21.

—— (1990), *Women and the law*, The Law Book Company, Sydney.

Sealey, R. (1990), *Women and the law in classical Greece*, The University of North Carolina Press, Chapel Hill and London.

Secretary's Committee to Study Extended Roles for Nurses (1972), *Report on Extending the Scope of Nursing Practice*, USGPO, Washington, reprinted in *Nursing Outlook*, 20(1), January, 1972, pp. 46–52.

Sellers, H. (Professional Officer, ANF — Victorian Branch) (unpub.), Letter to Megan-Jane Johnstone, 14 February, 1990.

Sevenhuijsen, S. (1986), 'Fatherhood and the political theory of rights: theoretical perspectives in feminism', *International Journal of the Sociology of Law*, 14(3/4), pp. 329–340.

Shalleck, A. (1988), 'Report of the women and the law project: gender bias and the school curriculum', *Journal of Legal Education*, 38, pp. 97–99.

Shanley, C. (1990), Letter-to-editor, *The Lamp*, 47(2), August, p. 3.

Shannon, M.L. (1975), 'Nurses in American history: our first four licensure laws', *American Journal of Nursing*, 75(8), pp. 1327–1329.

Sheehan, J. (1985), 'Legislation, 1: the Beveridge years', *Nursing Mirror*, 161(6), 7 August, pp. 18–21.

Shelden, R.G. (1981), 'Sex discrimination in the juvenile justice system Memphis, Tennessee, 1900–1917', in M.Q. Warren (ed), *Comparing female and male offenders*, Sage Publications, Beverley Hills, Calif., pp. 55–72.

Short, S.D. and Sharman, E. (1987), 'The nursing struggle in Australia', *Image*, 19(4), Winter, pp. 197–200.

Simpson, F.F. (1909), 'Factors which contribute to a reduction in mortality in abdominal surgery', *Journal of the American Medical Association*, 53(15), 9 October, pp. 1173–1176.

Sklar, C. (1979a), 'You and the law — On trial!', *Canadian Nurse*, 75(2), February, pp. 8–10.

Sklar, C.L. (1979b), 'Sinners or saints? The legal perspective', *The Canadian Nurse*, 75(10), November, pp. 14–16.

—— (1979c), 'Sinners or saints? The legal perspective, part two', *The Canadian Nurse*, 75(11), December, pp. 16–21.

Slack, P. (1982), 'Disciplinary procedures', *Nursing Times*, 78(2), 13 January, p. 49.

—— (1986), 'What future for the ward sister?', *Nursing Times*, 82(46), 12 November, pp. 28–30.

Slater, P. (1974), 'Nurse practitioner, family practice nurse or physician's assistant', *Australian Nurses Journal*, 3(6), December/January, pp. 31–34.

Sleeman, J.G. (1939), 'Tuberculosis and the nursing profession', *Australasian Nurses Journal*, 37(3), 15 March, pp. 41–45.

Smart, C. (1976), *Women, crime and criminology: a feminist critique*, Routledge and Kegan Paul, London.

—— (1984), *The ties than bind: law, marriage and the reproduction of patriarchal relations*, Routledge and Kegan Paul, London.

—— (1989), *Feminism and the power of law*, Routledge, London.

—— (1990a), 'Law's power, the sexed body, and feminist discourse', *Journal of Law and Society*, 17(2), Summer, pp. 194–210.

—— (1990b), 'Law's truth/women's experience', in R. Graycar (ed) *Dissenting opinions: feminist explorations in law and society*, Allen & Unwin, Sydney, pp. 1–20.

—— (1991), *The woman in legal discourse*, Vronwenstudies sociale Wetenschappen, Rijksuniversiteit te Utrecht, Utrecht, pp. 1–22.

—— and Brophy, J. (1985), 'Locating law: a discussion of the place of law in feminist politics', in J. Brophy and C. Smart (eds), *Women in law: explorations in law, family and sexuality*, Routledge and Kegan Paul, London, pp. 1–20.

Smith, C.M. (1983), 'Concepts of organizational dynamics: power', in S.F. Jacobson and H.M. McGrath (eds), *Nurses under stress*, John Wiley and Sons, New York, pp. 127–139.

Smith, F.B. (1982), *Florence Nightingale: reputation and power*, Croom Helm, London and Canberra.

Smith, S. (1990a), 'The new GP contract — make or break?', *Nursing Times*, 86(20), 16 May, pp. 29–31.

—— (1990b), 'Nurse prescribing — take with caution', *Nursing Times*, 86(29), 18 July, pp. 29–31.

Smoyak, S. (1987), 'Nurses and doctors: redefining roles', *Nursing Times*, 83(5), 28 January, pp. 35–37.

Snell, B.F., Mashford, M.L.M. and Moulds, R.F.W. (unpub.), *Pain experience and analgesic use: a study in three Victorian teaching hospitals*, unpublished study, Victorian Medical Post-Graduate Foundation Therapy Committee, Melbourne, (1988).

Social Services Committee (1984), *Griffiths NHS Management inquiry Report, together with the Proceedings of the Committee, the Minutes of Evidence and Appendices*, HMSO, London.

Solly, Mr (1915), Reported comments to the Assembly (16 September), *Victorian Parliamenary Debates, Session 1915*, Vol. 141, p. 2424.

Spence, D. (1989), 'Battlefronts: tender loving academics', *The independent monthly*, September, pp. 40–41.

Spender, D. (1982), *Women of ideas and what men have done to them*, Pandora, London.

—— (1985), *Man made language*, Routledge and Kegan Paul, London and New York.

Stanley, L. (1979), 'Doctors: what to do when the MD is wrong', *Registered Nurse*, 42(3), March, pp. 22–30.

Starr, P. (1982), *The social transformation of American medicine*, Basic Books Inc., New York.

Staunton, P. (1989), 'Regulate to fit the role', *Australian Nurses Journal*, 19(5), November, p. 9.

—— (1990), 'There, but for the grace of God . . .', *The Lamp*, 46(11), December/January, p. 24.

—— (1991a), Editorial, *The Lamp*, 48(3), April, p. 3.

—— (1991b), Editorial, *The Lamp*, 48(5), June, p. 3.

—— and Whyburn, B. (1993), *Nursing and the law*, 2nd edn, W.B. Saunders/Baillière Tindall, Sydney.

Stein, L.L. (1968), 'The doctor–nurse game', *American Journal of Nursing*, 68(1), January, pp. 101–105 (reprinted from the *Archives of General Psychiatry* (1967), 16, pp. 699–703).

Stewart, I.M. (1921), 'Popular fallacies about nursing education', *Modern Hospital*, 17(5), 1 November, pp. 424–428.

Stilwell, B. (1988), 'Should nurses prescribe?', *Nursing Times*, 84(12), 23 March, pp. 31–34.

—— (1990), 'The new GP contract — partners in practice', *Nursing Times*, 86(20), 16 May, pp. 32–34.

Strachey, R. (1978), *The cause: a short history of the women's movement in Great Britain*, Virago, London.

Stubbs, M. (1986), 'Feminism and legal positivism', *Australian Journal of Law and Society*, 3, pp. 63–91.

Styles, M.M. (1982), *On nursing: toward a new endowment*, The C.V. Mosby Company, St Louis, Mo.

—— (1989), *On specialization in nursing: toward a new empowerment*, American Nurses' Foundation Inc., Kansas City, Mo.

Sullivan, E.J., Bissell, L. and Leffler, D. (1990), 'Drug use and disciplinary actions among 300 nurses', *International Journal of the Addictions*, 25(4), pp. 375–391.

Summersgill, H.T. (1915), President's address, *Transactions of the American Hospital Association*, 17(7936), 22–25 June, pp. 90–96.

Sumner, E. (1981), 'Time to overturn "doctor's law"', *Nursing Times*, 77(43), 28 October, p. 1874.

Sun Herald (1990), 'Medically unfit', 17 June, p. 168.

Swaffield, L. (1990), 'Quest for quality', *Nursing Times*, 86(12), pp. 16–17.

Swendson, C. (unpub.), The regulation of nursing in Queensland: individual, organisational or societal control?, paper presented at the 13th national conference, Royal College of Nursing, Australia entitled 'Controlling nursing's destiny', Brisbane, 31 May (1991).

Symanski, M.E. (1990), 'Make room for care: challenges for faculty of undergraduate nursing curricula', in M. Leininger and J. Watson (eds), *The caring impertaive in education*, National League for Nursing, New York, pp. 137–144.

Symonds, M.A. (1914), 'Nursing etiquette, in hospital and private work', *Una*, 12(4), 30 June, pp. 112–113.

Szasz, S.S. (1982), 'The tyranny of uniforms', in J. Muff (ed), *Socialization, sexism, and stereotyping: women's issues in nursing*, The C.V. Mosby Company, St Louis, Mo., pp. 397–401.

Szasz, T.S. (1972), *The myth of mental illness*, Paladin, Frogmore, St Albans, Herts, UK.

Talbot, D. (1991a), 'Nurses protest at staff proposal', *The Age* (Melbourne), 5 August, p. 5.

—— (1991b), 'Nursing work bans will disrupt some elective surgery', *The Age* (Melbourne), 6 August, p. 6.

Taub, N. and Schneider E.M. (1982), 'Perspectives on women's subordination and the role of law', in D. Kairys (ed), *The politics of law: a progressive critique*, Pantheon Books, New York, pp. 117–139.

Taylor, E.W., Dwiggins, R., Albert, M. and Dearner, J. (1983), 'Male nurses: what they think about themselves — and others', *Registered Nurse*, 46(10), October, pp. 58–64.

Templeton, J. (1969), *Prince Henry's: the evolution of a Melbourne Hospital 1869–1969*, Robertson and Mullens, Melbourne.

Thompson, G. (1965), 'Duties and responsibilities of the nurse under the law', *Australian Nurses Journal*, 63(4), April, pp. 82–88.

Thompson, J. (1990), 'No vacancies', *Nursing Times*, 86(21), 23 May, p. 18.

Thompson, W.G. (1906), 'The over-trained nurse', *Journal of the American Medical Association*, 46(19), 12 May, p. 1476 (reprinted from the *New York Medical Journal*, 28 April).

Thornton, M. (1984), 'A fair day's pay for work of equal value', *The Lamp*, 41(8), pp. 11–16.

—— (1986), 'Feminist jurisprudence: illusion or reality?', *Australian Journal of Law and Society*, 3, pp. 5–29.

—— (1989), 'Hegemonic masculinity and the academy', *International Journal of the Sociology of Law*, 17(2), pp. 115–130.

—— (1990), *The liberal promise: anti-discrimination legislation in Australia*, Oxford University Press, Melbourne.

—— (1991), 'Feminism and the contradictions of law reform', *International Journal of the Sociology of Law*, 19(4), pp. 453–474.

Tingle, J. (1990a), 'Nurses and the law. Responsible and liable?', *Nursing Times*, 86(25), 20 June, pp. 42–43.

—— (1990b), 'Nurses and the law. A duty of care', *Nursing Times*, 86(30), 25 July, pp. 60–61.

The Trained Nurse (1921), 'The ethics of nursing', *Una*, 18(10), 1 February, pp. 200–202.

Trained Nurses and Hospital Review (1914), 'Nurses and labor laws', 52, January, pp. 37–38.

Trainer, M., King, J. and Zakowicz, H. (1981), 'Nurse practitioner or physician's assistant?',in J.C. McCloskey and H. Grace (eds), *Current issues in nursing*, Blackwell Scientific Publishers, Oxford, UK, pp. 232–241.

Trembath, R. and Hellier, D. (1987), *All care and responsibility: a history of nursing in Victoria 1850–1934*, Florence Nightingale Committee, Australia (Victorian Branch), Melbourne.

Trinosky-Lind, P. (1988), 'America's dwindling pool', *Nursing Times*, 84(31), 3 August, pp. 35–36.

Trubek, D.M. (1972), 'Max Weber on law and the rise of capitalism', *Wisconsin Law Review*, 3, pp. 720–753.

Tuma, J.L. (1977), 'Professional misconduct?', *Nursing Outlook*, 25(9), September.

Turkel, G. (1990), 'Michel Foucault: law, power, and knowledge', *Journal of Law and Society*, 17(2), pp. 170–193.

Turner, B.S. (1987), *Medical power and social knowledge*, Sage Publications, London.

Turner, T. (1990a), 'The new GP contract — a case for concern?', *Nursing Times*, 86(20), 16 May, pp. 27–29.

—— (1990b), 'Catch 22', *Nursing Times*, 86(22), 30 May, p. 19.

—— (1990c), 'Speaking out', *Nursing Times*, 86(26), 27 June, pp. 16–18.

—— (1990d), 'No guarantees', *Nursing Times*, 86(30), 25 July, p. 18.

Una (1914), 'State registration of nurses: deputation to minister', 12(4), 30 June, p. 110.

—— (1917), 'State registration', 14(12), 28 February, p. 390.

—— (1918), 'Redress for nurses', 16(1), 30 March, p. 3.

—— (1919), 'The Nurses' Registration Bill in the House of Commons, England', 17(5), 30 July, pp. 145–149.

—— (1922), 'State registration', 20(4), 1 June, p. 74.

—— (1923), 'Nurses' Registration Bill', 21(9), 1 November, pp. 167–168.

United Kingdom Central Council for Nursing, Midwifery and Health Visiting (UKCC) (1984), *Code of professional conduct for the nurse, midwife and health visitor*, 2nd edn, UKCC, London.

United States Bureau of Education (1901), *Annual report for 1899–1900*, Vol. 2, Government Printing Office, Washington DC.

Upton, A.M. (1905), 'Evidence to Select Committee on Registration of Nurses (16 May)', in *Report from the Select Committee on Registration of Nurses*, HMSO, London, pp. 46–48.

Uren, J. (1988), 'The erosion of the role of the clinical nurse', *Nurses' Action* (published by the ANF(Victorian Branch), Melbourne), March, p. 5.

Valenstein, E.S. (1986), *Great and desperate cures: the rise and decline of psychosurgery and other radical treatments for mental illness*, Basic Books Inc., New York.

Valentine, H.T. (1890), 'Evidence to the Select Committee on Metropolitan Hospitals (30 June)', in *Report from the Select Committee of the House of Lords on Metropolitan Hospitals*, Vol. 16, facsimile, The Irish University Press series of British Parliamentary Papers (1970), Dublin, pp. 316–331.

Vance, C., Talbott, S., McBride, A. and Mason, D. (1985), 'An uneasy alliance: Nursing and the women's movement', *Nursing Outlook*, 33(6), November/December, pp. 281–285.

Victorian Nursing Council (unpub.), Minutes of 28/7/33–11/5/48, Victorian Nursing Council, Melbourne.

Vidovich, M. (1990), 'Towards a national nurse registering authority', *Australian Nurses Journal*, 19(11), June, p. 21.

Vousden, M. (1985), 'Wasteful use of expensive personnel', *Nursing Mirror*, 161(3) 17 July, p. 9.

Waikato Times (1990), 'Ethical guidelines underway', 15 October, p. 3.

Walker, A.E. (1972), 'PRIMEX — The family nurse practitioner program', *Nursing Outlook*, 20(1), January, pp. 28–31.

Walsh, M. Roth (1977), *'Doctors wanted: no woman need apply': sexual barriers in the medical profession, 1835–1975*, Yale University Press, New Haven, Conn.

Waring, M. (1988), *Counting for nothing: what men value and what women are worth*, Allen & Unwin, Port Nicholson Press, Wellington, NZ.

Warner, G.T. (1930), *Landmarks in English industrial history*, Blackie and Son, London.

Wasserstrom, R.A. (1971), *Morality and the law*, Wadsworth Publishing Company, Belmont, Calif.

Waters, S. and Arbeiter, J. (1985), 'Nurse practitioners: how are they doing now?', *Registered Nurse*, October, pp. 38–39.

Watson, J. (1985a), *Nursing: human science and human care — a theory of nursing*, Appleton-Century-Crofts, Norwalk, Conn.

—— (1985b), *Nursing: the philosophy and science of caring*, Colorado Asociated University Press, Colo.

Watson Cheyne, Sir (1919), Debate on Nurses' Registration Bill, 2nd reading, 28 March, 114 HC Deb 5 s, HMSO, London, pp. 800–802.

Weinreb, L.L. (1987), *Natural law and justice*, Harvard University Press, Cambridge, Mass.

Weisberg, D.K. (ed) (1982a), *Women and the law: a social historical perspective, Vol. 1, Women and the criminal law*, Schenkman Publishing Co., Cambridge, Mass.

—— (1982b), *Women and the law: a social historical perspective, Vol. 2, Property, family and the legal profession*, Schenkman Publishing Co., Cambridge, Mass.

Wellwood, E.M. (1961), 'Medicine and the law: reasonable care and unreasonable fatigue', *The Lancet*, 8 April, pp. 763–764.

Wertheimer, M. (1990), 'Separate roles for doctors and nurses need to be recognised', *Medicine*, 2(7), 16 April, p. 11.

White, R. (1976), 'Some political influences surrounding the Nurses Registration Act 1919 in the United Kingdom', *Journal of Advanced Nursing*, 1(3), pp. 209–217.

—— (1985), 'Educational entry requirements for nurse registration: an historical perspective', *Journal of Advanced Nursing*, 10(6), pp. 583–590.

Whittaker, J. (1984), 'Distinguishing nurses "from other types of frauds"', *Registered Nurses Association of British Columbia News*, 16(4), July/August, pp. 20–23.

Whittlesea Post (Melbourne) (1990), 'Esmonde threatens to quit', 20 November, p. 1.

Wiles, M. (1925), 'District nursing ethics', *Una*, 23(10), 1 December, pp. 260–262.

Williams, C.L. (1989), *Gender differences at work: women and men in nontraditional occupations*, University of California Press, Berkeley.

Williams, J. (1890), Evidence to Royal Commission on Charitable Institutions (30 May), in *Papers presented to parliamentary, session 1892–3*, Vol. 4, Robt. S. Brain, Government Printer, Melbourne, pp. 105–133.

Williams, J.A. and Goodman, R.D. (1988), *Jane Bell, OBE (1873–1959), Lady Superintendent, The Royal Melbourne Hospital (1910–1934)*, The Royal Melborune Hospital Graduate Nurses' Association, Melbourne.

Williamson, A.A. (1914), 'California and the eight-hour law', *Trained Nurse and Hospital Review*, 53(5), November, pp. 258–265.

—— (1915), 'The eight-hour law, its present and its future', *Transactions of the American Hospital Association*, 17(7936), June, pp. 132–138.

Willig, S.H. (1970), *The nurse's guide to the law*, McGraw-Hill Book Company, New York.

Willis, E. (1989), *Medical dominance*, Allen & Unwin, Sydney.

Windschuttle, E. (1981), 'Women, crime and punishment', in S.K. Mukherjee and J.A. Scutt (eds), *Women and crime*, Allen & Unwin, Sydney. pp. 31–50.

Winfield, R. (ed) (1989), *The expert medical witness*, The Federation Press, Annandale, NSW.

Winslow, G.R. (1984), 'From loyalty to advocacy: a new metaphor for nursing', *Hastings Center Report*, 14(3), June, pp. 32–40.

Wishik, H. (1986), 'To question everything: the inquiries of feminist jurisprudence', *Berkeley Women's Law Journal*, 1, pp. 64–77.

Witz, A. (1992), *Professions and patriarchy*, Routledge, London and New York.

Wolf, Z.R. (1988), *Nurses' work, the sacred and the profane*, University of Pennsylvania Press, Philadelphia, Pa.

—— (1989), 'Uncovering the hidden work of nursing', *Nursing and Health Care*, 10(8), October, pp. 463–467.

Wolfe, S.M., Bergman, H. and Silver, G. (1985), *Public citizen health research group report*, cited in C.B. Inlander, L.S. Levin and E. Weiner (1988), *Medicine on trial: the appalling story of ineptitude, malfeasance, neglect, and arrogance*, Prentice Hall Press, New York, p. 277.

Woodham-Smith, C. (1964), *Florence Nightingale, 1820–1910*, Fontana Books, London.

World Health Organisation (1987), *Leadership for health for all: the challenge to nursing: a strategy for action*, Division of Health Manpower Development, World Health Organisation, Geneva.

Worrall, A. (1990), *Offending women: female lawbreakers and the criminal justice system*, Routledge, London.

Wortman, M.S. (ed) (1985), *Women in American law, Vol. 1, From Colonial times to the new deal*, Holmes and Meier Publishers, New York.

Wright, C.A. (1936), 'Hospitals — liability for negligence of nurses and doctors — respondeat superior', *The Canadian Bar Review*, 8, October, pp. 699–708.

Yarling, R.R. and McElmurry, B.J. (1986a), The moral foundation of nursing, *Advances in Nursing Science*, 8(2), pp. 63–73.

—— (1986b), 'Rethinking the nurse's role in "Do Not Resuscitate" orders: a clinical policy proposal in nursing ethics', in P. Chinn (ed), *Ethical issues in nursing*, Aspen Systems, Rockville, Md., pp. 123–134.

Yates, G.G. (1975), *What women want: the ideas of the Movement*, Harvard University Press, Cambridge, Mass.

Yatman, E.M. (1890), Evidence to The Select Committee on Metropolitan Hospitals (30 June and 3 July), in *Report from the Select Committee of the House of Lords on Metropolitan Hospitals*, Vol. 16, facsimile, The Irish University Press series of British Parliamentary Papers (1970), Dublin, pp. 293–307, 331–333.

Young, A.D. (1913), 'The nurse's duty to herself', *Trained Nurse and Hospital Review*, 60(5), November, pp. 265–270.

Young, A.P. (1991), *Law and professional conduct in nursing*, Scutari Press, London.

Young, I.M. (1990), *Justice and the politics of difference*, Princeton University Press, Princeton, NJ.

Young, L.S. (1972a), 'Physician's assistant: why, who and how?', *American Operating Room Journal*, 15(4), April, pp. 56–60.

—— (1972b), 'Physician's assistants and the law', *Nursing Outlook*, 20(1), January, pp. 36–41.

Young, M.S. and Lucas, C.M. (1984), 'Nursing diagnosis: common problems in implementation', *Topics in Clinical Nursing*, January, pp. 68–77.

Young, W.B. (1985), 'The competition approach to understanding occupational autonomy: expansion and control of nursing services', *Journal of Professional Nursing*, 1(5), September/October, pp. 283–291.

Zipper, J. and Sevenhuijsen, S. (1987), 'Surrogacy: feminist notions of motherhood reconsidered', in M. Stanworth (ed), *Reproductive Technologies*, Polity Press, Cambridge, UK.

INDEX

Index compiled by Glenda Browne.

In this index all entries refer to nurses unless otherwise specified; for example, *negligence* means *nursing negligence*. Initial articles are omitted; for example, *The Digest* is written as *Digest*. Filing order is word-by-word.